British Armour and Recce in the Second World War:

Units, Organization and Equipment

Richard A. Rinaldi

Orbat.com
for
Tiger Lilly Books
An imprint of
General Data LLC

ISBN 978-0-98205-419-2
2012

The front cover is cropped from a photograph of a Comet tank taken by AlfvanBeem at Marshallmuseum - Liberty Park - Oorlogsmuseum Overloon, The Netherlands. He generously placed this in the public domain for all purposes, including commercial. commons.wikimedia.org/wiki/File:Cromwell_%28A27M%29_pic2.JPG. Note that the hull machinegun and front idler wheel on the right of the tank are missing. The markings are more illustratitve than an accurate depiction of an actual wartime tank. A Cromwell with '51' in a red square would be from the senior regiment in 22nd Armoured Brigade, but markings would also include the formation sign of the brigade above the red square, and of 7th Armoured Division on the opposite side. A '3' inside a square would indicate the troop leader of 3rd Troop, 'C' Squadron.

The rear cover is cropped from another photograph of the same tank, again taken by AlfvanBeem.
commons.wikimedia.org/wiki/File:Cromwell_%28A27M%29_pic7.JPG

Table of Contents

x

Preface

Some years ago I began to combine the lineage information from Frederick[1] with assignment information from Joslen[2] to create a list of British units in the Second World War. Over the years I added further information as I acquired books and other material on the Second World War Army. In addition to works on units, uniforms, equipment, and battles and campaigns there were books that helped provide a look at some key issues, especially for the largest British force of the war, 21st Army Group.[3]

This work grew out of that project, the first of an intended three volumes on the major combat units of the Second World War British Army, the regiments and battalions or their equivalents. The succeeding volumes will feature the Infantry and the Artillery. The goal for each volume is provide details on the units themselves, their organization, and their principal items of equipment.[4]

This volume covers all of the Army's armoured and reconnaissance units, whatever their source. It thus contains some information on infantry units—in particular the Guards battalions converted to armour and the six motorcycle battalions of the 1939-40 period. However, complete detail on those units will be found in the later Infantry volume. This work also includes armoured units of the Royal Engineers and Royal Marines.

For material contained in the list of Sources at the end, all footnote references are to a short version of the title. For the occasional work that might be cited in a footnote but not contained in the Sources, a full citation is given.

The tank graphic used just below the part titles in the book shows, in order, a Firefly, Sherman, Churchill, Grant, Cromwell, and Valentine. The silhouettes are derived from the font, 'Tanks-WW2' created by Tom Mouat.[5] This is also the source for the illustrations used in the AFV part.

---

[1] The two-volume *Lineage Book of British Land Force* covering the cavalry, infantry and artillery. An earlier version only had information on cavalry and infantry.
[2] Anyone looking at the British Army in the Second World War is indebted to his *Orders of Battle*.
[3] Three especially interesting works, particularly if read together, are Timothy Harrison Place, *Military Training in the British Army, 1940-1944*, David French, *Raising Churchill's Army*, and Stephen Ashley Hart, *Montgomery and "Colossal Cracks"*; all were published in 2000.
[4] The Royal Engineers will be covered in a separate work, under preparation in collaboration with Graham Watson.
[5] From his map symbols web page, www.mapsymbs.com/fontstuf.html.

Introduction

British Armoured Units in the Second World War

Perhaps no other Second World War Army had such a heterogeneous collection of unit designations in their armoured forces as the British. No simple system of numbers and 'Tank' or 'Reconnaissance', etc., for them. In fact, outside of the Reconnaissance Corps and a very small number of special units, even knowing a designation does not necessarily give someone a full clue as to what kind of unit it was. Cavalry, Yeomanry, or Royal Tank Regiment could all be an armoured or tank regiment, a unit with specialized armour, or (except for the RTR) an armoured car or armoured recce regiment.

First there was the cavalry, whether Household or line. The oldest of these had lineages stretching back to the 1600s, and even some of the newest from the Nineteenth Century were 'retrofitted' with the honours of regiments serving in the Napoleonic Wars and disbanded after. Most of these held on to their horses into the 1930s, and four were still horsed when the war began.

Next came the Royal Tank Corps, dating from 1916 and surviving in the post-war Army probably because nobody else wanted anything to do with tanks and armoured cars.[6] These were the advocates of tanks and mobile warfare and the most zealous of them envisaged tank-only formations dominating the modern battlefield with little need for infantry or artillery.

Creation of the Royal Armoured Corps in 1939 did nothing to unify the cavalry and the Royal Tanks (changing from Corps to Regiment). The RAC was intended to comprise the RTR and all mechanized cavalry regiments. However, every regiment continued to exist as a distinct and separate entity, with its own capbadge and with officers commissioned in the regiment. Both then and later the Household Cavalry regiments were never part of the RAC, and the last of the cavalry regiments did not 'enter' the RAC until 1941. In essence, the RAC was a designation for a grouping of disparate units

---

[6] By contrast, the National Defense Act of 1920 in the US abolished the Tank Corps and made tanks part of the infantry. When some US cavalry regiments began to mechanize in the 1930s, this led to the silliness of calling their light tanks 'combat cars' because, legally, anything that was a tank belong to the Infantry. Only in 1940 did the US Army create the 'Armored Force' and designate former infantry (tank) and cavalry regiments as armored units, and only in 1950 did 'Armor' finally become a branch of the US Army. Similarly, in Canada, the first post-war tank units—even if they lacked tanks—were created in 1936 by designating six militia infantry regiments as tank regiments: e.g., The Ontario Regiment (Tank).

and not a corporate entity in its own right. The British Army is famously an army of regiments and that remained unchanged.

Thus, there was a Royal Armoured Corps, and there were many armoured units, but the former never included all of the latter.[7] As might be expected, there was little sense of collegiality among these disparate forces until the war and shared battle experiences.[8] There was also no real Army-wide doctrine for how armoured forces ought to operate. When the Mobile Division (later 1st Armoured Division) was formed in 1937—putting cavalry and the RTC in a common formation for the first time ever—the first commander appointed ended up being a gunner from the Royal Artillery, neatly side-stepping the issue of having a cavalry or tank general in command. Major General Alan Brooke (later Field Marshal and Chief of the Imperial General Staff Lord Alanbrooke) noted the problems of his new command:

> There was on the one hand the necessity to evolve correct doctrine for the employment of armoured forces in the field of battle, and on the other hand some bridge must be found to span the large gap that existed in the relations between the extremists of the Tank Corps and the cavalry. There was no love lost between the two. The cavalry naturally resented deeply losing their horses, giving up their mounted role and becoming dungaree mechanics.[9]

Put simply, in 1939 the cavalry and the Royal Tanks felt they had little in common with each other and making them a Corps did nothing to change that. In fact, a 1942 history of the RAC quoted one cavalry officer as saying 'The very idea of such a union of armoured units was loathed by everyone concerned, and this gave rise to considerable ill-feeling in the early days.'[10]

---

[7] The Household Cavalry have never been part of the RAC. In the Second World War, the armoured units in the RE and Royal Marines were likewise outside the RAC.

[8] And even this, apparently, could still have its limits. When 3rd Hussars absorbed the 6th Airborne Armoured Recce Regiment in February 1946, neither group seemed to mix well with the others. Flint, *Airborne Armour*, pp 190-191.

[9] Quoted in Peter Beale, 'Be Unprepared'. Beale then went on to note that '[i]t appears that tank doctrine was not documented until Army Training Instruction No 3, Handling of an Armoured Division (1941).' Discussions of inter-war doctrine, such as it was, and the evolution of armoured units and formations is beyond the scope of this work, but good discussions can be found in Duncan Crow, *British and Commonwealth Armoured Formations* and David French, *Raising Churchill's Army*.

[10] Quoted in Duncan Crow, *British and Commonwealth Armoured Formations*, p. 23. Not surprisingly, perhaps, the first 'official account' (*The Royal Armoured Corps*, prepared for the War Office by Frank Owen and H. W. Atkins in 1944) avoids any such discussions. Typical is this throwaway line in a chapter on training: 'When the cavalry regiments of the British Army were mechanized, few people realized how easily and naturally [!] the cavalry men would adapt themselves to tanks.' (p. 32)

The two might have been in one division, but they were not brigaded together, there or elsewhere. Cavalry regiments were in light armoured brigades, or serving as armoured car or divisional cavalry regiments. The RTR were in heavy armoured brigades or the separate army tank brigades. Mechanized Yeomanry, to the extent they had any vehicles, were brigaded together or nominally allocated as armoured car or divisional cavalry regiments. The remaining horsed regiments were off by themselves.

Whatever the feelings of their officers (or men) might have been, and whatever their origins, all of these units ended up training for war and many of them engaged in combat. Some regiments managed to serve throughout the war in 'segregated' brigades. The two notable examples are the 2nd Armoured Brigade, with the same three cavalry regiments in 1945 they had in 1939[11] and the 23rd Armoured Brigade, with the same three Territorial RTR regiments from first to last.[12]

The pre-war Army also had the Yeomanry, the mounted arm of the Territorial Army. Some regiments had become armoured car companies in the RTC, regaining their old titles and separate identities in 1939 when they became part of the new RAC. Like the Regular cavalry, the Yeomanry had horsed regiments when the war started. Some ultimately came under the RAC when they mechanized and others were converted, mainly to units in the Royal Regiment of Artillery or the Royal Corps of Signals.

As the Table on p 7 below shows, there were some 65 regiments of cavalry or armour in September 1939 and some of the cavalry was still on horse. Regular units of the RTR lacked most of the cruiser and infantry tanks necessary for their establishments; and the TA RTR and mechanized Yeomanry regiments all lacked armoured vehicles. Ultimately, however, these pre-war regiments were the units most likely to avoid disbanding or suspended animation during the course of the war.

Wartime brought more variety to the types of units, as well as increased numbers. There were six new cavalry regiments raised towards the end of 1940 and early 1941. These had no pre-war history and even those still around at the end of the war soon disappeared. Four more regiments were added to the RTR. In 1941, a number of Guards battalions were converted to armour. These kept their designations and formal connections to their regiments, simply adding a parenthetical: e.g., 2nd (Armoured) Bn Grenadier Guards. That same year, infantry battalions were converted to armour. Unlike the Guards, these had to give up their former titles and became regiments RAC; thus, 5th (Cumberland) Bn The Border Regiment became 110th Regiment RAC.[13] Some were TA

---

[11] Albeit the three regiments were briefly absent in 1942 to refit after losing all their tanks in combat.

[12] Although some of the regiments served away from the brigade for periods.

[13] These became the first combat units to actually have 'RAC' in their designation. Training regiments had been so designated since September 1939.

battalions with long histories, other were battalions formed only in 1940. Most of these regiments RAC would disappear during the war as the Army had to reduce its strength.

With the cavalry all gone off to be part of armoured formations from 1940, creation of recce units for infantry divisions presented the problem of what to call them. They became part of a new corps, the Reconnaissance Corps, raised in January 1941. A few infantry battalions were converted to battalions of the Reconnaissance Corps, but most recce battalions were new units. In January 1944 the regiments of the Reconnaissance Corps became reconnaissance regiments in the RAC. For these units, at least, their designation told you what they were, although the 2nd Derbyshire Yeomanry ended up reorganized during the war as a recce regiment for an infantry division.

As if this were not enough, in 1943 the Royal Engineers formed armoured units (designated 'assault' units at first) with specialized armour to help tackle fortified positions. And the Royal Marines also formed a unit with tanks, to help invasions from the sea get ashore.[14]

At the peak, in December 1942, there were some 126 armoured or recce regiments of one type of another, and the number of distinct units had been somewhat larger, as a few units were converted to other roles or lost during that year. As with the Army in general, it proved impossible to maintain all of these units, and reductions during 1943 and 1944 led to a December 1944 force of some 98 different regiments.[15] As is evident from the table at p 17, the largest reduction was in the wartime regiments RAC, with less than a third of those formed surviving into 1945. Other reductions occurred in wartime cavalry, the RTR (both wartime and TA), and the Yeomanry (mainly in duplicate units, although some regiments had been converted to other arms over the years).

But ultimately reassignments, consolidations and disbanding helped shuffle different kinds of units, and Regular cavalry, RTR, Yeomanry, and regiments RAC could be found in various combinations in different brigades. Regiments could also shift roles, regardless of their origins, during the course of the war. In the early years, especially, regiments sometimes exchanged squadrons for periods to balance out brigades, with a cavalry squadron (light tanks) going to an RTR regiment, and a squadron from an RTR regiment taking its cruisers to stiffen a cavalry regiment. In addition, officers and even groups of other ranks could be drafted from one regiment to another, especially where a unit was disbanded. After five years of war, the remaining active units were still distinct

---

[14] This unit is not included in the Table on p 6, since it only existed during 1944. Another RM regiment (with LVTs) was raised in 1945.
[15] Two regiments were disbanded in early 1945 and another armoured engineer regiment raised, giving the Army 99 regiments in May 1945.

regiments, but they had common experiences, and the RAC was less ephemeral post-war than it might have seemed in 1939.[16]

The first part of this book is a list of every known unit, with details of their assignments and service, and notes on their equipment. Details are also given on regimental badges and Second World War battle honours.

War Establishments

If the first section is 'who were they' then the next section is 'how were they organized'. What the US Army would call tables of organization and equipment, the British Army called war establishments. These were published documents, showing the organization of a unit. There was usually an overview summarizing the organization, often accompanied by a wire diagram with some details of personnel and equipment.

As much as possible, information in the middle section of the book is from war establishments, although use has been made of secondary sources where necessary. Details vary with the available source, but whenever possible I have given a detailed breakdown (similar to that in the war establishment) for all vehicles in the last wartime version of a unit. More summary data is given for earlier war establishments, but the reader desiring full details should be able to locate them from the sourcs.

Armoured Fighting Vehicles

After who they were and how they were organized, the final section of the book provides summary information on the major armoured fighting vehicles used by the British Army.

As the title implies, information here is primarily limited to vehicles such as tanks, armoured and scout cars, and various specialized armour. SP artillery and SP antitank vehicles, even where derived from a tank chassis, are omitted as both belonged to the Royal Artillery.

---

[16] In the smaller post-war Army, regiments in the RAC continued to shift roles and organization as they moved from posting to posting. The only exceptions were that the Household Cavalry regiments were always armoured car, and the armoured car role within the RAC was restricted to former cavalry regiments. (The RTR were 'tank units' and thus presumed not suitable for the more 'dashing' armoured car role.) That restriction actually lasted until 1963 when the 4th RTR became the first element of the regiment to convert to armoured cars. In 1969, the Royal Horse Guards and The Royal Dragoons amalgamated as The Blues and Royals, an armoured regiment, which The Royals were at the time; from then to 1992 the two Household regiments alternated with one in Germany as armoured and one in the UK as armoured car, later armoured recce. Following Options for Change, the single tactical Household Cavalry regiment was an armoured recce unit.

Exceptions to this general rule are the various amphibian vehicles, which equipped units in this volume, and the ubiquitous US-built White scout car and M5 halftrack, both of which often replaced 15cwt light trucks.

The information in this section is restricted to key information on the vehicles—weight, crew, armament, speed, etc.—along with information on production. Full volumes exist on this subject, often extensively illustrated, for those desiring more detail.[17]

---

[17] On tanks, Peter Chamberlain and Chris Ellis, *British and American Tanks of World War Two* is definitive. With less detail but coverage of a broader range of vehicles, see B. T. White, *British Tanks and Fighting Vehicles 1914-1945*. There are also a variety of specialist works on particular vehicles, especially the AFV/Weapons Profiles of Profile Publications Ltd.

Table: Armoured/Recce Regiment Totals

	Sep 1939	Dec 1940	Dec 1941	Dec 1942	Dec 1943	Dec 1944
Household Cavalry	2 [i]	1	2	2	2	2
Cavalry	20 [ii]	23	26	26	25	24
Royal Tank Regiment	20 [iii]	24	24	22	19	18 [iv]
Yeomanry	23 [v]	24	24	21	20	18
Converted Foot Guards	-	-	6	6	7	7
Regiments RAC [vi]	-	-	18	33	19	10 [vii]
Recce Corps/recce RAC	-	-	19	16	18	17 [viii]
Assault RE/Armoured Engineer	-	-	-	-	3	4 [ix]
Aggregate	65	72	119	126	113	98

[i] The two regiments, horsed in peacetime, formed a composite horsed regiment on mobilization. In 1941, the reserve regiment became operational, joining the former composite regiment as another armoured car unit.

[ii] Three still horsed (one in the process of dismounting) and not all mechanized regiments fully equipped.

[iii] Eight Regular, not all fully equipped; 12 TA essentially without equipment.

[iv] In 1945 the 4th RTR (lost in 1942) was reformed from a regiment RAC, giving the RTR 19 active units at the end of the war but not changing the overall number of armoured regiments.

[v] Eight were horsed regiments, one was a newly-raised Special Reserve armoured regiment, and 14 were former RTC armoured car companies and their duplicate units. None of the armoured units were actually equipped (beyond the old armoured cars in the former RTC companies). Additional horsed regiments that converted to Royal Artillery 1939-40 are not included.

[vi] Numbered regiments (107-116 and 141-163) only, excluding scorpion, replacement and training regiments.

[vii] One regiment RAC was disbanded January 1945, reducing the overall armoured total by one before the end of the war. Another (as noted) was redesignated 4th RTR, which did not affect the totals.

[viii] One regiment disbanded February 1945, reducing the overall total by one before the end of the war.

[ix] An additional regiment was formed January 1945 in Italy but was not operational by the end of the war there.

Part 1: Armoured and Reconnaissance Units

Introduction to Units

The Royal Armoured Corps was formed 30 April 1939, as noted, to comprise mechanized cavalry regiments and the Royal Tank Corps, which was concurrently redesignated as the Royal Tank Regiment. Also as noted, each regiment remained legally a distinct Corps. Gradually all of the cavalry regiments came within the RAC, as did Yeomanry units as they were mechanized. Infantry units converted to armour during the war were designated as 'Regiments RAC'. The Reconnaissance Corps was absorbed into the RAC 1 January 1944 and its units redesignated. However, not all of the wartime armoured units came under even the loose umbrella of the RAC. The Household Cavalry—neither then nor later—came within the scope of the RAC, and the converted battalions of Foot Guards were outside the RAC as well, along with armoured units of the RE and RM. Following the Second World War, few units other than training regiments retained a designation as part of the RAC and those quickly disappeared.

To repeat, it is difficult to overstate the heterogeneity of unit designations, sources, and organization in the RAC. However, as a 1944 history noted, there were five main roles, each with an associated type of unit:[18]

- Tank regiment: equipped with infantry ('I') tanks, to work closely with the infantry to break opposing forces and create opportunities for launching armoured divisions;
- Armoured regiment: equipped with cruisers, their purpose is to destroy enemy armoured formations, dislocate and destroy their headquarters, communications, and rear areas generally, and to keep the battle fluid;[19]
- Armoured recce regiment: this unit has the prime purpose of ensuring the march or maneuver of the armoured division: 'its prime duty is to keep the Division fully and promptly aware of all that is going on within its area of action';
- Armoured car regiment: virtually 'its sole business is advanced reconnaissance' to serve as the eyes and ears of the corps;
- Reconnaissance regiment: similar to armoured recce regiments except that it works in front of an infantry division.

---

[18] Frank Owen and H. W. Atkins, *The Royal Armoured Corps*, pp 46-47.
[19] While this matches closely with pre-war RTC views, the RAC history—unlike the old RTC zealots—makes explicit note of the artillery, engineers, motorized infantry and other elements of an armoured division, not just the tanks, and the need for the division to operate as a whole formation.

Much of the specialized armour came from former tank regiments, and their roles were roughly congruent with that of tank regiments: working closely with infantry to break opposing forces or positions.

As with the rest of the Army, the normal dress from 1937 was khaki battledress. The Royal Tank Corps/Regiment had always worn a black beret, and in July 1941 this was extended to the entire RAC, although not necessarily adopted by some regimens until 1942.[20] The Reconnaissance Corps wore a khaki beret until absorbed by the RAC in 1944, and there were a variety of regimental distinctions within the RAC, such as the 116th Regiment RAC (Gordon Highlanders) who retained the khaki Balmoral bonnet of their regiment. Uniforms had formation badges, arm of service stripes and (for many) coloured regimental titles at the top of the sleeves. There were a variety of outfits for wear in and around the tanks, including a khaki tank suit issued after 1943. The standard helmet was worn until 1943 when a distinct rimless RAC helmet was issued, like that of the paratroops but with a simpler web chinstrap.

RAC Badge: The first badge was the letters 'RAC' surrounded by a wreath and surmounted by a crown. This was later replaced by a mailed gauntlet (with 'RAC' on the wrist), within a double pincers, surmounted by the Crown. Officers in silver plate, other ranks in white metal. As with the original, this badge was little used during the war, except for training units and officers newly commissioned in the RAC.
Battledress: Red 'Royal Armoured Corps' on yellow

RAC personnel had an arm of service strip of yellow/red worn on the sleeve below any formation signs.

Household Cavalry

Best known for their ceremonial role in London, the Household Cavalry regiments were also expected to be able to go off to war. In 1939, they were the only two Regular regiments in the UK still mounted on horses. As was the case in 1914, they initially formed a composite regiment, which went to Palestine with the 1st Cavalry Division. From 1941, there were two composite regiments, organized with armoured cars. Unlike the case in the First World War, the regiments themselves were never reformed as distinct units, although 1st Household Cavalry Regiment ultimately consisted mainly of Life Guards and 2nd Household Cavalry Regiment mainly Royal Horse Guards. Since the two regiments remained composite units during the war, each regiment shares in all of the battle honours earned by the wartime units. Personnel retained their regimental badges throughout the war.

---

[20] The 11th Hussars (Prince Albert's Own) and the Inns of Court Regiment kept their own berets; the former rust brown with a bright red strip, the latter a distinctive green.

THE LIFE GUARDS

The 1st and 2nd Life Guards, with a complicated lineage dating back to 1658, were amalgamated in May 1922 to form The Life Guards (1st and 2nd); the subtitle was soon omitted. The regiment was still horsed in September 1939, located at Hyde Park Barracks, under the control of London District.

Personnel were divided 3 September 1939 among the Household Cavalry Composite Regiment [see 1st Household Cavalry Regiment], Household Cavalry Training Regiment [see 2nd Household Cavalry Regiment], and Household Cavalry Reserve Regiment.

The Life Guards were reformed 17 July 1945 in Germany with personnel from 1st Household Cavalry Regiment.

Badge: The Royal Cypher, within a circle containing legend 'The Life Guards', surmounted by a crown. Officers bright bronze, other ranks gilding metal.

ROYAL HORSE GUARDS (THE BLUES)

Raised in 1661 and designated from 1877 as Royal Horse Guards (The Blues). The regiment was still horsed in September 1939, located at Windsor, under the control of London District.

Personnel were divided 3 September 1939 among the Household Cavalry Composite Regiment [see 1st Household Cavalry Regiment], Household Cavalry Training Regiment [see 2nd Household Cavalry Regiment], and Household Cavalry Reserve Regiment.

The Royal Horse Guards were reformed 17 July 1945 in Germany with personnel from 2nd Household Cavalry Regiment, remaining assigned to Guards Division. Relieved 1946 and returned to the UK.

Badge: The Royal Cypher, within a circle containing legend 'Royal Horse Guards', surmounted by a crown. Officers bright bronze, other ranks gilding metal.

WARTIME UNITS

1st Household Cavalry Regiment Organized 3 September 1939 as Household Cavalry Composite Regiment, with personnel drawn from Life Guards and Royal Horse Guards (The Blues). Assigned 4th Cavalry Brigade 13 November 1939. Redesignated November 1940 as 1st Household Cavalry Regiment; remaining assigned to 4th Cavalry Brigade until 31 July 1941. By October 1940, one squadron was converted from horses to trucks. The regiment was slated for conversion to a motor battalion in March 1941, and was wholly mounted in trucks by June 1941. Assigned to 9th Armoured Brigade 3 August 1941 but apparently already slated for armoured car role; relieved 9 October 1941 and assigned 10th Armoured Division [an armoured car regiment by that date, if not earlier]; relieved 13 March 1942. A GHQ unit in Cyprus March to September 1942, then served with 7th Armoured Division September to December 1942. Returned to 10th Armoured Division 14 January 1943; relieved 5 November 1943. A GHQ unit with Eighth Army in Italy November-December 1943, then with Ninth Army in Palestine December 1943-January 1944. It returned to Eighth Army in Italy April to October 1944, operating with V Corps and II Polish Corps.[21] Sent to the UK (Home Forces) October 1944 to March 1945. Served with XXX Corps in NW Europe from March 1945. Disbanded 17 July 1945 in Germany (personnel used to reconstitute Life Guards).

Equipment notes: Originally horsed, then partly horsed and partly truck-born October 1940. By December 1941 in 15cwt trucks, later armoured cars. In October 1942 had 42 Marmon-Herrington and 11 Daimler armoured cars. By June 1943 a mix of Daimler and AEC armoured cars. Equipped with Daimler armoured cars by March 1944.

2nd Household Cavalry Regiment Organized 3 September 1939 as Household Cavalry Training Regiment, with personnel drawn from Life Guards and Royal Horse Guards (The Blues). Converted November 1940 as 2nd Household Cavalry Motor Bn. Reorganized 15 September 1941 as 2nd Household Cavalry Regiment [an armoured car regiment] and assigned Guards Armoured Division same date; relieved 27 February 1943. A GHQ unit with Home Forces from March 1943 and Second Army from July 1943. Served with VIII Corps in NW Europe from June to August 1944, then with XXX Corps to May 1945 (but often with Guards Armoured Division as its recce element). Assigned Guards Division 12 June 1945. Disbanded 17 July 1945 in Germany (personnel used to reconstitute Royal Horse Guards (The Blues)).

Equipment notes: Given Guy armoured cars on conversion to that role. June 1944: 45 Daimler I, 14 Staghound, 8 AEC III, 5 AA armoured cars, 52 Daimler and 13 Humber scour cars; October 1944 (AC only): 41 Daimler, 18 Staghound, and 8 AEC III.

Household Cavalry Reserve Regiment Formed 3 September 1939 with personnel from The Life Guards and Royal Horse Guards (The Blues). May have been reorganized ca November 1940 as a motor battalion. Disbanded ca March 1941.

Household Cavalry Battle Honours: Mont Pincon, SOULEUVRE, Noireau Crossing, Amiens 1944, BRUSSELS, Neerpelt, NEDERRIJN, Nijmegen, Lingen, Bentheim, NORTH-WEST EUROPE 1944-45, Baghdad 1941, IRAQ 1941, PALMYRA, SYRIA 1941, EL ALAMEIN, NORTH AFRICA 1942-43, Arezzo, Advance to Florence, Gothic Line, ITALY 1944

---

[21] For service with II Polish Corps, personnel of 1st Household Cavalry Regiment were authorized to wear that corps' formation sign (white mermaid of Warsaw on red shield with white border), which was placed on the lower sleeve.

Brigade of Guards

In September 1941, a number of Guards infantry battalions were converted to armour in the process of forming a Guards Armoured Division. These retained the badges of their parent regiment. Battle honours are not shown for these units, since the honours were earned by and granted to the regiment as a whole.

2nd (ARMOURED) BN GRENADIER GUARDS

A Regular infantry battalion in 7th Guards Infantry Brigade; converted to armour 15 September 1941 with its parent brigade becoming 5th Guards Armoured Brigade.[22] Converted back to infantry as 2nd Bn 12 June 1945 in Germany.

Equipment notes: Equipped initially with Covenanter tanks, replaced the end of 1942 with 6pdr Crusaders. The battalion was equipped entirely with Shermans by June 1943. In spring 1944 changed to a mix of Sherman V and Fireflys.

4th (ARMOURED) BN GRENADIER GUARDS

An infantry battalion organized in October 1940 and in 30th Guards Infantry Brigade; converted to armour 15 September 1941 with its parent brigade becoming 6th Guards Armoured Brigade. Redesignated 5 January 1943 as 4th (Tank) Bn and brigade redesignated 6th Guards Tank Brigade; redesignated 2 February 1945 as 4th (Armoured) Bn and brigade redesignated as 6th Guards Armoured Brigade. Converted back to infantry as 4th Bn 17 June 1945 in Germany.

Equipment notes: The initial tank was the Covenanter, replaced the end of 1942 with 6pdr Crusaders, changed in 1943 to the Churchill III. In June 1944, Churchill IV [6pdr] and V/VIII (CS). In December 1944, Churchills (about 2/3 75mm and 1/3 6pdr, plus CS). Final equipment the Churchill VII/VIII [75mm/CS].

Badge of the Grenadier Guards: A fired grenade. Officers have the badge in gold embroidery. Warrant officers, orderly room sergeants and band sergeants: grenade in bronze, with the Royal Cypher interlaced and reversed with crown above, in silver, on the grenade. Sergeants and musicians have the Royal Cypher and crown embossed on the grenade, the badge all in gilding metal. Other ranks have a plain grenade, with the badge in gilding metal.
Battledress: White 'Grenadier Guards' on scarlet.

---

[22] Frederick shows the formal redesignation for this and other battalions as occurring on 21 October 1941. The 5th and 6th Guards Armoured Brigades were redesignated as the 5th and 6th Guards Brigades 12 and 17 June 1945, respectively, upon conversion to infantry.

1st (ARMOURED) BN COLDSTREAM GUARDS

A Regular infantry battalion in 7th Guards Infantry Brigade; converted to armour 15 September 1941 with its parent brigade becoming 5th Guards Armoured Brigade. Converted back to infantry as 1st Bn 12 June 1945 in Germany.

Equipment notes: Equipped initially with Covenanter tanks, replaced the end of 1942 with 6pdr Crusaders. The battalion was equipped entirely with Shermans by June 1943. In spring 1944 changed to a mix of Sherman V and Fireflys.

4th (ARMOURED) BN COLDSTREAM GUARDS

An infantry battalion organized in October 1940 and in 30th Guards Infantry Brigade; reorganized as a motor battalion 15 September 1941 with its parent brigade becoming 6th Guards Armoured Brigade. Reorganized 15 January 1943 as 4th (Tank) Bn and brigade redesignated 6th Guards Tank Brigade; redesignated 2 February 1945 as 4th (Armoured) Bn and brigade redesignated as 6th Guards Armoured Brigade. Converted back to infantry as 4th Bn 17 June 1945 in Germany.

Equipment notes: Equipped initially with Covenanter tanks, replaced the end of 1942 with 6pdr Crusaders. The initial infantry tank was the Churchill III. In June 1944, Churchill IV [6pdr] and V/VIII (CS). In December 1944, Churchills (about 2/3 75mm and 1/3 6pdr, plus CS). Final equipment the Churchill VII/VIII [75mm/CS].

Badge of the Coldstream Guards: Star of the Order of the Garter. Officers: badge in silver plate, the Garter and motto on a blue ground and the cross in red enamel. Warrant officers, drum majors, orderly room sergeants and band sergeants: as for officers, but of a squarer design and not elongated. All other ranks: the badge in gilding metal. Battledress: White 'Coldstream Guards' on scarlet.

3rd (ARMOURED) BN SCOTS GUARDS

An infantry battalion organized in October 1940 and in 30th Guards Infantry Brigade; converted to armour 15 September 1941 with its parent brigade becoming 6th Guards Armoured Brigade. Redesignated 5 January 1943 as 4th (Tank) Bn and brigade redesignated 6th Guards Tank Brigade; redesignated 2 February 1945 as 4th (Armoured) Bn and brigade redesignated as 6th Guards Armoured Brigade. Converted back to infantry as 4th Bn 17 June 1945 in Germany. (The battalion was disbanded 28 February 1946 in Germany.)

Equipment notes: The initial tank was the Covenanter, replaced the end of 1942 with 6pdr Crusaders, and then changed in 1943 to the Churchill III. In June 1944, Churchill IV [6pdr] and V/VIII (CS). In December 1944, Churchills (about 2/3 75mm and 1/3 6pdr, plus CS). Final equipment the Churchill VII/VIII [75mm/CS].

Badge of the Scots Guards: Star of The Order of the Thistle. Officers: the badge in silver plate, with the circle, motto and center in gilt. Warrant officers wear the Star of the Order of St. Andrew in silver plate, with motto, circle and thistle in gilt. Colour sergeants, sergeants and musicians wear the Star of the Order of The Thistle in white and gilding medal. Other ranks wear the star all in gilding metal.
Battledress: Yellow 'Scots Guards' on blue.

2nd (ARMOURED) BN IRISH GUARDS

A Regular infantry battalion formed in 1939, serving ultimately with 20th Guards Infantry Brigade. Transferred 15 September 1941 to 5th Guards Armoured Brigade and officially converted 21 October 1941 as armour. Serving throughout the war with Guards Armoured Division,[23] it was converted back to infantry as 2nd Bn 12 June 1945 in Germany.

Equipment notes: Equipped initially with Covenanter tanks, replaced the end of 1942 with 6pdr Crusaders. The battalion was equipped entirely with Shermans by June 1943. In spring 1944 changed to a mix of Sherman V and Fireflys.

Badge of the Irish Guards: Star of The Order of St. Patrick. Officers: the badge in silver plate, with the motto 'Quis Separabit', date 'MDCCLXXXIII' and circle in gilt on a blue enamel ground. Within the circle, the shamrock in green enamel over the red cross of St. Patrick. Warrant officers, the badge in silver plate with gilt center. Colour sergeants and guardsmen, the badge in gilding metal. Pipers have a badge large and in white metal.
Battledress: White 'Irish Guards' on emerald green.

2nd (ARMOURED RECONNAISSANCE) BN WELSH GUARDS

A Regular infantry battalion formed in 1939, serving ultimately with 20th Guards Infantry Brigade. Assigned 15 September 1941 to 6th Guards Armoured Brigade and converted 21 October 1941 as 2nd (Armoured) Bn; relieved 11 January 1943. Regiment then began reorganization as an armoured recce unit. Assigned Guards Armoured Division 13 April 1943 and redesignated 28 April 1943 as 2nd (Armoured Recce) Bn. Serving throughout the war with the division, it was relieved 11 June 1945 in Germany. Converted back to infantry 20 June 1945.

Equipment notes: Equipped initially with Covenanter tanks, replaced the end of 1942 with 6pdr Crusaders. A conventional armoured recce regiment from 1943 (Shermans and Stuarts), changed by spring 1944 to Cromwells (with the Stuarts reduced to a single recce troop).

---

[23] Guardsman Edward C. Charlton was awarded a Victoria Cross for his actions 21 April 1945 at Wistedt, Germany. After his and the other tanks supporting infantry were knocked out of action, he seized a Browning; advancing while firing and then firing from a fence, he halted a German attack that was in the process of over-running the infantry. Charlton was wounded twice and later died of his wounds.

Badge of the Welsh Guards: A Leek. Officers: the badge in gold embroidery on black cloth. All others, badge in gilding metal.
Battledress: White 'Welsh Guards' on black.

Cavalry

Cavalry found little role in the First World War, although there were still three cavalry divisions on the Western Front in 1918 and additional mounted divisions in Palestine, where the arm was more useful. While horsed cavalry survived in the post-war Army, the retrenchments of 1922 saw it reduced from 28 regiments to 20 through amalgamations.

The first regiments to give up their horses for vehicles were the 11th Hussars and 12th Royal Lancers, which became armoured car regiments in 1928-29. They were chosen since they were the most junior regiments to have escaped amalgamation six years earlier. While the remaining regiments might have begun replacing horse-drawn transport with cars and trucks, their fighting personnel were still horse-mounted.

Ultimately, it was impossible to avoid facing the question of exactly what a horsed unit was supposed to do on the modern battlefield. In autumn 1934, the Inspector of Cavalry, Major General John Blakiston-Houston told the assembled colonels that 'he could no longer see any future for horsed cavalry as such and that he proposed to ask that the bulk of the cavalry regiments be converted to armour'.[24] At first there were plans for a mix, with some regiments in light tanks and others serving as mechanized infantry, but the latter organization was dropped before any regiments converted. In 1937, regiments serving as divisional cavalry were marked for mechanization, as well as cavalry regiments stationed in India. Officers may have pined for their horses and the old days, but once the decision was made to become armoured many endeavored to make it work.[25]

---

[24] Quoted in Duncan Crow, *British and Commonwealth Armoured Formations (1919-46)*, p. 16. Blakiston-Houston was commissioned in the 11th Hussars, and in command of the 12th Lancers when they were mechanized. He told them: 'We've been given this role and it's a very important role. And you're damn well going to do it. I won't have you bloody well bellyaching'. (Quoted in David French, *Raising Churchill's Army*, p. 61.) His next command, as a brigadier, was a horsed brigade. He was promoted major general in 1934, and remained Commandant of the Equitation School, Weedon, and Inspector of Cavalry until his 1938 retirement. He was considered for, but not selected, to command the Mobile Division when it was created in 1937. Command, as noted earlier, went to an artilleryman, Major General Alan Brooke (later Field Marshal the Viscount Alanbrooke).

[25] From Brig G. M. O .Davy, *The Seventh and Three Enemies*: 'Among the officers there was at first a certain amount of dismay, but they quickly adjusted themselves and entered wholeheartedly into the business of oil and spanners. One young officer was heard to say something about Indian cavalry and was at once told, by an equally young officer, that they must

Announcing mechanization was easier than accomplishing it, and many of the Regular regiments were still short tanks or other equipment when the war began in September 1939. However, only the two regiments in Palestine and one in India were still horsed units by that date. The remainder were light armoured, divisional cavalry, or (still only the 11th and 12th) armoured car regiments. Ultimately the bulk of the cavalry became armoured or armoured car regiments, with a small number of other organizations as well.

In late 1940, six new cavalry regiments were formed, raising the issue of what to designate them. One suggestion was to undo some of the 1922 amalgamations, giving six of the former regiments an independent life again. However, the colonels involved did not believe (correctly) that the additional regiments would survive post-war reductions, and also did not want to undo the creation of the new regimental identities of the amalgamated units. So, the new regiments simply received numbers 22 to 27and designations in order as dragoons, hussars and lancers.

1st KING'S DRAGOON GUARDS

Raised 1685, becoming 1st (King's) Dragoon Guards and restyled 1 January 1921. Mechanized December 1937 as a cavalry light tank regiment.

Stationed at Aldershot as part of 1st Light Armoured Brigade. (Brigade redesignated 14 April 1940 as 1st Armoured Brigade); relieved 24 January 1941. Began conversion as an armoured car regiment on arrival in Egypt January 1941; assigned 2nd Armoured Division 24 February 1941; relieved 9 May 1941 (operated with 3rd Armoured Brigade 26 February to 22 March 1941). A GHQ unit in Palestine from June 1941 to November 1942. Assigned 4th Armoured Brigade 3 December 1942; relieved 30 April 1943. A GHQ unit with V Corps in NW Africa, Sicily and Italy May 1943 to April 1944, then X Corps in Italy April to November 1944. Served in Greece December 1944 to April 1945, then with Ninth Army in Palestine from May 1945.

Equipment notes: Had Mk VI Light tanks as an armoured regiment. Upon conversion to armoured cars, began with a mix of Morris and Rolls Royce vehicles. Equipped with Marmon-Herrington II armoured cars by March 1941. (Without equipment May-August 1941, when they took over armoured cars from 11th Hussars.) Received Marmon-Herrington II armoured cars November 1941(at first 30, later 45). Began to receive AEC armoured cars in November 1942. Had Daimler armoured cars by 1943. Last Marmon-Harringtons withdrawn February 1943 and AECs in May 1943. First unit to use M3 75mm GMC, in Tunisian campaign. Began to receive Humber armoured cars February 1943, and then changed to Daimlers in November 1943. Began to receive Staghounds as well from December 1943.

---

all go into mechanization together and make a job of it - as indeed they did'. (Ch. 1). Cavalry regiments of the Indian Army basically remained horsed units until after the war started.

Battle Honours: BEDA FOMM, DEFENCE OF TOBRUK, Tobruk 1941, Tobruk Sortie, Relief of Tobruk, Gazala, Bir Hacheim, DEFENCE OF ALAMEIN LINE, Alam el Halfa, El Agheila, ADVANCE ON TRIPOLI, TEBAGA GAP, Point 201 (Roman Wall), El Hamma, Akarit, TUNIS, NORTH AFRICA 1941-43, Capture of Naples, Scafati Bridge, MONTE CAMINO, Garigliano Crossing, Capture of Perugia, Arezzo, GOTHIC LINE, ITALY 1943-44, Athens, Greece 1944-45

Badge: The Imperial Eagle of Austria [restored 1937, after being disused from 1915]. Officers in silver plate, other ranks in white metal.

QUEEN'S BAYS (2nd DRAGOON GUARDS)

Raised 1685, becoming 2nd Dragoon Guards (Queen's Bays) until restyled 1 January 1921. Mechanized 1936 as cavalry light tank regiment.

Stationed at Tidworth as part of 2nd Light Armoured Brigade (brigade redesignated 14 April 1940 as 2nd Armoured Brigade). Relieved from 2nd Armoured Brigade 26 June 1942 due to heavy losses and returned 2 August 1942. Except for the period away to reorganize, the regiments of 2nd Armoured Brigade served with that formation throughout the war.

Equipment notes: Began with Mk VI Light Tank. (The first Mk VIC arrived late 1939 without their armament installed.) First A9 cruisers received April 1940 and the first A10s and A13s just before going to France in May 1940.) By May 1940 had 29 cruisers [4 A9, 3 A10, 22 A13] and 21 Mk VI light tanks. Back up to strength as a cruiser regiment by October 1940. Began to receive Coventanters 1941 and then Crusaders. In August 1941, had 36 Crusaders ('A' and 'B' Sqns) and 16 Stuarts ('C' Sqn). In December 1941, re-equipping with Crusader (one squadron) and Stuart tanks (two squadrons). Received first Grants April 1942; in late May 1942 RHQ and 'A' and 'B' Sqns had Crusaders, 'C' Sqn had Grants. Tanks were withdrawn mid 1942 to replace losses in other units. Began to receive Shermans early September 1942, and late October 1942 had Crusader III in RHQ and 'A' Sqn and Sherman I in 'B' and 'C' Sqns.; in March 1943 still a mix of Crusaders in RHQ and 'A' Sqn and Shermans in 'B' and 'C' Sqns. Later fully equipped with Sherman III and V. In August 1944 received 12 Sherman IIA (76mm), allotted one per troop, and in September 1944 6 Sherman IB (105mm), issued 2 per squadron as HQ vehicles. Received some Sherman IC Fireflys by 1945.

Battle Honours: SOMME 1940, Withdrawal to Seine, North-West Europe 1940, Msus, GAZALA, Bir el Aslagh, Cauldron, Knightsbridge, Via Balbia, Mersa Matruh, EL ALAMEIN, Tebaga Gap, EL HAMMA, El Kourzla, Djebel Kournine, TUNIS, Creteville Pass, NORTH AFRICA 1941-43, CORIANO, Carpineta, LAMONE CROSSING, Lamone Bridgehead, RIMINI LINE, Ceriano Ridge, Cesena, ARGENTA GAP, Italy 1944-45

Badge: Old English script 'Bays' within a laurel wreath and Crown. Officers gilt or gilding metal and others ranks in gilding metal.

3rd CARABINIERS (PRINCE OF WALES'S DRAGOON GUARDS)

Formed 1922 by amalgamation of 3rd Dragoon Guards (Prince of Wales's) (raised 1685) and 6th Dragoon Guards (Carabiniers) (raised 1685), as 3rd/6th Dragoon Guards; redesignated December 1928 as 3rd Carabiniers (Prince of Wales's Dragoon Guards). Mechanized January 1938 as cavalry light tank regiment.

Stationed at Khanspur Hill, India (Sialkot Brigade). Moved from Khanspur Hill to Sialkot in September 1939. Assigned 2nd Indian Armoured Brigade 1 September 1940. Relieved June 1941 before brigade left for Iraq. Mobilized 1 October 1941. Assigned 5 November 1941 to 1st Indian Armoured Brigade (redesignated October 1941 as 251st Indian Armoured Brigade and 10 September 1942 as 251st Indian Tank Brigade); relieved October 1943. Formed separate group October to December 1943 in India, then assigned 254th Indian Tank Brigade 11 December 1943. (Between May and July 1944 split into squadrons operating in support of 23rd and 5th Indian Infantry Divisions, and only RHQ remained with brigade.) Relieved and operated with 2nd Infantry Division 28 January to 31 March 1945, 7th Indian Division 7 April 1945, and 20th Indian Division 24 April to 20 May 1945 when the regiment was relieved of all operational commitments. It moved to Rangoon May 1945, then returned to India June 1945 and was assigned 254th Indian Tank Brigade 8 July 1945; it remained with the brigade (redesignated December 1945 as 3rd Indian Armoured Brigade) until April 1946. The regiment left Bombay for the UK in early 1947, the last British cavalry regiment to leave India.

Equipment notes: Began with 41 Mk VIB light tanks. These (all but 3) were handed in at the end of 1941 and the regiment given 15cwt trucks. The trucks were themselves taken away and the regiment given some tracked carriers. By May 1942 it had some Lees, but these were handed in July 1942. Told September 1942 that they were to have two squadrons Stuarts and one of Lees, which were later issued. (Partly equipped February 1943, with Lees.) In July 1943 the Lees were withdrawn and replaced by Stuarts. That decision was soon reversed and by December 1943 the regiment converted to all Lees. Following its return to India in June 1945 the regiment converted to Shermans.

Battle Honours: IMPHAL, Tamu Road, NUNSHIGUM, BISHENPUR, KANGLATONGHI, KENNEDY PEAK, Shwebo, SAGAING, MANDALAY, AVA, IRRAWADDY, Yenangyaung 1945, Burma 1944-45

Badge: Prince of Wales's plume and motto over crossed carbines, with scroll '3rd Carabiniers' over carbine stocks. Officers: coronet and scroll in gilt, plume, motto and carbines in silver plate; other ranks in gilding metal and white metal.

4th/7th ROYAL DRAGOON GUARDS

Formed 1922 by amalgamation of 4th Royal Irish Dragoon Guards (raised 1685) and 7th Dragoon Guards (Princess Royal's) (raised 1688); title did not include 'Royal' until October 1936. Mechanized 1938; a divisional cavalry regiment in 1939.

Stationed at Aldershot as part of 2nd Infantry Division.[26] Officially relieved from 2nd Infantry Division 31 May 1940 in France and assigned to 1st Armoured Recce Brigade, although it did not leave the division and join the brigade until 18 June 1940 when it was back in the UK. 1st Armoured Recce Brigade redesignated 26 November 1940 as 27th Armoured Brigade and unit converted as armoured regiment. Trained from 1943 with DD tanks. Relieved from 27th Armoured Brigade 31 January 1944 and assigned to 8th Armoured Brigade 27 February 1944. Remained in Germany following the war.

Equipment notes: Original equipment of Mk VI light tanks and carriers all lost in France May 1940. Re-equipped at first with trucks. In September 1940 had around 60 Beaverettes. Later given Mk VI light tanks. Received Covenanters beginning April 1941 and fully equipped by November of that year. Later equipped with Shermans. In June 1944 had a mix of Sherman II DD, Sherman III and Fireflys. (DD tanks withdrawn after Normandy landing.) In December 1944 a mixture of Shermans and Fireflys.

Battle Honours: Dyle, DUNKIRK 1940, NORMANDY LANDING, ODON, MONT PINCON, Seine 1944, NEDERRIJN, GEILENKIRCHEN, Roer, RHINELAND, Cleve, RHINE, Bremen, North-West Europe 1940 '44-45

Badge: Princess Royal's Coronet backed against the Star of the Order of St. Patrick (eight-pointed star, containing a circle inscribed 'Quis Separabit MCMXXII', within the circle St. George's Cross). Officers in silver with St. George's cross on background of red enamel; others ranks in gilding metal. Badge worn pinned through a maroon patch. Regimental flash: the regiment wore a black diamond with one gold above two maroon chevrons, high on the left arm.

5th ROYAL INNISKILLING DRAGOON GUARDS

Formed 1922 by amalgamation of 5th Dragoon Guards (Princess Charlotte of Wales's) (raised 1685) and The Inniskillings (6th Dragoons) (raised 1689); designated as 5th/6th Dragoons until restyled May 1927 and then designated as Royal 3 June 1935. Mechanized in 1938; a divisional cavalry regiment by 1939.

Stationed at Colchester, assigned to 4th Infantry Division.[27] Officially relieved from 4th Infantry Division in France 31 March 1940 and assigned 2nd Armoured Recce

---

[26] One squadron was at Sarafand, Palestine, attached to the Royal Scots Greys and later absorbed by that regiment.
[27] One squadron was at Gedera, Palestine, attached to 1st Royal Dragoons and later absorbed by that regiment.

Brigade but did not actually join until 16 May 1940. Due to losses, 15th/19th Hussars formed a composite regiment with 5th Royal Inniskilling Dragoon Guards from 18 May 1940. The regiment was reformed June 1940 in the UK. Parent brigade redesignated 23 June 1940 as 3rd Motor MG Brigade and 1 December 1940 as 28th Armoured Brigade; regiment reorganized from December 1940 as armoured. Relieved 13 July 1944 and sent to France, joining 22nd Armoured Brigade 29 July 1944. Remained with brigade on occupation duties with BAOR.

Equipment notes: Original equipment of Mk VI Light Tanks and carriers all lost in France May 1940. Re-equipped at first with trucks. In September 1940 around 90 Beaverettes and Humberettes. By March 1941 still had only one squadron with any tanks (1 Crusader, 5 Mk VIB Light, 6 Covenanters, 2 Vickers light tanks, along with 4 'Humberettes': civilian cars with Vickers MMG). Received Coventanters later in 1941 and fully equipped by November. From September 1942 began to receive Cromwells and Centaurs. Given Shermans in May 1944, but then had to convert to Cromwells (with Fireflys) on assignment to 22nd Armoured Brigade late July 1944, remaining so equipped for the remainder of the war.

Battle Honours: WITHDRAWAL TO ESCAUT, ST. OMER-LA BASSEE, DUNKIRK 1940, MONT PINCON, St. Pierre le Vielle, Lisieux, Risle Crossing, LOWER MAAS, Roer, Ibbenburen, North-West Europe 1940 '44-45

Badge: Monogram 'VDG' and crown, in white metal. Badge worn pinned through a green patch.

1st THE ROYAL DRAGOONS

Raised 1661, becoming 1st (Royal) Dragoons and designated 1st The Royal Dragoons from 1 January 1921. Stationed at Gedera, Palestine, the Royals were still a horsed regiment when the war began. (One squadron of 5th Royal Inniskilling Dragoon Guards with light tanks was attached and later absorbed.)

Mobilized with 8th Infantry Division, the regiment may have been temporarily in Egypt September 1939, but was back in Palestine by 28 February 1940 when the division was disbanded. Converted ca December 1940 as an armoured car regiment, coming under the RAC. The regiment served in North Africa from January 1941, but did not operate as a complete regiment until that November. Assigned 1st Armoured Division 12 May 1942; relieved 13 September 1942. Assigned 10th Armoured Division 22 September 1942; relieved 31 October 1942. Served as a GHQ unit in North Africa November 1942 to July 1943, and in Sicily and Italy July 1943 to January 1944. ('A' Sqn served in Sicily and Italy; the full regiment did not move to Italy until November 1943.) Sent to 21st Army Group February 1944 and operated with XII Corps in NW Europe from June 1944. Assigned 1st Parachute Brigade for period 10 May to 18 July 1945. Remained in Germany on occupation duties.

Equipment notes: Marmon-Herrington II armoured cars in May 1941. In May 1942 Marmon-Herrington III armoured cars. In late October 1942 had 46 Humber II and Daimler armoured cars. A mix of Daimler and AEC armoured cars by July 1943. June 1944: 45 Daimler I, 14 Staghound, 8 M3 H/T 75mm, 5 AA armoured cars, 52 Daimler and 13 Humber scour cars; October 1944 (AC only): 45 Daimler, 15 Staghound, and 7 M3 H/T 75mm.

Battle Honours: NEDERRIJN, Veghel, RHINE, NORTH WEST EUROPE 1944-45, SYRIA 1941, Msus, Gazala, KNIGHTSBRIDGE, Defence of Alamein Line, EL ALAMEIN, El Agheila, ADVANCE ON TRIPOLI, NORTH AFRICA 1941-43, SICILY 1943, ITALY 1943

Badge: The Royal Crest above scroll 'The Royal Dragoons', scroll in silver, rest in gold.

THE ROYAL SCOTS GREYS (2nd DRAGOONS)

Raised 1678, becoming 2nd Dragoons (Royal Scots Greys), restyling the title 1 January 1921. Stationed at Rehovath, Palestine and still a horsed unit. (One squadron 4th/7th Royal Dragoon Guards with light tanks attached and later absorbed.)

Mobilized in Lydda Area, under 7th Infantry Division. Assigned 6th Infantry Division for period 25 March to 30 May 1940. Assigned 6th Cavalry Brigade 1 March 1941; brigade redesignated 1 August 1941 as 8th Armoured Brigade. (Came under the RAC 19 July 1941.) Relieved from 8th Armoured Brigade 30 June 1942 and assigned to 4th Armoured Brigade for period 16 September to 23 November 1942. Regiment then became a GHQ unit under Eighth Army January to July 1943, in Sicily July to September 1943, and then in Italy September to November 1943. (Supported 56th (London) Infantry Division in September 1943 landing at Salerno.) The regiment then went to the UK and was assigned 27 January 1944 to 4th Armoured Brigade. Relieved 29 April 1945 and attached 1 May 1945 to 6th Airborne Division. Assigned 6 June 1945 to 31st Armoured Brigade. The regiment remained in Germany on occupation duties following the war.

Equipment notes: Began as mounted unit, later in 15cwt trucks. (In spring 1941, RHQ, MG Troop and one squadron were in trucks for Syrian campaign; remaining horses given up and converted to trucks during August 1941.) Stuart light tanks 1941 when added to RAC. Handed over tanks to other units ca. May 1942. Re-equipped with Grants and Lees ('A' and 'C' Sqns) by September 1942, along with one squadron ('B') of Stuarts. (October 1942: 19 Stuarts and 21 Grants.) Received first Shermans early December 1942, dividing them and remaining 4 Grants among two heavy squadrons, with one squadron still in Stuarts. Re-equipped with Shermans during 1943. In June 1944 had Sherman II and Fireflys. In December 1944, proportion of Fireflys up to around 34%.

Battle Honours: Caen, HILL 112, FALAISE, Venlo Pocket, HOCHWALD, ALLER, BREMEN, North West Europe 1944-45, MERJAYUN, Syria 1941, ALAM EL HALFA, EL ALAMEIN, El Agheila, NOFILIA, Advance on Tripoli, North Africa 1942-43, SALERNO, Battipaglia, Volturno Crossing, ITALY 1943

Badge: An Eagle (French Napoleonic) on plinth labeled 'Waterloo' above scroll 'Royal Scots Greys'. Officers eagle in silver plate and scroll in gilt, other ranks in white and gilding metal. Badge worn pinned through black patch.

3rd THE KING'S OWN HUSSARS

Raised 1685, becoming 3rd (King's Own) Hussars and restyled 1 January 1921. Mechanized 1935-36; a cavalry light tank regiment by 1939.

Stationed at Tidworth as part of 1st Light Armoured Brigade (redesignated 14 April 1940 as 1st Armoured Brigade). (One troop served in Norway April-May 1940.) Relieved from 1st Armoured Brigade 14 August 1940 and sent to North Africa. Assigned 7th Armoured Brigade 13 October 1940; relieved 22 January 1941. Assigned 3rd Armoured Brigade 26 February 1941; relieved 14 April 1941. Served as a GHQ unit in North Africa April 1941 to February 1942 (including service on Cyprus). ('B' Sqn sent to Java early 1942 and captured there.) Assigned 9th Armoured Brigade 16 March 1942; relieved 27 May 1943. (Regiment was in Syria, Palestine and Lebanon from January 1943 to April 1944 when it went to Italy.) Returned to 9th Armoured Brigade 23 to 30 August 1943. Again assigned to 9th Armoured Brigade 6 October 1944; relieved 30 December 1944. Left Italy 7 January 1945, serving thereafter in Egypt, Syria and Lebanon. Moved to Palestine December 1945 upon selection as recce regiment for 6th Airborne Division. Absorbed personnel of 6th Airborne Recce Regiment RAC 1 February 1946.

Equipment notes: In October 1940: Mk VI Light. In March 1941 had Mk VI light in 'A' and 'C' Sqns (26) and 12 Italian M13/40 in 'B' Sqn. In December 1941 while on Cyprus had Mark VIB light tanks and carriers. In May 1942 Stuarts in 'A' Sqn and Crusaders in 'B' and 'C' Sqns (probably understrength). Received first Grants and Shermans in mid-September 1942; October 1942 had 16 Crusaders in 'A' Sqn, 12 Shermans in 'B' Sqn and 9 Grants in 'C' Sqn; RHQ tanks unknown. (Lost 47 of 51 tanks at El Alamein.) Later (by June 1943) equipped all with Shermans. After leaving Italy, converted with 'A' Sqn in Sherman tanks and remainder in Staghound armoured cars.

Battle Honours: SIDI BARRANI, BUQ BUQ, BEDA FROMM, SIDI SULEIMAN, EL ALAMEIN, NORTH AFRICA 1940-42, CITTA DELLA PIEVE, CITTA DI CASTELLO, ITALY 1944, CRETE

Badge: The White Horse of Hanover above scroll '3rd The King's Own Hussars'. Officers horse and ground in silver plate and scroll in gilt; other ranks white and gilding metal.

4th QUEEN'S OWN HUSSARS

Raised 1685, becoming 4th (Queen's Own) Hussars until restyled 1 January 1921. Mechanized 1936 as cavalry light tank regiment.

Stationed at Tidworth as part of 1st Light Armoured Brigade (redesignated 14 April 1940 as 1st Armoured Brigade) (Almost all of the regiment was lost in Greece April 1941 and reconstituted June 1941 in Cairo.) Relieved 5 June 1942. Due to losses, formed combined regiment with 8th King's Royal Irish Hussars as 4th/8th Hussars; assigned 4th Armoured Brigade 14 July 1942 to 23 November 1942, then resumed separate identity; moved to Cyprus to refit (absorbed personnel of 'F' Sqn, 2nd Royal Gloster Hussars early January 1943) and then to Egypt in June 1943 and began conversion as armoured recce regiment. Assigned 1st Armoured Division 23 May 1944; relieved 25 September 1944. Assigned 9th Armoured Brigade 26 October 1944; converted November 1944 to APC regiment; relieved 6 May 1945. Moved into Austria on occupation duties following the end of the war. Assigned 26th Armoured Brigade 28 July 1945.

Equipment notes: Originally Mk VI light; still all Mk VIC light (52) in Greece April 1941. In December 1941 had some armoured cars. Received first Grants April 1942, in May 1942 had Stuarts in RHQ and 'A' Sqn and Grants in 'B' and 'C' Sqns. As composite regiment with 8th Hussars, equipped with Stuarts (48 in October 1942). Mixture of Shermans and Stuarts when reorganized as armoured recce regiment. When converted November 1944, 'A' and 'C' Sqns had APCs (modified Priests) and 'B' Sqn retained gun-armed Shermans. Final organization was 17 Shermans in 'B' Sqn, 53 converted Priests in 'A' Sqn, and 53 Kangaroos in 'C' Sqn. Probably converted to Shermans following the war.

Battle Honours: Gazala, Defence of Alamein Line, RUWEISAT, ALAM EL HALFA, EL ALAMEIN, North Africa 1942, CORIANO, San Clemente, SENIO POCKET, RIMINI LINE, Conventello-Comacchio, Senio, Santerno Crossing, ARGENTA GAP, Italy 1944-45, PROASTEION, CORINTH CANAL, GREECE 1941

Badge: Ornamented Roman numeral IV within circle inscribed 'Queen's Own Hussars' and containing spray of laurel in bottom center. Crown above and scroll 'Mente Et Manu' (With might and main) below. Officers: circle and crown in gilt and 'IV' and motto scroll in silver plate; other tanks gilding and white metal.

7th QUEEN'S OWN HUSSARS

Raised 1690, becoming 7th (Queen's Own) Hussars, with the title restyled 1 January 1921. Mechanized beginning May 1936 as a cavalry light tank regiment.

Stationed at Gerwala, Egypt as part of Light Armoured Brigade (Egypt) (brigade redesignated 16 February 1940 as 7th Light Armoured Brigade). Transferred 10 April 1940 to 4th Armoured Brigade; relieved 3 May 1941. Assigned 7th Armoured Brigade 7

July 1941; relieved November 1943. Assigned 10th Armoured Division as its armoured recce regiment 5 November 1943; relieved 25 April 1944. A GHQ unit in North Africa April to May 1944 when the regiment landed in Italy.[28] Assigned 9th Armoured Brigade 26 October 1944. Transferred 8 July 1945 to 7th Armoured Brigade. The regiment remained in Italy on occupation duties until October 1946 when it moved through Austria to Germany.

Equipment notes: Fully equipped with 58 Mk VI light tanks on mobilization. The first A9 arrived in October 1939 ('C' Sqn was training with them by January 1940, but the whole regiment only had 7 of its establishment of 16). In May 1941 establishment was to be 32 A9 and 20 A10 cruisers, but those actually on hand were given up on the 31st. 'C' Sqn was the first to re-equip in June 1941 (A10s); 'A' Sqn received A10s in July while 'C' Sqn switched to A9s (later a mix of A9/A10), and 'B' Sqn A13s. In September 1941, 'A' Sqn began to receive Crusaders, 'C' Sqn became all A10s. November 1941: 57 cruisers (21 A10, 16 A13, 20 Crusader). All but two tanks were lost during the fighting in November 1941, and at the end of the month the regiment withdrew; it began to reform with Stuart tanks January 1941, just before sailing for Burma. It withdrew to India May 1941, having lost all of its tanks in Burma. It began to receive Grants July 1941. In Iraq, Stuarts replaced the Grants, and by 1943 the regiment had Crusaders and three worn Shermans; 'B' Sqn was still in Stuarts. Around September 1943 it had Stuarts and Shermans, becoming an armoured recce regiment in November. Presumably converted back to conventional armoured regiment (Shermans) April-May 1944 before going to Italy. The regiment began to train with DD tanks October 1944. ('C' Sqn received Valentine DD tanks in November.) The regiment was dismounted December 1944 when 9th Armoured Brigade took over a sector of the front as infantry. The regiment remounted February 1945; 'A' Sqn increased and given Kangaroos while 'B' and 'C' Sqns had Shermans; however by the end of the month 'A' Sqn was changed to Valentine and Sherman DD tanks. Final wartime organization was three squadrons of 16 Shermans (DD variants in 'A' and 'B' Sqns and regular tanks in 'C' Sqn).

Battle Honours: EGYPTIAN FRONTIER 1940, BEDA FROMM, SIDI REZEGH 1941, NORTH AFRICA 1940-41, ANCONA, RIMINI LINE, ITALY 1944-45, PEGU, PAUNGDE, BURMA 1942

Badge: Monogram 'QO' reversed and intertwined within circle inscribed '7th Queen's Own Hussars', surmounted by Crown. Officers gilding metal with monogram in silver plate, other ranks gilding and white metals.

---

[28] The published regimental history (Brig G. M. O. Davy, *The Seventh and Three Enemies*) indicates that the 7th was back under 7th Armoured Brigade as a fourth regiment in May 1944, but Joslen, *Orders of Battle*, does not show it under that brigade again until 1945. In any case, the regiment seems to have operated in support of various infantry divisions (especially II Polish Corps) during the June-September 1944, when it came under Eighth Army and then AAI before passing to 9th Armoured Brigade.

8th KING'S ROYAL IRISH HUSSARS

Raised 1693, becoming 8th (King's Royal Irish) Hussars; title restyled 1 January 1921. Mechanized 1935 as a cavalry light tank regiment.

Stationed at Gerwala, Egypt as part of Light Armoured Brigade (Egypt) (brigade redesignated 16 February 1940 as 7th Light Armoured Brigade and 14 April 1940 as 7th Armoured Brigade); relieved 19 January 1941. Assigned 7th Armoured Brigade 7 March 1941; relieved 16 April 1941 and assigned the next day to 4th Armoured Brigade; relieved 3 May 1941. Assigned 1st Armoured Brigade 10 May 1941; relieved 8 August 1941. Assigned 4th Armoured Brigade 31 July 1941;[29] relieved 8 February 1942; returned 14 February 1942 and relieved 2 June 1942. Due to losses, formed combined regiment with 4th Queen's Own Hussars as 4th/8th Hussars; assigned 4th Armoured Brigade 14 July 1942 to 23 November 1942, then resumed separate identity; moved to Cyprus to refit (absorbed personnel of 'H' Sqn, 2nd Royal Gloster Hussars early January 1943). Moved to the UK November 1943 and converted as armoured recce regiment; assigned to 7th Armoured Division 16 December 1943. Remained in Germany on occupation duties following the end of the war.

Equipment notes: At mobilization, 'A' Sqn had tanks (11 Mk III and 7 Mk VIB lights); 'B' and 'C' Sqns were in 15cwt trucks. (Became all-tank but details unknown.) The first shipments to North Africa of the Stuart (July 1941) were used to equip the regiment entirely with that tank. November 1941: 51 Stuarts. Received Grants March 1942; late May 1942 had Stuarts in RHQ and 'C' Sqn, Grants in 'A' and 'B' Sqns. As composite regiment with 4th Hussars equipped with Stuarts (48 in October 1942). Conventional armoured recce regiment (Cromwells and Stuarts) from November 1943; by spring 1944 normal 21st Army Group pattern of all Cromwells with Stuarts only in the recce troop.

Battle Honours: VILLERS BOCAGE, Mont Pincon, Dives Crossing, Nederrijn, Best, LOWER MAAS, ROER, RHINE, NORTH WEST EUROPE 1944-45, Egyptian Frontier 1940, Sidi Barrani, BUQ BUQ, SIDI REZEGH 1941, Relief of Tobruk, GAZALA, Bir el Igela, Mersa Matruh, Alam el Halfa, EL ALAMEIN, NORTH AFRICA 1940-42,

Badge: Irish Harp and with Crown resting on the wing, above scroll '8th King's Royal Irish Hussars'. Harp in white metal and crown and scroll in gilding metal. (This is actually the other ranks badge. Officers wore a harp surmounted by a Royal Crest in silver plate, below the harp a Roman numeral 'VIII' in gilt; below all a scroll 'Pristinae Virtutis Memores' (Mindful of our former valor) in gilt.

---

[29] The discrepancy between leaving 1st Armoured Brigade in August and joining the 4th on 31 July exists within Joslen/

9th QUEEN'S ROYAL LANCERS

Raised 1715, becoming 9th (Queen's Royal) Lancers and altering the title somewhat 1 January 1921. Mechanized 1936 as a cavalry light tank regiment.

Stationed at Tidworth as part of 2nd Light Armoured Brigade (brigade redesignated 14 April 1940 as 2nd Armoured Brigade). Relieved from 2nd Armoured Brigade 30 June 1942 due to losses and returned 2 August 1942.

Equipment notes: Began with Mk VI Light Tanks. In May 1940 probably similar to Queen's Bays (29 cruisers and 21 Mark VI light). In December 1941, re-equipping with Crusader and Stuart tanks. Received first Grants April 1942, late May 1942 had Crusaders in RHQ and 'A' and 'C' Sqns and Grants in 'B' Sqn (plus 2 Stuarts and 1 Crusader). Began to receive Shermans early September 1942; in late October 1942 had Crusader III in RHQ and 'A' Sqn and Sherman I in 'B' and 'C' Sqns. Tanks were removed mid November 1942 for other units. Re-equipped by February 1943; in late March 1943 had Crusaders (mix of II/III) in RHQ and 'A' Sqn and a mixture of Shermans and Grants for 'B' and 'C' Sqns. Later fully equipped with Sherman III and V. In August 1944 received 12 Sherman IIA (76mm), allotted one per troop, and in September 1944 6 Sherman IB (105mm), issued 2 per squadron as HQ vehicles.

Battle Honours: SOMME 1940, Withdrawal to Seine, NORTH WEST EUROPE 1940, Saunnu, GAZALA, Bir el Aslagh, Sidi Rezegh 1942, Defence of Alamein Line, RUWEISAT, Ruweisat Ridge, EL ALAMEIN, Tebaga Gap, EL HAMMA, El Kourzia, Tunis, Creteville Pass, NORTH AFRICA 1942-43, Coriano, Capture of Forli, Lamone Crossing, Pideura, LAMONE BRIDGEHEAD, ARGENTA GAP, ITALY 1944-45

Badge: Crossed lances with pennons flying outwards, with figure '9' on the cross of the lances; Crown above and scroll 'Lancers' resting on lower portion of the lances below. Officers in silver plate and other ranks in white metal.

10th ROYAL HUSSARS (PRINCE OF WALES'S OWN)

Raised 1715, becoming 10t (Prince of Wales's Own Royal) Hussars; title restyled 1 January 1921. Mechanized 1936; a cavalry light tank regiment by 1939.

Stationed at Tidworth as part of 2nd Light Armoured Brigade (brigade redesignated 14 April 1940 as 2nd Armoured Brigade). Relieved from 2nd Armoured Brigade 4 July 1942 due to losses and returned 2 August 1942.

Equipment notes: Began with Mk VI Light Tanks. In May 1940 probably similar to Queen's Bays (29 cruisers and 21 Mark VI light). In December 1941, re-equipping with Crusader and Stuart tanks. Received first Grants April 1942, late May 1942 had Crusaders in RHQ and 'A' and 'B' Sqns and Grants in 'C' Sqn. Began to receive Shermans early September 1942; in late October 1942 had Crusader III in RHQ and 'B' Sqn and Sherman I in 'A' and 'C' Sqns. Tanks were removed mid November 1942 for other units. Re-equipped by February 1943; in late March 1943 had Crusaders (II/III) in

RHQ and 'B' Sqn and a mixture of Shermans and Grants for 'A' and 'C' Sqns. Later fully equipped with Sherman III and V. In August 1944 received 12 Sherman IIA (76mm), allotted one per troop, and in September 1944 6 Sherman IB (105mm), issued 2 per squadron as HQ vehicles.

Battle Honours: SOMME 1940, North West Europe 1940, SAUNNU, GAZALA, Bir el Aslagh, Alam el Halfa, EL ALAMEIN, EL HAMMA, El Kourzia, Djebel Kournine, TUNIS, North Africa 1942-43, CORIANO, SANTARCANGELO, Cosina Canal Crossing, Senio Pocket, Cesena, VALLI DI COMMACCHIO, ARGENTA GAP, Italy 1944-45

Badge: The Prince of Wales's Feathers and motto above scroll '10th Royal Hussars'. Officers plume and motto in silver plate, coronet and title scroll in gilt; other ranks in white and gilding metal. Badge worn pinned through a black patch.

11th HUSSARS (PRINCE ALBERT'S OWN)

Raised 1715, becoming 11th (or Prince Albert's Own) Hussars; title restyled in January 1921. Mechanized 1928 as an armoured car regiment.

Stationed at Gerwala, Egypt as part of Light Armoured Brigade (Egypt) (brigade redesignated 16 February 1940 as 7th Light Armoured Brigade); relieved 14 April 1940 and assigned to 7th Armoured Division. (Came under 4th Armoured Brigade 16 July to 22 November 1942.) Relieved from 7th Armoured Division 3 November 1943 and sent to the UK, coming under 21st Army Group by April 1944. Served with XXX Corps in NW Europe from June 1944. Remained in Germany on occupation duties, coming under 7th Armoured Division by 1946.

Equipment notes: A combination of 1920/1924 Rolls Royce and Morris CS9 armoured cars on mobilization. By summer 1941, Marmon-Herrington II armoured cars. November 1941: ca. 50 Humber II armoured cars. In October 1942 had 61 Humber III armoured cars. Changed over to Daimler armoured cars by March 1943. June 1944: 45 Daimler I, 14 Staghound, 8 M3 H/T 75mm, 5 AA armoured cars, 52 Daimler and 13 Humber scour cars; October 1944 (AC only): 43 Daimler, 17 Staghound, and 8 M3 H/T 75mm.

Battle Honours: VILLERS BOCAGE, Bourgebus Ridge, Mont Pincon, Jurques, Dives Crossing, La Vie Crossing, Lisieux, La Touques Crossing, Risle Crossing, ROER, RHINE, Ibbenburen, Aller, North West Europe 1944-45, EGYPTIAN FRONTIER 1940, Withdrawal to Matruh, Bir Enba, SIDI BARRANI, Buq Buq, Bardia 1941, Capture of Tobruk, BEDA FROMM, Halfaya 1941, Sidi Suleiman, Tobruk 1941, Gubi I, II, Gabr Saleh, SIDI REZEGH 1941, Taieb el Essom, Gubi II, Relief of Tobruk, Saunnu, Msus, Defence of Alamein Line, Alam el Halfa, EL ALAMEIN, Advance on Tripoli, Enfidaville, TUNIS, North Africa 1940-43, Capture of Naples, Volturno Crossing, ITALY 1943

Badge: Crest of the late Prince Consort. Officers in gilt and other ranks in gilding metal. The regiment had a distinctive rust coloured (reddish brown) beret with a cherry-picker red band,[30] and their colonel-in-chief (HM King George VI) allowed them to retain it in lieu of adopting the RAC black beret.

12th ROYAL LANCERS (PRINCE OF WALES'S)

Raised 1715, becoming 12th (Prince of Wales's Royal) Lancers; title restyled 1 January 1921. Mechanized 1928 as an armoured car regiment.

Stationed at Aldershot as a GHQ unit; served with BEF in France October 1939-May 1940, then under Home Forces control. Assigned 1st Armoured Division 1 November 1940; relieved 12 May 1942. Assigned 4th Armoured Brigade 18 July 1942; relieved 12 September 1942 and assigned the next day to 1st Armoured Division; relieved 6 April 1944. Served as a GHQ unit in Italy from April 1944 (with V Corps at least part of the time).

Equipment notes: Began the war with 38 Morris armoured cars. In December 1941 re-equipping with Humber II armoured cars. Humber II armoured cars May 1942 and 55 Humber II armoured cars October 1942. Had Daimler armoured cars by mid 1943.

Battle Honours: DYLE, Defence of Arras, Arras Counterattack, DUNKIRK 1940, NORTH WEST EUROPE 1940, CHOR ES SUFAN, GAZALA, Alam el Halfa, EL ALAMEIN, Advance on Tripoli, Tebaga Gap, El Hamma, Akarit, El Kourzla, Djebel Kournine, TUNIS, Creteville Pass, NORTH AFRICA 1941-43, Citerna, Gothic Line, Capture of Forli, Conventello-Comacchio, BOLOGNA, Sillaro Crossing, Idice Bridgehead, ITALY 1944-45

Badge: Crossed lances with pennons flying outwards, on the cross of the lances the Prince of Wales's plume, coronet and motto; above and within the upper portion of the lances the Crown; below and within the lower portion of the lances the Roman numeral 'XII'. Officers have the three feathers of the plume, the motto, and the lower half of each pennon in silver plate and the remainder of the badge in gilt. Other ranks in white metal and gilding metal.

---

[30] Their nickname was The Cherry Pickers, supposed to have originated in the Peninsula when a detachment was captured in an orchard.

13th/18th Royal Hussars (Queen Mary's Own)

Formed 1922 as 13th/18th Hussars by amalgamation of 13th Hussars (raised 1715) and 18th Royal Hussars (Queen Mary's Own) (raised 1858);[31] redesignated 13th/18th Royal Hussars (Queen Mary's Own) December 1935. Mechanized January 1939 (following return from India) as a divisional cavalry regiment.

Stationed at Shorncliffe and assigned to 1st Infantry Division. Officially relieved 31 March 1940 in France and assigned 1st Armoured Recce Brigade (but remained with the division and did not actually join it until 18 June 1940 when back in the UK). Brigade redesignated 26 November 1940 as 27th Armoured Brigade (and regiment converted as armoured regiment); trained with DD tanks from 1943 and operated them at Normandy, June 1944. Transferred to 8th Armoured Brigade 29 July 1944. Remained in Germany on occupation duties following the war.

Equipment notes: Began with Mk VI Light tanks and carriers; all were lost by Dunkirk May 1940. Re-equipped initially with trucks. In September 1940 around 60 Beaverettes. Received Covenanters beginning August 1941 and fully equipped by November. Trained with Valentine DD tanks from 1943 but converted to Sherman III DD tanks April-May 1944. In June 1944, Sherman (V?) DD in 'A' and 'B' Sqns, Sherman III and Firefly in 'C' Sqn. (DD tanks replaced after Normandy landing with conventional Shermans and Fireflys.) In December 1944 a mixture of Shermans and Fireflys.

Battle Honours: Dyle, Withdrawal to Escaut, YPRES-COMINES CANAL, NORMANDY LANDING, Bretteville, CAEN, Bourgebus Ridge, MONT PINCON, St Pierre la Vielle, GEILENKIRCHEN, ROER, RHINELAND, Waal Flats, GOCH, Rhine, Bremen, NORTH WEST EUROPE 1940 '44-45

Badge: Monogram 'QMO', superimposed on which is a scroll in shape of letter 'Z' with 'XIII' on top, 'XVIII' on bottom, and 'Royal Hussars' in center; Crown above. Officers in gilt and other ranks in gilding metal.
Regimental Flash: the regiment wore a diamond divided vertically (white and dark blue) on the upper left arm; this was originally the flash worn on the sun helmets of the 13th Hussars in the Boer War.

14th/20th King's Hussars

Formed 1922 as 14th/20th Hussars by amalgamation of 14th King's Hussars (raised 1715) and 20th Hussars (raised 1858);[32] restyled December 1936 as 14th/20th King's Hussars. Mechanized October 1938 as a cavalry light tank regiment.

---

[31] The new regiment was considered a successor to the prior 18th Light Dragoons, raised 1759 and disbanded 1821, whose battle honours were regranted to the new regiment.

[32] Raised by Hon. the East India Company and taken over by the British Army in 1862. In 1890 it was granted the honours of the earlier 20th Light Dragoons, raised 1792 and disbanded 1818.

Stationed at Trimulgherry, India and assigned to 4th (Secunderabad) Cavalry Brigade. Assigned 2nd Indian Armoured Brigade July 1941 (brigade redesignated December 1941 as 252nd Indian Armoured Brigade). Relieved 16 January 1945 and sent to Italy, coming under Eighth Army 1 February 1945. Operated mainly with 43rd Gurkha Infantry Brigade and one squadron converted to APCs. (Became an armoured car regiment July 1945.) Remained in Italy until February 1946 when they went to Germany.

Equipment notes: Began with 41 Mk VIB light tanks. Still had Mark VIB lights December 1941. By September 1942 equipped with Grant tanks. Final organization was 40 modified Priest APCs in 'A' Sqn and Shermans in 'B' and 'C' Sqns (14 tanks each). Converted July 1945 to Staghound and Greyhound armoured cars, but left them in Italy when transferred February 1946 to Germany, where they were equipped with Archer SP antitank guns.

Battle Honours: BOLOGNA, MEDECINA, ITALY 1945

Badge: The Prussian Eagle. Black japanned metal for officers and gilding metal for other ranks. (Badge was worn by 14th King's Hussars until 1915, and restored to the amalgamated regiment in 1931.)

15th/19th THE KING'S ROYAL HUSSARS

Formed 1922 by amalgamation of 15th The King's Hussars (raised 1759) and 19th Royal Hussars (Queen Alexandra's Own) (raised 1858);[33] known as 15th The King's Royal Hussars until restyled as 15th/19th early 1934. Mechanized 1938; a divisional cavalry regiment by 1939.

Stationed at York and assigned to 3rd Infantry Division. Officially relieved 31 March 1940 and assigned 2nd Armoured Recce Brigade but did not actually come under command until 16 May 1940. Due to heavy losses, formed a composite regiment with 5th Royal Inniskilling Dragoon Guards from 18 May 1940; regiment reformed June 1940 in the UK. (Brigade redesignated 23 June 1940 as 3rd Motor MG Brigade and 1 December 1940 as 28th Armoured Brigade; regiment converted ca. December 1940 as an armoured regiment). Relieved from 28th Armoured Brigade 20 June 1944. Converted July 1944 as an armoured recce regiment and assigned to 11th Armoured Division 17 August 1944. Remained in Germany on occupation duties following the war.

Equipment notes: Began with Mk VI Light Tanks and carriers; all lost by Dunkirk May 1940. Re-equipped initially with trucks. In September 1940 around 90 Beaverettes and Humberettes. Received Covenanters 1941 and fully equipped by November. From September 1942 began to receive Cromwells and Centaurs. Issued Sherman V DD tanks (75) in May 1944 as a sort of holding unit for DDs. Given

---

[33] Raised by Hon. the East India Company and taken over by the British Army in 1862. It inherited battle honours at various dates between 1874 and 1912 from the 19th Light Dragoons raised 1781 and disbanded 1821.

Cromwells on conversion July 1944. These were replaced with Comets April 1945 (although Cromwell CS tanks retained).

Battle Honours: WITHDRAWAL TO ESCAUT, SEINE 1944, Hechtel, NEDERRIJN, Venraij, RHINELAND, HOCHWALD, RHINE, IBBENBUREN, ALLER, NORTH WEST EUROPE 1940 '44-45

Badge: The Royal Crest within Garter, numbers 'XV.XIX' attached below, with scroll 'Merebinum' (Let us be worthy) below the numerals. Officers have the Garter and Roman numerals in gilt, the Royal Crest in silver plate, and the motto scroll and motto in silver plate with blue groundwork. Other ranks in gilding and white metals. Badge worn pinned through a red patch.

16th/5th LANCERS

Formed 1922 by amalgamation of 16th The Queen's Lancers (raised 1759) and 5th Royal Irish Lancers.[34] The regiment was supposed to begin mechanization but was still horsed at the out break of war.

Stationed at Risalpur, India and assigned 1st (Risalpur) Cavalry Brigade. Last mounted parade held January 1940 at Risalpur, at which time the regiment turned over its horses. Left for the UK March 1940. Assigned 1st Motor MG Brigade 30 May 1940 (brigade redesignated 12 October 1940 as 26th Armoured Brigade and regiment converted as an armoured regiment); relieved 9 January 1944. Returned to 26th Armoured Brigade 29 March 1944. Moved into Austria on occupation duties following the end of the war, later going to Schleswig-Holstein in Germany.

Equipment notes: By May 1940 had some Medium tanks and trucks. By March 1941 had 42 Valentines and 4 Matildas. All Valentines by December 1941. By August 1942 had a mix of Crusaders and Valentines (four troops in each squadron, half of each type). In February 1943 began to replace existing tanks with Shermans; re-drew old equipment for Kasserine, then began to refit again with Shermans; by April 1943 a homogenous regiment (Sherman III). Received 6 Sherman IB (105mm) for squadron HQs in September 1944, and began conversion to Sherman IIA (76mm) in March 1945.

Battle Honours: Kasserine, FONDOUK, Kairouan, BORDJ, DJEBEL KOURNINE, TUNIS, Grombaila, Bou Ficha, NORTH AFRICA 1942-43, CASSINO II, LIRI VALLEY, Monte Piccolo, Capture of Perugia, Arezzo, ADVANCE TO FLORENCE, ARGENTA GAP, Traghetto, ITALY 1944-45

---

[34] The inversion of the numbers is caused by the fact that the 5th were disbanded in 1799 and reformed 1858. The new regiment was allowed to claim the honours of the earlier one (raised in 1689) but lost its seniority. It is not clear why the amalgamated regiment lost the honour titles of the prior regiments in its title (note the cap badge); on 16 June 1954 it was redesignated 16th/5th The Queen's Royal Lancers.

Badge: Crossed lances with pennons flying outward; '16' on the cross of the lances; Crown between the upper portion of the lances and scroll 'The Queen's Lancers' on the lower portion of the lances. Officers in gilt, with figure '16', scroll, and the lower portion of each pennon in silver plate. Other ranks in gilding and white metals.

17th/21st LANCERS

Formed 1922 by amalgamation of 17th Lancers (Duke of Cambridge's Own) (raised 1759) and 21st Lancers (Empress of India's) (raised 1858).[35] Mechanization began 1938 but was still incomplete on return from India.

Stationed at Colchester, a GHQ unit. Assigned 1st Motor MG Brigade 30 May 1940 (brigade redesignated 12 October 1940 as 26th Armoured Brigade and regiment converted as an armoured regiment). The regiment moved into Austria on occupation duties following the end of the war, going to Greece in October 1946.

Equipment notes: At the outbreak of war, without equipment (including any transport) other than personal arms. First armour, within a few weeks, was 4 old Medium tanks. By May 1940 had some Medium tanks and trucks. As late as September 1940 only had 6 Matilda II infantry tanks. By the end of 1940 at one-third strength, with a mix of Valentines and Matildas. All Valentines by December 1941. By August 1942 a mix of Crusaders and Valentines (four troops in each squadron, half of each type). In February 1943 began to replace existing tanks with Shermans; re-drew old equipment for Kasserine, then began to refit again with Shermans; by April 1943 a homogenous regiment (Sherman III). Received 6 Sherman IB (105mm) for squadron HQs in September 1944, and began conversion to Sherman IIA (76mm) in March 1945.

Battle Honours: TEBOURBA GAP, Bou Arada, KASSERINE, Thala, FONDOUK, EL KOURZIA. TUNIS, Hammam Lif, NORTH AFRICA 1942-43, CASSINO II, Monte Piccolo, CAPTURE OF PERUGIA, Advance to Florence, Argenta Gap, Fossa Cembalina, ITALY 1944-45

Badge: Skull and Crossbones (Death's Head) with scroll 'Or Glory' on the bones. Officers in silver plate and other ranks in white metal.
Battledress: White '17/21 Lancers' on black[36]

---

[35] Raised by Hon. the East India Company and taken over by the British Army in 1862.
[36] Apparently the only Regular cavalry regiment to wear a shoulder title.

22nd DRAGOONS

Raised 30 December 1940 (cadre from 4th/7th and 5th Dragoon Guards) and assigned 29th Armoured Brigade; transferred 8 January 1941 to 30th Armoured Brigade. Placed in suspended animation ca November 1945. Disbanded June 1948.

Equipment notes: Received Valentines 1941 (from March?). Changed to flail tanks from October 1943. In June 1944 had a mix of Sherman V and Sherman V Crab tanks. Same in December 1944.

Battle Honours: Normandy Landing, Caen, Falaise, Le Havre, Lower Maas, Venlo Pocket, Reichswald, Rhine, North-West Europe 1944-45

Badge: Letter 'D' containing number 'XXII'; Crown above and scroll 'Dragoons' below. Officers in bronze and other ranks in white metal.

23rd HUSSARS

Raised 30 December 1940 (cadre from 10th and 15th/19th Hussars) and assigned 30th Armoured Brigade. Transferred 8 January 1941 to 29th Armoured Brigade. (Brigade withdrawn December 1944 to convert to Comets; but re-equipped with its original tanks for service in the Ardennes and not converted until March 1945.) Placed in suspended animation ca February 1946 when brigade disbanded. Disbanded June 1948.

Equipment notes: Probably only a few Matildas and old Vickers Mediums at first. Began to receive Valentines March 1941. Began to reorganize with Valentines and Crusaders from July 1942; changed back to all Valentines January 1943. Changed to Shermans May-June 1943; also included some Centaurs to early 1944. In June 1944 a mix of Sherman V and Fireflys. Changed to Comets (with Cromwell CS) ca March 1945.

Battle Honours: Bourgebus Ridge, Le Perier Ridge, Antwerp, Venraij, Venlo Pocket, Ourthe, North-West Europe 1944-45

Badge: Letter 'H', with Crown above and scroll '23rd Hussars' below. Officers badges in bronze; other ranks have 'H' in white metal and the remainder in gilding metal.

24th LANCERS

Raised 30 December 1940 (cadre from 9th and 17th/21st Lancers) and assigned to 29th Armoured Brigade; relieved 6 February 1944. Assigned 8th Armoured Brigade 8 February 1944; relieved 29 July 1944 and disbanded in France.

Equipment notes: By February 1941, only had 6 Matilda II and some Medium IIs. Began to receive Valentines March 1941. Began to reorganize with Valentines and Crusaders from July 1942; changed back to all Valentines January 1943. Changed to

Shermans May-June 1943; also included some Centaurs to early 1944In June 1944 had a mix of Sherman V and Fireflys.

Battle Honours: Putot en Bessin, Fontenay le Pesnil, Defence of Rauray, North-West Europe 1944

Badge: Circle with 'Lancers' on the lower portion and crown on the top portion; within the circle and extending above to the outer rim a pair of crossed lances with pennons flying outwards; numeral 'XXIV' in center of circle in front of the cross of lances. Officers in bronze and other ranks in white metal.

25th DRAGOONS

Raised 1 February 1941 at Sialkot Area, India (cadre from 3rd Carabiniers) and mobilized 23 May 1942 at Risulpur when assigned to 254th Indian Armoured Brigade. A GHQ unit from 5 December 1943 and moved to the Arakan front under XV Indian Corps. Assigned to 166th L of C (Poona) in India 27 June 1944, 168th L of C (Cocanada) in India 27 September 1944. ('A' Sqn served in Burma May-June 1945.) Assigned 50th Indian Tank Brigade 1 July 1945; relieved August 1945. Disbanded ca March 1947.
    Equipment notes: Had some old light tanks on formation. Equipped with Valentines by February 1943. Equipped with Lees (and possibly some Grants) by the end of 1943. Equipped with Sherman DD tanks by 1945.

Battle Honours: North Arakan, Buthidaung, Razabil, Ngakeydauk Pass, Burma 1944-45

Badge: Pair of crossed swords, Crown on the upper portion, numeral 'XXV' on the cross of the swords, with scroll '25th Dragoons' below the numerals. Officers in bronze; other ranks swords in white metal and remainder in gilding metal.

26th HUSSARS

Raised 1 February 1941 in India (cadre from 14th/20th Hussars) and attached to 2nd Indian Armoured Brigade until June 1941 for training. Mobilized 6 May 1942 and assigned to 255th Indian Armoured Brigade. Disbanded 31 October 1943 in India (personnel absorbed into Special Force).[37]
    Equipment notes: Had Mark IIB and VIC light tanks and Crossley armoured cars on formation. By October 1942 had some Grants, 5 Lees, and 15 armoured cars. Gained some more Grants December 1942.

Battle Honours: none awarded

---

[37] Special Force is better known as the Chindits: long range penetration infantry.

Badge: Prussian Eagle above scroll 'XXVI Hussars'. Officers in bronze and other ranks in white metal.

27th LANCERS

Raised February 1941 (or December 1940?) (cadre from 12th Lancers) as an armoured car regiment. Assigned 11th Armoured Division 10 March 1941; relieved 25 March 1943. A GHQ unit with Home Forces March 1943 to June 1944, then in Italy from June 1944. Placed in suspended animation ca September 1947. Disbanded June 1948
     Equipment notes: Had Guy and Daimler armoured cars in December 1941. Daimler or Humber vehicles later.

Battle Honours: Gothic Line, Savio Bridgehead, Capture of Ravenna, Menate, Filo, Argenta Gap, Bologna, Galana Crossing, Italy 1944-45

Badge: Pair of crossed lances, pennons flying outwards; an elephant's head on the cross of lances, with a Crown above and within the upper portion of the lances; figure '27' within the lower portion of the lances. Officers in bronze; other ranks gilding metal except elephant's head and lower part of the pennons in white metal.

Royal Tank Regiment

Raised in 1916 and made permanent in 1923 as Royal Tank Corps. On 4 April 1939, when made part of the new Royal Armoured Corps, it was redesignated as Royal Tank Regiment. This was the home of those who believed the tank would be the dominant weapon in future wars and, at their worst, had a disdain for the traditional arms. It was the RTC and its supporters who felt that armoured formations should be tank-heavy, with minimal infantry or artillery assigned.[38] At the same time, they did believe (unlike much of the Army before the war) in the value of the tank in modern warfare, and the individual regarded as the best armoured division commander of the war came from the RTR.[39]

The RTR contained two completely different kinds of units at the beginning of the war. There were those equipped (in theory) with the cruiser tanks, intended to be part of

---

[38] Thus, Major General Sir Percy Hobart, who thought there should be a distinct tank army, and whose doctrinal differences with his superiors led to his removal early in the war from command of what became 7th Armoured Division. He later commanded 79th Armoured Division and its specialized armour ('Hobo's funnies'), but that was just a holding organization whose components were parceled out to support other formations for particular operations. See Timothy Harrison Place, *Military Training in the British Army*, p. 86, and his entry in Nick Smart, *Biographical Dictionary of British Generals of the Second World War*.

[39] Major General George P. B. 'Pip' Roberts (11th Armoured Division). See his entry in Smart, as well as an interesting review of that division's training (under Hobart and then Roberts) in Place, Ch 7.

armoured brigades and operate in a decisive mobile fashion. Then there were those with the heavily armoured but slow infantry tanks, assigned a supporting role as part of army tank brigades. While cavalry regiments would ultimately get cruisers as well, the infantry tank role remained largely with units of the RTR or newly-raised regiments RAC converted from infantry battalions.

Component units were designated as battalions of the RTC until April 1939. At that point, units in armoured brigades were designated as 'Regiment' while those in tank brigades were 'Battalion, RTR'. (Regiments had squadrons and troops, battalions had companies and platoons.) Usage was later standardized with all components designated as 'Regiment'.[40] The RTR Depot was at Bovington Camp, Wareham, Dorset. In September 1939 it was redesignated as 52nd Training Regiment RAC.

Battle Honours: Arras Counter-Attack, Calais 1940, St. Omer-La Bassee, Somme 1940, Odon, Caen, Bourgebus Ridge, Mont Pincon, Falaise, Nederrijn, Scheldt, Venlo Pocket, Rhineland, RHINE, Bremen, NORTH-WEST EUROPE 1940 '44-45, ABYSSINIA 1940, Sidi Barrani, Beda Fromm, Sidi Suleiman, TOBRUK 1941, Sidi Rezegh 1941, Belhamed, Gazala, Cauldron, Knightsbridge, Defense of Alamein Line, Alam el Halfa, EL ALAMEIN, Mareth, Akarit, Fondouk, El Kourzia, Madjez Plain, Tunis, NORTH AFRICA 1940-43, Primosole Bridge, Gerbini, Adrano, SICILY, Sangro, Salerno, Volturno Crossing, Garigliano Crossing, Anzio, Advance to Florence, Gothic Line, Coriano, Lamone Crossing, Rimini Line, Argenta Gap, ITALY 1943-45, GREECE 1941, BURMA 1942

Badge: Crowned laurel wreath with the left profile side view of a stylized Mark IV tank across the center, above the scroll 'Fear Naught'. Officers in silver plate and other ranks in white metal.
Battledress: Cloth stylized Mark IV tank on the sleeve (worn below formation badges and arm of service strip).
    Regiments also had cloth slip-overs worn on the shoulder strap: 1st RTR red (replaced by a red lanyard), 2nd RTR yellow (with crosswise central stripe of green/red/brown), 3rd RTR green, 4th RTR dark blue, 5th RTR red/light blue, 6th RTR red/yellow, 7th RTR red/green, 8th RTR red/dark blue,
    9th RTR red/brown, 10th RTR red/white, 11th RTR white/black, 12th RTR red/purple,
    40th RTR blue with vertical red/blue, 41st RTR yellow/green, 42nd RTR yellow/blue, 43rd RTR green/maroon (or purple?), 44th RTR yellow/maroon (or purple?), 45th RTR green/thin yellow/black, 46th RTR green with red Welsh dragon superimposed, 47th RTR white/green/white (or grey/pink/grey?), 48th RTR yellow/black, 49th RTR green/maroon (or purple/grey?), 50th RTR black, vertical

---

[40] This was not made official until 19 September 1945, but it appears few units other than 48th RTR used the 'battalion' appellation after 1941.

green/black (or dark blue in place of black?), 51st RTR green/black (or grey/black?). The slip-overs were not worn consistently, especially at the front in NW Europe.

1st ROYAL TANK REGIMENT

Stationed at Gerwala, Egypt, part of Heavy Armoured Brigade (Egypt); brigade redesignated 16 February 1940 as 4th Heavy Armoured Brigade. Transferred 10 April 1940 to 7th Armoured Brigade; relieved 3 April 1941. Assigned 9 April 1941 to 3rd Armoured Brigade. Transferred 18 September 1941 to 32nd Army Tank Brigade. Transferred 21 January 1942 to 1st Armoured Brigade; relieved 1 June 1942. Assigned 4th Armoured Brigade 3 June 1942; relieved 7 July 1942. Assigned 22nd Armoured Brigade 17 September 1942. Remained in Germany on occupation duties following the end of the war.

Equipment notes: Began the war with 58 Mk VIB light tanks. In June 1940 it had 23 A9/A10 cruisers and 26 Mk VI light tanks. It was still a mix of A9/A10 cruisers and Mk VI lights in December 1940. November 1941: 26 cruisers (6 A9, 9 A10, 11 A13) and 19 Mk VI light tanks. Received first Grants April 1942; by May 1942 Stuarts in RHQ and 'C' Sqn and Grants in 'A' and 'B' Sqns. (October 1942: 24 Grants and 19 Stuarts.) By March 1943 had Crusaders in 'A' Sqn and Shermans and Grants in 'B' and 'C' Sqns. Re-equipped 1943 with Shermans. Re-equipped spring 1944 in UK with Cromwells and Sherman Fireflys.

2nd ROYAL TANK REGIMENT

Stationed at Farnborough[41] as part of 1st Heavy Armoured Brigade (brigade redesignated 14 April 1940 as 3rd Armoured Brigade); relieved 11 August 1940 and shipped to North Africa. Assigned 4th Armoured Brigade 13 October 1940; relieved 16 April 1941 and assigned to 7th Armoured Brigade; relieved 10 July 1941. Returned to 7th Armoured Brigade 6 September 1941. Moved into Austria on occupation duties following the end of the war; then moved at the end of the year to Italian-Yugoslav border.

Equipment notes: Initially equipped with Mark VIB lights (21 May 1940) and cruisers (8 A9, 1 A10 and 18 A13 in May 1940). Following return from France began to re-equip with A13s. In October 1940 had two squadrons A10 and one squadron A13 cruisers, plus A9 CS tanks. In December 1940 it had 'A' and 'C' Sqns with A13 cruiser tanks; 'B' Sqn with A10's was with 3rd Hussars, and a squadron 3rd Hussars (Mk VI light) was with 2nd RTR. In February 1941 it was down to 12 A13 cruisers and 7 light tanks. May 1941: RHQ (A13), 'A' Sqn (A9/A10), 'C' Sqn (A9/A10/A13): total 6 A9, 17 A10 and 7 A13. June 1941: still a mix of A9 (10), A10 (11), and A13 (21) cruisers. November 1941: 52 A13 cruisers. The regiment was then re-equipped with Stuart tanks,

---

[41] When companies were redesignated squadrons in 1939, the 2nd RTR adopted a unique system of giving them names; thus, instead of being 'A', 'B', 'C' and HQ Squadrons, they were simply termed Ajax, Badger, Cyclops and Nero.

all of which were lost during the initial campaign in Burma. The regiment marched on foot back into India, where it was reformed and re-equipped with Grants. Re-equipped during 1943 with Shermans. By December 1944 had Sherman IB (105mm) in squadron HQs and mix of Sherman II and IIA (76mm), along with 1 Firefly. At the end of 1945, 'A' Sqn was in Churchills, 'C' Sqn in Shermans, Recce Trp in Stuart Recce and scout cars, and 'B' Sqn non-operational due to demobilization.

3rd ROYAL TANK REGIMENT

Stationed at Warminster as part of 1st Heavy Armoured Brigade (brigade redesignated 14 April 1940 as 3rd Armoured Brigade); relieved 22 May 1940 and sent to Calais, where it was lost 26 May (about 80 personnel escaped back to the UK). The regiment was reformed in the UK, coming under 3rd Armoured Brigade 19 to 30 June 1940. It was then assigned to 1st Armoured Brigade 11 August 1940; relieved 28 October 1940 and assigned 3rd Armoured Brigade the next day; relieved 25 January 1941. Assigned 1st Armoured Brigade 13 February 1941; relieved 8 August 1941. Assigned 4th Armoured Brigade 31 July 1941; relieved 7 June 1942. Formed a composite regiment with 5th RTR as 3rd/5th RTR for period 7 July to 1 August 1942 in 2nd Armoured Brigade. Assigned 8th Armoured Brigade 12 August 1942; transferred 6 February 1944 to 29th Armoured Brigade. (Brigade withdrawn December 1944 for conversion to Comets; re-drew its old equipment for the Ardennes and conversion delayed.) Remained in Germany on occupation duties following the end of the war.

Equipment notes: Went to Calais May 1940 with 27 cruisers and 21 Mk VI Light tanks. In October 1940 had 6 A10 CS cruisers, one squadron with A10 and two squadrons with A13 cruisers. April 1941 in Greece, had A9 CS and A10 cruisers (52 tanks total). In November 1941 equipped with 52 Stuarts. Received Grants March 1942; late May 1942 had Stuarts (and 1 Grant) in RHQ, Stuarts in 'A' Sqn, and Grants in 'B' and 'C' Sqns. Started getting Shermans September 1942; October 1942 had Grants in RHQ and 'C' Sqn , Crusaders in 'A' Sqn and Sherman II in 'B' Sqn. By March 1943 had Crusaders in 'A' Sqn and Shermans in 'B' and 'C' Sqns. Later changed to Shermans. Fully equipped with Sherman V and Fireflys after assignment to 29th Armoured Brigade. Converted to Comet (with Cromwell CS) by March 1945.

4th ROYAL TANK REGIMENT

Tank battalion at Farnborough, part of 1st Army Tank Brigade. Relieved 18 September 1939 and sent to BEF as GHQ unit. Assigned 1st Army Tank Brigade 30 April 1940; relieved 10 December 1940 and transferred to North Africa. ('B' Sqn served in East Africa 1941.) Assigned 7th Armoured Brigade 16 April 1941; transferred 8 (4?) May

1941[42] to 4th Armoured Brigade; relieved 27 July 1941. Assigned 32nd Army Tank Brigade 18 September 1941.[43] Destroyed in Tobruk 21 June 1942.

Reformed 1 March 1945 by redesignation of 144th Regiment RAC, an LVT-equipped element of 33rd Armoured Brigade; relieved 30 March 1945 and assigned to 30th Armoured Brigade; relieved 24 (15?) April 1945 and assigned 31st Armoured Brigade; relieved 9 June 1945 and assigned 34th Armoured Brigade. Remained in Germany on occupation duties following the end of the war. Earmarked for service in the Far East against Japan but the end of the war canceled that deployment. Remained with 34th Armoured Brigade until it was disbanded January 1946 and then the regiment moved to Italy.

Equipment notes: In May 1940 had 50 A10 infantry and 5 Mk VI light tanks, all of which were lost in France. Re-equipped with Matilda II by September 1940. In June 1941: 36 Matilda II. November 1941: 50 Matildas and 4 Mk VI light tanks. Had Valentine tanks May 1942. When reformed in 1945 it was an LVT unit. It presumably changed to tanks after the war ended.

5th ROYAL TANK REGIMENT

Stationed at Perham Down as part of 1st Heavy Armoured Brigade (brigade redesignated 14 April 1940 as 3rd Armoured Brigade); relieved 18 February 1941. Returned to 3rd Armoured Brigade 24 March 1941; relieved 14 April 1941. Assigned 4th Armoured Brigade 4 May 1941; relieved 27 July 1941; returned 31 July 1941 and relieved 7 June 1942. Formed a composite regiment with 3rd RTR as 3rd/5th RTR for period 7 July to 1 August 1942 in 2nd Armoured Brigade. Assigned 22nd Armoured Brigade 17 September 1942. Remained in Germany on occupation duties following the end of the war.

Equipment notes: In May 1940 probably 21 Mark VIB light and 26 or so cruisers. Late June 1940: four light and seven cruisers, all that were returned from France; by late July 1940 nearly at strength in A9 and A10 cruisers. In October 1940 had A10 CS cruisers, one squadron with A10 and two squadrons with A13 cruisers. In March 1941 establishment was A10 CS and A13 cruisers, but under strength (25 A13s). After heavy losses, reformed May-June 1941 with mix of A9 cruisers (2), Matilda 'I' tanks (33), and Light tanks Mks VIB.C (4 and 1). Handed these over to 44th RTR late June 1941 and gradually received and trained on US M3 Stuarts. November 1941 had 52 Stuarts. Received Grants March 1942; late May 1942 Stuarts in RHQ and 'A' Sqn, Grants in 'B' and 'C' Sqns. October 1942: 'A' Sqn 16 Crusaders, 'B' Sqn 10 Shermans and 'C' Sqn 14 Grants. By March 1943 had Crusaders in 'A' Sqn and Shermans and Grants in 'B' and 'C' Sqns. Later changed to all Shermans. Re-equipped spring 1944 in the UK with Cromwells and Sherman Fireflys.

---

[42] Where alternate dates are shown, the discrepancy is in Joslen and there is usually no way to reconcile it.

[43] Capt. Philip J. ('Pip') Gardner was awarded a Victoria Cross for his actions 23 November 1941 at Tobruk, Libya, where he went to the rescue of two destroyed armoured cars. Dismounting, he rescued an officer who had lost both legs and returned to British lines.

6th ROYAL TANK REGIMENT

Stationed at Gerwala, Egypt as part of Heavy Armoured Brigade (Egypt) (brigade redesignated 16 February 1940 as 4th Heavy Armoured Brigade and 14 April 1940 as 4th Armoured Brigade); relieved 19 January 1941. ('B' Sqn served in the Sudan 1940.) Assigned 3rd Armoured Brigade 26 February 1941; relieved 14 April 1941. Assigned 7th Armoured Brigade 8 June 1941; relieved 24 January 1942. Assigned 1st Armoured Brigade 5 February 1942; relieved 5 June 1942. Assigned 4th Armoured Brigade 7 June 1942; relieved 7 July 1942 and assigned 2nd Armoured Brigade; relieved 1 August 1942. The regiment was then stationed in Iraq, Syria and Egypt as a GHQ unit. Assigned 7th Armoured Brigade 30 December 1942; relieved 8 June 1944. Returned to 7th Armoured Brigade 24 June 1944; relieved 20 August 1944. Returned to 7th Armoured Brigade 16 September 1944. Moved into Austria on occupation duties following the end of the war. Transferred to 2nd Armoured Brigade 17 September 1945. Moved to Italy October 1945.

Equipment notes: In September 1939 equipped with mix of 8 A9 cruisers and 7 Mk VIB lights in 'A' Coy, 8 Medium Mk II and 2 MK VIB lights in 'B' Coy and 8 Medium Mk II and 7 Mk VIB lights in 'C' Coy.[44] By January 1940 it was at 'full establishment' of 23 cruiser tanks, along with the mediums and lights. In June 1940 it had 23 A9/A10 cruisers and 13 Mk VI light tanks. In December 1940 still a mixture of A9/A10 cruisers and Mk VI lights. In March 1941, had Mk VI lights in 'B' Sqn and 36 Italian M13/40 tanks in 'A' and 'C' Sqns. June 1941: fully equipped with 52 Crusader I cruisers (first regiment in N Africa to receive them). November 1941: 49 Crusaders. Received first Grants April 1942; by May 1942 Stuarts in RHQ and 'A' Sqn and Grants in 'B' and 'C' Sqns. Began to receive Shermans by March 1943 but may not have been completed until landing in Taranto May 1944. Began conversion to Churchills in February 1945, and period after that largely spent in conversion and training. Received 12 Crocodiles 4-5 May 1945, forming a troop of 4 in each squadron.

7th ROYAL TANK REGIMENT

Tank battalion at Catterick as part of 1st Army Tank Brigade; relieved 10 December 1940 and sent to North Africa. GHQ unit with XIII Corps January to May 1941. Assigned 4th Armoured Brigade 4 May 1941; relieved 11 July 1941. ('D' Sqn assigned 3rd Armoured Brigade 16 April 1941 to 18 September 1941.) Assigned 32nd Army Tank Brigade 18 September 1941; relieved 21 February 1942. Assigned 32nd Army Tank Brigade 10 April 1942. Destroyed in Tobruk 21 June 1942.[45]

---

[44] 6th Bn RTR redesignated as 6th RTR November 1939 and companies redesignated as squadrons. HQ Squadron was formed December 1939.

[45] Lt. Col. Henry R. B Foote was awarded a Victoria Cross for his actions during the period 27 May to 15 June 1942 in Libya. This included one instance when he went on foot from tank to tank, encouraging the crews who were under artillery and anti tank fire; he had been wounded a week earlier but continued to lead his regiment on that occasion.

Reformed 22 February 1943 from 10th RTR, an element of 31st Tank Brigade (brigade redesignated 2 February 1945 as 31st Armoured Brigade). [Re-equipped with flame-thrower tanks by December 1944.] Remained in Germany on occupation duties following the end of the war, and probably converted to normal tanks. Relieved from 33rd Armoured Brigade September 1945 and placed under I Corps District.

Equipment notes: In May 1940 had 27 A11 and 23 A12 infantry and 7 Mk VI light tanks, all of which were lost in France.[46] Re-equipped with Matilda II by September 1940; had 50 in December. June 1941: 47 Matilda II, 6 Mk VI light, 2 A10 cruisers. In December 1941 all but one squadron (with Matildas) was serving as a tank delivery unit. Had Matildas May 1942 and a mix of Valentine and Matilda the next month. In June 1944 mainly Churchill III/IV [6pdr], with a few Churchill VI [75mm] and V/VIII [CS]. In December 1944 mainly Crocodiles, with some 75mm and CS Churchills.

8th ROYAL TANK REGIMENT

Tank battalion at Perham Down under 1st Army Tank Brigade; relieved 28 April 1940 (remained in UK when brigade HQ went to BEF). Assigned 1st Army Tank Brigade 24 June 1940; relieved 23 July 1941. Assigned 1st Army Tank Brigade 1 Sep1941; relieved 3 June 1942. (Served with 4th Indian Division January-February 1942.) Assigned 4th Armoured Brigade 7 June 1942; relieved 7 July 1942. Assigned 1st Army Tank Brigade 10 July 1942; relieved 30 September 1942. Dismounted November 1942 and converted to a 'beach brick' May 1943 in Syria. Remounted by January 1944 when assigned 7th Armoured Brigade 29 January 1944; relieved 8 July 1945. Assigned 9th Armoured Brigade 11 July 1945. Personnel flown back to the UK in August 1945. Regiment earmarked for service in the Far East against Japan but the end of the war canceled deployment to that theater. Sent to Austria for occupation duties January 1946.

Equipment notes: In September 1939 equipped with trucks; in May 1940 had perhaps 30 A11 infantry tanks; gradually gained Matilda II (A12) tanks (complete by September 1940). In November 1941 had 52 Valentines, with 6 Matilda CS tanks. Same equipment May 1942. First given Shermans on landing in Taranto May 1944. Final organization was normal Churchills in 'A' and 'C' Sqns (16 tanks each) and Crocodiles (16) in 'B' Sqn.

9th ROYAL TANK REGIMENT

Organized beginning 27 November 1940 at Gateshead (cadre from 3rd RTR) as a tank battalion; assigned 31st Army Tank Brigade 15 January 1941 (brigade redesignated May 1942 as 31st Tank Brigade). Relieved 31 August 1944. Assigned 34th Tank Brigade 4 September 1944. (Brigade redesignated 2 February 1945 as 34th Armoured Brigade.)

---

[46] Probably all A10 on the outbreak of war, as the 1st Tank Brigade had only two of the A11 (all that had been produced!) at that time.

Relieved 1 July 1945, but remained in Germany on occupation duties. Disbanded 30 November-13 December 1945.

Equipment notes: The regiment was one of the first to receive the Churchill in the summer of 1941. In June 1944 mainly Churchill III/IV [6pdr], with a few Churchill VI [75mm] and V/VIII [CS]. In December 1944 about 1/3 6pdr and 2/3 75mm Churchills plus CS versions.

10th ROYAL TANK REGIMENT

Organized November 1940 as a tank battalion; assigned 31st Army Tank Brigade 15 January 1941 (brigade redesignated May 1942 as 31st Tank Brigade). Disbanded 22 February 1943 to reform 7th RTR.

Equipment notes: About 3/4 strength (Churchills) in December 1941. Later brought up to strength.

11th ROYAL TANK REGIMENT

Organized November 1940 and assigned 25th Army Tank Brigade 22 November 1940 [brigade designated 2nd Motor MG Brigade until 10 December]; relieved 26 April 1941. GHQ unit with Home Forces April 1941 to February 1942. Assigned 25th Army Tank Brigade 29 February 1942; relieved 5 August 1942. Equipped with CDL tanks late 1942 and assigned 1st Army Tank Brigade 18 October 1942. (Brigade redesignated 23 April 1944 as 1st Tank Brigade.) Relieved from 1st Tank Brigade 2 October 1944 and re-equipped ca late September 1944 with LVTs; assigned 79th Armoured Division 2 October to 1 November 1944. Assigned 31st Tank Brigade 2 November 1944 to 22 December 1944 when transferred to 30th Armoured Brigade; relieved 27 February 1945. Assigned 30th Armoured Brigade 31 March 1945; relieved 25 April 1945. Assigned 33rd Armoured Brigade 26 April 1945; relieved 19 August 1945. Disbanded 1945 in Germany.

Equipment notes: Fully equipped with Matilda (58) tanks by December 1941. Equipped with CDL tanks by June 1943.

12th ROYAL TANK REGIMENT

Organized December 1940 and assigned 25th Army Tank Brigade 10 December 1940; relieved 26 April 1941 and assigned to 21st Army Tank Brigade (brigade redesignated 6 June 1942 as 21st Tank Brigade and 11 June 1945 as 21st Armoured Brigade.) Moved to Austria on occupation duties following the end of the war and disbanded later 1945.

Equipment notes: Initially equipped with Matilda tanks; received first Churchill Is July 1941 and converted to them. Mix of Churchill I/II by December 1941. Slated to convert to Valentine V before going overseas late 1942 but decision reversed and Churchills restored February 1943. By March 1943 had Churchill III/IV and I CS. Changed to an organization with two troops Churchills and two troops Shermans in each squadron by August 1943 when in Italy. Began to add the Churchill NA75 by late autumn 1944, although Shermans remained on strength to February 1945.[47]

40th (THE KING'S) ROYAL TANK REGIMENT

TA unit formed 28 November 1938 by conversion of 7th Bn The King's Regiment (Liverpool), at Bootle; part of 23rd Army Tank Brigade. Embodied 3 September 1939. (Brigade redesignated 1 November 1940 as 23rd Armoured Brigade). Utilized as infantry in Greece from August 1944; re-equipped with tanks and armoured cars January 1945. Placed in suspended animation April 1946 in Greece.

Equipment notes: In September 1939 equipped with trucks. Equipped with Matilda CS and Valentine infantry tanks by November 1941. In July 1942 still Matilda CS and Valentines. October 1942: 42 Valentines. Converted to Shermans ca September 1943. Operated a mixture of Shermans and Staghound and Daimler armoured cars following the war.

41st (OLDHAM) ROYAL TANK REGIMENT

TA unit formed 28 November 1938 by conversion of 10th Bn The Manchester Regiment, at Oldham, Manchester as part of 24th Army Tank Brigade. Embodied 3 September 1939. (Brigade redesignated 1 November 1940 as 24th Armoured Brigade). Relieved 9 December 1942. Placed in suspended animation March 1943 (personnel and equipment to 1st Scorpion Regiment RAC).

Equipment notes: In September 1939 equipped with trucks. Valentines by December 1941. Began to receive Shermans September 1942, by late October 1942 had Crusaders in 'A' Sqn and Shermans in 'B' and 'C' Sqns. Personnel and equipment distributed to other units 1 November 1942.

42nd ROYAL TANK REGIMENT

TA unit formed 1 November 1938 by conversion of 7th (23rd London) Bn The East Surrey Regiment, at London, part of 21st Army Tank Brigade. Embodied 3 September 1939. Relieved 12 April 1941 and assigned 1st Army Tank Brigade 21 April 1941; relieved 23 July 1941. A GHQ unit in Egypt August to November 1941. Assigned 1st Army Tank Brigade 11 November 1941; relieved 11 December 1941. Returned to 1st Army Tank Brigade 28 December 1941; relieved 8 June 1942. Again assigned to 1st Army Tank Brigade 27 June 1942. [Equipped with Scorpions autumn 1942 and CDL tanks from 1943.] (Brigade redesignated 1st Tank Brigade 23 April 1944.) Relieved from 1st Tank Brigade 17 November 1944 and placed in suspended animation.

---

[47] For actual tank strength (excluding Stuarts) for the period December 1944-April 1945 see Appendix D.

Equipment notes: In September 1939 equipped with trucks. Began to receive a small number of Mediums and Mk II Light tanks and some Matildas in 1940; received first Valentine Is in August 1940 and gradually built to strength with Valentine I. In November 1941 50 Matildas and 6 or 7 Mk VIC light tanks. Equipped only with Matilda in May 1942. In October 1942, two troops had Matilda Scorpion tanks. Equipped with CDL tanks by June 1943.

43rd ROYAL TANK REGIMENT

TA unit formed 1 November 1938 by conversion of 6th (City) Bn The Royal Northumberland Fusiliers, at Newcastle-on-Tyne, as part of 25th Army Tank Brigade. Embodied 3 September 1939. (Brigade redesignated as 2nd Motor MG Brigade 1 June 1940 and reverted to 25th Army Tank Brigade 12 December 1940); relieved 9 November 1940 and assigned to 21st Army Tank Brigade; relieved 26 April 1941 and assigned 25th Army Tank Brigade the next day; relieved 17 October 1941 and assigned 33rd Army Tank Brigade 18 October 1941. (Brigade redesignated June 1942 as 33rd Tank Brigade.) Relieved 5 August 1943. Assigned 79th Armoured Division 6 August 1943, served as experimental unit [flail tanks initially]; relieved 14 May 1944. Assigned 35th Tank Brigade 13 July 1944; relieved 30 May 1945. Left July 1945 for India, arriving early September. Unit redesignated May 1947 as 2/43rd RTR when 43rd RTR reformed in the TA; it left India that September and was disbanded on arrival back in the UK.

Equipment notes: In September 1939 equipped with trucks. In September 1940, around 54 Beaverettes and Humberettes. Converting from Matilda to Churchill tanks in December 1941. Miscellaneous equipment from 1943. In February 1945 changed to a mixture of Shermans and Grant CDL tanks.

44th ROYAL TANK REGIMENT

TA unit formed 1 November 1938 by conversion of 6th Bn The Gloucestershire Regiment, at Bristol as part of 21st Army Tank Brigade. Embodied 3 September 1939. Relieved 11 September 1940. Assigned 1st Army Tank Brigade 10 December 1940; relieved 26 June 1941. Assigned 4th Armoured Brigade 1 July 1941; relieved 27 July 1941 and returned to 1st Army Tank Brigade. [Equipped with flail tanks 1942, then dismounted for period August-October 1942, when equipped with CDL tanks.] Relieved from 1st Army Tank Brigade 10 May 1943 and re-equipped May 1943 as an armoured regiment; GHQ unit in Egypt May to July 1943. Assigned 4th Armoured Brigade 13 July 1943. [Re-equipped with specialist armour by 79th Armoured Division for period 9 to 24 March 1945, then reverted to normal organization as armoured regiment.] Remained in Germany on occupation duties following the end of the war and placed in suspended animation there ca the end of 1945.

Equipment notes: In September 1939 equipped with trucks. Began to receive a small number of Mediums and Mk II Light tanks and some Matildas in 1940; received first Valentine Is in August 1940 and gradually built to strength. November 1941 48 Matildas and 5 Mk VIC light tanks. In May 1942, equipped with Valentines plus Matilda CS tanks. In October 1942, two troops had Matilda Scorpion tanks. Re-equipping with Shermans by June 1943. In June 1944 a mix of Sherman II and Fireflys. Same mix December 1944, but Sherman mark unknown.

45th (LEEDS RIFLES) ROYAL TANK REGIMENT

TA unit formed 1 November 1938 by conversion of 7th Bn (Leeds Rifles) The West Yorkshire Regiment (The Prince of Wales's Own), at Leeds as part of 24th Army Tank Brigade. Embodied 3 September 1939. (Brigade redesignated 1 November 1940 as 24th Armoured Brigade). Relieved 28 February 1943. Placed in suspended animation 8 March 1943.

Equipment notes: In September 1939 equipped with trucks. Valentines by December 1941. Began to receive Shermans September 1942, by late October 1942 Crusaders in one squadron ('B'?) and Shermans in the other two. Personnel and equipment distributed to other units 1 November 1942.

46th (LIVERPOOL WELSH) ROYAL TANK REGIMENT

TA unit formed 1939 as Liverpool Welsh Bn The King's Regiment (Liverpool), and then converted as duplicate of 40th RTR. Embodied 3 September 1939 at Liverpool as part of 23rd Army Tank Brigade (redesignated 1 November 1940 as 23rd Armoured Brigade). Relieved 1 December 1942. GHQ unit in Egypt December to June 1943. Assigned 23rd Armoured Brigade 28 June 1943; relieved 4 January 1944. GHQ unit in Italy and North Africa February to June 1944. Returned to 23rd Armoured Brigade 22 July 1944. In Greece, formed one squadron with armoured cars and two of infantry; re-equipped with tanks and armoured cars January 1945. Placed in suspended animation April 1946 in Greece.

Equipment notes: In September 1939 equipped with trucks. Equipped with Matilda CS and Valentine infantry tanks by November 1941. Same equipment in July 1942. October 1942: 49 Valentines. Converted to Shermans by July 1943. (October 1944, while in Greece, 'A' Sqn had 18 Humber IV armoured cars; 'B' and 'C' Sqns were infantry. By December 1944, 'C' Sqn had 10 Sherman and 2 Stuart tanks.) Operated a mixture of Shermans and Staghound and Daimler armoured cars following the war.

47th (OLDHAM) ROYAL TANK REGIMENT

TA unit formed 1939 at Manchester as duplicate of 41st RTR; part of 24th Army Tank Brigade. Embodied 3 September 1939. (Brigade redesignated 1 November 1940 as 24th Armoured Brigade). Relieved 15 January 1943. Placed in suspended animation March 1943.

Equipment notes: In September 1939 equipped with trucks. Valentines by December 1941. Began to receive Shermans September 1942, by late October 1942 Crusaders in 'C' Sqn and Shermans in 'A' and 'B' Sqns. Personnel and equipment distributed to other units 1 November 1942.

48th ROYAL TANK REGIMENT

TA unit formed 1939 at London as duplicate of 42nd RTR; part of 21st Army Tank Brigade. Embodied 3 September 1939. (Brigade redesignated 21st Tank Brigade 6 June 1942 and 21st Armoured Brigade 11 June 1945). (Served with 25th Tank Brigade May-August 1944, then returned to 21st.) Moved into Austria on occupation duties following the end of the war and disbanded later 1945.

Equipment notes: In September 1939 equipped with trucks. Began to receive a small number of Mediums and Mk II light tanks and some Matildas in 1940; received first Valentine Is in August 1940 and gradually built to strength with Valentine I and (from April 1941) Valentine II. Later in 1941 began to switch to Churchills. Mix of Churchill I/II by December 1941. Slated to convert to Valentine V before going overseas late 1942 but decision reversed and Churchills restored February 1943. By March 1943 had Churchill III/IV and I CS. Changed to an organization with two troops Churchills and two troops Shermans in each squadron by August 1943 when in Italy. Began to add the Churchill NA75 by late autumn 1944, although Shermans remained on strength to February 1945.[48]

49th ROYAL TANK REGIMENT

TA unit formed 1939 at Newcastle-on-Tyne as duplicate of 43rd RTR; part of 25th Army Tank Brigade. Embodied 3 September 1939. (Brigade redesignated 1 June 1940 as 2nd Motor MG Brigade, reverted 10 December 1940 to 25th Army Tank Brigade but 49th RTR was relieved 9 December 1940). Assigned 1st Army Tank Brigade 10 December 1940; relieved 20 April 1941. Assigned 25th Army Tank Brigade 27 April 1941; relieved 28 February 1942. Assigned 35th Tank Brigade 16 August 1942 [converted 1943 to CDL tanks]. Relieved 30 April 1944 and assigned to 1st Tank Brigade; relieved 25 October 1944. Converted November 1944 to APCs and designated as 49th Armoured Personnel Carrier Regiment.[49] Assigned 31st Tank Brigade 22 December 1944 (brigade redesignated 2 February 1945 as 31st Armoured Brigade.) Disbanded 1945.

Equipment notes: In September 1939 equipped with trucks. In September 1940, around 54 Beaverettes and Humberettes. Probably about 2/3 strength and a mix of

---

[48] For actual tank strength (excluding Stuarts) for the period December 1944-April 1945 see Appendix D.

[49] Sometimes shown as 49th Regiment RAC or 49th APC Regiment RAC after conversion. Whether significant or not, Kenneth Macksey, *The Tanks*, does not include the 49th in his list of RTR regiments in 1945.

Matilda and Churchill tanks in December 1941. Later a Churchill unit, then CDL tanks from August 1943. Kangaroo APCs from November 1944.

50th ROYAL TANK REGIMENT

TA unit formed 1939 at Bristol as duplicate of 44th RTR, part of 23rd Army Tank Brigade. Embodied 3 September 1939. (Brigade redesignated 1 November 1940 as 23rd Armoured Brigade). Served as infantry in Greece from August 1944; re-equipped with tanks and armoured cars January 1945. Placed in suspended animation April 1946 in Greece.

Equipment notes: In September 1939 equipped with trucks. Matilda CS and Valentine infantry tanks by November 1941. Same equipment July 1942. October 1942: 44 Valentines. Converted to Shermans by July 1943. ('B' Sqn received Sherman tanks again 15 December 1944.) Operated a mixture of Shermans and Staghound and Daimler armoured cars following the war.

51st (LEEDS RIFLES) ROYAL TANK REGIMENT

TA unit formed 1939 at Morley (from 'A' Coy/45th RTR) as duplicate of 45th RTR; part of 25th Army Tank Brigade. Embodied 3 September 1939. (Brigade redesignated 1 June 1940 as 2nd Motor MG Brigade, reverted 10 December 1940 to 25th Army Tank Brigade).[50] (Brigade converted 5 January 1945 as 'B' Assault Brigade RAC/RE, then 6 April 1945 as 25th Armoured Engineer Brigade.) [Converted 1945 with 'A' and 'C' Sqns in flame-thrower tanks and 'B' Sqn in flail tanks.] Relieved 13 May 1945, with 'C' Sqn remaining with 25th Armoured Engineer Brigade until 22 June 1945. Served in Italy and Austria following the war and placed in suspended animation 1946.

Equipment notes: In September 1939 equipped with trucks. In September 1940, around 54 Beaverettes and Humberettes. Probably about 2/3 strength and a mix of Matilda and Churchill tanks in December 1941. All Churchills in 1942. Prior to April 1944 replaced two Churchill troops in each squadron with Shermans.[51] The final organization was 'A' and 'C' Sqns with Churchill Crocodiles (16 each) and 'B' Sqn with 15 Sherman Crab II flail tanks. Possibly re-equipped following the war.

LIGHT TANK COMPANIES

In 1938, the RTC had six light tank companies active in India; three (2nd, 6th and 9th) were disbanded before September 1939 and their personnel and equipment used to help mechanize cavalry units in India. In September 1939 the 1st and 7th Light Tank Coys

[50] The regiments of 25th Tank Brigade were awarded a silver maple leaf July 1944 for service with I Canadian Corps, to be worn on the upper left arm (the brigade also added a maple leaf to its diabolo badge); it is not know if 51st RTR added this device to their uniforms.
[51] For actual tank strength (excluding Stuarts) for the period May-November 1944 see Appendix D.

RTR were assigned to the Peshawar District and the 11th Light Tank Coy RTR was assigned to the Razmak Brigade. These were disbanded after that date, again to help mechanize cavalry in India. Their exact date of inactivation is apparently unknown. Each had and establishment of 25 Mk VI light tanks.

Yeomanry

The Yeomanry were the mounted arm of the Territorial Force, with units originally raised locally at private initiative beginning in the 1790s. Most of them raised one or more companies for service in South Africa (1900-1902) as part of the Imperial Yeomanry, and a few regiments trace their lineage to units originally raised for that war. During the First World War, many ended up converted to infantry, with only a few regiments serving as cavalry to the end of the war. As the now-renamed Territorial Army was reformed after the war, it was clear that it would have no need for the more than 40 regiments of Yeomanry. A few were handed over to the Royal Tank Corps to become armoured car companies; one went to the Royal Signals; and several were converted to artillery (often becoming effectively amalgamated with another regiment). Nine of them were kept as part of three cavalry brigades (to form a wartime cavalry division) and a few other horsed regiments survived as GHQ units, albeit with no clear role.

With creation of the Royal Armoured Corps in April 1939, the Yeomanry armoured car companies of the RTC reverted to their former designations and began to expand to regiments. At the end of August 1939 they were ordered to form duplicate units, as other parts of the TA had been doing during the year.

Following mobilization, the horsed regiments not forming part of 1st Cavalry Division ended up converted as field or medium regiments of the Royal Artillery. The regiments going abroad with 1st Cavalry Division either ended up part of the RAC or were converted as infantry or as part of the Royal Corps of Signals. This section includes all of the horsed regiments, even if they did not end up part of the RAC. (A number of those would be reformed in the RAC in 1947.) One of the scout (horsed recce) regiments served as infantry for the bulk of the war.

AYRSHIRE YEOMANRY (EARL OF CARRICK'S OWN)

Formed 1794, a GHQ horsed regiment at Ayr (Scottish Command). Embodied 3 September 1939. Transferred to the Royal Artillery 15 February 1940 as The Ayrshire Yeomanry Regiment RA and formed a duplicate unit; redesignated 15 April 1940 as 151st (Ayrshire Yeomanry) Field Regiment RA; duplicate unit became 152nd (Ayrshire Yeomanry) Field Regiment RA. The regiment reformed in the RAC 1947.
Equipment notes: horsed regiment on mobilization.

In lieu of battle honours, the regiment received an Honorary Distinction: Royal Regiment of Artillery badge with yeardates '1942-45' and three scrolls, 'North-West Europe', 'North Africa', and 'Italy'

Badge: The crest of the Earl of Carrick: a Griffin with a lion's head, flaming tongue and eagle's wing, on a wreath inscribed 'Ayrshire Earl Of Carrick's Own Yeomanry'. In gilding metal.

THE CHESHIRE YEOMANRY (EARL OF CHESTER'S)

Formed 1797; a horsed regiment at Chester, part of 6th Cavalry Brigade. Transferred 21 March 1941 to 5th Cavalry Brigade; relieved 7 June 1941. Returned 15 July 1941; relieved 21 March 1942. Converted July 1942 as 5th [renumbered March 1945 as 17th] Lines of Communications Signals, Royal Signals. The regiment reformed in the RAC 1947.

Battle Honours: SYRIA 1941, and Honorary Distinction: Badge of the Royal Corps of Signals with year-date '1945' and one scroll 'North-West Europe'
Battledress: Red 'Cheshire Yeomanry' on yellow

Badge: The Prince of Wales's plume, coronet and motto, above a scroll 'Cheshire (Earl Of Chester's) Yeomanry'. In bronze.

THE DERBYSHIRE YEOMANRY

Derbyshire Yeomanry formed in 1794; transferred 1922 to the RTC as 24th (Derbyshire Yeomanry) Armoured Car Coy, RTC. Transferred to RAC 30 April 1939 under old title and intended for reorganization as armoured car regiment. Doubled 24 August 1939.

1st Derbyshire Yeomanry   Original unit redesignated 24 August 1939 as 1st Derbyshire Yeomanry, located at Derby. Embodied 3 September 1939 as GHQ unit with Home Forces. Assigned 10 November 1940 to 6th Armoured Division; converted ca. January-March 1943 as an armoured recce regiment.[52] Redesignated 1 January 1947 as 2/1st Derbyshire Yeomanry (because of reconstitution of TA regiment); 2/1st Derbyshire Yeomanry disbanded 14 June 1947.
   Equipment notes: By December 1941 had Humber light recce cars and Daimler scout cars. Later equipped with Humber armoured cars. By March 1943, Daimler armoured cars. A conventional armoured recce regiment (Shermans and Stuarts) from early 1943.

---

[52] 1st Derbyshire Yeomanry was the only armoured car regiment assigned an armoured division to convert to an armoured recce regiment.

2nd Derbyshire Yeomanry   Raised 24 August 1939 as duplicate unit, also located at Derby. Embodied 3 September 1939 as GHQ unit with Home Forces. Assigned 8th Armoured Division 27 November 1940; relieved 20 August 1942 and assigned the next day to 10th Armoured Division; relieved 10 September 1942. Assigned 4th Armoured Brigade 4 October 1942 to 15 November 1942. A GHQ unit with Ninth Army in Palestine January to May 1943 and then under GHQ MEF May to June 1943 in North Africa. Returned to the UK as GHQ unit with Home Forces July 1943. Converted as a recce regiment when assigned to 51st (Highland) Infantry Division 20 January 1944. Placed in suspended animation ca March 1946.

Equipment notes: Guy armoured cars by December 1941. In October 1942 had 50 Humber II and Daimler armoured cars. (In March 1943 served as tank reorganization group for Eighth Army.) Armoured cars and light recce cars from 1944 (but equipped with Daimler rather than the Humber armoured cars normally used by recce regiments).

Battle Honours: DIVES CROSSING, La Vie Crossing, Lisieux, LOWER MAAS, Ourthe, RHINELAND, Reichswald, North West Europe 1944-45, ALAM EL HALFA, EL ALAMEIN, MEDJEZ EL BAB, Tebourba Gap, Bou Arada, Kasserine, Steamroller Farm, Maknassy, Fondouk, KAIROUAN, El Kourzia, Tunis, North Africa 1942-43, CASSINO II, Liri Valley, Aquino, Arezzo, Advance to Florence, ARGENTA GAP, Fossa Cembalina, Italy 1944-45

Badge: A rose within a laurel wreath surmounted by a crown; on the laurel wreath scrolls inscribed 'South Africa 1900 1901', below a scroll inscribed 'Derbyshire Yeomanry' [central part of scroll blank]. Officers in gilt with laurel wreath in silver. Other ranks white metal.

EAST RIDING YEOMANRY

East Riding of York Yeomanry raised 1902 and transferred 1922 to the RTC as 26th (East Riding of York Yeomanry) Armoured Car Co, RTC. Transferred to the RAC 30 April 1939 under former title[53] and slated for organization as a divisional cavalry regiment. Doubled 24 August 1939.

1st East Riding Yeomanry   Original unit designated 24 August 1939 as 1st East Riding Yeomanry, located at Hull. Embodied 3 September 1939 as GHQ unit with Home Forces. Sent to BEF January 1940. Assigned 1st Armoured Recce Brigade 30 March 1940 (brigade redesignated 26 November 1940 as 27th Armoured Brigade) and regiment converted as an armoured regiment]. Relieved 8 October 1943 and assigned 33rd Tank Brigade; returned 14 (17?) February 1944 to 27th Armoured Brigade; relieved 29 July 1944. Assigned 33rd Armoured Brigade 16 August 1944; converted January-

---

[53] The official title until 1951 was East Riding of York Yeomanry, but the unit is almost always referred to simply as the East Riding Yeomanry.

March 1945 to LVTs, then reverted to armour; relieved 23 April 1945, becoming a GHQ unit in 21st Army Group. Assigned 4th Armoured Brigade 14 June 1945; brigade disbanded later 1945 and regiment placed in suspended animation.

Equipment notes: Presumably brought up to establishment of 28 Mk VI light tanks and 44 carriers before going to France, where all equipment was lost. In September 1940 around 60 Beaverettes. Received Covenanters 1941 and fully equipped by November. Trained with Valentine DD tanks from 1943; may have had Sherman DD tanks but in June 1944 was a conventional regiment with Sherman IIIs and Fireflys. In December 1944 same mix, but about 1/3 of strength was Fireflys. Changed to LVTs January 1945 then re-equipped after Rhine crossing (March 1945) with Sherman tanks and Fireflys.

2nd East Riding Yeomanry   Duplicate unit raised 24 August 1939, also at Hull. Embodied 3 September 1939 with Home Forces. Probably intended as divisional cavalry regiment, but may never have been equipped. Converted 25 June 1940 as 10th (East Riding Yeomanry) Bn, The Green Howards (Alexandra, Princess of Wales's Own Yorkshire Regiment), and later converted as 12th Bn (Yorkshire), The Parachute Regiment.

Battle Honours: Withdrawal to Escaut, ST. OMER-LA BASSEE, CASSEL, NORMANDY LANDING, CAMBES, CAEN, BOURGEBUS RIDGE, La Vie Crossing, LISIEUX, Foret de Bretonne, LOWER MAAS, VENLO POCKET, Ourthe, RHINE, North West Europe 1940 '44-45

Badge: A fox in full cry, above a scroll 'Forrard'. Fox in gilding metal and scroll in white metal.

FIFE AND FORFAR YEOMANRY

Raised 1860 and transferred 1922 to the RTC as 20th (Fife and Forfar) Armoured Car Co, RTC. Transferred to the RAC 30 April 1939 under former title and slated for conversion to a divisional cavalry regiment. Doubled 24 August 1939.

1st Fife and Forfar Yeomanry   Original unit designated 24 August 1939 as 1st Fife and Forfar Yeomanry; located at Kircaldy. Embodied 3 September 1939 with 51st Highland) Infantry Division; relieved 30 March 1940. Assigned 1st Armoured Recce Brigade 7 April 1940; relieved 17 June 1940 and assigned 2nd Armoured Recce Brigade 18 June 1940 (brigade redesignated 23 June 1940 as 3rd Motor MG Brigade and 1 December 1940 as 28th Armoured Brigade); relieved 20 August 1944. Converted August 1944 to flame-thrower tanks. Assigned 79th Armoured Division 7 October to 1 November 1944. Assigned 31st Tank Brigade 2 November 1944 (brigade redesignated 2 February 1945 as 31st Armoured Brigade); relieved 6 June 1945 and assigned 34th

Armoured Brigade. Relieved later and placed under I Corps District. Placed in suspended animation after March 1946.

Equipment notes: Presumably brought up to establishment of 28 Mk VI light tanks and 44 carriers before going to France, where all equipment was lost. In September 1940 around 90 Beaverettes and Humberettes. Received Covenanters 1941 and fully equipped by November. From September 1942 began changing to Cromwells and Centaurs. Crocodiles from August 1944.

2nd Fife and Forfar Yeomanry   Raised 24 August 1939 at Dundee as duplicate unit. Embodied 3 September 1939 and served as GHQ unit with Home Forces. Assigned 29th Armoured Brigade 7 June 1941. (Brigade withdrawn December 1944 for conversion to Comet, but re-drew old equipment for the Ardennes and not converted until later.) Placed in suspended animation ca September 1945.

Equipment notes: Limited equipment before Valentines began to arrive March 1941; at full strength by mid 1942 Began to reorganize with Crusaders and Valentines from July 1942; reverted to all Valentines January 1943. Changed to Shermans May-June 1943. In June 1944 a mixture of Sherman V and Fireflys. Converted to Comet (and Cromwell CS) by March 1945.

Battle Honours: DUNKIRK 1940, CHEUX, BOURGEBUS RIDGE, LE PERIER RIDGE, SCHELDT, OURTHE, RHINE, NORTH WEST EUROPE 1940 '44-45

Badge: The County badge [armoured knight, known as the 'Thain of Fife']. In white metal.

ROYAL GLOUCESTERSHIRE HUSSARS

Raised 1830 and transferred to RTC 1922 as 21st (Gloucestershire Yeomanry) Armoured Car Co, RTC. Transferred to the RAC 30 April 1939 under former title and slated for conversion as a light tank regiment. Doubled 24 August 1939.

1st Royal Gloucestershire Hussars   Original unit, at Gloucester, designated 24 August 1939 as 1st Royal Gloucestershire Hussars, an element of 20th Light Armoured Brigade. Embodied 3 September 1939. (Brigade redesignated 14 April 1940 as 20th Armoured Brigade). Converted 15 January 1943 as armoured recce regiment; relieved and assigned 9th Armoured Division 16 January 1943; relieved 10 July 1944. Converted as [infantry] reconnaissance regiment when assigned 55th (West Lancashire) Infantry Division 1 August 1944; relieved 15 June 1945. Assigned 35th Tank Brigade, a training formation, 16 June 1945 (brigade redesignated 14 July 1945 as 35th Armoured Brigade). Tasked for service in the Far East but the war ended before it deployed. Moved to Austria in 1946 for occupation duties and placed in suspended animation there later that year.

Equipment notes: At first just some carriers and armoured cars. By the end of 1940 1/3 strength in Matildas and Valentines. All Valentines by December 1941. A conventional armoured recce regiment from January 1943 and recce regiment from August 1944. Equipment on move to Austria unknown.

2nd Royal Gloucestershire Hussars   Duplicate unit raised 24 August 1939 at Bristol, an element of 22nd Heavy Armoured Brigade. Embodied 3 September 1939. (Brigade redesignated 14 April 1940 as 22nd Armoured Brigade); relieved 16 September 1942. Assigned 24th Armoured Brigade 9 December 1942; relieved 15 January 1943. Much of regiment posted away early January 1943, 'F' Sqn mainly to 4th QO Hussars, 'G' Sqn mainly to Royal Wilts Yeomanry, and 'H' Sqn to 8th KRI Hussars. Placed in suspended animation 15 January 1943; remnants existed for a period as 'K' Royal Tank Regiment (RAC Holding Regiment).

Equipment notes: Most cruisers sent to Egypt first half of 1941, later equipped with Crusaders. November 1941: 51 Crusaders. Received Grants March-April 1942; late May 1942 had Crusaders in RHQ and 'G' and 'H' Sqns, Grants in 'F' Sqn ['F' Sqn also had 1 Crusader and RHQ had 1 Grant]. Had no tanks in October 1942.

Battle Honours: TOBRUK 1941, GUBI I, SIDI REZEGH 1941, CHOR ES SUFAN, GAZALA, BIR EL ASLAGH, CAULDRON, ALAM EL HALFA, WEST POINT 23, NORTH AFRICA 1941-42

Badge: The insignia of the Duke of Beaufort (a portcullis or with azure nails, chains or surmounted by a ducal coronet), above a scroll in Beaufort blue 'Royal Gloucestershire Hussars'. Officers wear the badge embroidered in colors when wearing a beret. Other ranks badge is gilding metal.

THE INNS OF COURT REGIMENT

Formed 1859 and served from 1908 as officer-producing unit for the TF, then the TA.[54] (From 1932 organized with a squadron of cavalry and two companies of infantry.) Embodied 3 September 1939 as an officer-producing unit. Transferred to RAC November 1940 and reorganized as armoured car regiment. Assigned 9th Armoured Division 23 January 1941; relieved 15 January 1943. GHQ unit with I Corps February 1943 to August 1944 and then VIII Corps from August 1944. Remained in Germany on occupation duties following the war. Placed in suspended animation there March 1947 (and concurrently reformed in the TA).

Equipment notes: Equipping with Daimler armoured cars in December 1941. June 1944: 45 Daimler I, 14 Staghound, 8 AEC III, 5 AA armoured cars, 52 Daimler and

---

[54] The regiment has a claim to the earlier Inns of Court trained bands (formed 1584) which became the Bloomsbury and Inns of Court Volunteers in 1797. Formed from lawyers of the four Inns, their nickname 'The Devil's Own' is credited to a remark of King George III during a parade. The Volunteers were disbanded ca 1816.

13 Humber scour cars; October 1944 (AC only): 43 Daimler, 17 Staghound, and 8 AEC III.

Battle Honours: NORMANDY LANDING, CAEN, BOURGEBUS RIDGE, Cagny, CATHEOLIES, AMIENS 1944, ANTWERP, Hechtel, RHINE, LEESE, ALLER, NORTH WEST EUROPE 1944-45

Badge: Within a laurel wreath surmounted by a crown, four shields placed in the form of a cross with bottom points touching in the center. On the bottom of the wreath, a scroll 'Inns Of Court Regt'. Each shield bears the arms of one of the following Inns: Lincoln's Inn at top (a number of mill-rinds, in the top left canton a lion rampant); Inner Temple on the right (a Pegasus); ; Gray's Inn at bottom (a griffin); Middle Temple on left (St. George's Cross with the Paschal Lamb on the center). The badge is in gilding metal.
Beret badge: The Inns of Court had a distinctive green beret (different from commando green), with an embroidered badge of a red devil on a black oval.
Battledress: White 'Inns Of Court Regiment' on dark green (although often replaced by the normal Royal Armoured Corps flash on normal duty battledress)

NORTH IRISH HORSE

Unit originally raised 1900 and disbanded 1922. Reconstituted 31 August 1939 in the Militia (Supplementary Reserve) as an armoured car regiment.[55] Actual authorization was received 8 September 1939 and the first recruits enlisted 26 September 1939. The regiment formed slowly: only HQ and 'A' Sqns formed by December, and did not organize 'B' and 'C' Sqns until mid January 1940. The regiment was a GHQ unit with Home Forces, remaining in Northern Ireland until October 1941. Began conversion to an army tank regiment in April 1941. Assigned 34th Army Tank Brigade 1 December 1941 (brigade redesignated June 1942 as 34th Tank Brigade); relieved 6 September 1942 and assigned 25th Tank Brigade; relieved 3 December 1944 and assigned 21st Tank Brigade the next day (brigade redesignated 11 June 1945 as 21st Armoured Brigade). Remained on occupation duties in Italy until October 1945 when it moved to Austria and began conversion to recce regiment; it absorbed personnel of 56th Recce Regiment RAC in November, replacing that unit in 78th Infantry Division. In January 1946 it moved to Germany and was assigned to 53rd (Welsh) Infantry Division (absorbed personnel of 53rd Recce Regiment RAC in February). Disbanded 7 July 1946 in Germany.[56]

Equipment notes: The first three armoured cars were not received until January 1940, and gradually gained more. In April 1941, 'A' Sqn took over Valentine tanks as the first element of the regiment to convert; by September the regiment still had only 36 tanks. Began training with the Churchill tanks in February 1942; equipped with III/IV and CS I before going overseas with brigade. (Stuarts replaced carriers in the recce troop

---

[55] The TA was not extended to Northern Ireland until 1947, so the reserve units formed there were Militia and the regiment, technically, was not part of the Yeomanry before 1947.
[56] Personnel probably absorbed by 14th/20th King's Hussars.

October 1943.) In April 1944 gained some Sherman tanks, ultimately replacing two Churchill troops in each squadron with Shermans (made official 30 May 1944). The Shermans began to be replaced with Chnurchill NA75 tanks October 1944 (although the last few Shermans made it to March 1945).[57] In May 1945 it handed in all tanks but three per squadron. Converted to a recce regiment in October 1945 and re-equipped accordingly.

This regiment was one that designated its recce troop a recce squadron. In February 1945 the recce squadron had four troops, three tanks each: Honeys, 95mm Churchills, 6pdr Churchills and Shermans. On 1 March 1945 it added a 6pdr Churchill to SHQ.

Battle Honours: HUNT'S GAP, Sedjenane I, Tamera, Mergueb Chaouach, DJEBEL RMEL, LONGSTOP HILL 1943, TUNIS, North Africa 1943, Liri Valley, HITLER LINE, ADVANCE TO FLORENCE, GOTHIC LINE, Monte Farneto, Monte Cavallo, CASA FORTIS, Casa Bettini, Lamone Crossing, Valli di Commacchio, SENIO, ITALY 1944-45

Badge: The Irish Harp with a crown above the wings; below the harp a scroll 'North Irish Horse'. In gilding metal.
Battle Dress: White 'North Irish Horse' on green
The regiments of 25th Tank Brigade were awarded a silver maple leaf July 1944 for service with I Canadian Corps, to be worn on the upper left arm (the brigade also added a maple leaf to its diabolo badge).

THE LANARKSHIRE YEOMANRY

Raised 1819, a GHQ horsed regiment at Lanark (Scottish Command). Embodied 3 September 1939. Transferred to Royal Artillery 15 February 1940 as The Lanarkshire Yeomanry Regiment RA and formed a duplicate unit; redesignated 15 April 1940 as 155th (Lanarkshire Yeomanry) Field Regiment RA. Duplicate unit became 156th (Lanarkshire Yeomanry) Field Regiment RA. Reformed in the RAC 1947.
Equipment notes: a horsed regiment on mobilization.

In lieu of battle honours, the regiment received an Honorary Distinction: Royal Regiment of Artillery badge with yeardates '1941-45' and four scrolls, 'North-West Europe', 'Sicily', 'Italy', and 'Malaya'

Badge: A double-headed eagle grasping a bell in its right claw, surmounted by a crown; below, a scroll inscribed 'Lanarkshire Yeomanry'. In gilding metal.

---

[57] For actual tank strength (excluding Stuarts) May 1944-April 1945 see Appendix D.

The Duke of Lancaster's Own Yeomanry

Raised 1819, a horsed regiment at Manchester (Western Command). Embodied 3 September 1939. Transferred to Royal Artillery 15 February 1940 as The Duke of Lancaster's Own Yeomanry Regiment RA and formed a duplicate unit; redesignated 15 April 1940 as 77th (Duke of Lancaster's Own Yeomanry) Medium Regiment RA. Duplicate unit became 78th (Duke of Lancaster's Own Yeomanry) Medium Regiment RA. Reformed in the RAC 1947.

Equipment notes: a horsed regiment on mobilization.

In lieu of battle honours the regiment received an Honorary Distinction: Royal Regiment of Artillery badge with year-dates '1944-45' and two scrolls, 'North-West Europe' and 'Italy'

Badge: A rose within a wreath (laurel on the left and oak on the right), a scroll inscribed 'Duke Of Lancaster's Own' on the wreath; the whole ensigned with a ducal coronet. In gilding metal.

The Leicestershire Yeomanry (Prince Albert's Own)

Raised 1794, a GHQ horsed regiment at Leicester (Northern Command). Embodied 3 September 1939. Transferred to Royal Artillery 15 February 1940 as Leicestershire Yeomanry Regiment RA and formed a duplicate unit; redesignated 15 April 1940 as 153rd (Leicestershire Yeomanry) Field Regiment RA. Duplicate unit became 154th (Leicestershire Yeomanry) Field Regiment RA. Reformed in the RAC 1947.

Equipment notes: a horsed regiment on mobilization.

In lieu of battle honours the regiment received an Honorary Distinction: Royal Regiment of Artillery badge with year-dates '1942, '44-45' and three scrolls, 'North-West Europe', 'North Africa', and 'Italy'

Badge: The crest of the Prince Consort with a scroll above inscribed 'Leicestershire' with a scroll below inscribed 'Prince Albert's Own Yeo' and another scroll below that inscribed 'South Africa 1900-02'. In gilding metal.

2nd County of London Yeomanry (Westminster Dragoons)

Raised 1902 and transferred 1922 to RTC as 22nd (London) Armoured Car Coy RTC. Reorganized 1938 as 22nd Bn (Westminster Dragoons), RTC, an officer-producing unit; RTC redesignated RTR April 1939. Embodied 3 September 1939 and redesignated

102nd OCTU (WD). Converted 30 November 1940 as an armoured regiment;[58] GHQ unit with Home Forces. Assigned to 30th Armoured Brigade 8 March 1941. [Equipped with flail tanks from November 1943.] Placed in suspended animation after September 1945 (possibly November).

Equipment notes: Little armour until Valentines began to arrive March 1941. Valentines and some Matildas in December 1941. Began to change to Covenanters from May 1942 and at strength October 1942. Sherman Crabs from November 1943.

Battle Honours: NORMANDY LANDING, VILLERS BOCAGE, VENRAIJ, MEIJEL, VENLO POCKET, ROER, NORTH WEST EUROPE 1944-45

Badge: The Arms of the City of Westminster, above a scroll 'Westminster Dragoons'. This is the other ranks badge, in white metal. Officers wear the Royal Crest.

3rd/4th COUNTY OF LONDON YEOMANRY (SHARPSHOOTERS)

3rd County of London Yeomanry (Sharpshooters) raised 1902 and transferred 1922 to the RTC as 23rd (London) Armoured Car Co, RTC; expanded 1938 as 23rd Cavalry Armoured Car Regiment and transferred to RAC 30 April 1939 under original title. Slated for organization as an armoured regiment. Embodied 3 September 1939 at London, part of 22nd Heavy Armoured Brigade (brigade redesignated 14 April 1940 as 22nd Armoured Brigade). Assigned 2nd Armoured Brigade for period 7 to 13 July 1942 and then returned to 22nd. Relieved from 22nd Armoured Bde16 September 1942. GHQ unit in North Africa September 1942 to July 1943. Assigned 13 July 1943 to 4th Armoured Brigade. Amalgamated 1 August 1944 with duplicate unit to form *3rd/4th County of London Yeomanry (Sharpshooters)*. Relieved from 4th Armoured Brigade 28 July 1945. However, remained in Germany on occupation duties to ca May 1946 when placed in suspended animation.

Equipment notes: Trucks and a few light tanks after mobilization. Tanks received later sent to Egypt 1941, replaced later by Crusaders. November 1941: 51 Crusaders. Received Grants in March-April 1942; late May 1942 had Crusaders in RHQ and 'A' and 'C' Sqns and Grants in 'B' Sqn. Had Sherman III tanks in July 1943. In June 1944 had Sherman II and Fireflys. A mix of Shermans and Fireflys in December 1944 (about 1/3 the latter).

4th County of London Yeomanry (Sharpshooters) raised ca August 1939 in London as a duplicate unit.[59] Embodied 3 September 1939; assigned to 22nd Armoured Brigade

---

[58] The regiment was normally referred to as the Westminster Dragoons, although it was not until 1 September 1951 that it reversed the order of its designation, becoming The Westminster Dragoons (2nd County of London Yeomanry).

[59] Instead of becoming 2/3rd County of London Yeomanry, the duplicate unit resurrected the title originally used by King Edward's Horse: 4th County of London Imperial Yeomanry (King's Colonials), a corps for overseas subjects resident in the UK. King Edward's Horse (The King's

(brigade redesignated 14 April 1940 as 22nd Armoured Brigade); relieved 29 July 1944. Amalgamated 1 August 1944 in France with parent unit.

Equipment notes: Had 1 light tank on mobilization, which it gave to parent unit. Gained another light tank and a Rolls Royce armoured car the end of the month. By the end of the year it had given up the armoured car but had three medium tanks in addition to the light one. It first gained real strength in June 1940, ending the month with 37 Mk VIC light tanks; later increased to 46. In November 1940 it began to reduce the number of lights and gained its first (three) A13 cruisers. In February 1941 it gained its first Crusaders (Cruiser Mk VI). In July 1941, the month before it left the UK, the regiment's armoured strength was still below establishment: 5 Light tanks Mk VIC, 2 Cruisers A13, 9 Cruiser Mk V, 11 Cruiser Mk VI (Crusader), 6 American Light tanks M2A4, 4 American light 'cruisers' M3 [the Honey], along with 10 scout cars. It did not take that equipment, and began to draw tanks from workshops after arrival in Egypt in December (51 Crusaders). The regiment lost virtually all of its armour in combat that month. Received Grants in March-April 1942; late May 1942 had Crusaders in RHQ and 'B' and 'C' Sqns and Grants in 'A' Sqn. (October 1942: 9 Grants and 28 Crusaders.) In December 1942 the regiment had a tank strength of six CS, one 2pdr and 14 6pdr Cruisers, plus 18 (5 Shermans and 13 Grants). It was little different the next month: 8 Shermans, 20 Grants, 15 6pdr and 6 CS cruisers. It continued with this tank mix through the end of the fighting in Tunisia (May 1943). (March 1943 had Crusaders in 'C' Sqn and Shermans and Grants in 'A' and 'B' Squadrons.) The regiment converted to Shermans before going to Italy that autumn. In February 1944 it began to convert to the Cromwell tank, along with the Sherman Firefly.

Battle Honours: Villers Bocage, Odon, Defence of Rauray, CAEN, Bourgebus Ridge, Falaise, Lower Maas, Rhineland, Hochwald, RHINE, Aller, NORTH WEST EUROPE 1944-45, Tobruk 1941, Gubi I, Gabr Saleh, SIDI REZEGH 1941, Chor es Sufan, Gazala, Cauldron, Hagiag er Rami, Mersa Matruh, Minqar Qaim, Defence of Alamein Line, Deir el Shein, Ruweisat, Point 93, Ruweisat Ridge, ALAM EL HALFA, EL ALAMEIN, Akarit, Djebel Roumana, TUNIS, North Africa 1941-43, Landing in Sicily, Lentini, Simeto Bridgehead, SICILY 1943, Termoli, SANGRO, Fossacesia, Volturno Crossing, ITALY 1943

Badge: Circle inscribed 'County Of London Yeomanry' enclosing the letters 'CLY' in front of a pair of crossed rifles, with a crown above the circle and a scroll 'Sharpshooters' below. In gilding metal with 'CLY' in white metal.
Battledress: Yellow 'Sharpshooters' on dark green

Overseas Dominions Regiment) was disembodied in 1919 and disbanded in 1924. While Frederick (*Lineage Book of British Land Forces*) has it formed 27 September 1939, the regiment's war diary has it in existence by September 1, albeit it was very small and largely without equipment.

LOTHIANS AND BORDER HORSE

Raised 1797 and transferred 1922 to the RTC as 19th (Lothians and Border) Armoured Car Coy, RTC. Transferred to the RAC 30 April 1939 under former title[60] and slated for conversion as a divisional cavalry regiment. Regiment divided 24 August 1939.

1st Lothians and Border Horse   Original unit redesignated 24 August 1939 as 1st Lothians and Border Horse, at Edinburgh. Embodied 3 September 1939 with 48th (South Midland) Infantry Division; relieved 27 April 1940. Served with BEF April-June 1940. GHQ unit with Home Forces from July 1940. Later converted as armoured regiment; and assigned 30th Armoured Brigade 9 March 1941. [Converted 1943 to flail tanks.] Placed in suspended animation after August 1945 (possibly November).
      Equipment notes: Early equipment unknown. Began to receive Valentines March 1941. Valentines and some Matildas in December 1941. Converted to Covenanters from May 1942. Sherman Crabs from November 1943.

2nd Lothians and Border Horse   Duplicate unit raised 24 August 1939 at Ladybank. Embodied 3 September 1939 as GHQ unit with Home Forces. Assigned 1st Motor MG Brigade 30 May 1940 (brigade redesignated 12 October 1940 as 26th Armoured Brigade). Relieved 17 July 1945. Placed in suspended animation ca July or August 1945.
      Equipment notes: Little armour at first, about 1/3 strength in Valentines and Matildas by the end of 1940. All Valentines by December 1941. A mixture of Crusaders and Valentines August 1942. In February 1943 began to replace tanks with Shermans; re-drew old equipment for Kasserine, then began to refit again with Shermans; by April 1943 a homogenous Sherman regiment (Sherman III). Received 6 Sherman IB (105mm) for squadron HQs in September 1944, and began conversion to Sherman IIA (76mm) in March 1945.

Battle Honours: Somme 1940, Withdrawal to Seine, St Valery-en-Caux, FALAISE, Falaise Road, Laison, Le Havre, BOULOGNE 1944, Calais 1944, Scheldt, WESTKAPELLE, Geilenkirchen, Roer, Reichswald, NORTH WEST EUROPE 1940 '44-45, Bou Arada, KASSERINE, Thala, Fondouk, Sidi Ali, Bordj, Djebel Kournine, Tunis, HAMMAM LIF, Bou Ficha, NORTH AFRICA 1942-43, CASSINO II, Liri Valley, Monte Piccolo, Monte Rotondo, Capture of Perugia, Arezzo, Advance to Florence, ARGENTA GAP, ITALY 1944-45

Badge: A sheaf of wheat. In gilding metal.

---

[60] The official title was The Lothians and Border Horse Yeomanry, but the regiment was commonly referred to simply as The Lothians and Border Horse.

THE LOVAT SCOUTS

Units raised for the Boer War reformed 1903; transferred to Scouts 1920 [horsed recce], at Inverness (Scottish Command). Embodied 3 September 1939. Sent to the Faroe Islands May 1940; returned to the UK June 1942 and trained as infantry in Scotland, going to the School of Mountain Warfare near Braemar. Assigned 227th Independent Infantry Brigade 30 September 1942 and moved to north Wales; relieved 9 July 1943. Sent to Canada December 1943 for mountain and ski training. Sent to Italy July 1944, going to Austria after the German surrender and then to Greece early 1946. Placed in suspended animation there 20 January 1947.

Equipment notes: a horsed regiment on mobilization; dismounted by May 1940 and infantry from that point on.

Battle Honours: No battle honours awarded[61]

Badge: The crest and motto of Clan Fraser (of which Lord Lovat was chief): Within a strap inscribed 'Je Suis Prest' (I am ready) a stag's head. In white metal.

NORTHAMPTONSHIRE YEOMANRY

Originally raised 1794; later disbanded and reformed in 1902; transferred 1922 to the RTC as 25th (Northamptonshire Yeomanry) Armoured Car Coy, RTC. Transferred to the RAC 30 April 1939 under former title and slated for conversion as a light tank regiment. Regiment divided 24 August 1939.

1st Northamptonshire Yeomanry Original unit redesignated 24 August 1939 as 1st Northamptonshire Yeomanry. Embodied 3 September 1939 at Northampton as part of 20th Light Armoured Brigade (brigade redesignated 14 April 1940 as 20th Armoured Brigade). Converted 15 January 1943 as an armoured recce regiment; relieved 3 April 1943. Assigned 42nd Armoured Division 18 April 1943; relieved 16 September 1943. Converted as an armoured regiment and assigned 33rd Tank Brigade 21 September 1943 (brigade redesignated 17 March 1944 as 33rd Armoured Brigade); relieved 18 August 1945. Converted January 1945 to LVTs. Transferred August 1945 to XXX Corps District. Placed in suspended animation March 1946 or later.

Equipment notes: Little armour at first, at 1/3 strength in Valentines and Matildas by the end of 1940. All Valentines by December 1941. A conventional armoured recce regiment April-September 1943. Converted to Shermans March 1944. In June 1944, a mix of Sherman I and II. In December 1944 a mix of Shermans and Fireflys. LVTs from January 1945.

---

[61] Since they clearly would have qualified at least for Italy 1944-45, this is probably because they became part of the Royal Artillery in 1949, well before any of the Second World War battle honours were determined.

2nd Northamptonshire Yeomanry   Raised 27 September 1939 at Northampton as duplicate unit, also part of 20th Light Armoured Brigade (brigade redesignated 14 April 1940 as 20th Armoured Brigade). Converted 15 January 1943 as an armoured recce regiment; relieved 3 April 1943. Assigned 79th Armoured Division 10 January 1943; relieved 25 March 1943 and assigned 11th Armoured Division; relieved 17 August 1944 and placed in suspended animation 18 August 1944 in France.

   Equipment notes: Little armour at first, at 1/3 strength in Valentines and Matildas by the end of 1940. All Valentines by December 1941. Organized January 1943 as a conventional armoured recce regiment; changed spring 1944 to 21st Army Group pattern (Cromwells, with Stuarts only in the recce troop).

Battle Honours: ODON, CHEUX, Defence of Rauray, CAEN, Noyere, BOURGEBUS RIDGE, MONT PINCON, FALAISE, Falaise Road, Dives Crossing, Lisieux, LE HAVRE, LOWER MAAS, Venlo Pocket, OURTHE, RHINE, North West Europe 1944-45

Badge: 1st Northamptonshire Yeomanry wore the original badge: The White Horse of Hanover on a ground, in white metal. 2nd Northamptonshire Yeomanry wore the White Horse of Hanover enclosed in an oval inscribed 'Northamptonshire Yeomanry', in white metal.

THE NORTHUMBERLAND HUSSARS

Raised 1797, a GHQ horsed regiment at Newcastle-on-Tyne (Northern Command). Embodied 3 September 1939. Converted 15 February 1940 as 102nd LAA/Atk Regiment RA (The Northumberland Hussars); later 102nd Atk Regiment RA (The Northumberland Hussars). Reformed in the RAC 1947.

   Equipment notes: a horsed regiment on mobilization.

Instead of battle honours, the regiment received an Honorary Distinction: badge of the Royal Regiment of Artillery with year-dates '1940-45' and five scrolls, 'North Africa', 'Greece', 'Middle East', 'Sicily', 'North-West Europe'

Badge: A circle inscribed 'Northumberland Hussars' with a crown above; within the circle a Norman castle (from the Arms of Newcastle-on-Tyne); below the circle a scroll inscribed 'South Africa 1900-02'. In gilding metal.

The Nottinghamshire Yeomanry (Sherwood Rangers)

Raised 1794. A horsed regiment at Newark, part of 5th Cavalry Brigade. Embodied 3 September 1939.[62] Relieved 2 February 1941. A GHQ unit in Palestine February to July 1941; assigned to RAC 12 April 1941 as an armoured regiment. Assigned 8th Armoured Brigade 1 August 1941. Placed in suspended animation 1 March 1946 in Germany.

*Equipment note*s: Began as horsed unit. By December 1941 in 15cwt trucks and a few Stuart tanks (those later withdrawn?). Received some Grants for training March 1942, but they were withdrawn. Equipped with Grants and Crusaders August 1942, may have received some Lees in September 1942 along with first Shermans. October 1942 had Grants in RHQ and 'B' Sqn (20), Crusaders in 'A' Sqn (13), and Shermans in 'C' Sqn (11). By March 1943 had Crusaders in 'A' Sqn and Shermans in 'B' and 'C' Sqns. Later all Shermans. In June 1944, Sherman II DD in 'B' and 'C' Sqs, Sherman III and Fireflys in 'A' Sqn. Changed after Normandy landing to normal pattern of Shermans and Fireflys. In December 1944 the same.

Battle Honours: NORMANDY LANDING, Villers Bocage, Odon, Fontenay le Pesnil, Defence of Rauray, Mont Pincon, Jurques, Noireau Crossing, Seine 1944, GHEIL, Nederrijn, GEILENKIRCHEN, Roer, Rhineland, Cleve, Goch, Weeze, RHINE, NORTH WEST EUROPE 1944-45, ALAM EL HALFA, EL ALAMEIN, El Agheila, ADVANCE ON TRIPOLI, TEBAGA GAP, Point 201 (Roman Wall), El Hamma, Chebket en Nouiges, Enfidaville, Takrouna, NORTH AFRICA 1940-43

Badge: A horn with lanyard, within a strap inscribed 'Notts Sherwood Rangers Yeomanry', surmounted by a crown. Officers badge in silver plate and other ranks in gilding metal.

Scottish Horse Scouts

Raised 1900 for the Boer War and reformed 1903; made Scouts [horsed recce] 1920 at Dunkeld (Scottish Command). Embodied 3 September 1939. Taken over as The Scottish Horse Regiment RA 15 February 1940 and formed a duplicate unit; redesignated 15 April 1940 as 79th (The Scottish Horse) Medium Regiment RA; duplicate unit became 80th . (The Scottish Horse) Medium Regiment RA. Reformed in the RAC 1947.
Equipment notes: a horsed regiment on mobilization.

Instead of battle honours the regiment received an Honorary Distinction: badge of the Royal Regiment of Artillery 0with year-dates '1943-45' and three scrolls, 'North-West Europe', 'Sicily', and 'Italy'

---

[62] The regiment was almost invariably known by its subtitle, and on 1 September 1951 was retitled as The Sherwood Rangers Yeomanry.

Badge: An oval inscribed 'Scottish Horse 1900' with scrolls below inscribed 'South Africa 1900 1901 1902'. A wreath of juniper and bay encloses the oval; St Andrew's Cross is superimposed on the oval, with a crown above the oval. In white metal.

THE SHROPSHIRE YEOMANRY

Raised 1814, a GHQ horsed regiment at Shrewsbury (Western Command). Embodied 3 September 1939. Transferred to the Royal Artillery 15 February 1940 as The Shropshire Yeomanry Regiment RA and formed a duplicate unit; redesignated 15 April 1940 as 75th (Shropshire Yeomanry) Medium Regiment RA. Duplicate unit became 76th (Shropshire Yeomanry) Medium Regiment RA. Reformed in the RAC 1947.
   Equipment notes: a horsed regiment on mobilization.

Instead of battle honours the regiment received an Honorary Distinction: Badge of the Royal Regiment of Artillery with year-dates '1943-45' and two scrolls, 'Sicily' and 'Italy'

Badge: Three leopards' faces (from the Arms of Shrewsbury) within a strap inscribed 'Shropshire Yeomanry' surmounted by a crown. In gilding metal.

THE NORTH SOMERSET YEOMANRY

Raised 1798; a GHQ horsed regiment at Bath (Southern Command). Embodied 3 September 1939. Assigned 4th Cavalry Brigade 15 November 1939; transferred 21 March 1941 to 5th Cavalry Brigade; relieved 20 March 1942. Converted 21 March 1942 as 4th Air Formation Signals (North Somerset Yeomanry), absorbing unit in the Middle East with that number. On 25 September 1944, 14th Formation Signals (North Somerset Yeomanry) formed by detachment from the 4th, ending affiliation with the former unit; served with 21st Army Group. Regiment reformed in the RAC 1947.
   Equipment notes: Began as horsed regiment, later changing over to 15cwt trucks.

Battle Honours: JEBEL MAZAR, SYRIA 1941, and Honorary Distinction: badge of the Royal Corps of Signals with year-dates '1942-45' and four scrolls, 'North Africa', 'Sicily', 'Italy', 'North-West Europe'

Badge: A ten-pointed star, the top point displaced by a crown; in the center a circle inscribed 'Arma Pacis Fulcra' (Arms the mainstay of peace); within the circle the Royal Cypher with crown above. In white metal.

THE STAFFORDSHIRE YEOMANRY (QUEEN'S OWN ROYAL REGIMENT)

Raised 1794. A horsed regiment at Stafford, assigned to 6th Cavalry Brigade. Embodied 3 September 1939. Relieved 28 April 1941 Assigned 5th Cavalry Brigade 30 April 1941; relieved 4 June 1941 and assigned 6th Cavalry Brigade the next day (brigade redesignated 1 August 1941 as 8th Armoured Brigade). Relieved 13 February 1944 and assigned the next day to 27th Armoured Brigade; equipped with DD tanks for Normandy June 1944; relieved 29 July 1944. From that date operated as an independent DD tank unit, serving at times with 4th and 33rd Armoured Brigades. Assigned 79th Armoured Division 17 September 1944; relieved 17 April 1945. Assigned 31st Armoured Brigade 18 to 28 (26?) April 1945 and then assigned 33rd Armoured Brigade; relieved 26 June 1945. Placed in suspended animation 1 March 1946 in Germany.

Equipment notes: Began as horsed regiment, later in 15cwt trucks. December 1941 in 15cwt trucks and 3ton lorries, with a few Stuarts (later withdrawn?). Received some Grants for training March 1942, but they were withdrawn. Equipped with Grants ('A' and 'B' Sqns) and Crusaders ('C' Sqn) August 1942, may have received some Lees in September 1942 along with first Shermans. October 1942: Grants in RHQ and 'B' Sqn (15), Shermans in 'A' Sqn (10) and Crusaders in 'C' Sqn (15). May have received some Valentine DD tanks February 1944; converted to Sherman III DD tanks April-May 1944.

Battle Honours: NORMANDY LANDING, CAEN, Troarn, RHINE, Lingen, North West Europe 1944-45, Syria 1941, ALAM EL HALFA, EL ALAMEIN, EL AGHEILA, ADVANCE ON TRIPOLI, TEBAGA GAP, Point 201 (Roman Wall), El Hamma, Akarit, Sebkret en Noual, Djebel el Telli, ENFIDAVILLE, Takrouna, North Africa 1942-43

Badge: Officers: The Stafford Knot within the Garter inscribed 'Honi Soit Qui Maly Y Pense' (Evil be to them who evil think), a crown above the Garter and scroll below inscribed 'Pro Aris Et Focis' (For our altars and our hearths); in bronze. Other ranks: The Stafford Knot surmounted by a crown, in gilding metal.

THE WARWICKSHIRE YEOMANRY

Raised 1794. A horsed regiment at Warwick, assigned to 6th Cavalry Brigade. Embodied 3 September 1939. Relieved 21 March 1941 and assigned 4th Cavalry Brigade the next day (brigade redesignated 3 August 1941 as 9th Armoured Brigade); relieved 27 May 1943. A GHQ unit Syria and/or Palestine May-August 1943. Returned to 9th Armoured Brigade 23 August 1943; relieved 8 October 1944 and returned to UK; GHQ unit with Home Forces December 1944 to March 1945. Assigned 35th Tank Brigade, a training formation, 27 March 1945 (brigade redesignated 14 July 1945 as 35th Armoured Brigade). Placed in suspended animation after August 1945.

Equipment notes: Began as horsed regiment, later in 15cwt trucks. In May 1942 Stuarts in 'A' Sqn and Crusaders in 'B' and 'C' Sqns (probably understrength). Received first Grants and Shermans in mid-September 1942; October 1942 had 17 Crusaders in RHQ and 'A' Sqn, 13 Shermans in 'B' Sqn and 14 Grants in 'C' Sqn. By June 1943 equipped with Shermans.

Battle Honours: IRAQ 1941, SYRIA 1941, EL ALAMEIN, NORTH AFRICA 1942, FICULLE, TRASIMENE LINE, SANTATUCCHIO, ADVANCE TO FLORENCE, CAMPRIANO, ITALY 1944

Badge: The Bear and Ragged Staff [crest of the Warwick family]. Officers in silver and other ranks in gilding metal.

THE ROYAL WILTSHIRE YEOMANRY (PRINCE OF WALES'S OWN)

Raised 1794. A GHQ horsed regiment at Trowbridge (Southern Command). Embodied 3 September 1939 as GHQ unit with Home Forces. Assigned 4th Cavalry Brigade 3 December 1939; transferred 3 October 1940 to 6th Cavalry Brigade; relieved 7 January 1941. [Began training in searchlight role July 1940; two squadrons served on rotation as searchlight unit in North Africa.[63] Remainder of the regiment converted to lorried infantry; returned to 4th Cavalry Brigade 8 January 1941 (brigade redesignated 3 August 1941 as 9th Armoured Brigade); relieved 27 May 1943. (Absorbed personnel of 'G' Sqn, 2nd Royal Gloucester Hussars early January 1943.) Returned to 9th Armoured Brigade 13 August 1943; relieved 8 October 1944 returned to UK; GHQ unit with Home Forces December 1944 to March 1945. Assigned 35th Tank Brigade, a training formation, 27 March 1945 (brigade redesignated 14 July 1945 as 35th Armoured Brigade). Upon arrival of trainees in March 1945, the regiment trained on the Churchill tank, later adding Sherman, Cromwell and Comet as well. Placed in suspended animation 1 February 1946.
    Equipment notes: Began as horsed regiment; January 1941 began conversion from horsed to 15cwt trucks. In May 1942 Stuarts in 'B' Sqn and Crusaders in 'A' and 'C' Sqns (probably understrength). Received first Grants and Shermans in mid September 1942; October 1942 had Grants in RHQ and 'C' Sqn (9),10 Shermans in 'A' Sqn and 14 Crusaders in 'B' Sqn. By June 1943 equipped with Shermans. As a training unit, had Sherman, Cromwell, Comet and Churchill tanks.

Battle Honours: Iraq 1941, PALMYRA, Syria 1941, EL ALAMEIN, North Africa 1942, LIRI VALLEY, ADVANCE TO TIBER, CITTA DELLA PIEVE, TRASIMENE LINE, ADVANCE TO FLORENCE, MONTE CEDRONE, CITTA DI CASTELLO, Italy 1944

---

[63] 'C' Sqn went to Egypt in the role September 1940, replaced ca. December 1940 by 'B' Sqn. (January 1941 under 2nd AA Brigade.) 'B' Sqn ended up in Tobruk until evacuated by sea December 1941. They returned to the regiment August 1942.

Badge: The Prince of Wales's plume, coronet and motto. Officers have coronet in gilding metal and remainder in silver plate; other ranks in gilding and white metals.

THE QUEEN'S OWN YORKSHIRE DRAGOONS

Raised 1794. A horsed regiment at Doncaster assigned to 5th Cavalry Brigade. Embodied 3 September 1939. Relieved from 5th Cavalry Brigade 18 March 1942. Then served as a GHQ unit in Palestine North Africa to August 1942. (The last mounted regiment in the Army, they were dismounted in February 1942.) There were to become an armoured regiment but the shortage of tanks resulted in their conversion as a motor battalion, assigned to 2nd Armoured Brigade 24 August 1942. Redesignated 19 December 1942 as 9th Bn The King's Own Yorkshire Light Infantry and later placed in suspended animation. They were reformed 1947 in the RAC.

Equipment notes: Began as horsed regiment; January 1941 began conversion from horses to 15cwt trucks.

Battle Honours: [as cavalry] SYRIA 1941, [as infantry] EL ALAMEIN, Tebaga Gap, EL HAMMA, El Kourzia, TUNIS, NORTH AFRICA 1942-43, ANZIO, ROME, Coriano, RIMINI LINE, CERIANO RIDGE, ITALY 1944

Badge: The Rose of York surmounted by a Royal Crown. In gilding metal.

THE YORKSHIRE HUSSARS (ALEXANDRA, PRINCESS OF WALES'S OWN)

Raised 1794. A horsed regiment at York, assigned to 5th Cavalry Brigade. Embodied 3 September 1939. Transferred 23 March 1941 to 6th Cavalry Brigade; relieved 31 July 1941. GHQ unit in Palestine July to October 1941. Assigned 9th Armoured Brigade 10 October 1941; relieved 13 March 1942. GHQ unit in Middle East March 1942 to November 1943. Converted as an [infantry] recce regiment and assigned 50th (Northumbrian) Infantry Division 12 December 1943; relieved 18 January 1944. Assigned 61st Infantry Division 24 January 1944; relieved 16 June 1945 and assigned 35th Tank Brigade, a training formation (brigade redesignated 14 July 1945 as 35th Armoured Brigade). (The regiment ran D Day embarkation camps in the Sussex area , and then served as a recce holding unit and were responsible for training tank crews.) Placed in suspended animation ca 1945.

Equipment notes: Began as horsed regiment, later in 15cwt trucks. First equipped as armoured unit with Stuart tanks, moved to Cyprus March 1942 and equipped with cruiser and Valentine tanks. Moved to Egypt January 1943 and equipped with Crusader and Sherman tanks. Moved to the UK November 1943 and became a normal recce regiment, then a holding/training unit.

Battle Honours: None awarded

Badge: The Rose of York surmounted by the Prince of Wales's plume, coronet, and motto. The coronet in gilding metal, the remainder of the badge in white metal.

Royal Armoured Corps Units

The need for new armoured units was met in part by conversion of infantry battalions to armour. As the war progressed and the number of units needed and supportable decreased, these 'regiments RAC' were often disbanded or converted back to infantry, leaving only a small number of those formed still in the field at the end of the war. Neither the RAC itself or units designated as part of it received separate battle honours, any earned went to the infantry regiment.

The converted infantry battalions all retained their normal cap badges. A summary of those regiments providing regiments RAC and their cap badges follows.

The Buffs (The Royal East Kent Regiment) [141st Regiment RAC]: A dragon above a scroll inscribed 'The Buffs'. In silver plate for officers and gilding metal for other ranks.

The King's Own Royal Regiment (Lancaster) [107th and 151st Regts RAC]: The Lion of England from the Royal Arms on a bar inscribed 'The King's Own'. Officers in silver plate and other ranks in gilding metal.

The King's Regiment (Liverpool) [152nd Regiment RAC]: The White Horse of Hanover in a prancing position, its hind legs standing on a scroll inscribed 'King's' in Old English lettering. Officers, the White Horse in silver plate and the remainder in gilt or gilding metal; other ranks use white metal and gilding metal.

The Suffolk Regiment [142nd Regiment RAC]: The Castle of Gibraltar with a scroll above inscribed 'GIBRALTAR' and a key descending from the center of the base turned to the left, within a circle inscribed 'Montis Insignia Calpe' [The Arms of Gibraltar], the whole within an oak leaf wreath; above the circle a Crown and below the circle a scroll inscribed 'The Suffolk Reg^t.' In silver plate (gilt scroll) for officers, white metal (scroll in gilding metal) for other ranks.

The West Yorkshire Regiment (The Prince of Wales's Own) [113th Regiment RAC]: The White Horse of Hanover, galloping on a ground, below the ground a scroll inscribed 'West Yorkshire'. Officers have the horse and ground in silver plate and the scroll in gilt or gilding metal, other ranks white metal and gilding metal.

The Green Howards)Alexandra, Princess of Wales's Own Yorkshire Regiment) [161st Regiment RAC]: The letter 'A' (cipher of Queen Alexandra) with 'Alexandra' inscribed on the cross-bar; combined with the cipher is the Dannebrog [Danish Cross] inscribed '1875'; above the cipher and cross a Crown; immediately below the cipher a scroll inscribed 'The Yorkshire Reg^t' with 'Yorkshire' forming a straight base for the cipher; below that another scroll inscribed 'Princess Of Wales's Own' with a rose in the center of the scroll. In bronze for officers and gilding metal for other ranks.

The Lancashire Fusiliers [108th, 109th and 143rd Regts RAC]: A grenade, on the ball a laurel wreath within which is a Sphinx resting on a tablet inscribed 'Egypt'; below the grenade a scroll inscribed 'The Lancashire Fusiliers'. For officers, the grenade is in gilt or gilding metal and the scroll in silver plate; for other ranks, the whole badge is in gilding metal.

The South Wales Borderers [158th Regiment RAC]: Within a wreath of immortelles, a Sphinx resting on a tablet inscribed 'Egypt'; on the lower portion of the wreath the letters 'SWB'. In silver plate for officers; for other ranks, the wreath is in gilding metal and the rest in white metal.

The Gloucestershire Regiment [159th Regiment RAC]: The Sphinx resting on a tablet inscribed 'Egypt' within two springs of laurel; below, a scroll inscribed 'Gloucestershire'. Officers have the badge in gold embroidery, other ranks in white metal. Uniquely, the regiment wears the Sphinx badge on the back of their head gear as well as the front or side.

The East Lancashire Regiment [144th Regiment RAC]: The Sphinx resting on a tablet inscribed 'Egypt', below the tablet a rose, the whole within a laurel wreath with a Crown above the wreath; resting on the lower portion of the wreath is a scroll inscribed 'East Lancashire'. In silver plate, except that the rose is in gilt for officers and gilding metal for other ranks.

The Duke of Wellington's Regiment (West Riding) [114th, 115th, 145th and 146th Regts RAC]: The crest and motto of the Duke of Wellington[64] above a scroll inscribed 'The West Riding'. In silver plate for officers (title scroll in gilt or gilding metal); white metal and gilding metal for other ranks.

The Border Regiment [110th Regiment RAC]: A star similar to that of the Order of the Garter, with a Crown displacing the uppermost point; on the star a Maltese Cross, with the battle honours inscribed on the four arms; in the center of the cross a circle inscribed 'Arroyo Dos Molinos 1811', within the circle a dragon superscribed 'China'; below the Maltese Cross a scroll inscribed 'The Border Regt.'. In silver plate for officers and white metal for other ranks.

The Royal Sussex Regiment [160th Regiment RAC]: The Star of the Order of the Garter over the Roussillon plume, with a scroll below inscribed 'The Royal Sussex Reg[t].'. For officers, the star is in silver plate, the Cross of St. George in red enamel, the Garter and motto are on a blue ground, the plume is in silver with a gilt stem. For other ranks, white metal with the scroll in gilding metal.

The Hampshire Regiment [147th and 157th Regts RAC]: The Hampshire Rose with the Royal Tiger above standing on a scroll, the whole enclosed in a laurel wreath, with a scroll inscribed 'Hampshire' superimposed on the lower part of the wreath. The tiger and wreath in white metal and the rose and scroll in gilding metal. [This is the other ranks badge. Officers wore an eight-pointed silver-plated star, on the center the Garter with motto on a ground of blue enamel,

---

[64] Out of a ducal coronet, a demi-lion rampant, holding a forked pennon, flowing to the left, charged with the Cross of St. George, and the motto "Virtutis Fotuna Comes" [Fortune favors the brave].

surmounted by a Crown displacing the topmost point of the star; within the Garter the Hampshire Rose in gilt and red enamel; on the lower part of the star a scroll inscribed 'Hampshire' on a ground of blue enamel.]

The Essex Regiment [153rd Regiment RAC]: The Castle of Gibraltar with the key hanging from the center of the base; above the Castle the Sphinx resting on a tablet inscribed 'Egypt'; all but the Sphinx enclosed in an oak wreath, with a scroll inscribed 'The Essex Reg^t.' on the lower portion of the wreath. In silver plate for officers; for other ranks, castle and wreath in gilding metal and Sphinx and scroll in white metal.

The Sherwood Foresters (Nottinghamshire and Derbyshire Regiment) [112th and 163rd Regts RAC]: A Maltese Cross surmounted by a Crown; in the center a wreath of oak leaves, within the wreath a stag lodged; on the left arm of the cross and across the left branch of the wreath a straight scroll inscribed 'Sherwood'; on the right arm of the cross and across the right branch of the wreath, a straight scroll inscribed 'Foresters'; below the cross, a scroll inscribed 'Notts &Derby'. In bronze for officers; white metal for other ranks, with the scroll in gilding metal.

The Loyal Regiment (North Lancashire) [148th Regiment RAC]: The Royal Crest; below the crown a rose; below the rose a scroll inscribed 'The Loyal Regiment'. For officers, the rose is in gilt with red enamel petals and green points; the Royal Crest is in silver plate and the scroll in gilt or gilding metal. For other ranks, the Royal Crest is in white metal and the remainder in gilding metal.

The Queen's Own Royal West Kent Regiment [162nd Regiment RAC]: The White Horse of Kent standing on a scroll inscribed 'Invicta' (Unconquered) in Old English lettering; below that a scroll inscribed 'Royal West Kent'. In silver plate for officers and white metal for other ranks.

The King's Own Yorkshire Light Infantry [149th Regiment RAC]: A French hunting horn with a rose in the twist. In silver plate for officers, with the roles on a black ground; other ranks all in white metal.

The Manchester Regiment [111th Regiment RAC]: A fleur-de-lis. In silver plate for officers and white metal for other ranks.

The North Staffordshire Regiment (The Prince of Wales's) [154th Regiment RAC]: The Stafford Knot with the Prince of Wales's plume, coronet and motto above; below the knot a scroll inscribed 'North Stafford'. Officers have the knot and coronet in gilt or gilding metal and the plume and scroll in silver plate. Other ranks have the knot and coronet in silver plate and the rest in white metal.

The York and Lancaster Regiment [150th Regiment RAC]: The Royal Tiger with the Union Rose above and a coronet above the rose; the tiger is within a scroll inscribed 'York And Lancaster' with laurel continuing each arm of the scroll upwards to meet at the coronet. Officers have the tiger, wreath and scroll in gilt or gilding metal, the coronet in silver plate, and the rose in red and white enamel on silver plate. Other ranks use gilding metal and white metal.

The Durham Light Infantry [155th Regiment RAC]: A bugle (ornamented with a leaf motif) with the strings taken upwards in a Crown; within the strings the letters 'DLI'. In silver plate for officers and white metal for other ranks.

The Highland Light Infantry (City of Glasgow Regiment) [156th Regiment RAC]: The Star of the Order of the Thistle; on the star a bugle horn; in the twist of the horn the monogram 'HLI'; above the horn a Crown, and below it an elephant superscribed 'Assaye' on a scroll. Officers have the star and horn in silver plate, the remainder in gilt or gilding metal, with a crimson cap for the Crown. The badge for other ranks is all in white metal.

The Gordon Highlanders [116th Regiment RAC]: A stag's head above a ducal coronet within a wreath of ivy; on the bottom of the wreath a scroll inscribed 'Bydand' (Stand Fast). Officers in silver plate and other ranks in white metal.

Although retaining their regimental cap badges, the regiments RAC wore the Royal Armoured Corps regimental flash on battledress, rather than that of their former infantry regiment.

107th (KING'S OWN) REGIMENT RAC

Formed 1 November 1941 by conversion of 5th Bn The King's Own Royal Regiment, an element of 11th Armoured Brigade. (Brigade redesignated 25 July 1942 as 11th Tank Brigade.) Tasked 1942 as advanced training regiment for units converting to Churchills. Redesignated 15 February 1943 as 107th Training Regiment RAC (King's Own). Relieved 23 November 1943 and placed in suspended animation 31 December 1943.

Equipment notes: Began to receive some Covenanters[65] but by May-June 1942 was converting to the Churchill III.

107th (KING'S OWN) REGIMENT RAC [ex 151st]

Formed 1 January 1942 as 151st (King's Own) Regiment RAC by conversion of 10th Bn The King's Own Royal Regiment, an element of 35th Army Tank Brigade; relieved 4 August 1942. Assigned 25th Tank Brigade 5 August to 2 September 1942. Assigned 3 September 1942 to 34th Tank Brigade (brigade redesignated 2 February 1945 as 34th Armoured Brigade). Renumbered 31 December 1943 as 107th. Placed in suspended animation ca December 1945.

Equipment notes: Equipped with some carriers on formation. First Churchill IIs arrived February 1942. By September around 45 Churchills (Mainly III). In June 1944, primarily Churchill III/IV [6pdr], about 30% VI/VII [75mm], plus V/VIII CS versions. In December 1944, proportion of 6pdr/75mm reversed (about 31% 6pdr).

---

[65] On 31 March 1942 the 42nd Armoured Division (10th and 11th Armoured Brigades) had only 94 Coventers all told, along with 95 carriers being used as training vehicles.

108th REGIMENT RAC

Formed 1 November 1941 by conversion of 1/5th (Bury) Bn The Lancashire Fusiliers, an element of 10th Armoured Brigade. (Brigade redesignated 25 July 1942 as 10th Tank Brigade.) Relieved 24 November 1943 (and possibly converted back to infantry, but more likely effectively dissolved the next month). Officially placed in suspended animation 7 February 1944.

Equipment notes: Began to receive some Covenanter tanks, then converted to Churchill III. In a training role, also received some Shermans in June 1943.

109th REGIMENT RAC

Formed 1 November 1941 by conversion of 1/6th Bn The Lancashire Fusiliers, an element of 10th Armoured Brigade. (Brigade redesignated 25 July 1942 as 10th Tank Brigade.) Relieved 24 November 1943 (and possibly converted back to infantry, but more likely effectively dissolved the next month). Officially placed in suspended animation 7 February 1944.

Equipment notes: Began to receive some Covenanter tanks, then converted to Churchill III. In a training role, also received some Shermans in June 1943.

110th REGIMENT RAC

Formed 1 November 1941 by conversion of 5th (Cumberland) Bn, The Border Regiment, an element of 11th Armoured Brigade. (Brigade redesignated 25 July 1942 as 11th Tank Brigade.) Relieved 23 November 1943. Converted back to infantry February 1944 as 5th Bn The Border Regiment.

Equipment notes: Began to receive some Covenanters but by May-June 1942 was converting to the Churchill III.

111th (MANCHESTER REGIMENT) REGIMENT RAC

Formed 1 November 1941 by conversion of 5th Bn The Manchester Regiment, an element of 11th Armoured Brigade. (Brigade redesignated 25 July 1942 as 11th Tank Brigade.) Relieved 23 November 1943 and placed in suspended animation 1 December 1943.

Equipment notes: Began to receive some Covenanters but by May-June 1942 was converting to the Churchill III.

112th REGIMENT RAC

Formed November 1941 by conversion of 9th Bn The Sherwood Foresters as an armoured car regiment, assigned 42nd Armoured Division 17 November 1941. Relieved 24 February 1943 and placed under Home Forces (allotted for XII Corps to February

1944). Handed over equipment to 1st Royal Dragoons when that regiment returned to the UK December 1943 and replaced it in XII Corps. Placed in suspended animation 19 November 1944.

Equipment notes: No armoured cars assigned as of December 1941. Later a conventional armoured car regiment.

113th REGIMENT RAC

Formed 20 July 1942 by conversion of 2/5th Bn The West Yorkshire Regiment, an element of 137th Armoured Brigade; relieved 25 September 1943. Converted September 1943 as a tank delivery squadron in 2nd Armoured Delivery Regiment. Officially placed in suspended animation 7 February 1944 and concurrently converted to infantry as 14th Bn The West Yorkshire Regiment.

Equipment notes: Equipped with Covenanter tanks.

114th REGIMENT RAC

Formed 20 July 1942 by conversion of 2/6th Bn The Duke of Wellington's Regiment (West Riding), an element of 137th Armoured Brigade; relieved 25 September 1943. Converted September 1943 as a tank delivery squadron in 2nd Armoured Delivery Regiment. Officially placed in suspended animation 7 February 1944 and concurrently converted to infantry as 11th Bn The Duke of Wellington's Regiment.

Equipment notes: Equipped with Covenanter tanks.

115th REGIMENT RAC

Formed 20 July 1942 by conversion of 2/7th Bn The Duke of Wellington's Regiment (West Riding), an element of 137th Armoured Brigade; relieved 25 September 1943. Converted September 1943 as a tank delivery squadron in 2nd Armoured Delivery Regiment. Officially converted to infantry as 12th Bn The Duke of Wellington's Regiment 7 February 1944 and placed in suspended animation.

Equipment notes: Equipped with Covenanter tanks.

116th (GORDON HIGHLANDERS) REGIMENT RAC

Formed 24 July 1942 in India by conversion of 9th Bn The Gordon Highlanders and assigned 267th Indian Armoured Brigade 27 July 1942. Relieved 31 October 1943 and transferred to 255th Indian Armoured Brigade (brigade redesignated 15 April 1944 as 255th Indian Tank Brigade). Relieved 31 January 1945 and placed under command 7th Indian Infantry Division and then IV Corps 24 May 1945. Placed in suspended animation ca September 1945.

Equipment notes: Equipping with Grant and Lee tanks February 1943. Equipped with Shermans by 1944.

141st REGIMENT RAC

Formed 8 November 1941 by conversion of 7th Bn The Buffs, an element of 31st Army Tank Brigade (brigade redesignated May 1942 as 31st Tank Brigade); relieved 21 June 1944. Reorganized by spring 1944 with flame-thrower tanks. Assigned 30th Armoured Brigade 2 July 1944; relieved 4 September 1944 and returned to 31st Tank Brigade (brigade redesignated 2 February 1945 as 31st Armoured Brigade). Relieved 27 August 1945 from 31st Armoured Brigade (may have returned before brigade was disbanded that October). Placed in suspended animation November 1945.

Equipment notes: About 3/4 strength (Churchills) in December 1941. In June 1944, 45 Crocodile and 7 Churchill IV [6pdr]. By December 1944, the non-Crocodiles were 75mm and CS Churchill variants.

142nd REGIMENT RAC

Formed 9 November 1941 by conversion of 7th Bn The Suffolk Regiment, an element of 25th Army Tank Brigade (brigade redesignated 1 June 1942 as 25th Tank Brigade); relieved 18 December 1944.[66] Disbanded January 1945 in Italy.

Equipment notes: Probably about 2/3 strength and a mix of Matilda and Churchill tanks in December 1941. All Churchills during 1942. Prior to April 1944 replaced two Churchill troops in each squadron with Shermans.[67]

143rd REGIMENT RAC

Formed 1 November 1941 by conversion of 9th Bn The Lancashire Fusiliers, an element of 10th Armoured Brigade. (Brigade redesignated 25 July 1942 as 10th Tank Brigade.) Relieved 24 November 1943 and disbanded December 1943.

Equipment notes: Began to receive some Covenanter tanks, then converted to Churchill III. In a training role, also received some Shermans in June 1943.

144th REGIMENT RAC

Formed 22 November 1941 by conversion of 8th Bn The East Lancashire Regiment, an element of 33rd Army Tank Brigade (brigade redesignated June 1942 as 33rd Tank Brigade and 17 March 1944 as 33rd Armoured Brigade). Assigned 31st Tank Brigade 23 to 31 August 1944 and then returned to 33rd. Reorganized autumn 1944 with LVTs. Relieved 28 February 1945 and disbanded 1 March 1945 to reform 4th RTR.

---

[66] The regiments of 25th Tank Brigade were awarded a silver maple leaf July 1944 for service with I Canadian Corps, to be worn on the upper left arm (the brigade also added a maple leaf to its diabolo badge).

[67] For actual tank strength (excluding Stuarts) for the period May–November 1944 see Appendix D.

Equipment notes: Equipping with Churchill tanks in December 1941. Converted to Shermans March 1944. In June 1944 a mixture of Sherman I/II. LVTs autumn 1944.

145th REGIMENT RAC

Formed 15 November 1941 by conversion of 8th Bn The Duke of Wellington's Regiment, an element of 21st Army Tank Brigade (brigade redesignated 6 June 1942 as 21st Tank Brigade); relieved 4 December 1944. Disbanded 12 January 1945 in Italy.

Equipment notes: Equipped with the Churchill I/II on formation. Slated to convert to Valentine V before going overseas late 1942 but decision reversed and Churchill's restored February 1943. By March 1943 had Churchill III/IV and I CS. Changed to mix of two troops Churchills and two troops Shermans in each squadron by August 1943 when in Italy.

146th REGIMENT RAC

Formed 22 October 1941 in India by conversion of 9th Bn The Duke of Wellington's Regiment and assigned to 50th Indian Tank Brigade (brigade designated until 31 October 1941 as Heavy Armoured Brigade). Absorbed 'B' Special Service Sqn RAC ca June 1943. Transferred August 1945 to 254th Indian Tank Brigade; relieved October 1945. Survived to January 1947, when 7th RTR arriving in India that month absorbed its personnel.

Equipment notes: Equipped with Valentine infantry tanks by the end of 1942. Changed to Lees by early 1944. May have changed to Stuarts and Fox armoured cars following the end of the war.

147th REGIMENT RAC

Formed November (December?) 1941 by conversion of 10th Bn The Hampshire Regiment, an element of 34th Army Tank Brigade from 1 December 1941 (brigade redesignated June 1942 as 34th Tank Brigade and 2 February 1945 as 34th Armoured Brigade); relieved 30 June 1945. Disbanded ca October 1945.

Equipment notes: Began to receive Churchills in early 1942. In June 1944, primarily Churchill III/IV [6pdr], about 30% VI/VII [75mm], plus V/VIII CS versions. In December 1944, proportion of 6pdr/75mm reversed (about 31% 6pdr).

148th REGIMENT RAC

Formed 22 November 1941 by conversion of 9th Bn The Loyal Regiment, an element of 33rd Army Tank Brigade (brigade redesignated June 1942 as 33rd Tank Brigade); relieved 8 October 1943 and assigned 27th Armoured Brigade; relieved 31 January 1944. Returned 17 February 1944 to 33rd Tank Brigade (redesignated 17 March 1944 as 33rd Armoured Brigade); relieved 16 August 1944. Disbanded August 1944 in France.

Equipment notes: Equipping with Churchill tanks in December 1941. Converted to Shermans March 1944. In June 1944, a mixture of Sherman I/II.

149th REGIMENT RAC

Formed 22 November 1941 in India by conversion of 7th Bn The King's Own Yorkshire Light Infantry but already assigned Heavy Armoured Brigade [in India] 24 October 1941 (brigade redesignated 31 October 1941 as 50th Indian Tank Brigade). Transferred 4 July 1944 to 254th Indian Tank Brigade. Relieved 18 August 1944 and assigned to 166th L of C. Returned to 50th Indian Tank Brigade 20 April 1945; relieved August 1945. Disbanded ca December 1945.

Equipment notes: Equipped with Valentines by February 1943. Equipped with Lees by 1944.

150th REGIMENT RAC

Formed 22 November 1941 in India by conversion of 10th Bn The York and Lancaster Regiment and assigned 50th Indian Tank Brigade 1 December 1941. (Operated in support of 19th Indian Infantry Division June to October 1942 and 2nd Infantry Division 16 April 1943 to 30 April 1944.) Returned to 50th Indian Tank Brigade 30 April 1944; relieved 3 November 1944 and assigned to 254th Indian Tank Brigade. Relieved October 1945; disbanded ca December 1945.

Equipment notes: Equipped with Lees by February 1943.

151st (KING'S OWN) REGIMENT RAC
See [second] 107th (King's Own) Regiment RAC

152nd REGIMENT RAC

Formed 1 January 1942 by conversion of 11th Bn The King's Regiment, an element of 35th Army Tank Brigade (brigade redesignated 12 August 1942 as 35th Tank Brigade and 14 July 1945 as 35th Armoured Brigade). Converted 1943 to CDL tanks. Operated as a training unit from ca May 1944. Disbanded ca November 1945.

Equipment notes: Equipped with some carriers on formation. Began to receive Churchills in early 1942. CDL tanks 1943. Changed after April 1944 to Churchill tanks.

153rd REGIMENT RAC

Formed 1 December 1941 by conversion of 8th Bn The Essex Regiment, an element of 34th Army Tank Brigade (brigade redesignated June 1942 as 34th Tank Brigade); relieved 24 August 1944. Disbanded August 1944 in France.

Equipment notes: Began to receive Churchills in early 1942. In June 1944, primarily Churchill III/IV [6pdr], about 30% VI/VII [75mm], plus V/VIII CS versions.

154th REGIMENT RAC

Formed 1 January 1942 by conversion of 9th Bn The North Staffordshire Regiment, an element of 36th Army Tank Brigade (brigade redesignated 12 August 1942 as 36th Tank Brigade); relieved 3 July 1943. Disbanded ca August 1943.

Equipment notes: Equipped with carriers on formation, later Churchill III.

155th REGIMENT RAC

Formed 1 January 1942 by conversion of 15th Bn The Durham Light Infantry, an element of 35th Army Tank Brigade (brigade redesignated 12 August 1942 as 35th Tank Brigade and 14 July 1945 as 35th Armoured Brigade). Converted 1943 to CDL tanks. Reduced to cadre May 1944; later operated as a training unit. Disbanded ca November 1945.

Equipment notes: Equipped with some carriers on formation. Began to receive Churchills in early 1942. CLD tanks 1943. Changed after April 1944 to Churchill tanks.

156th REGIMENT RAC

Formed December 1941 by conversion of 11th Bn The Highland Light Infantry, an element of 36th Army Tank Brigade from 10 January 1942 (brigade redesignated 12 August 1942 as 36th Tank Brigade); relieved 3 July 1943. Placed in suspended animation September 1943 and concurrently converted to infantry under former title.

Equipment notes: Equipped with carriers on formation, later Churchill III.

157th REGIMENT RAC

Formed January 1942 by conversion of 9th Bn The Hampshire Regiment, an element of 36th Army Tank Brigade from 17 January 1942 (brigade redesignated 12 August 1942 as 36th Tank Brigade); relieved 3 July 1943. Disbanded August 1943.

Equipment notes: Equipped with carriers on formation, later Churchill III.

158th REGIMENT RAC

Formed 15 July 1942 by conversion of 6th Bn The South Wales Borderers and then sent to India October 1942. Assigned 255th Indian Armoured Brigade 20 December 1942. Converted back to infantry 25 March 1943 as 6th Bn The South Wales Borderers, although not officially relieved from brigade until 1 April 1943.

Equipment notes: Arrived with 23 Grant and 7 Stuart tanks; gained 11 more Grants December 1942.

159th REGIMENT RAC

Formed 15 July 1942 by conversion of 10th Bn The Gloucestershire Regiment and then sent to India October 1942. Assigned 255th Indian Armoured Brigade 20 December 1942. Relieved and converted back to infantry 1 April 1943 as 10th Bn The Gloucestershire Regiment.

Equipment notes: Arrived with 37 Lee and 7 Stuart tanks.

160th REGIMENT RAC

Formed 15 July 1942 by conversion of 9th Bn The Royal Sussex Regiment and then sent to India October 1942. Assigned 267th Indian Armoured Brigade 22 December 1942. Relieved and converted back to infantry 1 April 1943 as 9th Bn The Royal Sussex Regiment.

Equipment notes: Equipping with Grant and Lee tanks February 1943.

161st (GREEN HOWARDS) REGIMENT RAC

Formed 28 July 1942 by conversion of 12th Bn The Green Howards as an armoured car regiment. Intended for assignment to 80th Armoured Division October 1942, but that formation was never organizaed and its planned creation abandoned December 1942. Converted 24 October 1943 as 161st (Green Howards) Regiment Reconnaissance Corps.

Equipment notes: Conventional armoured car regiment.

162nd REGIMENT RAC

Formed 28 July 1942 by conversion of 9th Bn The Queen's Own Royal West Kent Regiment as armoured car regiment and assigned to 79th Armoured Division 10 September 1942. Relieved 10 January 1943. Served as GHQ unit with Home Forces to August 1943 and then disbanded.

Equipment notes: Conventional armoured car regiment.[68]

163rd REGIMENT RAC

Formed 30 July 1942 in India by conversion of 13th Bn The Sherwood Foresters and assigned 267th Indian Armoured Brigade. Relieved 31 March 1943. Converted back to infantry 1 December 1943 as 13th Bn The Sherwood Foresters.

Equipment notes: Equipping with Grant and Lee tanks February 1943.

---

[68] This has been shown in some sources as an armoured recce regiment, but there was no war establishment for such units published until April 1943.

SCORPION UNITS RAC

1st Scorpion Regiment RAC   Formed 15 February 1943 (from 41st RTR) as 'T' Scorpion Regiment RAC. Later redesignated 1st Scorpion Regiment RAC (sometimes also shown as No. 1 Scorpion Regiment RAC). Served in North and Northwest Africa. 'B' and 'C' Sqns served in Sicily; RHQ and 'A' Sqn remained in North Africa. 'C' Sqn landed at Salerno early October 1943 and 'B' Sqn at Taranto November 1943. The entire regiment was in Italy by April 1944. Redesignated 1 May 1944 as 1st Assault Regiment RAC/RE.
       Equipment notes: Began with Matilda Scorpion tanks, replacing many with the Grant Scorpion by the end of the campaign in North Africa. Entirely equipped with Grant Scorpions by the time of Sicily.

'T' Scorpion Regiment RAC   *See* 1st Scorpion Regiment RAC

400th Independent Scorpion Squadron RAC   Formed by 21 November 1943 when arrived in India from the ME. Operated under command of 50th Indian Tank Brigade from 21 November 1943 to 11 November 1944 and 254th Indian Tank Brigade from 16 November 1944 to May 1945. Later disbanded (probably summer 1945).

ARMOURED DELIVERY/REFITTING/HOLDING UNITS RAC

1st Armoured Replacement Group   Served in CMF. Controlled 1st and 200th Armoured Delivery Regiments and 1st Armoured Reinforcement Regiment. In 1945 at least also had control over 'A' Maintenance Sqn of the group.

2nd Armoured Replacement Group   Served in 21st Army Group. Controlled 2nd Armoured Delivery Regiment .and 2nd Armoured Refitting Regiment.

1st Armoured Delivery Regiment RAC   Formed May 1943 in N Africa. Assigned 1st Armoured Replacement Group and served in Italy from September 1943. Disbanded following the war.

2nd Armoured Delivery Regiment RAC   Formed September 1943 in the UK from the regiments of 137th Armoured Brigade. Assigned 2nd Armoured Replacement Group; served with 21st Army Group and Second Army in NW Europe 1944-45. Disbanded following the war.

200th Armoured Delivery Regiment RAC   Formed October 1942 in Iraq as 'X' Armoured Delivery Regiment RAC; redesignated January 1943 as 200th Tank Delivery Regiment; renamed armoured delivery by April 1944. Assigned 1st Armoured Replacement Group and served in Italy from September 1943. Disbanded following the war.

201st Armoured Delivery Regiment RAC   Existed at least January to March 1943 in Iraq under PAIForce. No other details available.

Tank Delivery Regiment   Existed under First Army in NW Africa ca. summer 1943 and then disbanded.[69]

1st Armoured Reinforcement Regiment RAC   Assigned 1st Armoured Replacement Group; served in Italy 1944-45. Disbanded following the war.

2nd Armoured Refitting Regiment RAC   Assigned 2nd Armoured Replacement Group; served in NW Europe 1944-45. Disbanded following the war.

2nd Armoured Reinforcement Group   Served in 21st Army Group.

21st RAC Training Regiment   Listed in Joslen[70] as part of 21st Army Group in November 1944 and May 1945. It has surviving war diaries for the period September to December 1944, but as 21st Training Regiment RTR.

'K' Royal Tank Regiment (RAC Holding Regiment)   Formed January 1943 in the Middle East, originally from remnants of 2nd Royal Gloucestershire Hussars. Disbanded ca November 1943.

Holding Battalion RAC   Existed in the Middle East at least for the period March to September 1943.

Armoured Delivery Squadrons
The following armoured delivery squadrons have been identified in the catalogues of war diaries. Some or all of them presumably formed part of the larger units listed above. This list is presumably incomplete.

21st Army Group
        Armoured Delivery Sqn: 2
        Army Delivery Sqn: 256
        Corps Delivery Sqns: 254, 257, 258, 259,
        Forward Delivery Sqns: 261, 262, 263, 264, 265, 266, 268, 269, 270, 271
Central Mediterranean Force (Italy)
        Army Delivery Sqn: 'E'
        Delivery Sqn: 'H', 250, 253, 272, 273, 274, 175, 276, 277, 278, 279, 280, 311[71]

---

[69] Joslen, *Orders of Battle*, p. 465 lists it under 10 July 1943 but not under the prior (February 1943) column.
[70] *Orders of Battle*, p. 463. This unit is not listed in Frederick.
[71] This may be a cataloguing error, as units with 300 numbers were normally troops.

Forward Delivery Sqns:[72] 250, 278
Tank Delivery Sqn: 272
Allied Force HQ (NW Africa)
Corps Tank Delivery Sqn: 1
Tank Delivery Sqn: 254
Home Forces
Corps Delivery Sqns: 1, 2
Tank Delivery Sqn: 251[73]
Forward Delivery Sqns: 260, 268

SQUADRONS RAC

Tank Squadron   Existed at Gibraltar for at least the period March to October 1943.

39th Squadron RAC   Existed in the Middle East in June 1943.

40th Squadron RAC   Formed from 'D' Sqn, 3rd County of London Yeomanry; existed in the Middle East for at least the period April to June 1943.

52nd Tank Squadron RAC   Existed under Home Forces for at least the period September 1943 to December 1944.

73rd Squadron RAC   Existed in the Middle East at least in September and October 1943.

76th Squadron RAC   Existed in the Middle East for at least the period June to October 1943.

SPECIAL SERVICE SQUADRONS RAC

These were created in 1941 for 'special services', such as amphibious operations.

'A' Special Service Squadron RAC   Formed 29 April 1941 at Wickham Market with personnel from 48th RTR. Sent to Inverary, Scotland for training. Sent by sea September 1941 to Freetown, Sierra Leone and returned home March 1942. Disbanded 15 June 1942. Equipped with Valentine infantry tanks and Mark VI light tanks.

'B' Special Service Squadron RAC   Formed 6 July 1941 at Shoreham-by-Sea with personnel from 47th RTR. Sent to Inverary, Scotland for training. Sent by sea September 1941 to Freetown, Sierra Leone and returned home March 1942. Assigned 29th Infantry Brigade Group 20 August 1942 to 1 June 1943. Served with brigade in occupation of

---

[72] By 1945 both were simply delivery squadrons.
[73] The former 2 Corps Delivery Sqn, redesignated February 1943.

Madagascar. Went to India with brigade 1943 and absorbed ca June 1943 into 146th Regiment RAC. Equipped with Valentine infantry tanks and Mark VI light tanks.

'C' Special Service Squadron (Light) RAC   Formed 31 July 1941at Ogbourne St. George (Salisbury Plain) with personnel from the three regiments of 2nd Armoured Brigade (Queen's Bays, 9th Lancers, and 10th Hussars). Sent to Inverary, Scotland for training. Elements sent by sea September 1941 to Freetown, Sierra Leone and returned home March 1942. (Elements served in Madagascar under 'B' Special Service Squadron RAC.) Disbanded 24 June 1942 and reformed the next day as Airborne Light Tank Squadron RAC [see Airborne Units under Reconnaissance Corps below]. Equipped with Tetrarch light tanks.

LIGHT SCOUT CAR COMPANIES

1st Light Scout Car Company   Under 21st Army Group in 1944.

3rd Light Scout Car Company   Under 21st Army Group in 1944.

4th Light Scout Car Company   Served in Burma 1943.

5th Light Scout Car Company   Served in Burma 1943.

ARMOURED TRAIN GROUPS

1st Armoured Train Group RAC   Existed under Home Forces in 1940.

2nd Armoured Train Group RAC   Existed under Home Forces for at least the period June 1940 to April 1941.

3rd Armoured Train Group RAC   Existed under Home Forces for at least the period June 1940 to June 1941. Included 'B', 'H' and 'M' Trains.

4th Armoured Train Group RAC   Existed under Home Forces for at least the period July 1940 to March 1941. Included 10th, 11th and 12th Train Detachments.

Reconnaissance Corps

The withdrawal of the few divisional cavalry regiments from divisions in spring 1940 left them without any assigned recce units. By that autumn, the Army determined that infantry divisions needed a recce element, and the ultimate decision was to create a new Corps for that purpose. In the interim, divisions on the higher establishment had formed brigade recce groups, small organizations with motorcycles and light vehicles.

The Reconnaissance Corps was established by Royal Warrant of 14 January 1941, although some units were actually formed prior to that date. Divisions on the higher establishment received battalions and divisions on the lower establishment companies. Brigade recce groups and the remaining brigade antitank companies were one source of personnel, as were the four motorcycle battalions, and some other infantry battalions.

In 1942 it was decided to change from infantry-type to cavalry-type designations, and all battalions were redesignated as regiments 6 June 1942 and separate companies as squadrons. One result of these changes was that units could have a variety of designations depending on when they were formed and disbanded. Some sources suggest that most of the battalions or regiments assigned to a TA division added that formation's parenthetical designation to their own, although only a few are known for sure.[74]

On 1 January 1944 the Corps was absorbed into the Royal Armoured Corps, and existing units were restyled as reconnaissance regiment RAC. This left the Reconnaissance Corps with no units, although it was not disbanded until August 1946, by which date all of its former units had been disbanded or placed in suspended animation.

As with the case of the Royal Armoured Corps, the Reconnaissance Corps was not awarded any battle honours.

Badge: Spearhead flanked by two bolts of lightning, above a scroll reading 'Reconnaissance Corps'. White metal with bronze or gilded spearhead for officers and gilding metal for other ranks. Officers in Scottish regiments had the badge in all white metal.

There are two variant badges. Officers in the 15th (Scottish) Recce Regiment had their division badge (red heraldic Scottish lion rampant on a yellow circle with a white border) over the center. The officers of the 49th Recce Regiment had the white rose of York added where the lightning bolts first meet the spear above the scroll.

Battle Dress: Yellow 'Reconnaissance' on green [original shoulder title in 1942 had full wording 'Reconnaissance Corps'; however, that flash was withdrawn and later replaced in 1943]

The Reconnaissance Corps had a green and yellow arm of service stripe.[75] The Corps wore a distinctive khaki beret, although the 56th Recce Regiment wore green.

Generally there are no equipment notes for units in this section unless something sets them apart from the equipment set out in the section on their war establishments. Some

---

[74] I have generally followed Richard Doherty's Osprey volume on the Reconnaissance Corps for parenthetical designations.

[75] 4th Recce Regiment wore a long rectangle, divided diagonally yellow and green, with a leaping black panther above the arm of service stripe. These were designed in pairs with the panther always facing forward.

regiments in 21st Army Group began to receive Daimler armoured cars in lieu of the normal Humbers around March 1945. Only the 15th used these to somewhat alter their organization.

1st RECONNAISSANCE REGIMENT RAC

Formed 8 January 1941 as 1st Bn Recce Corps (from personnel of the Hampshire Regiment and 2nd and 3rd Infantry Brigade Atk Coys), an element of 1st Infantry Division. Restyled 6 June 1942 as 1st Regiment Recce Corps and 1 January 1944 as 1st Recce Regiment RAC. Disbanded ca May 1946.

2nd RECONNAISSANCE REGIMENT RAC

Formed 3 April 1941 as 2nd Bn Recce Corps, an element of 2nd Infantry Division, by conversion of 6th Bn The Loyal Regiment. Restyled 6 June 1942 as 2nd Regiment Recce Corps and 1 January 1944 as 2nd Reconnaissance Regiment RAC. Placed in suspended animation 1 July 1946.

Equipment notes: Regiment underwent major reorganizations in 1943 and then again in 1944 for operations in Burma.

3rd RECONNAISSANCE REGIMENT RAC (NORTHUMBERLAND FUSILIERS)

Formed 30 April 1941 as 3rd Bn Recce Corps, an element of 3rd Infantry Division, by conversion of 8th Bn The Royal Northumberland Fusiliers. Restyled 6 June 1942 as 3rd Regiment Recce Corps and 1 January 1944 as 3rd Reconnaissance Regiment RAC. Relieved 10 August 1945, but presumably returned later. Placed in suspended animation July 1946.

Equipment notes: Began to receive Daimler armoured cars as replacements as early as September 1944.

4th RECONNAISSANCE REGIMENT RAC

Formed 8 January 1941 as 4th Bn Recce Corps, an element of 4th Infantry Division (from 10th, 11th and 12th Infantry Brigade Atk Coys).[76] Restyled 6 June 1942 as 4th Regiment Recce Corps and 1 January 1944 as 4th Reconnaissance Regiment RAC. Disbanded after August 1945.

---

[76] This was the first unit in the Recce Corps to receive a light recce car in place of the Beaverettes, on 6 January 1942 (Doherty, *Only the Enemy in Front*, p. 12).

5th RECONNAISSANCE REGIMENT RAC

Formed 22 January 1941 as 5th Bn Recce Corps, an element of 5th Infantry Division, by conversion of 3rd Bn The Tower Hamlets Rifles. Restyled 6 June 1942 as 5th Regiment Recce Corps and 1 January 1944 as 5th Reconnaissance Regiment RAC. Placed in suspended animation July 1946.[77]

Equipment notes: Received Daimler armoured cars to replace its Humbers after arrival in NW Europe March 1945.

15th BATTALION RECCE CORPS

Formed 8 January 1941, an element of 15th (Scottish) Infantry Division (from 44th, 45th and 46th Infantry Brigade Atk Coys); relieved 3 December 1941 [see 15th Independent Squadron]. Broken up 1 January 1942

15th (SCOTTISH) RECONNAISSANCE REGIMENT RAC

Formed 15 February 1943 as 15th (Scottish) Regiment Recce Corps, an element of 15th (Scottish) Infantry Division. (54th and 45th Sqns Recce Corps redesignated as 'B' and 'C' Sqns of new regiment; with existing 15th Independent Sqn Recce Corps as 'A' Sqn.) Restyled 1 January 1944 as 15th Reconnaissance Regiment RAC. Disbanded in Germany the end of March 1946.

Equipment notes: Began to receive Daimler armoured cars in March 1945 and used them to replace the two light recce cars in the third scout troop of each squadron, making the troop two Humber and two Daimler armoured cars. From that point on, any lost Humber armoured cars were replaced by Daimlers.

18th BATTALION RECCE CORPS

Formed 25 April 1941, an element of 18th Infantry Division, by conversion of 5th Bn The Loyal Regiment. Lost at Singapore 15 February 1942.

38th RECONNAISSANCE REGIMENT RAC

Formed 13 November 1943 as 38th Regiment Recce Corps from existing 38th, 47th and 55th Independent Squadrons and assigned 38th (Welsh) Infantry Division 1 January 1944; relieved 14 August 1944 and disbanded.

---

[77] Personnel probably absorbed by 13th/18th Royal Hussars, which joined the division ca. March 1946 to become its recce regiment.

A new 38th Reconnaissance Regiment RAC formed when 80th Reconnaissance Regiment RAC was renumbered as 38th and assigned to 38th Infantry (Reserve) Division 2 October 1944.[78] Disbanded after August 1945.

43rd (WESSEX) RECONNAISSANCE REGIMENT RAC

Formed 14 October 1941 as 48th Bn Recce Corps, an element of 48th (South Midland) Infantry Division, by conversion of 5th Bn The Gloucestershire Regiment; relieved 18 November 1941 and assigned to 43rd (Wessex) Infantry Division 20 November 1941. Renumbered 8 January 1942 as 43rd. Restyled 6 June 1942 as 43rd (Wessex) Regiment Recce Corps and 1 January 1944 as 43rd (Wessex) Reconnaissance Regiment RAC. Placed in suspended animation May 1946.[79]

44th RECONNAISSANCE REGIMENT RAC

Formed 8 January 1941 as 44th Bn Recce Corps, an element of 44th (Home Counties) Infantry Division (from Atk coys 131st, 132nd and 133rd Infantry Brigades). Restyled 6 January 1942 as 44th Regiment Recce Corps. Relieved from 44th (Home Counties) Infantry Division 24 November 1942. Assigned 8 March 1943 to 56th (London) Infantry Division. Restyled 1 January 1944 as 44th Reconnaissance Regiment RAC. Relieved 16 February 1944 and served as GHQ unit in Italy. Returned 2 June 1944 to 56th (London) Infantry Division. Disbanded after August 1945.

45th REGIMENT RECCE CORPS

Formed 8 January 1941 as 45th Bn Recce Corps, an element of 45th Infantry Division (from Atk coys 134th, 135th and 136th Infantry Brigades). Relieved ca December 1941. Restyled 6 June 1942 as 45th Regiment Recce Corps. Assigned 70th Infantry Division 21 October 1942 and relieved 16 September 1943 when converted to infantry role and assigned 16th Infantry Brigade [formed 45 and 54 Columns, part of Special Force, or Chindits]. Disbanded 17 October 1944.

46th RECONNAISSANCE REGIMENT RAC

Formed 11 July 1941 as 46th Bn Recce Corps, an element of 46th Infantry Division, by conversion of 23rd Bn The Royal Fusiliers and Atk coys from 137th, 138th and 139th Infantry Brigades. Restyled 6 June 1942 as 46th Regiment Recce Corps and 1 January 1944 as 46th Reconnaissance Regiment RAC. Placed in suspended animation after August 1945.

---

[78] The existing 38th (Welsh) Infantry Division was dissolved and the 80th Infantry (Reserve) Division renumbered.

[79] Personnel probably absorbed by 14th/20th King's Hussars, who joined by March 1946 as the division's recce regiment.

48th BATTALION RECCE CORPS
See 43rd Reconnaissance Regiment RAC

49th (WEST RIDING) RECONNAISSANCE REGIMENT RAC

Organized 5 September 1942 as 49th (West Riding) Regiment Recce Corps, an element of 49th (West Riding) Infantry Division (absorbing 29th and 148th Independent Sqns Recce Corps). Restyled 1 January 1944 as 49th (West Riding) Reconnaissance Regiment RAC. Disbanded after August 1945.

50th REGIMENT RECCE CORPS

Formed 30 April (6 March?) 1941 as 50th Bn Recce Corps, an element of 50th (Northumbrian) Infantry Division, by conversion of 4th Bn The Royal Northumberland Fusiliers. (Detached with 150th Infantry Brigade November-December 1941 then served as GHQ unit in North Africa December 1941-February 1942.) Assigned 22nd Armoured Brigade 16 February to 19 June 1942. Restyled 6 June 1942 as 50th Regiment Recce Corps but overrun and effectively destroyed that date in North Africa. Returned to UK June 1942 although not relieved from 50th (Northumbrian) Infantry Division until 26 November 1942. Converted back to infantry March 1943 as 4th Bn The Royal Northumberland Fusiliers.

51st (HIGHLAND) REGIMENT RECCE CORPS

Formed 22 January 1941 as 51st (Highland) Bn Recce Corps, an element of 51st (Highland) Infantry Division, by conversion of 14th Bn The Highland Light Infantry. Restyled 6 June 1942 as 51st (Highland) Regiment Recce Corps. Relieved 26 November 1942. Converted to infantry 14 January 1943 as 14th Bn The Highland Light Infantry.

52nd (LOWLAND) RECONNAISSANCE REGIMENT RAC

Formed 8 January 1941 as 52nd (Lowland) Bn Recce Corps, an element of 52nd (Lowland) Infantry Division, from recce groups of 155th, 156th and 157th Infantry Brigades. Restyled 6 June 1942 as 52nd (Lowland) Regiment Recce Corps and 1 January 1944 as 52nd (Lowland) Reconnaissance Regiment RAC. Relieved 11 August 1944 when division reorganized for airlanding role and returned to 1 December 1944. Absorbed 61st Recce Regiment RAC in February 1945. Relieved 16 July 1945, but presumably returned later. Disbanded June 1946.
Equipment notes: had a special organization from May 1942 when division reorganized for mountain warfare and then again from August 1944 to February 1945.

53rd (WELSH) RECONNAISSANCE REGIMENT RAC

Formed 1 January 1941 as 53rd (Welsh) Bn Recce Corps, an element of 53rd (Welsh) Infantry Division (from 158th, 159th and 160th Infantry Brigade Atk Coys). Restyled 6 June 1942 as 53rd (Welsh) Regiment Recce Corps and 1 January 1944 as 53rd (Welsh) Reconnaissance Regiment RAC. Disbanded February 1946 in Germany (personnel to North Irish Horse).

54th BATTALION RECCE CORPS

Formed 15 July 1941, an element of 54th (East Anglian) Infantry Division, with personnel from disbanded 21st Bn The Royal Fusiliers. Broken up 1 January 1942 into 54th, 45th and 76th Independent Coys Recce Corps.

56th RECONNAISSANCE REGIMENT RAC

Formed 8 January 1941 as 56th Bn Recce Corps, an element of 56th (London) Infantry Division, from Atk coys 167th, 168th and 169th Infantry Brigades.[80] Restyled 6 June 1942 as 56th Regiment Recce Corps. Relieved 15 August 1942 from 56th (London) Infantry Division. Assigned 1 September 1942 to 78th Infantry Division. Restyled 1 January 1944 as 56th Recce Regiment RAC. Disbanded late November 1945 in Austria (personnel to North Irish Horse).

59th (STAFFORDSHIRE) RECONNAISSANCE REGIMENT RAC

Formed 27 January 1941 as 59th (Staffordshire) Bn Recce Corps, an element of 59th (Staffordshire) Infantry Division, possibly from Atk coys of 176th, 177th and 197th Infantry Brigades. Restyled 6 June 1942 as 59th (Staffordshire) Regiment Recce Corps and 1 January 1944 as 59th (Staffordshire) Reconnaissance Regiment RAC. Relieved 31 August 1944 and disbanded then or later in France.

61st RECONNAISSANCE REGIMENT RAC

Formed 14 September 1941 as 61st Bn Recce Corps, an element of 61st Infantry Division; from Atk coys 182nd, 183rd and 184th Infantry Brigades. Restyled 6 June 1942 as 61st Regiment Recce Corps and 1 January 1944 as 61st Reconnaissance Regiment RAC. Relieved 23 January 1944 from 61st Infantry Division. Assigned 14 February 1944 to 50th (Northumbrian) Infantry Division. Relieved 30 November 1944.

---

[80] An attempt was made by The Artists' Rifles, then serving as 163rd OCTU, to have the 56th Recce assume their identity in order to earn battle honours. This was rejected by the 56th, although it may have been approved by the Army, and some sources show the 56th as having been formed from The Artists' Rifles. See Richard Doherty, *Only the Enemy In Front*, p 32.

Operated as GHQ unit with 21st Army Group until disbanded February 1945 (personnel absorbed by 52nd Recce Regiment RAC).

80th RECONNAISSANCE REGIMENT RAC

Formed 21 January 1943 as 80th Regiment Recce Corps, an element of 80th Infantry (Reserve) Division, from 48th, 76th and 77th Independent Sqns Recce Corps; restyled 1 January 1944 as 80th Reconnaissance Regiment RAC. Relieved 31 August 1944. Redesignated 2 October 1944 as 38th Reconnaissance Regiment RAC and assigned 38th Infantry (Reserve) Division.[81]

161st (GREEN HOWARDS) RECONNAISSANCE REGIMENT RAC

Formed 24 October 1943 as 161st (Green Howards) Regiment Recce Corps by redesignation of 161st (Green Howards) Regiment RAC and assigned 38th (Welsh) Infantry Division; relieved 12 November 1943. Assigned 55th (West Lancashire) Infantry Division 23 December 1943. Restyled 1 January 1944 as 161st (Green Howards) Reconnaissance Regiment RAC. Relieved 24 July 1944 from 55th (West Lancashire) Infantry Division. Assigned 45th Infantry Division 13 September 1944. Disbanded after August 1945. This was basically a reserve and training unit.

AIRBORNE RECONNAISSANCE UNITS[82]

6th Airborne Armoured Reconnaissance Regiment RAC   Formed 14 January 1944, absorbing existing Airborne Light Tank Squadron RAC and presumably 6th Airborne Division's existing airlanding recce squadron. Assigned 11 February 1944 to 6th Airborne Division. Served with division at Normandy, in the Ardennes, and the final campaigns in Germany. Moved with division to Palestine October 1945. Disbanded 1 February 1946 (personnel absorbed by 3rd The King's Own Hussars).

1st Airborne Reconnaissance Squadron RAC   Formed 10 December 1941 as 1st Airlanding Coy Recce Corps by redesignation of 31st Independent Brigade Gp Recce Coy. Restyled 24 April 1942 as 1st Airlanding Sqn Recce Corps. Relieved 30 December 1942 from 1st Airlanding Brigade and assigned 1st Airborne Division. (Lost 'B' Trp in Italy 1943.) Redesignated 1 January 1944 as 1st Abn Recce Squadron RAC. Destroyed at Arnhem September 1944. Reformed, it was disbanded along with 1st Airborne Division in November 1945.

---

[81] The new 38th Infantry (Reserve) Division was simply the 80th renumbered.

[82] All of these most likely wore the airborne red beret. This is known for sure of the 6th Airborne Armoured Recce Regiment, all of whose personnel otherwise wore their prior regimental capbadges.

Airborne Light Tank Squadron RAC   Formed 25 July 1942 at Blackford, Perthshire from 'C' Special Service Sqn (Light) RAC. Moved to Salisbury Plain, and assigned 1st Airborne Division 17 August 1942. Did not go to NW Africa with division and relieved 11 April 1943. Assigned 26 May 1943 to 6th Airborne Division. Absorbed 14 January 1944 into new 6th Airborne Armoured Recce Regiment RAC.

PHANTOM [GHQ LIAISON REGIMENT]

Created in 1939 as a small signals reporting/liaison force, Phantom expanded during the war to a force of some 150 officers and 1,500 men, serving in North Africa, Italy, NW Europe, and with the SAS. (Of this, about 105 officers and 800 men were in the 21st Army Group area 1944-45.) Transferred 1945 to the Royal Signals.[83]

The role of Phantom was primarily to move around what in modern times would be called the 'forward edge of the battle area' to determine the location of friendly and enemy forces, monitor friendly radio traffic, and provide first-hand reports of the situation back to senior commanders. While often traveling in armoured vehicles, they could also be parachuted in with SAS or airborne forces.

Members of Phantom wore a formation sign of a white 'P' on a black square, which was also the sign on their vehicles; there was no other distinguishing mark, and personnel wore the cap badges of their parent regiments.[84] Wireless operators came from the Royal Corps of Signals.

No. 2 GHQ Liaison Regiment (Phantom)   Formed ca 1939 as No. 3 Air Mission for special signals reporting role, and known initially as the 'Hopkinson Mission'. Reorganized ca. February 1940 as Advanced Report Centre (with Headquarters, Phantom Squadron [six Guy armoured cars, the most modern in the Army], and Intelligence Squadron [officers and NCOs on motorcycles]). Disbanded after Dunkirk but soon reformed at Richmond Park, London, under Lt Col G. F. 'Hoppy' Hopkinson.[85]

---

[83] This may have occurred late that year, since the recent official history (Cliff Lord and Graham Watson, *The Royal Corps of Signals*) has only a passing reference to the wartime units, contained in the lineage of the TA successor, Princess Louise's Kensington Regiment (which furnished machine gun battalions in the Second World War). The final designations as Nos. 2 and 3 GHQ Liaison Regiment are from J. B. M. Frederick, *Lineage Book of British Land Force*; Lord and Watson refer to them as 'No. 3 Air Mission, No. 1 GHQ Reconnaissance Unit, and GHQ Liaison Regiment RAC, which…played a valuable intelligence-gathering role for 21st Army Group. At the same time, No 2 GHQ Liaison Regiment operated in Italy'. (p. 150). The official history for the campaign in NW Europe lists the unit under 21st Army Group simply as GHQ Liaison Regiment, placing it under the RAC: Maj L. F. Ellis, *Victory in the West*, Volume II (originally HMSO 1968, reprinted by Imperial War Museum [London] and The Battery Press, Inc. [Nashville], 1994), p 370.

[84] After becoming part of the RAC they adopted the black beret of that corps.

[85] The reformed unit began with 48 officers and 407 other ranks.

Designated GHQ Liaison Regiment 30 January 1941. Expanded January 1943 as A, B, C, D, F, L Phantom Sqns. Made part of the Reconnaissance Corps 1 December 1943 and the RAC 1 January 1944. This was reorganized before D-Day into two army squadrons ('A' Sqn for Second Army and 'B' Sqn for First Canadian Army), a squadron for operating with the airborne forces, an army group squadron, and 'F' Sqn for working with the SAS. Reorganized late 1944 as No. 2 GHQ Liaison Regiment. Transferred 1945 to the Royal Signals but probably soon disbanded.

No. 3 GHQ Liaison Regiment (Phantom) Organized ca late 1944. Transferred 1945 to the Royal Signals and reorganized as Independent (Phantom) Squadron; probably soon disbanded.

INDEPENDENT SQUADRONS/COMPANIES

15th Independent Squadron Recce Corps Formed 4 December 1941 as 15th Independent Coy Recce Corps, an element of 15th (Scottish) Infantry Division, from part of 15th Bn Recce Corps. Restyled 6 June 1942 as 15th Independent Sqn Recce Corps. Absorbed 15 February 1943 into new 15th Regiment Recce Corps.

24th Independent Brigade Group (Guards) Recce Squadron Formed 10 February 1941 as 24th Independent Brigade Group (Guards) Recce Coy; restyled 6 June 1942 as 24th Independent Brigade Group (Guards) Recce Squadron. Relieved 29 October 1942. Restyled 24th Independent Recce Squadron and assigned 10 November 1942 to 33rd Guards Infantry Brigade Group. Relieved 9 February 1943 and disbanded.

29th Independent Brigade Group Recce Company Formed 19 January 1941; relieved 5 May 1941 and disbanded.

29th Independent Squadron Recce Corps Formed 22 June 1942, an element of 78th Infantry Division. Relieved 23 August 1942 and absorbed 5 September 1942 into 49th (West Riding) Regiment Recce Corps.

31st Independent Brigade Group Recce Company Formed 8 January 1941. Redesignated 10 December 1941 as 1st Airlanding Coy Recce Corps [see under Airborne Reconnaissance Units above].

38th Independent Squadron Recce Corps Formed 2 January 1942 as 38th Independent Coy Recce Corps, an element of 38th (Welsh) Infantry Division, and restyled 6 June 1942 as 38th Independent Sqn Recce Corps; relieved 18 October 1943 and absorbed 13 November 1943 into 38th Regiment Recce Corps.

45th Independent Squadron Recce Corps Formed 1 January 1942 from part of 54th Bn Recce Corps. Absorbed 15 February 1943 into 15th Regiment Recce Corps.

47th Independent Squadron Recce Corps   Formed 3 December 1941 as 47th Independent Coy Recce Corps , an element of 47th (London) Infantry Division. Restyled 6 June 1942 as 47th Independent Sqn Recce Corps. Relieved 27 October 1943 and absorbed 13 November 1943 into 38th Regiment Recce Corps.

48th Independent Squadron Recce Corps   Formed 4 January 1942 as 48th Independent Coy Recce Corps, an element of 48th (South Midland) Infantry Division, and restyled 6 June 1942 as 48th Independent Sqn Recce Corps. Relieved 2 January 1943 and absorbed 21 January 1943 into 80th Regiment Recce Corps.

54th Independent Squadron Recce Corps   Formed 1 January 1942 from part of 54th Bn Recce Corps as 54th Independent Coy Recce Corps, remaining with 54th (East Anglian) Infantry Division; restyled 6 June 1942 as 54th Independent Sqn Recce Corps. Relieved 9 February 1943. Absorbed 15 February 1943 into 15th Regiment Recce Corps.

55th Independent Squadron Recce Corps   Formed 27 December 1941 as 55th Independent Coy Recce Corps, an element of 55th (West Lancashire) Infantry Division, and restyled 6 June 1942 as 55th Independent Sqn Recce Corps. Relieved 29 October 1943 and absorbed 13 November 1943 into 38th Regiment Recce Corps.

76th Independent Squadron Recce Corps   Formed 1 January 1942 from part of 54th Bn Recce Corps and assigned 76th Infantry Division 15 January 1942. Restyled 6 June 1942 as 76th Independent Sqn Recce Corps. Relieved 6 January 1943 and absorbed 21 January 1943 into 80th Regiment Recce Corps.

77th Independent Squadron Recce Corps   Formed 5 January 1942 as 77th Independent Coy Recce Corps, an element of 77th Infantry Division. Restyled 6 June 1942 as 77th Independent Squadron Recce Corps. Relieved 3 January 1943 and absorbed 21 January 1943 into 80th Regiment Recce Corps.

148th Independent Brigade Group Recce Squadron   Formed 8 January 1941 as 148th Independent Brigade Group Recce Coy and restyled 6 June 1942 as 148th Independent Brigade Group Recce Sqn. Relieved 24 July 1942 and disbanded.

Motorcycle Battalions

In 1939, three of the existing TA infantry divisions were restyled as motor divisions during the TA's doubling. This was partly the result of pulling battalions away for conversion to the machine gun role, leaving a deficit: a motor division only had two brigades (six battalions) instead of three brigades (and nine battalions). There was also, it appears, some intent of copying the German practice of having a fully motorized infantry division. As it happened, these divisions never functioned as such, lacking the requisite

RASC transport companies to convey the infantry. In 1940, they were disbanded or reorganized as conventional infantry divisions.

Each motor division had a motorcycle battalion assigned as its recce element. These survived to autumn 1940 or early 1941, with four becoming part of The Reconnaissance Corps and two converted to motor battalions. At that point motorcycle battalions disappeared from the British Army.

4th BN THE ROYAL NORTHUMBERLAND FUSILIERS

TA infantry battalion at Newburn, formerly with 149th Infantry Brigade. Converted 1939 to a motorcycle battalion. Embodied 3 September 1939 with 50th (Northumbrian) Division. Relieved 23 June 1940. Served as a GHQ unit with Home Forces until 30 April 1941 when converted as 50th Bn Reconnaissance Corps and returned to 50th (Northumbrian) Infantry Division.

8th BN THE ROYAL NORTHUMBERLAND FUSILIERS

Raised 1939 at Prudhoe as a duplicate of 4th Bn of regiment and organized as a motorcycle battalion. Embodied 3 September 1939 with 23rd (Northumbrian) Division. Relieved 29 June 1940. Served as a GHQ unit with Home Forces until 20 November 1940 when assigned to 3rd Infantry Division in a recce role. Converted 26 April 1941 as 3rd Bn Reconnaissance Corps.

Badge, The Royal Northumberland Fusiliers: A grenade; on the ball a circle inscribed 'Quo Fata Vocant' (Whither the fates call); within the circle St. George killing the dragon. For officers, grenade in gilt or gilding metal with the circle and St. George in silver plate. Other ranks in gilding metal and white metal.
Battledress: white 'R. Northumberland Fus.' On scarlet

5th BN THE LOYAL REGIMENT (NORTH LANCASHIRE)

A TA infantry battalion at Bolton, formerly with 164th Infantry Brigade. Converted as a motorcycle battalion and embodied 3 September 1939 with 55th (West Lancashire) Division. Relieved 23 April 1940. Assigned briefly to 20th Guards Infantry Brigade. Assigned 18th Infantry Division 13 January 1941 in recce role and converted 25 April 1941 as 18th Bn Recce Corps.

6th BN THE LOYAL REGIMENT (NORTH LANCASHIRE)

Raised May 1939 at Bolton as a duplicate of 5th Bn of regiment; organized then or later as a motorcycle battalion. Embodied 3 September 1939 with 55th (West Lancashire) Division and transferred 15 September 1939 to 59th (Staffordshire) Division. Relieved

23 June 1940 and survived as a GHQ unit until 13 November 1940 when assigned to 2nd Infantry Division in recce role; converted 29 April 1941 as 2nd Bn Recce Corps.

Badge of The Loyal Regiment: The Royal Crest; below the crown a rose; below the rose a scroll inscribed 'The Loyal Regiment'. For officers, the rose is in gilt with red enamel petals and green points; the Royal Crest is in silver plate and the scroll in gilt or gilding metal. For other ranks, the Royal Crest is in white metal and the remainder in gilding metal.
Battledress: white 'Loyals' on scarlet

QUEEN VICTORIA'S RIFLES

This was a TA regiment, part of the Corps of The King's Royal Rifle Corps. In July 1939 it was doubled, forming two battalions.

1st Bn Queen Victoria's Rifles   The original unit, at Berkley Square W1, London, was redesignated 31 March 1939 as 1st Bn of regiment and began, then or later, to reorganize as a motorcycle battalion. Embodied 3 September 1939 with 1st London Division. Relieved 21 May 1940, the battalion was and sent to Calais where it was destroyed 26 May 1940.[86] Reconstituted 18 July 1940 as a GHQ unit and reorganized 23 October 1940 as a motor battalion. It would be redesignated in 1941 as 7th Bn (QVR), The King's Royal Rifle Corps.

2nd Bn Queen Victoria's Rifles   Raised July 1939 at Grosvenor Square, London as a duplicate unit and organized as a motorcycle battalion. Embodied 3 September 1939 with 2nd London Division. Relieved 13 June 1940 and served as GHQ unit with Home Forces until assigned to 28th Armoured Brigade 1 December 1940 and reorganized as a motor battalion. It would be redesignated in 1941 as 8th Bn (QVR), The King's Royal Rifle Corps.

Badge: A Maltese Cross with a circle in the center inscribed 'Queen Victoria's' enclosing St. George killing the dragoon; resting on the top arm of the cross a tablet inscribed 'South Africa 1900-02' with a Crown above that.

Training Regiments RAC

Until Primary Training Centres were established in 1942, the training regiments RAC handled initial recruit training as well as specialized Corps training. From 1942, they handled only the latter function. There were three main wings in a training regiment, to handle driving and maintenance, gunnery, and wireless. Finally, there was a wing for troop training and tactics, probably teaching little more than troop formations and

---

[86] The battle honours Calais 1940 and North-West Europe 1940 were awarded for this service.

evolutions. Actual collective training occurred later, in the armoured units themselves.[87] Training was intended to leave all RAC personnel the master of at least two trades. This resulted in eight main categories in the RAC:[88]

1. Driver mechanic (primarily a tank driver)
2. Driver operator (primarily a wireless operator)
3. Gunner operator (primarily a gunner)
4. Gunner mechanic (hull gunner and second driver)
5. Driver IC (driving only wheeled vehicles)
6. Mechanist (vehicle mechanic, electrician, or fitter and gunner)
7. Technical storeman
8. Motorcyclist.

Reviews of war establishments show how crews and personnel can be specified according to this scheme. For example, one of the cruiser tanks at RHQ in the November 1943 armoured recce regiment has a subaltern, sergeant, gunner operator, driver mechanic and driver operator. One of the cruisers in a sabre squadron of the regiment, to take another example, is crewed by a sergeant, driver mechanic, gunner operator, and driver operator.

Prior to the war, cavalry training was handled by three cavalry training regiments: 3rd at Edinburgh, 4th at Colchester and 6th at Maidstone. These all closed in 1940.[89] Armoured training was done at the RTC (later RTR) Depot at Bovington. New training regiments were formed on the outbreak of war; these were concentrated in the Catterick-Barnard Castle area from 1942.

51st Training Regiment RAC   Organized September 1939 at Catterick from the Cavalry Depot. Initially known as 51st Training Regiment (Light Tank) RAC. Disbanded between May and August 1945.

52nd Training Regiment RAC   Organized September 1939 at Bovington by redesignation of RTR Depot. Later moved to Catterick. Disbanded between May and August 1945.

53rd Training Regiment RAC   Organized September 1939 at Tidworth. Initially known as 53rd Light Training Regiment RAC. Later moved to Catterick. Disbanded between May and August 1945.

---

[87] Summarized from Timothy Harrison Place, *Military Training in the British Army, 1940-1944*, pp. 82-83. Chapter 6 covers armoured training.

[88] Frank Owen and H. W. Atkins, *The Royal Armoured Corps*, p. 18. This publication was written during the war; Ch 3 covers turning 'civilian into soldier' for the RAC; Ch 4 covers the jobs themselves; and Ch 5 discusses selection and development of officers.

[89] The 3rd and 4th lasted to at least November 1940.

54th Training Regiment RAC   Organized September1939 at Perham Down; later moved to Barnard Castle. Became an armoured regiment training unit; still active into 1947.

55th Training Regiment RAC   Organized September1939 at Farnborough. Later moved to Catterick. Disbanded between May and August 1945.

56th Training Regiment RAC   Organized September1939 at Catterick. Initially known as 56th Army Training Regiment RAC. Disbanded between May and August 1945.

57th Training Regiment RAC   Organized Sep1939 at Warminster; later moved to Catterick. Initially known as 57th Heavy Training Regiment RAC. Became an armoured regiment training unit; still active after August 1945.

58th Training Regiment RAC   Organized 1940 at Bovington; a young soldiers unit. Later moved to Catterick. Disbanded between May and August 1945.

59th Training Regiment RAC   Organized ca 1940 at Tidworth. Later moved to Catterick. Became an armoured car training unit; still active after August 1945.

60th Training Regiment RAC   Organized ca 1940 at Tidworth. Later moved to Catterick. Disbanded between May and August 1945.

61st Training RAC   Organized ca 1940 at Tidworth. Later moved to Catterick. Became an armoured regiment training unit; still active after August 1945.

62nd Training RAC   Organized 1944 at Catterick from the Recce Training Centre.[90] Still active after August 1945.

Armoured Engineer Units

The Royal Engineers began forming specialized assault (later armoured) engineer units in 1943 (the UK) and 1944 (Italy). Former chemical warfare (4.2" mortar) companies recently converted as field companies were used in spring 1943 to devise techniques for land assault on defended positions. These were then married up with the Churchill infantry tank and came under 79th Armoured Division to determine modifications to the tank for RE use. Additional RE units were converted, becoming a full brigade. In Italy, the armoured engineers were created from a combination of RAC personnel and the RE

---

[90] A Recce Corps training center was first established at Winchester (1 February 1941), but then relocated and expanded to form Nos. 1 and 2 Recce Training Centers at Halleaths Camp, Lochmaben in Dumfriesshire and at Scarborough. In August 1943 these were consolidated at Catterick.

from two disbanded armoured divisions. In either theater, these units tended to be farmed out by squadron (or even troop) to help other units attack fortifications or other obstacles, rather than operating as brigades or regiments.

The RE do not earn battle honours.

Badge: The Royal Cypher within the Garter, the whole enclosed in a laurel wreath; above (resting on the top) of the Garter is a crown; below the Garter and resting on the lower portions of the laurel wreath, a scroll inscribed 'Royal Engineers'. For officers, the Garter, motto, Royal Cypher, crown and scroll are in gilt and raised above the laurel wreath, which is in silver plate. For other ranks, the badge is in gilding metal and white metal.
Battledress: 'Royal Engineers' in dark blue on scarlet.

The arm of service stripe for the RE was blue/red.

ASSAULT/ARMOURED ENGINEER REGIMENTS

1st Assault Regiment RAC/RE   Formed in Italy 1 May 1944 by redesignation of 1st Scorpion Regiment RAC. Redesignated 5 January 1945 as **'A' Armoured Regiment RE** and assigned 'B' Assault Brigade RAC/RE. Redesignated 6 April 1945 as **1st Armoured Engineer Regiment** (and brigade redesignated as 25th Armoured Engineer Brigade.) Disbanded ca. November 1945.
    Controlled 'D', 'E', and 'F' (Cheshire) Assault Squadrons RE (later armoured engineer squadrons).
    Equipment notes: Originally equipped with Grant Scorpion tanks, squadrons were a mixture of AVREs, ARKs, and Sherman dozer tanks.

2nd Armoured Engineer Regiment   Formed 5 January 1945 in Italy as **'B' Armoured Regiment RE** (from 1st Armoured Division RE and other sources) and assigned 'B' Assault Brigade RAC/RE. Redesignated 6 April 1945 as **2nd Armoured Engineer Regiment** (and brigade redesignated as 25th Armoured Engineer Brigade.) The regiment was incompletely trained and thus not operational at the end of the war. Disbanded ca October 1945.
    Controlled 'G', 'H', and 'I' Assault Sqns RE (later armoured engineer squadrons).
    Equipment notes: A mixture of AVREs, ARKs, and Sherman dozer tanks in each squadron.

5th Armoured Engineer Regiment   5th GHQ Troops RE assigned 27 April 1943 to 79th Armoured Division. Redesignated 6 May 1943 as 5th Assault Troops RE. Redesignated 26 October 1943 as **5th Assault Regiment RE**. Relieved 26 November 1943 from 79th Armoured Division and assigned 1st Assault Brigade RE. Redesignated

22 April 1945 as **5th Armoured Engineer Regiment** (and brigade redesignated 23 April 1945 as 1st Armoured Engineer Brigade). Relieved 14 July 1945. Disbanded then or shortly later.

Formed with 77th, 79th and 80th Field Coys RE, which were converted to assault squadrons RE with the same numbers. 26th Field Coy RE assigned October 1943 and also converted as assault squadron RE.

26th, 77th and 79th Assault Sqns RE converted to LVTs summer 1944; 26th and 79th converted back to AVRE early 1945. 80th Assault Squadron RE converted to Terrapins November 1944 and operated apart from regiment.

6th Armoured Engineer Regiment   6th GHQ Troops RE assigned 27 April 1943 to 79th Armoured Division. Redesignated 6 May 1943 as 6th Assault Troops RE. Redesignated 26 October 1943 as **6th Assault Regiment RE**. Relieved 26 November 1943 from 79th Armoured Division and assigned 1st Assault Brigade RE. Redesignated 22 April 1945 as **6th Armoured Engineer Regiment** (and brigade redesignated 23 April 1945 as 1st Armoured Engineer Brigade). Relieved 14 July 1945. Disbanded then or shortly after.

Formed with 81st, 82nd, and 87th Field Coys RE, which were converted to assault squadrons RE with the same numbers. 284th Field Coy RE assigned October 1943 and also converted as assault squadron RE. The regiment converted from AVRE to LVTs in August 1944, and then reverted to AVREs early 1945..

87th Assault Squadron RE left 1 March 1945 and converted as 87th Assault Dozer Squadron RE.

42nd Armoured Engineer Regiment   42nd Armoured Division RE relieved 17 September 1943; assigned 28 September 1943 to 79th Armoured Division as 42nd Assault Troops RE (redesignated 6 October 1943 as **42nd Assault Regiment RE**). Relieved 26 November 1943 and assigned 1st Assault Brigade RE. Redesignated 22 April 1945 as **42nd Armoured Engineer Regiment** (and brigade redesignated 23 April 1945 as 1st Armoured Engineer Brigade). Relieved 14 July 1945. Remained in Germany through the end of 1946.[91]

Formed with 16th and 617th Field Squadrons RE and 222nd and 557th Field Coys RE, all of which were converted to assault squadrons RE with the same numbers.

557th Assault Squadron RE left summer 1944, becoming experimental unit under 1st Assault Brigade RE.

557th Assault Training Regiment RE   Formed summer-fall 1944 by expansion of 557th Assault Sqn RE, which may have been designated 557th Assault Training Sqn, although a war establishment as a regiment (XIV/951/1) was effective July 1944. In December 1944 took over the role of F Wing, an experimental unit tasked with the

[91] Relocated later to the UK and renumbered in 1948 as 32nd; disbanded and reformed twice in the post-war years and currently stationed in Germany as 32 Engineer Regiment (The Assault Engineers); its regimental sign is the former formation sign of 79th Armoured Division.

general development of armoured engineer equipment. Assigned 1st Assault Brigade RE 8 January 1945. Redesignated 24 April 1945 as **557th Armoured Engineer Training and Experimental Establishment** (and brigade redesignated as 1st Armoured Engineer Brigade); relieved 12 July 1945. Disbanded ca September 1945. The regiment comprised three training squadrons, but their designations are unknown.

'A' Armoured Regiment RE   *See* 1st Armoured Engineer Regiment

'B' Armoured Regiment RE   *See* 2nd Armoured Engineer Regiment

ASSAULT/ARMOURED ENGINEER SQUADRONS

26th Assault Squadron RE   Formed October 1943 by conversion of 26th Field Coy RE and assigned 5th GHQ Troops RE (that unit redesignated 26 November 1943 as 5th Assault Regiment RE). Redesignated 22 April 1945 as **26th Armoured Engineer Squadron** (and regiment redesignated 5th Armoured Engineer Regiment). Remained in Germany through the end of 1946 (transferred to 42nd Armoured Engineer Regiment).
Equipment notes: Conventional AVRE squadron to autumn 1944 when converted to LVTs; reverted to AVRE early 1945.
    The squadron had a square with the number '26' immediately below the Royal Engineers battledress flash.

77th Assault Squadron RE   Formed ca April 1943 by conversion of 77th Field Coy RE, part of 5th GHQ Troops RE (that unit redesignated 6 June 1943 as 5th Assault Tps RE and 26 November 1943 as 5th Assault Regiment RE). Redesignated 22 April 1945 as **77th Armoured Engineer Squadron** (and regiment redesignated 5th Armoured Engineer Regiment). Disbanded 1945.
Equipment notes: Conventional AVRE unit until conversion to LVTs in August 1944. The only LVT squadron not converted back to AVREs.

79th Assault Squadron RE   Formed ca. April 1943 by conversion of 79th Field Coy RE, part of 5th GHQ Troops RE (that unit redesignated 6 June 1943 as 5th Assault Tps RE and 26 November 1943 as 5th Assault Regiment RE). Redesignated 22 April 1945 as **79th Armoured Engineer Squadron** (and regiment redesignated 5th Armoured Engineer Regiment). Disbanded 1945.
Equipment notes: Conventional AVRE squadron to August 1944 when converted to LVTs; reverted to AVRE March 1945.

80th Assault Squadron RE   Formed ca. April 1943 by conversion of 80th Field Coy RE, part of 5th GHQ Troops RE (that unit redesignated 6 June 1943 as 5th Assault Tps RE and 26 November 1943 as 5th Assault Regiment RE). Redesignated 22 April 1945 as **80th Armoured Engineer Squadron** (and regiment redesignated 5th Armoured

Engineer Regiment). Converted ca November 1944 to Terrapin amphibious trucks and operated apart from regiment, although still officially assigned. Disbanded 1945.

Equipment notes: Conventional AVRE squadron until converted to Terrapins.

81st Assault Squadron RE   Formed ca April 1943 by conversion of 81st Field Coy RE, part of 6th GHQ Troops RE (that unit redesignated 6 June 1943 as 6th Assault Tps RE and 26 November 1943 as 6th Assault Regiment RE). Redesignated 22 April 1945 as **81st Armoured Engineer Squadron** (and regiment redesignated 6th Armoured Engineer Regiment). Disbanded 1945.

Equipment notes: Conventional AVRE squadron throughout.

82nd Assault Squadron RE   Formed ca April 1943 by conversion of 82nd Field Coy RE, part of 6th GHQ Troops RE (that unit redesignated 6 June 1943 as 6th Assault Tps RE and 26 November 1943 as 6th Assault Regiment RE). Redesignated 22 April 1945 as **82nd Armoured Engineer Squadron** (and regiment redesignated 6th Armoured Engineer Regiment). Disbanded 1945.

Equipment notes: Conventional AVRE squadron throughout.

87th Assault Squadron RE   Formed ca. April 1943 by conversion of 87th Field Coy RE, part of 6th GHQ Troops RE (that unit redesignated 6 June 1943 as 6th Assault Tps RE and 26 November 1943 as 6th Assault Regiment RE). Reorganized ca. November 1944 as **87th Assault Dozer Squadron** and transferred to 1st Assault Brigade RE 1 March 1945; relieved 22 April 1945. Disbanded 1945.

Equipment notes: Conventional AVRE squadron until conversion to dozer unit.

149th Assault Park Squadron RE   149th Field Park Squadron RE assigned 79th Armoured Division 19 Sep1943. Reorganized 29 September 1943 as 149th Assault Park Squadron RE. Relieved 10 May 1944 and combined with HQ 1st Assault Brigade RE. Separated as 149th Assault Park Squadron RE 18 January 1945 and assigned 1st Assault Brigade RE. Redesignated 23 April 1945 as **149th Armoured Engineer Park Squadron** (brigade redesignated as 1st Armoured Engineer Brigade); relieved 12 July 1945. Redesignated ca 1946 as 203rd Armoured Park Squadron RE, and assigned 42nd Armoured Engineer Regiment.

Equipment notes: held 12 lightly armoured D7 angledozers (bulldozers) for use by other units as needed.

222nd Assault Squadron RE   Formed ca. October 1943 by conversion of 222nd Field Coy RE and assigned 42nd Assault Tps RE (that unit redesignated 26 November 1943 as 42nd Assault Regiment RE). Redesignated 22 April 1945 as **222nd Armoured Engineer Squadron** (and regiment redesignated 42nd Armoured Engineer Regiment). Disbanded 1945.

Equipment notes: Conventional AVRE squadron throughout.

284th Assault Squadron RE   Formed ca. October 1943 by conversion of 284th Field Coy RE and assigned 6th GHQ Troops RE (that unit redesignated 26 November 1943 as 6th Assault Regiment RE). Redesignated 22 April 1945 as **284th Armoured Engineer Squadron** (and regiment redesignated 6th Armoured Engineer Regiment). Disbanded 1945.

Equipment notes: Conventional AVRE squadron throughout.

557th Assault Squadron RE   Formed ca October 1943 by conversion of 557th Field Coy RE and assigned 42nd Assault Regiment RE. Reorganized from July 1944 as training unit, becoming *557th Assault Training Regiment RE.*

Equipment notes: Conventional AVRE squadron; remained AVRE unit in training role.

631st Armoured Engineer Park Squadron RE   631st Field Park Squadron RE relieved 29 September 1944 from 1st Armoured Division. Redesignated by 5 January 1945 as *'C' Armoured Park Squadron RE* when assigned 25th Armoured Engineer Brigade. Redesignated 6 April 1945 as 631st Armoured Engineer Park Squadron. Relieved 19 August 1945. Disbanded ca November 1945.

'C' Armoured Park Squadron RE   *See* 631st Armoured Engineer Park Squadron RE

'D' Assault Squadron RE   Formed autumn 1944 in Italy from elements 10th Armoured Division RE and 1st Scorpion Regiment RAC and assigned 1st Assault Regiment RAC/RE. (Regiment redesignated 5 January 1945 as 'A' Armoured Regiment RE.) Redesignated 6 April 1945 as **'D' Armoured Engineer Squadron** (and regiment redesignated as 1st Armoured Engineer Regiment). Disbanded ca November 1945.

Equipment notes: Final organization was 6 Sherman dozer tanks, 6 AVRE and 6 Arks.

'E' Assault Squadron RE   Formed autumn 1944 in Italy from elements 10th Armoured Division RE and 1st Scorpion Regiment RAC and assigned 1st Assault Regiment RAC/RE. (Regiment redesignated 5 January 1945 as 'A' Armoured Regiment RE.) Redesignated 6 April 1945 as **'E' Armoured Engineer Squadron** (and regiment redesignated as 1st Armoured Engineer Regiment). Disbanded ca November 1945.

Equipment notes: Final organization was 6 Sherman dozer tanks, 6 AVRE and 6 Arks.

'F'(Cheshire) Assault Squadron RE   Formed autumn 1944 from 3rd or 622nd (Cheshire) Field Sqn RE and elements 1st Scorpion Regiment RAC and assigned 1st Assault Regiment RAC/RE. (Regiment redesignated 5 January 1945 as 'A' Armoured Regiment RE.) Redesignated 6 April 1945 as **'F' (Cheshire) Armoured Engineer Squadron** (and regiment redesignated as 1st Armoured Engineer Regiment). Disbanded ca. November 1945.

Equipment notes: Final organization was 6 Sherman dozer tanks, 6 AVRE and 6 Arks.

'G' Assault Squadron RE   Formed 5 January 1945 in 'B' Armoured Regiment RE from elements 1st Armoured Division RE. Redesignated 6 April 1945 as **'G' Armoured Engineer Squadron** (and regiment redesignated as 2nd Armoured Engineer Regiment).Disbanded ca. October 1945.

Equipment notes: Final organization was 6 Sherman dozer tanks, 6 AVRE and 6 Arks.

'H' Assault Squadron RE   Formed 5 January 1945 in 'B' Armoured Regiment RE from elements 1st Armoured Division RE. Redesignated 6 April 1945 as **'H' Armoured Engineer Squadron** (and regiment redesignated as 2nd Armoured Engineer Regiment). Disbanded ca October 1945.

Equipment notes: Final organization was 6 Sherman dozer tanks, 6 AVRE and 6 Arks.

'I' Assault Squadron RE   Formed 5 January 1945 in 'B' Armoured Regiment RE from elements 1st Armoured Division RE. Redesignated 6 April 1945 as **'I' Armoured Engineer Squadron** (and regiment redesignated as 2nd Armoured Engineer Regiment). Disbanded ca October 1945.

Equipment notes: Final organization was 6 Sherman dozer tanks, 6 AVRE and 6 Arks.

Royal Marine Armour/Recce

The Royal Marines performed a wide variety of roles during the Second World War, including ship's gunners (at least one turret on each battleship was crewed by RM personnel), anti-aircraft artillery, commandos and landing craft crews. An offshoot of the experiments with armed landing craft was (by 1944) the RM Armoured Support Group with tanks carried to shore in LCT(A)s: Landing Craft Tank (Armoured). These tanks could fire from the LCT, and then be landed and move inshore. Although without heavy tools or maintenance equipment, the unit remained in action until withdrawn 24 June 1944. By that point at least half of the tanks which had landed were out of action for mechanical failures. The tanks were given up and the personnel assembled as a battalion (29th RM Battalion, organized 3 October 1944). That battalion was later used as the basis for the LVT-equipped 34th Amphibious Assault Regiment RM. However, the actual first armoured-type RM unit was the recce battalion for the RM Division.

Badge: The globe, showing the eastern hemisphere, surmounted by the Royal Crest, within a laurel wreath. For officers: globe in silver and gilt and remainder in gilt; for other ranks, all in gilding metal. From 1943 (adoption of the blue beret), worn with a red backing by all RM personnel except those in commando units wearing the green beret.

Battledress: RM other than commando units appear not to have worn a regimental flash on battledress.

The Royal Marines do not earn battle honours.

18th RM (Mobile) Battalion   Formed December 1940 from existing mobile companies (the first of which formed in January 1940). The companies were a mix of carriers and motorcycles. This was the recce unit for the RM Division. The Army Recce Training Centre agreed to train them in March 1941. The unit later added Daimler scout cars as well, and could have had some Mk VIC light tanks in December 1941. The RM Division itself was disbanded in September 1943 but the battalion survived until it was disbanded August 1944 without service.

RM Armoured Support Group   Formed ca 31 July 1943 at Merley Park Camp as RM Support Craft Regiment, with 1st to 3rd Support Craft Btys. Redesignated 14 March 1944 as HQ, RM Armoured Support Group. Disbanded 30 September 1944 (personnel to 29th RM Bn).

1st RM Armoured Support Regiment   Organized 31 July 1943 as 2nd RM Support Craft Bty by conversion of 31st RM Light Bty. Reorganized 10 March 1944 as 1st RM Armoured Support Regiment (with 1st and 2nd RM Armoured Support Btys), an element of RM Armoured Support Gp. Disbanded at Hawthorn 30 September 1944 (personnel to 29th RM Bn).

2nd RM Armoured Support Regiment   Organized 31 July 1943 as 3rd RM Support Craft Bty by conversion of 1st RM Atk Bty. Reorganized 1-4 March 1944 as 2nd RM Armoured Support Regiment (with 3rd and 4th RM Armoured Support Btys), an element of RM Armoured Support Gp. Disbanded 3 October 1944 (personnel to 29th RM Bn).

34th Amphibious Assault Regiment RM   Organized 1 March 1945 from most of the personnel 29th RM Bn[92] (itself built around personnel of the former RM Armoured Support Group); contained HQ, HQ Squadron, and four batteries. Sent to the Far East. Redesignated 14 June 1945 as **34th Amphibious Support Regiment RM**. The unit saw no active service in its intended role, but did spend some time as infantry on internal security duties in SE Asia. Returned to the UK April 1946 and disbanded that autumn.
   Equipment notes: Unlike the earlier regiment, this was equipped solely with LVTs. The 1st and 2nd RM Support Btys had LVT(A)s, the 3rd RM (Rocket) Bty had the LVT(R), and the 4th RM Bty the LVT (Flamethrower).

---

[92] Despite losing almost all its personnel 1 March 1945, the battalion was not actually disbanded until the following February.

1st RM Armoured Support Battery   Organized 10 March 1944 as part of 1st RM Armoured Support Regiment. Disbanded 30 September 1944 (personnel to 29th RM Bn).

Equipment notes: Shermans for troop commanders and Centaur IVs.

2nd RM Armoured Support Battery   Organized 10 March 1944 as part of 1st RM Armoured Support Regiment. Disbanded 30 September 1944 (personnel to 29th RM Bn).

Equipment notes: Shermans for troop commanders and Centaur IVs.

3rd RM Armoured Support Battery   Organized 10 March 1944 as part of 2nd RM Armoured Support Regiment. Disbanded 30 September 1944 (personnel to 29th RM Bn).

Equipment notes: Shermans for troop commanders and Centaur IVs.

4th RM Armoured Support Battery   Organized 10 March 1944 as part of 2nd RM Armoured Support Regiment. Disbanded 30 September 1944 (personnel to 29th RM Bn).

Equipment notes: Shermans for troops commanders and Centaur IVs.

5th (Independent) RM Armoured Support Battery   Organized by 7 December 1943 at Devizes as 1st RM Support Craft Bty. Redesignated 17 March 1944 as 5th (Independent) RM Armoured Support Bty, an element of RM Armoured Support Gp. Disbanded 30 September 1944 (personnel to 29th RM Bn).

Equipment notes: Shermans for troops commanders and Centaur IVs.

1st RM Support Craft Battery   See 5th (Independent) RM Armoured Support Bty

Equipment notes: Centaur IVs without engines.

2nd RM Support Craft Battery   See 1st RM Armoured Support Regiment

Equipment notes: Centaur IVs without engines.

3rd RM Support Craft Battery   See 2nd RM Armoured Support Regiment

Equipment notes: Centaur IVs without engines.

Royal Army Service Corps

'Fantail' Regiment   The LVT—known as the Buffalo in NW Europe—was termed the Fantail in Italy. The RASC was to form a regiment with LVTs, created initially from 15th RASC Transport Column and supplemented by a squadron drawn from the 27th Lancers. There was also a US Army tank battalion (755th) converted to LVTs. In practice, the two units ended up consolidated (albeit with separate headquarters).[93] The unit came under 9th Armoured Brigade for operations. It was relieved ca July 1945 and probably soon disbanded.

Dummy Tank Units

The British created a number of deceptive armoured units. These might in some cases have dummy tanks (cloth or other mock-ups) to appear in aerial photographs, or just consist of a small group to generate signals traffic. In most cases, these were assigned to deceptive armoured brigades.

39th Royal Tank Regiment   Dummy tank unit designation used in 1942; also referred to as 39th Army Tank Bn (Special), an element of dummy 74th Armoured Brigade. Later, dummy tank unit assigned 29 August 1943 to dummy 24th Armoured Brigade.

54th Royal Tank Regiment   Dummy tank unit designation used 1941, assigned to dummy 74th Armoured Brigade.

60th Royal Tank Regiment   Dummy tank unit designation used 18 February-17 September 1944. Assigned to dummy 74th Armoured Brigade 12 July 1944 (brigade redesignated 14 July 1944 as dummy 24th Armoured Brigade); relieved 17 September 1944.

62nd Royal Tank Regiment   Dummy tank unit designation used 18 February-17 September 1944. Assigned to dummy 74th Armoured Brigade 12 July 1944 (brigade redesignated 14 July 1944 as dummy 24th Armoured Brigade); relieved 17 September 1944.

66th Royal Tank Regiment   Dummy tank unit designation used 26Aug 1943-14 February 1944.

99th Royal Tank Regiment   Dummy tank unit designation used October-November 1940.

100th Royal Tank Regiment   Dummy tank unit designation used October-November 1940.

---

[93] In addition to HQ RASC Regiment and HQ 755th Tank Battalion, there were two squadrons manned by the British, one by the Americans, an 'artillery' squadron manned by the British (intended to lift artillery rather than infantry), and two British detachments of engineers, REME and ROAC personnel. See Hughes et al., *The British Armies in World War Two*, Volume Four, pp 35-36.

101st Royal Tank Regiment   Dummy tank unit designation used 1 December 1941-25 August 1943, assigned to dummy 74th Armoured Brigade. (Brigade redesignated 23 August 1943 as dummy 24th Armoured Brigade.)[94]

102nd Royal Tank Regiment   Dummy tank unit designation used 1 December 1941-25 August 1943, assigned to dummy 74th Armoured Brigade (brigade redesignated 23 August 1943 as dummy 24th Armoured Brigade).

118th Royal Tank Regiment   Dummy tank unit designation used 29 May 1943-ca January 1944.

124th Royal Tank Regiment   Dummy tank unit designation used 29 May 1943-ca January 1944.

3rd Royal Gloucestershire Hussars   Designation used for dummy tank unit 26 May to 11 July 1944 (assigned dummy 87th Armoured Brigade).

4th Northamptonshire Yeomanry   Designation used for dummy tank unit 26 May to 11 July 1944 (assigned dummy 87th Armoured Brigade).

---

[94] The designation may have been used again, since WO170/866 has war diaries from January to December 1944 for a 101st Royal Tank Regiment under CMF.

Part 2: Armoured and Reconnaissance Establishments

Introduction to War Establishments

The British had an extremely wide variety of armoured unit types and establishments during the course of the war, not even counting the specialized armour ('funnies') such as mine-clearing tanks. First there was the basic division between *armoured regiments* with cruiser tanks and *tank battalions* (later regiments) with infantry tanks. The former were intended to operate as part of armoured divisions engaging in swift and mobile operations, while the latter were to be more heavily armoured and slower, to support infantry. This distinction remained until the end of the war, although the two types of regiments tended to converge in organization as the war progressed.

At the beginning of the war, the armoured division had no reconnaissance element at all; the *armoured car regiment* was a GHQ formation. These were later also assigned to armoured divisions for the recce role. With the creation of an *armoured recce regiment* in 1943, armoured car regiments (much expanded) became GHQ units again, generally assigned one per corps.[95]

The recce role for infantry divisions was to be handled by *divisional cavalry regiments*. The four fully-formed Regular divisions had these, and a few Yeomanry regiments were designated as such. However, most of the latter never had the equipment for the role, and were in any case much fewer than even the number of first-line TA divisions. Following the 1940 debacle in France, these began a gradual conversion to armoured regiments. In 1941, the Reconnaissance Corps was established and *reconnaissance battalions* began forming for infantry divisions. In 1943, these changed from infantry designations (battalion and company) to cavalry (regiment and squadron) as *reconnaissance regiments*, and on 1 January 1944 the Reconnaissance Corps was absorbed into the Royal Armoured Corps.

The first type of specialized armour was the mine-clearing tank, and ultimately some regiments would be organized solely with mine-clearing tanks. Another major type (albeit of less use in operations) was the searchlight-equipped tank, hidden under the deception title of Canal Defence Light (CDL). There were also regiments with flamethrower tanks, and then regiments equipped with the landing vehicle, tracked (LVT), or Buffalo. The Royal Engineers developed the Armoured Vehicle RE (AVRE)

---

[95] However, in 21st Army Group from the summer of 1944 on, armoured car regiments tended to be attached to armoured divisions for the recce role,. since the armoured recce regiments in those divisions had become organized and used as a fourth armoured regiment.

and formed some regiments equipped with them. During the 1944 campaign, some of these would switch from AVREs to LVTs, and then back again.

A *war establishment* listed all of the personnel of the unit, with their ranks, grouping and summarizing them as officers, warrant officers, staff sergeants and sergeants, corporals and troopers (or equivalent). Another re-summing of personnel showed the numbers of tradesmen (clerks, driver operators, storemen, etc.) and non tradesmen (batmen, drivers, motor cyclists, mortarmen, etc.). There were also summaries of the vehicles and armament.

For vehicles, a war establishment would then include details for each sub-part of the unit, with vehicles and who was in them. For example, the regimental headquarters of an airborne armoured recce regiment RAC in October 1944 was organized as follows:

Motor cycle	Liaison officer
Motor cycle	Corporal motorcyclist
Motor cycles 3-10	Motor cyclists
5cwt car 4x4	Lieutenant colonel
	Adjutant
5cwt car 4x4	Intelligence officer
	Driver operator
5cwt car 4x4	Major second in command
	Sergeant clerk
	Driver operator
Scout car	Signal officer
	Corporal driver operator
Scout car	Regimental sergeant major
	Driver operator

This RHQ had six officers, one warrant officer (the regimental sergeant major), one sergeant, two corporals and 11 troopers—21 all ranks in total. There are two scout cars, three 5cwt 4x4 cars (jeeps), and 10 solo motorcycles. From another part of the war establishment we know that there are four .303" light machine guns [Bren guns]; two of these have to be on the scout cars, but there is no indication where the other two are. There are also three PIATs carried at RHQ. Small arms are not shown on this version.

There are two problems with weapons in any war establishment. The first is that they may include weapons mounted on vehicles. The second is that they do not always show the distribution of individual or crew-served weapons within a unit, simply—where shown at all—the aggregate for a troop or headquarters.

Wherever possible, I have worked from a copy of a war establishment, these are designated by the number and date. The war establishments reviewed were those available in a published form, which can generally be determined from the Sources in the end.[96] However, in some cases I have used information from secondary sources without having seen a copy of the relevant official war establishment. The most detail is always given for the last major version of a unit, generally from late 1943 or 1944.

Most war establishments also provided for an orderly room sergeant and sometimes a few other personnel to be left at base. These are omitted here. Some also provided for 'first reinforcements' which were to be available for replacing losses. For example, a 1940 war establishment for an armoured car regiment had an orderly room sergeant left at base ('Note: Base in this case meant GHQ 2nd Echelon.') and first reinforcements of five officers, a warrant officer, two sergeants, and 33 rank and file. These provisions seem to have continued to the end. The last war establishment for an armoured regiment (from May 1945) still showed the orderly room sergeant under 'Details left at base'. First reinforcements were supposed to total 101 personnel: two captains, eight subalterns, a squadron quartermaster sergeant, three sergeants, four corporals, eight lance corporals, and 75 troopers. It also specified the tradesmen to be included among the rank and file: two clerks, 16 driver mechanics AFV, 20 driver operators, 17 gunner operators, 16 gunner mechanics, an electrician, three vehicle mechanics, and a storeman (technical).

In addition to the personnel of the unit, there were a small number of non-RAC personnel listed separately as attached. For a typical regiment, there would be a medical officer from the RAMC, fitters and vehicle mechanics from the RAOC (early years, later REME), and cooks from the ACC. Thus, the May 1945 armoured regiment had 670 personnel and 29 attached personnel, for an overall total of 699.

The major types of armoured fighting vehicles are examined in the next part of this work. Details on all of the softskin wheeled vehicles in use by 21st Army Group 1944-45 can be found online.[97] Information on earlier, later superseded vehicles, is probably only available in out of print works.[98]

---

[96] However, since these are from secondary sources and sometimes in different formats, there are discrepancies among them. I have made my best judgment in each case. In places of some there are obvious typos, so all of these are transcriptions and not reproductions. As one overview noted, 'Many of the original documents are in the form of complex tables which are difficult to reproduce with accuracy.' www.ww2talk.com/forum/home/28389-contents-about-trux-information.html.

[97] www.ww2talk.com/forum/vehicles/28539-transport.html. This begins with bicycles and motorcycles and ends with specialized vehicles (dark room lorries, truck mounted cranes) and trailers.

[98] The most complete is probably Bart H. Vanderveen, *The Observer's Fighting Vehicles Directory of World War II* (London and New York: Frederick Warne and Co Ltd (Inc), 1972. It's not all that good on fighting vehicles, but comprehensive on softskins. More restricted is David E. Jane, *British Military Transport of World War Two* (London: Almark Publishing Co Ltd, 1978), which covers light utilities, lorries, and heavy general service trucks.

Armoured Regiments

As if the division between armoured regiments and army tank battalions were not sufficient, the Army began with two types of armoured regiments. In 1939, former cavalry regiments were equipped with light tanks while elements of the Royal Tank Regiment had (in theory) cruisers. The former were in light armoured brigades and the latter in heavy armoured brigades. Cruisers also came in two types, heavy and light, although there was little genuine difference between them. The all-light tank regiment officially disappeared in early 1940, replaced by the armoured (cruiser) regiment. However, there weren't actually enough cruiser tanks to accomplish this, so all regiments ended up with some light tank troops. Armoured regiments went through a number of revisions, although the basic form was set in 1943 as all of them converted to the Sherman tank. The Sherman would remain the most-used tank in armoured regiments until the end of the war, joined by only a single brigade in the Cromwell from 1944 and another in the Comet in 1945.

HEAVY ARMOURED REGIMENT 1939-40

War Establishment I/1931/5C

	Officers/Men	Equipment
RHQ	5/16	2 light cruisers, 2 CS cruisers
HQ Squadron	5/124	
▶ Squadron HQ	1/4	
▶ Intercomm Trp	1/23	12 scout cars
▶ Admin Trp	3/97	
Squadron x3	7/145	
▶ Squadron HQ	2/92	1 light cruiser, 2 CS cruisers
▶ Light Half-Squadron	3/25	7 light cruisers
▶ Heavy Half-Squadron	2/28	5 heavy cruisers

Aggregate personnel was 606 all ranks (31 Officers and 575 men). There were also a medical officer RAMC and two armourers RAOC, for a grand total of 609. The armoured strength was 26 light cruiser tanks, 15 heavy cruiser tanks, and eight CS cruiser tanks (49 tanks all told). At the beginning of the war, the scout cars in the intercommunications troop might or might not have been fitted with a Bren gun.

Regimental HQ was little beyond the commanding officer, second in command, adjutant, and intelligence officer, along with the tank crews themselves and two drivers in a 4-seater car. HQ squadron had the bulk of the regiment's support vehicles, although squadron HQ of the sabre squadrons had a fighting portion and an administrative portion as well.

The squadrons had a total of five troops. The heavy half-squadron had two troops and the light half-squadron three. Each troop had two tanks, with an additional tank for the half-squadron leader. Actual personnel strength of the half-squadrons could vary depending on equipment. The intended heavy cruiser was the A13, with a crew of four, and the intended light cruiser was the A10, with a crew of four or five depending on the mark. However, there was also the A9 with a crew of six, so a squadron or regiment might have a mix of cruiser types.

Overall the regiment had 15 motorcycles (three combination), five cars (a 4-seater and four 2-seater), two 8cwt trucks, 15 15cwt trucks (12 GS, and one each office, FFW and water), 11 30cwt GS lorries, 22 3ton 4x2 GS lorries, and four 3ton 6x4 GS lorries.

LIGHT ARMOURED [CAVALRY LIGHT TANK] REGIMENT 1939-40

War Establishment 1/1931/8F/1 (effective May 1938)

	Officers/Men	Equipment
RHQ	5/12	4 light cruisers, 2 scout carriers
HQ Squadron	5/118	
► Squadron HQ	1/3	
► Intercomm Trp	1/23	12 scout cars
► Admin Trp	3/92	
Light Cruiser Squadron	5/140	
► Squadron HQ	2/83	3 light cruisers, 1 scout carrier
► Troop x5	(12)[99]	3 light cruisers
Light Tank Squadron x2	5/112	
► Squadron HQ	2/70	3 light tanks, 1 scoutcarrier
► Troop x5	(9)[100]	3 light tanks

Aggregate personnel was 519 all ranks (25 Officers and 494 men). There were six attached personnel: medical officer RAMC, two armourers, an electrician, armamement artificer and fitter RAOC; the grand total was 525.[101] The armoured strength was 22 light cruisers and 36 light tanks (58 total), although in 1939 all 58 tanks would have been the machine-gun armed Light Tank Mk VI. The strengths shown suggest that the A13 cruiser (with a crew of four) was the intended tanks for the light cruiser squadron.[102]

---

[99] Each troop could have an officer (3) or NCO (2) and 11 men.

[100] Each troop could have an officer (3) or NCO (2) and 8 men.

[101] Note the greater number of RAOC personnel (five) than for an armoured regiment (two).

[102] One source (from the 1940 portion of the former Trux Models web site) shows a strength of 20 officers and 434 other ranks (454 in all without the attached personnel), which may reflect the actual strength of a regiment with 58 light tanks.

Other than the variations in tank type, the regiment is roughly similar to its heavy cousin. The transport was different, however. There were 41 motorcycles, no cars, five 8cwt trucks, 15 15cwt GS trucks, and 20 30cwt 6x4 GS lorries.

Light armoured regiments in India had a different establishment, with 481 personnel, 41 light tanks, and 15 scout cars.

In April 1940 the distinction between heavy and light armoured brigades and their associated regiments were abolished. A 22 May 1940 war establishment (I/1931/5E/1) provided for regiments with only cruiser tanks. This had 31 officers and 546 other ranks (577 total, exclusive of attached personnel) with 46 cruisers and six CS cruisers. RHQ had four cruisers, squadron HQs each had two cruisers and two CS cruisers, and the four troops of each squadron had three cruisers each. However, there were nowhere near enough cruiser tanks to replace all of the lights.

In the interim, the regiments of 1st Armoured Division swapped equipment. The convoluted half-squadron of the old heavy armoured regiment disappeared, and all regiments now had three squadrons of four troops each. Squadron HQ would have four tanks (two CS if available), two troops of cruiser tanks (three each), and two troops of light tanks (three each). RHQ would have three cruiser tanks.

In practice, the results are somewhat variable. We have details on one regiment in each brigade. The Queen's Bays had 29 cruiser tanks (four A9, three A10 and 22 A13) along with 21 Mark VIC light tanks. Two squadrons had four cruisers at HQ, and two troops each of cruisers and light tanks. The third squadron had three cruisers at HQ, one troop of cruisers, and three of light tanks. 2nd RTR had 27 cruisers (eight A9, one A10 and 18 A13) and 21 Mark VIB light tanks. In the Bays, some of their CS tanks were the newer A13, while 2nd RTR only had A9 CS tanks.

ARMOURED REGIMENT 1940-42

	Officers/Men	Equipment
RHQ	5/12	4 cruisers
HQ Squadron	6/122	
► Squadron HQ	2/4	
► Intercomm Trp	-/18	9 scout cars
► Admin Trp	4/99	
Squadron x3	7/138	
► Squadron HQ	3/94	2 cruisers, 2 CS cruisers
► Trp x4	1/11	3 cruisers

This detail differs marginally—580 all all ranks (32 Officers and 548 men)—from the earlier personnel strength (577) from Joselen.[103] Squadron strength assumes tanks with four-man crews, although the Crusader III (introduced in the summer of 1942) only had a crew of three. Attached personnel are unknown.

ARMOURED REGIMENT 1942-43 (UK PATTERN)

War Establishment II/101/2, effective 26 August 1942

	Officers/Men	Equipment
RHQ	5/36	4 cruisers, 8 AA tanks
HQ Squadron	7/158	
▶ Squadron HQ	2/4	
▶ Recce Trp	1/19	9 carriers
▶ Intercomm Trp	1/17	9 scout cars
▶ Admin Trp	3/118	
Squadron *x3*	8/150	
▶ Squadron HQ	3/95	2 cruisers, 2 CS cruisers
▶ Trp *x5*	1/11	3 cruisers

Various changes in 1942 led to a larger regiment, at 680 all ranks (36 Officers and 644 men). The only (partial) copy of this war establishment seen did not show attached personnel or other vehicles.

Increasing each squadron by another troop gave the revised armoured regiment a tank strength of 61 (55 cruisers and six CS cruisers). Personnel strength could vary somewhat depending on tank types. The Crusader (Cruiser VI) had a crew of four or three depending on model, the Cavalier (Cruiser VII) had a crew of five, and the Centaur (Cruiser VIII) was back to four. The US-supplied Sherman had a crew of five.

This remained the basic pattern for armoured regiments, with some changes made in November 1943 and minor alterations after that.

ARMOURED REGIMENT (MIDDLE EAST) 1942-43

The 'basic' organization in North Africa was as follows:

	Officers/Men	Equipment
RHQ	5/12	4 cruisers
HQ Squadron	7/122	
▶ Squadron HQ	2/4	
▶ Recce Trp	1/19	10 scout cars
▶ Intercomm Trp	-/16	8 scout cars or jeeps
▶ Admin Trp	4/83	

---

[103] *Orders of Battle*, p 139. I have not seen a copy of the actual war establishment.

	Officers/Men	Equipment
Squadron *x3*	7/114	
▶ Squadron HQ	3/70	2 cruisers, 2 CS cruisers
▶ Trp *x4*	1/11	3 cruisers

The theoretical strength was 33 officers and 476 other ranks (509 all told). In late 1942 the admin troop was reduced by one man, and the squadron HQs were each increased by six men. However, actual strength of the regiment depended on the type of tanks assigned, and increments of 36 to 88 were possible depending on the mix. Only units with Crusader tanks would have CS versions, and it was not unusual to replace those with normal gun-armed tanks.

From March 1942 there were a variety of establishments for armoured regiments in the Middle East. One type of regiment had Stuarts (RHQ and one squadron) and Grants (two squadrons), with 44 tanks (20 Stuarts and 24 Grants). Another type of regiment had Crusaders (RHQ and two squadrons) and Grants (one squadron), with 48 tanks (36 Crusaders and 12 Grants).

In fact, there were other variations as well, and heavy tank losses during the 1942 fighting affected the actual as opposed to theoretical establishments. As late as El Alamein in October 1942 there was still a regiment equipped entirely with the Stuart light tank. There were also mixes of Crusaders and Shermans instead of Crusaders and Grants. However, a 'variable' war establishment was issued in August 1942.

War Establishment VI/560/1, effective 13 August 1942

	Officers/Men	Equipment
RHQ	5/12	4 tanks
HQ Squadron	6/112	
▶ Squadron HQ	2/4	
▶ Recce Trp	1/19	10 scout cars
▶ Intercomm Trp	1/15	8 scout cars
▶ Admin Trp	3/73	
Squadron *x3*	7/114	
▶ Squadron HQ	3/70	2 tanks, 2 CS tanks
▶ Trp *x4*	1/11	3 tanks

The basic strength for this regiment was 498 (32 officers and 466 other ranks). Attached were a medical officer RAMC, two armourers RAOC, and eight cooks ACC, for an aggregate of 509. The regiment had 52 tanks (46 gun and six CS). Most regiments probably did not have the CS tanks. If scout cars were not available for the intercommunications troop, then 5cwt FWD cars could be substituted.

RHQ had a 4-seater utility car in addition to the tanks. All told, the HQ squadron had six 5cwt FWD cars, six 15cwt trucks (two GS, FWD armoured, wireless, water and office), and nine 3ton lorries (eight GS, one stores). The sabre squadrons had a 5cwt FWD car, two 15cwt trucks (GS and water), and seven 3ton lorries.

However, there were seven possible tank configurations specified, each with an increment of other ranks and 3ton lorries:

	Troopers	3ton lorries
30 Grant, 16 Crusader 2-pdr. and 6 Crusader, CS	87	20
30 Grant and 22 Crusader III	70	24
30 Sherman, 16 Crusader 2-pdr and 6 Crusader, CS	54	18
30 Sherman and 22 Crusader III	37	22
14 Sherman, 32 Crusader 2-pdr and 6 Crusader, CS	26	9
30 Grant and 22 Stuart	83	17
14 Grant and 38 Start	41	10

There was no requirement that all three regiments in a brigade be the same, so the fitters and armourers of the light aid detachments had their hands full.

This was followed in November (after El Alamein), with an establishment for uniform regiments, with 52 Crusader II, or 52 Valentine, or 52 Stuart tanks. Note that it had the same war establishment number. However, it would also apply to other regiments.

War Establishment VI/560/1, effective 21 November 1942

	Officers/Men		Equipment
RHQ	5/12		4 tanks
HQ Squadron	6/115		
▶ Squadron HQ		2/4	
▶ Recce Trp		1/19	10 scout cars
▶ Intercomm Trp		1/15	8 scout cars
▶ Admin Trp		3/76	
Squadron *x3*	7/117		
▶ Squadron HQ		3/73	4 tanks
▶ Trp *x4*		1/11	3 tanks

This establishment had 32 officers and 478 other ranks, for a strength of 510. Attached were the medical officer RAMC, two armourers (now REME), and 13 cooks ACC. Apparently scout cars were still in short supply, since a note reads 'Until scout cars are available for intercommunication troops, cars, 5-cwt., 4 x 4, will be issued in lieu.' A new addition to the establishment is four 6ton, 4-wheeled breakdown tractors: one in the HQ squadron and one in each sabre squadron. Otherwise the supporting vehicles are roughly similar.

However, this establishment came with *ten* possible variants, each with an increment in troopers and lorries:

	Troopers	3ton lorries
30 Grant and 22 Crusader II (four man)	87	20
30 Grant and 22 Crusader III	69	23
30 Sherman and 22 Crusader II (four man)	54	18
30 Sherman and 22 Crusader III	36	21
30 Sherman and 22 Stuart (four man)	53	17
30 Grant and 22 Stuart	85	19
30 Sherman, 14 Crusader II, and 8 Crusader III	47	19
52 Grant	144	30
52 Sherman	88	27

With the increasing supply of Shermans and phasing out of earlier types, the final Middle East armoured regiment war establishment was issued in July 1943. However, it was still possible to have some variety of tanks within a regiment.

War Establishment VI/560/4, effective 14 July 1943

	Officers/Men		Equipment
RHQ	5/20		4 tanks, 1 AA tank
HQ Squadron	7/147		
▶ Squadron HQ		2/7	
▶ Recce Trp		2/40	6 scout cars, 10 carriers
▶ Intercomm Trp		-/16	8 scout cars
▶ Admin Trp		3/84	
Squadron *x3*	7/138		
▶ Squadron HQ		3/18	3 tanks, 1 AA tank
▶ Admin Trp		-/64	
▶ Trp *x4*		1/14	3 tanks

This regiment had 33 officers and 581 other ranks (614 aggregate). With, of course, the medical officer RAMC, two armourers REME, 13 cooks ACC, bringing it to 630. The number of tanks fell to 49, and there were now four AA tanks as well. The recce troop was changed to a mix of scout cars and carriers, each of the latter with a .5-inch HMG. As before, if scout cars were not available, the intercommunications troop could substitute 5cwt 4x4 cars (by now, and probably earlier, the ubiquitous jeep). There were eight PIATs in the regiment.

RHQ had a single four-seater 4x2 car in addition to the tanks. The HQ squadron had a single four-seater 4x2 car, four 5cwt 4x4 cars, six motorcycles, two 15cwt 4x4 armoured personnel trucks, six 15cwt 4x2 trucks (two GS, two FFW, water and office), ten 3ton 4x2 lorries (eight GS, one for cooking and one for stores), a 4x2 heavy ambulance, and a 6x4 breakdown tractor.

In the sabre squadrons, HQ had a 5cwt 4x4 car in addition to the tanks and had become purely a command element. There was now a distinct admin troop, with yet another four-seater 4x2 car, three motorcycles, two 15cwt 4x2 trucks (GS and water), 19 3ton 4x2 lorries (17 GS, one for cooking, one stores), and a 6x4 breakdown tractor.

There were two variants to the all-Sherman regiment. One with 34 Shermans and 15 others (eight Crusader III and seven Crusader II, or 15 Stuarts) and four AA tanks, and one with 49 Crusader or Stuart tanks and four AA tanks. The former would deduct 27 troopers and nine 3ton GS lorries; the latter would deduct 85 troopers and 27 3ton GS lorries. These regiments would finally convert to the November 1943 war establishment.

ARMOURED REGIMENT 1944-45

War Establishment II/151/3, effective 30 November 1943

	Officers/Men	Equipment
RHQ	5/16	4 cruisers
HQ Squadron	8/193	
▶ Squadron HQ	2/4	
▶ Recce Trp	1/43	11 light tanks
▶ AA Trp	1/23	6 AA tanks
▶ Intercomm Trp	1/17	9 scout cars
▶ Admin Trp	3/106	
Squadron *x3*	8/149	
▶ Squadron HQ	3/22	2 cruisers, 2 CS cruisers
▶ Admin Trp	-/57	
▶ Trp *x5*	1/14	3 cruisers

The final version of the wartime armoured regiment had a strength of 693 all ranks (37 officers and 656 men), as well as the normal attachments: medical officer RAMC, nine armourers and vehicle mechanics REME, and 19 cooks ACC, or 722 all told. Tank strength remained at 61 (55 cruisers and six CS cruisers). The recce troop changed from carriers to 11 light tanks. The number of AA tanks was reduced from eight to six and moved from RHQ to an AA troop in HQ squadron.

However, this structure is as much theoretical as real. The AA troops were all disbanded following D-Day—given the lack of real threat from the Luftwaffe and the increasing need for tank crews they served no real purpose. However, they remained part of the official establishment.

In the recce troop, some regiments removed the turret from the Stuart and substituted a pintle-mounted .50-caliber machine gun for a lower profile. (By that point, the Stuart's 37mm gun was of little value against any target.) It appears that by the end of the war a theater commander could authorize an alternative organization, with six light tanks and six scout cars. However, the official establishment remained 11 light tanks.

By 1944, the US Sherman was the main vehicle for all British armoured regiments. In 21st Army Group, there were no CS Shermans (with a 105mm howitzer), all were normal gun-armed tanks. The 22nd Armoured Brigade (7th Armoured Division) re-equipped with the Cromwell before D-Day, and its regiments did include the Cromwell CS tank (95mm howitzer) at squadron HQ.

The major change for 21st Army Group regiments, however, was the introduction of the Sherman Firefly: a Sherman modified to carry the 17pdr anti-tank gun. The original goal was to have one Firefly per troop of three tanks. However, initial production was insufficient, so the squadron was changed to four troops of four tanks each (one a Firefly), and squadron HQ reduced to three tanks. This kept the regiment at 61 cruisers (49 Shermans and 12 Fireflys in Sherman regiments, 43 Cromwells, six Cromwell CS and 12 Fireflys in 7th Armoured Division). Ultimately regiments were built up to have more than one Firefly per troop, and the fourth tank in squadron HQ was restored, making 64 cruisers all told. Cromwell-equipped regiments were supposed to receive the Challenger (a Cromwell variant with the 17pdr) but almost none of these were received by the end of the war.

Regiments in Italy, with few or no Fireflys, received the 76mm variant of the Sherman and also the 105mm Sherman CS variant, retaining the structure of five troops of three tanks each in the squadron.

Supporting vehicles would have been roughly the same as the final war establishment. The details in Appendix 6 (the May 1945 war establishment) also show changes made after November 1943 as well as variations particular to 21st Army Group.

ARMOURED REGIMENT MAY 1945

War Establishment II/157/I, effective 1 May 1945

	Officers/Men	Equipment
RHQ	5/17	4 tanks
HQ Squadron	9/186	
▶ Squadron HQ	3/4	
▶ Recce Trp	2/42	11 light tanks
▶ AA Trp	1/23	6 AA tanks
▶ Intercomm Trp	1/17	9 scout cars
▶ Admin Trp	2/100	
Squadron x3	8/143	
▶ Squadron HQ	3/21	2 tanks, 2 CS tanks, 1 scout car, 1 ARV
▶ Admin Trp	-/52	
▶ Trp x5	1/14	3 tanks

With the end of the war in Europe, armoured regiments were changed again. A January 1945 Standardization Conference determined that both armoured and tank units should be designated as armoured, and have the same organization. They would differ only in their tanks (cruiser or infantry) while waiting re-equipping with a single 'capital' or 'universal' tank to replace the two distinct wartime types. The tank battalions in 21st Army Group changed over to this organization in February-March 1945, before the war establishment was published.[104] Full details of this war establishment are contained in Appendix 6.

The regiment had 38 officers and 632 other ranks (670 personnel aggregate). Attached personnel were the normal medical officer RAMC, three armourers (one sergeant) and six vehicle mechanics (three sergeants) REME, and 19 cooks (one sergeant) ACC, or 699 all told. There were 55 gun-armed and six close support tanks, either cruisers or infantry. Authorization of threatre commanders to change the recce troop to six light tank cars and six scout cars is contained in a note to the war establishment.

DD-EQUIPPED ARMOURED REGIMENTS

D-Day

These were essentially a standard armoured regiment, with two squadrons equipped with DD Shermans and the remaining squadron with Shermans and Fireflys. Each regiment received 40 DD tanks, making a squadron four troops of four and four at squadron HQ. Once ashore the surviving DD tanks were withdrawn and the squadrons re-equipped with Shermans and Fireflys.

The Scheldt

In autumn 1944 the Staffordshire Yeomanry were re-equipping with DD tanks. The one trained squadron assisted in the attack on South Beveland Island 25 October 1944. Again, it appears that the intent was to simply replace the normal tank mixture with DD tanks throughout the regiment. Problems with the operation led 79th Armoured Division to establish a group to examine DD tank operations.

Rhine Crossing

DD regiments lost the normal recce troop and gained one with the Buffalo LVT, some of which were equipped with the ability to lay a carpet on the banks to help the DD tanks come out of the water; this was adapted from the AVRE carpet layer. The intercommunications troop changed from scout cars to the tracked Weasel (M29 basic, or M29C amphibious). Finally, 3ton 4x4 vehicles in the squadrons were replaced by the amphibious DUKW.

---

[104] However, they did not reform the AA troops during the final months of the war or immediately after.

RHQ had three Sherman DD tanks. The recce troop had two LVT II command/control, six LVT II carpet layers, and three LVT II carrying airborne bulldozers. The intercommunications troop had nine M29 or M29C Weasels. Each squadron had three DD Shermans at squadron HQ and four troops of four DD Shermans each.

REGIMENTS (INDIA AND BURMA)

I have not seen any published war establishments for the British armoured regiments serving in India and Burma. One secondary source[105] shows a regiment with 49 tanks (four at RHQ, and three squadrons each with three at squadron HQ and four troops of three tanks each), and also shows a recce troop with three Humber armoured cars. Another source[106] shows a basic regiment of 52 tanks (four at RHQ, and three squadrons, each with four tanks at squadron HQ and four troops of three tanks each). In addition, it shows a recce troop with 11 Daimler scout cars. The only other vehicles shown are an OP carrier at RHQ and three ARV Mk II (either Grant or Sherman).

Tank Battalions/Regiments

The army tank (later tank) battalion was intended to have a slow, heavily armoured vehicle to assist infantry formations. Until May 1945 these always had a separate organization from armoured regiments, although by 1944 there were generally similar. Officially the units were battalions until 1945, but all save one appear to have self-referred as regiments before that date.

ARMY TANK BATTALION 1939-40

War Establishment III/1931/8A/3, effective 4 October 1939

	Officers/Men	Equipment
Bn HQ	5/176	2 infantry tanks, 3/4 light tanks, 2 carriers
Company x3	8/122	
▶ Company HQ	3/67	1 infantry tank, 1 light tank, 2 carriers
▶ Section x5	1/11	3 infantry tanks

The battalion had 29 officers and 542 other ranks, including attached (RAMC officer and RAOC armourer), for a total of 570 personnel.[107] There were 50 infantry and 7 light tanks.

---

[105] David Hughes, David A. Ryan and Steve Rothwell, *The British Armies in World War Two*, Vol Ten (The Indian Army—Part 3) (West Chester, OH: The Nafziger Collection, Inc, 2008), p 102.

[106] Mark Bevis, *British and Commonwealth Armies 1944-45*, pp 69-70.

[107] Joslen (p 192) shows 29 and 484, for a total of 513. I have followed a detailed version of the war establishment once available at the old Trux Models web site. WOIIIs were replaced in 1940 by subalterns.

Battalion HQ was organized into No 1 Group (Fighting) and No 2 Group (Administrative). No 1 Group had a car, six motorcycles, and four 8cwt trucks (one fitted with a wireless set). No 2 Group had six more motorcycles, two 8cwt GS trucks, a 15cwt water truck, and 15 3ton lorries (one with stores and fitters tools, the rest GS). Three of the lorries each carried a Bren LMG and Atk rifle.

The tank company HQ was not formally divided into fighting and administrative portions. In addition to the carriers and tanks, there was a car, a motorcycle combination and six motorcycles, three 15cwt trucks (two GS, one water), and four 3ton GS lorries. One lorry carried a Bren LMG and Atk rifle. Sections consisted of the three infantry tanks and 12 personnel (subaltern or WOIII and 11 other ranks). (Four-man crews are for the Infantry Tank Mk II. The MG-armed Mk I had a crew of two; all of these were lost in France in 1940.)

ARMY TANK BATTALION 1941

War Establishment III/1931/33A/4, effective 7 April 1941

	Officers/Men	Equipment
RHQ		4 infantry tanks
HQ Squadron		
Squadron *x3*		
▶ Sqn HQ		1 infantry tank, 2 CS infantry tanks
▶ Troop *x5*		3 infantry tanks

Army tank battalions remained unchanged until April 1941, when companies and sections were redesignated squadrons and troops, and a HQ squadron was organized. Light tanks were completely gone, and each squadron gained two CS tanks. The battalion was somewhat larger, with 35 officers and 547 other ranks, for a total of 582 personnel. (Details for attached personnel are not known.) There were 58 infantry tanks, six of them CS versions.

TANK BATTALION 1942

War Establishment II/154/1, effective 16 August 1942

	Officers/Men	Equipment
RHQ		4 infantry tanks, 8 AA tanks, 10 scout cars
HQ Squadron		
Squadron *x3*		
▶ Sqn HQ		1 infantry tank, 2 CS infantry tanks
▶ Troop *x5*		3 infantry tanks

From June 1942 tank brigades began dropping 'army' whether assigned to mixed divisions or as independent tank brigades. Battalion HQ gained a recce troop with 10 scout cars in May 1942, and then added 8 AA tanks in August. Personnel strength increased to 37 officers and 588 other ranks, 625 overall. (Again, details on attached personnel are not known.) Infantry tank strength remained unchanged (52 gun and six CS).

TANK BATTALION 1943

The last change to the tank battalion came in November 1943. However, there is no internally consistent and reliable copy of that war establishment.

War Establishment II/154/2, effective 30 November 1943

	Officers/Men		Equipment
RHQ	5/27		4 infantry tanks, 2 OP tanks
HQ Squadron	7/?		
► Sqn HQ		3/6	
► Recce Troop		1/43	11 light tanks
► Intercom Troop		2/16	9 scout cars
► AA Troop		1/23	6 AA tanks
► Admin Troop		1/?	
Squadron *x3*	8/?		
► Sqn HQ		3/?	1 infantry tank, 2 CS infantry tanks, 1 scout car, 1 ARV
► Troop *x5*		1/14	3 infantry tanks

According to Joslen, the regiment (including attached personnel) should have 38 officers and 670 other ranks, or 708 in aggregate.[108] However, he provides no breakdown below that level, or other information beyond the AFVs. The complete war establishment from Tux Models,[109] gives at one point 38 officers and 629 other ranks (667) plus 29 attached, or 696 all told. That document is internally consistent and the details of personnel and vehicles cannot be made to add up.The information on the fighting troops and (probably) RHQ is reliable, but working from the document still leaves two officers and a number of other ranks unaccounted for. This is discussed in Appendix 7.

Battalion HQ gave up AA tanks and the recce troop, but gained two OP tanks. HQ squadron now had a recce troop with 11 light tanks—the same as in an armoured regiment, an intercommunications troop with nine scout cars, and an AA troop with six AA tanks, in addition to its own HQ and the administrative troop.[110] There were still 58 infantry tanks (52 gun and six CS), along with 11 light tanks, six AA tanks, and two OP tanks. In 21st Army Group, the OP tanks were withdrawn in March 1944 and consolidated in the tank brigade HQ squadron.

---

[108] *Orders of Battle*, p 194.
[109] www.ww2talk.com/forum/armour/28483-tank-battalion.html. There is also a published edition from Trux Models (their WE 2115) which has some differences with the later web version.
[110] As with the armoured regiment, the AA troops were withdrawn and disbanded following Normandy.

TANKS 1945

A Standardization Conference in January 1945 determined that all armoured/tank brigades and regiments would be designated as armoured, and would differ only in the equipment: cruisers or infantry tanks. The new war establishment for the former tank battalions was not issued until May 1945, although 21st Army Group changed over during February and March (see above, under Armoured Regiments). For the former tank battalions, this also involved replacing some of the earlier supporting vehicle types with larger versions (e.g., 3ton office lorry in lieu of 15cwt office truck).

Armoured Car Regiments

At the beginning of the war, armoured car regiments were GHQ units, although the one stationed in Egypt was initially part of the light armoured brigade there. For a period of time in 1940 they were called light tank regiments (wheeled) and the armoured cars retitled accordingly. Reverting to the more sensible armoured car designations, the regiments became the recce element of armoured divisions, but could also be GHQ units. Finally, in 1943, the Army made all armoured car regiments GHQ units, normally operating one per corps.

ARMOURED CAR REGIMENTS 1939

The initial War Establishment for a cavalry armoured car regiment, as it was officially designated, was from 1938.

War Establishment I/1931/5/3, effective 29 June 1938

	Officers/Men	Equipment
RHQ	8/81	2 armoured cars
Squadron x3	6/92	
▶ Squadron HQ	3/41	3 armoured cars
▶ Troop x3	1/17	3 armoured cars

Personnel strength was 26 officers and 357 other ranks, for an aggregate of 383 personnel. There was a medical officer RAMC and three RAOC other ranks (an electrician and two fitters MV) attached to RHQ, giving an overall strength of 387. The regiment had 38 armoured cars, and no other type of armoured vehicle, such as scout cars.

Notable at first glance is the lack of any HQ squadron for the regiment; the RHQ was divided between Group 1 (command) and Group 2 (administrative). The command element had two 4-seater 4-wheeled cars, an 8cwt 4-wheeled GS truck, and nine motorcycles in addition to the two armoured cars. The admin element had another 8cwt 4-wheeled GS truck, a motorcycle, two 30cwt 4-wheeled GS lorries (one for cooking), and nine 3ton, 4-wheeled GS lorries (including one for petrol).

Squadron HQ for the three fighting squadrons also included support personnel and vehicles. It had a 4-seater, 4-wheeled car, two motorcycles, four 30cwt, 4-wheeled GS lorries (including one for cooking), and two 3ton, 4-wheeled GS lorries. The troops contained only the three armoured cars and two motorcycles. Some of the other ranks in each troop were relief drivers, who rode in admin vehicles.

In 1938 the Army had also created a war establishment for a cavalry armoured car regiment (colonial).

	Officers/Men	Equipment
RHQ	7/112	2 armoured cars
Squadron *x3*	5/95	
▶ Squadron HQ	2/32	3 armoured cars
▶ Trp *x3*	1/21	3 armoured cars

This regiment had 23 officers (one squadron was given an additional subaltern) and 387 other ranks, for an aggregate of 410. It had two RAOC armourers attached, and would also get some Royal Signals personnel.

Although organizing them differently, this regiment had the same 38 armoured cars as the domestic one, but more personnel. One reason is that the establishment included horses: every armoured car troop had two, squadron HQ had four, and the RHQ had 12; the regiment thus had 44 horses.[111]

The other vehicles for the colonial armoured car regiment were 30 solo motorcycles, 16 2-seater and one 4-seater cars, and ten 30cwt 6-wheeled lorries (one in each troop and one at RHQ). This amounted to a fairly skimpy support element, and was much below the domestic establishment. A squadron HQ had only four cars and two motorcycles, along with a training chassis. It does not appear that any regiment was ever organized under this war establishment; the 11th Hussars and 12th Royal Lancers were both organized under the normal 1938 establishment shown at the beginning.

It may be that the 12th Lancers were reorganized before going to France in October 1939. There is a war establishment III/1931/8C/1, without an exact effective date shown in the source.[112] However, it contains the same 38 armoured cars but a personnel strength of 436.

RHQ had a command group and an administrative group. The command group had a car, nine motorcycles, and an 8cwt truck for the signal officer. The admin group had a car

---

[111] Which is two more than the establishment detail would give. The extra subaltern in one squadron got his two horses as well, along with a groom.
[112] This is another of the BEF 1940 establishments formerly found on the old Trux Models site. It does not give a complete breakdown of the personnel and is internally inconsistent.

and motorcycle, along with one 15cwt truck for the medical officer and 11 3ton GS lorries (one for petrol and one for small arms ammunition, the remainder for stores, baggage, cooks, etc.). Squadron HQ had a car, two motorcycles, and 8cwt GS truck, four 30cwt GS lorries (cooks, petrol, small arms ammunition and spare personnel), and two 3ton GS lorries (personnel, stores and fitters) in addition to the armoured cars. Each troop had three armoured cars and two motorcycles.

ARMOURED CAR REGIMENT 1940

Armoured car regiments were changed January 1940. Actually, since armoured cars had become light tanks (wheeled), the official name for this organization was Light Armoured Regiment (Wheeled). However, I will call light tanks (wheeled) armoured cars. This establishment did not apply to the 12th Lancers until after their return from France.

War Establishment I/1931/5D/1, effective 3 January 1940

	Officers/Men	Equipment
RHQ	5/10	4 armoured cars
HQ Squadron	5/118	
▶ Squadron HQ	1/3	
▶ Intercomm Trp	1/23	12 scout cars
▶ Admin Trp	2/92	
Squadron x3	7/105	
▶ Squadron HQ	2/65	3 armoured cars
▶ Trp x5	1/8	3 armoured cars

This was clearly a larger unit than the pre-war regiments. It had 24 officers and 447 other ranks, for an aggregate of 471.[113] There were three personnel attached: an RAMC officer and two RAOC armourers, making for 474 personnel all told.

The new regiment has a distinct HQ squadron, and clearly more personnel and vehicles than the old RHQ. The number of armoured cars has risen to 58, and there are also 12 scout cars in the intercommunications troop. In addition to vehicle weapons, the regiment had 14 .303" Bren light machine guns and 14 of the .55" anti-tank rifles carried one each on various of the supply trucks.

This regiment had 13 motorcycles (10 solo in the intercommunications troop and one combination in each squadron HQ). There were a larger number of vehicles, and the change to wartime variants from older types is evident: one 4-seater car, a utility car, one 8cwt wireless truck, 16 15cwt GS trucks, one 15cwt water tank truck, one 15cwt office

---

[113] Six of the 'officer' slots in the regiment were filled by the six WOIII's on establishment (two in each squadron: 2nd and 4th Troops). The WOIII ranks was abolished in 1940 and replaced by subalterns.

truck, seven 4-wheeled 30cwt lorries, 14 4-wheeled 3ton lorries, and three 28-seater coaches. The armoured car troops were exclusively armoured car units (no motorcycle or other vehicle) but each squadron HQ included seven trucks or lorries. RHQ was austere: four armoured cars and the single utility car. The remaining vehicles were in the admin troop, except for the 8cwt wireless truck carrying the four personnel in the HQ Squadron's own HQ.

ARMOURED CAR REGIMENT 1942

The next change came in 1942 where, for whatever reason, there were two almost identical war establishments published a month apart. The first war establishment had a late August 1942 effective date.

War Establishment II/153/2, 26 August 1942

	Officers/Men	Equipment
RHQ	6/19	2 armoured cars
HQ Squadron	6/115	
▶ Squadron HQ	2/4	
▶ Intercomm Trp	1/30	13 scout cars
▶ Admin Trp	3/81	
Squadron x4	9/151	
▶ Squadron HQ	4/71	4 armoured cars
▶ Trp x5	1/18[114]	2 armoured cars, 2 scout cars
▶ Trp	1/14	2 armoured cars, 2 scout cars

The two major changes are the increase in squadrons from three to four, and the changes in the troops from armoured cars to a mix of armoured and scout cars. This larger regiment had 48 officers and 778 other ranks, for an aggregate of 826. Attachments included one officer (RAMC) and 28 other ranks (3 RAOC and 25 ACC), for a grand total of 855 personnel..

The number of armoured cars remained the same as before, 58, with the scout cars increasing dramatically to 53 (40 in the squadrons, 13—an increase of one—in the intercommunications troop).

RHQ remained fairly austere, with two armoured cars and three cars (two 4-seater and one two-seater) along with six motorcycles. The intercommunications troop had a car, two trucks and a motorcycle in addition to its scout cars. Most of the soft vehicles of the regiment were in the admin troop. In the armoured car squadron, the squadron HQ had four armoured cars, a 4-seater car and five motorcycles in its fighting element, along with two motorcycles, two 15cwt trucks and eight lorries (seven 3ton and a 30cwt slave

---

[114] One troop has a subaltern and 14 personnel (twp armoured cars, two scout cars, and a 5cwt 4x4 car); the other four troops each have a subaltern and 18 personnel (two armoured cars, two scout cars, two 5cwt 4x4 cars and two motorcycles).

battery) in the admin element. Armoured car troops were now a mix of armoured and scout cars, and differed somewhat in the number of additional vehicles.

This was followed by another war establishment for an armoured car regiment, effective late September 1942. This one was just a variant on the 1940 establishment, going back to three squadrons and a 'pure' armoured car troop.

War establishment II/152/2, effective 24 September 1942

	Officers/Men	Equipment
RHQ	6/27	4 armoured cars
HQ Squadron	5/114	
▶ Squadron HQ	2/4	
▶ Intercomm Trp	1/26	12 scout cars
▶ Admin Trp	2/84	
Squadron *x3*	7/129	
▶ Squadron HQ	2/74	3 armoured cars
▶ Trp *x5*	1/11	3 armoured cars

Still at 58 armoured cars, and with scout cars only in the intercommunications troop, the regiment had 32 officers and 528 other ranks, for an aggregate of 560 personnel. This made it larger than the 1940 regiment, albeit with no additional combat strength. Attached personnel were the standard medical officer (RAMC) and 21 other ranks (two REME armourers and 19 ACC cooks).

In addition to the four armoured cars, RHQ had a 6-seater 4x2 car, two 4-seater 4x2 cars, and a motorcycle. HQ of the HQ squadron was unchanged (4-seater 4x2 car and a 15cwt 4x2 GS truck). The intercommunications troop had a motorcycle and 15cwt 4x2 GS truck (one fewer) in addition to the 12 scout cars (also one fewer). The admin troop was somewhat smaller, with five motorcycles, a 4-seater 4x2 car, five 15cwt 4x2 trucks (two GS, one each FFW, water and office), and 11 3ton 6x4 lorries (one store and 10 GS):

The fighting part of a sabre squadron HQ had a 4-seater 4x2 car and five motorcycles in addition to the three armoured cars (a reduction of one). The admin portion had a motorcycle (reduction of one), two 15cwt 4x2 trucks (water and FFS), and seven 3ton 6x4 lorries. Each troop had three armoured cars.

Completely gone are the four 30cwt 4x2 slaver battery vehicles of the prior war establishment, which had one in each squadron.

ARMOURED CAR REGIMENT (MIDDLE EAST) 1942-43

As was the case with armoured regiments, there were distinct war establishments for armoured car regiments in North Africa. The first came in August 1942.

War Establishment VI/554/1, effective 15 August 1942

	Officers/Men	Equipment
RHQ	6/21	4 armoured cars
HQ Squadron	5/103	
▶ Squadron HQ	2/3	
▶ Intercomm Trp	1/26	12 scout cars
▶ Admin Trp	2/74	
Squadron *x3*	7/105	
▶ Squadron HQ	2/40	3 armoured cars
▶ Trp *x5*	1/13	3 armoured cars

The regiment had 32 officers and 439 other ranks (471 total), along with a medical officer RAMC, two armourers REME, and 13 cooks ACC—487 overall. There were 58 armoured cars and 12 scout cars. While it had the same armoured and scout car complement of the August 1942 home regiment, its personnel strength was smaller.

RHQ had two 5cwt FWD cars (probably jeeps) and a utility car in addition to its armoured cars. In addition to the scout cars, the intercommunications troop had a 5cwt FWD car and 15cwt GS truck. Overall, the HQ squadron had two 5cwt FWD cars, a utility car, an armoured 15cwt truck, seven 15cwt trucks (four GS, and one each office, wireless, and water), and ten 3ton GS lorries.

In the squadrons, HQ had a 5cwt FWD car and utility car in addition to the armoured cars. The admin portion of the squadron had another 5cwt FWD car, two 15cwt trucks (wireless and water), and five 3ton GS lorries.

This was succeeded by a new establishment in November 1942.

War Establishment VI/554/2, effective 9 November 1942

	Officers/Men	Equipment
RHQ	5/19	4 armoured cars
HQ Squadron	6/93	
▶ Squadron HQ	3/10	
▶ Admin Trp	3/83	
Squadron *x3*	7/114	
▶ Squadron HQ	2/61	3 armoured cars
▶ Trp *x5*	1/11	3 armoured cars

The revised regiment had 32 officers and 454 other ranks (486 aggregate), a slight increase. The medical officer RAMC and two armourers REME remained, but the ACC cooks were reduced to 12, for 501 personnel overall. The regiment still had 58 armoured cars, but the intercommunications troop and its scout cars were gone.

RHQ now had a two-seater 4x2 car, two 5cwt 4x4 cars (jeeps), and a 3ton GS lorry in addition to the armoured cars. HQ squadron all told had another two-seater 4x2 car, three

5cwt 4x4 cars, an armoured 15cwt 4x2 truck, nine 15cwt 4x2 trucks (four GS, two FFW, two water, one office), and ten 3ton 4x2 GS lorries.

The fighting portion of a squadron HQ included a two-seater 4x2 car and a 5cwt 4x4 car and two 3ton 4x2 GS lorries along with the armoured cars. The admin portion had four 15cwt 4x2 trucks (two FFW, two water) and seven 3ton 4x2 GS lorries.

The final Middle East pattern armoured car regiment (War Establishment VI/554/3, effective 19 April 1943) came in April 1943, shortly before the end of the fighting in Tunisia. However, the organization and personnel strength are identical with the earlier war establishment. There are still 58 armoured cars and no scout cars. The overall vehicle count is unchanged. Absent some changes in ranks or trades, it is not clear why this war establishment was issued.

ARMOURED CAR REGIMENT 1943

The final wartime establishment for armoured car regiments came the end of November 1943. By this point, armoured car regiments had returned to their role as GHQ units and all were organized with four squadrons; the squadrons were larger and more varied than the 1942 patterns. The complete war establishment can be found in Appendix 8.

War establishment III/236/2, effective 30 November 1943

	Officers/Men	Equipment
RHQ	5/22	3 armoured cars
HQ Squadron	6/125	
▶ Squadron HQ	2/4	
▶ AA Trp	-/20	5 AA armoured cars
▶ Intercomm Trp	1/25	13 scout cars
▶ Admin Trp	3/75	
Squadron x4	11/134	
▶ Squadron HQ	4/61	4 armoured cars, 1 scout car
▶ Trp x5	1/9	2 armoured cars, 2 scout car
▶ Support Trp	1/19	3 15cwt trucks, 1 scout car
▶ Heavy Trp	1/9	2 armoured cars, 1 scout car

This regiment had 67 armoured cars, plus the five AA armoured cars, and 65 scout cars. Its personnel included 55 officers and 683 other ranks, for an aggregate of 738. The attachments were little different than before: one officer RAMC and 28 other ranks (four REME and 24 ACC). Total strength, then, was 767 all ranks.

RHQ and the HQ Squadron are generally similar to prior versions, with the addition of an AA troop. As in the case with armoured regiments, the AA troop did not survive the summer of 1944.

The big difference between the 1942 and 1943 versions of the four-squadron regiment lies in the armoured car squadron itself. The five troops are now a mixture of two armoured and two scout cars. New is the support troop, with infantry (sergeant and 14 troopers) along with the subaltern and four drivers. This is basically a rifle section from a motor battalion. The 15cwt trucks would be replaced by White scout cars or, in some cases, M5 halftracks. The heavy troop was intended to have the AEC III armoured car with its 75mm gun. Units in the Mediterranean had the T12 halftrack (an M3 halftrack variant with a 75mm gun mounted) until the barrels wore out during 1944. Some regiments grouped the heavy troops into a provisional battery during operations.

Armoured Reconnaissance Regiments

In 1943 the Army decided that armoured car regiments would become GHQ (normally corps) troops, and that a distinctive armoured recce regiment would be established for armoured divisions. The first war establishment was issued in April 1943. However, the resulting units were not deemed satisfactory and a revised establishment was published in November of that year.

ARMOURED RECCE REGIMENT

The first armoured recce regiment had a mix of tank and carrier troops in its squadrons.

War establishment ?, effective 13 April 1943

	Officers/Men	Equipment
RHQ	6/44	4 cruiser tanks, 8 AA tanks, 1 carrier
HQ Squadron	6/141	
▶ Squadron HQ	2/4	
▶ Recce Trp	2/22	12 scout cars
▶ Intercomm Trp	-/14	7 scout cars
▶ Admin Trp	2/101	
Squadron *x3*	9/150	
▶ Squadron HQ	3/75	3 cruiser tanks, 1 CS cruiser tank
▶ Tank Trp *x3*	1/11	2 cruiser tanks, 1 CS cruiser tank
▶ Carrier Trp *x3*	1/14	4 carriers, 2 2" mortars

Overall the regiment had 39 officers and 635 other ranks, for an aggregate of 674 personnel. There were 24 attached personnel (medical officer RAMC, three armourers REME, and 20 ACC cooks), bringing the total to 698 personnel. The regiment had 31 cruisers, 12 CS cruisers, and eight AA tanks.

RHQ had four cruiser and eight AA tanks, along with a carrier and a 4-seater car. The small HQ of the HQ squadron had a 2-seater car and a 15cwt FFW truck. The recce and intercommunications troops both had scout cars. The admin troop had 13 motorcycles, a 2-seater car, seven 15cwt 4x2 trucks (five GS, one office, two water), two 15cwt 4x4 personnel trucks, nine 3ton 4x4 lorries (seven GS and two store), and a slave battery carrier.

Squadron HQ of the recce squadron had the conventional division into 'A' (fighting) and 'B' (administrative) portions. In addition to the four tanks, it had a 2-seater car, two 4x2 15cwt GS trucks, a 15cwt 4x4 personnel truck, eight 3ton lorries (seven GS, one store), and a slave battery carrier. The tank troops were simply the three tanks, and the carrier troops the four carriers. Each carrier troop had two 2" mortars (18 for the regiment); except for 12 Bren LMGs carried in wheeled vehicles (six in HQ squadron and two in each fighting squadron) these were the only weapons other than individual or vehicle mounted.

ARMOURED RECCE REGIMENT, TYPE B

The next, and final, war establishment for armoured recce regiments clearly used the armoured car regiment as a pattern, substituting cruiser and light tanks in the troops for armoured and scout cars. The complete war establishment can be found in Appendix 9.

War establishment II/156/1, effective 5 November 1943

	Officers/Men	Equipment
RHQ	5/14	4 cruiser tanks
HQ Squadron	9/151	
▶ Squadron HQ	3/6	
▶ AA Trp	1/19	5 AA tanks
▶ Recon Trp	2/22	12 scout cars
▶ Intercomm Trp	1/13	7 scout cars
▶ Admin Trp	2/91	
Squadron *x3*	9/157	
▶ Squadron HQ	4/72	2 cruiser tanks, 2 CS cruiser tanks, 1 scout car
▶ Trp *x5*	1/17	2 cruiser tanks, 2 light tanks

The regiment had 41 officers and 636 other ranks, for an aggregate of 677. There were 30 attached personnel (medical officer RAMC, three armourers and six vehicle mechanics AFV from the REME, and 20 ACC cooks), for a total of 707. The regiment had 40 cruiser, six CS cruiser, and 30 light tanks. It may be presumed that the AA troop and its five AA tanks were disbanded in the summer of 1944, as was the case with armoured regiments.

This type of regiment only saw service in Italy, as those in 21st Army Group had a completely different organization.

ARMOURED RECCE REGIMENT, 21st ARMY GROUP

In 21st Army Group, the armoured recce regiments were reorganized in early 1944 as regular armoured regiments under that war establishment (see above). Unlike the armoured regiments, however, they did not receive any Firefly tanks. All of the British regiments were equipped with the Cromwell tank. This is discussed in Appendix 9.

ARMOURED RECCE REGIMENT, MAY 1945

Like its armoured counterpart, the armoured recce regiment received a new establishment in May 1945. Or, more accurately, it was simply organized exactly like a May 1945 armoured regiment. This recognized what had happened in 21st Army Group: the armoured recce regiment was just a fourth armoured regiment for the division. This meant that the 1945 armoured division, like that of 1939, had no organic recce element beyond the troops in the armoured regiments.

Specialized Regiments

The British Army had a variety of specialized armoured regiments, mainly from 1943, of which only the flail, flamethrower and LVT regiments saw combat. One regiment was converted from tanks to armoured personnel carriers. Finally, the RE had a variety of assault (later armoured engineer) squadrons.

FLAIL TANK REGIMENT

War Establishment[115]

	Personnel	Equipment
RHQ	9/64	3 cruiser tanks
Squadron *x3*	6/149	
▶ Sqn HQ	3/24	1 cruiser tank, 2 CS cruiser tanks, 3 scout cars
▶ Admin Trp	-/53	
▶ Trp *x3*	1/24	5 Flail tanks

The regiment had 538 personnel (27 officers and 511 other ranks), plus attachments (RAMC officer, 8 REME other ranks, and 18 ACC cooks). There were 12 cruiser tanks for control (six normal, six CS) and 45 'cruiser tanks, special': the Sherman Crab. RHQ was simply a command element; the squadrons were expected to operate independently, administrative support was moved to that level. In addition to its tanks, RHQ had two

---

[115] The first war establishment was VIII/633/1, effective January 1944. There were two later ones: XIV/1641/1 of July 1944 and XIV/1641/2 of January 1945. This table reflects the July 1944 or January 1945 war establishment. The original is titled as 'A Regiment of 30 Armoured Brigade' while the last two are for 'A Flail Regiment'.

cars, three jeeps, three motorcycles, two halftracks, three armoured 15cwt trucks, two 15cwt GS trucks, and six 3ton lorries (five GS, one stores).

Squadron HQ had three tanks (two CS) for control, three scout cars, a jeep, three motorcycles, and an ARV. Each troop had five flail tanks; normal operation was to sweep three abreast, with two tanks in reserve for fire support or as a replacement. The admin troop had a halftrack, two 15cwt GS trucks, 17 3ton lorries (1 stores, 16 GS), and a starting and charging (slave battery) carrier.

The flail regiments were originally much larger. A squadron had four troops, each with five flail tanks, and a reserve troop with five Shermans that could mount the roller anti-mine device. RHQ and squadron HQs each had three regular Shermans. Thus a regiment had 87 tanks. In July 1944 the roller device was abandoned and the squadrons reduced to three troops of five flail tanks each.

CROCODILE [FLAMETHROWER] REGIMENT

A regiment equipped with the Crocodile flamethrower tank had the same establishment as a 1944 tank regiment. However, there were some differences in equipment.

The most obvious is the replacement of the normal Churchill tanks in the regiment's troops with Crocodiles, giving it 15 in each squadron or 45 overall. The three tanks at each squadron HQ (one normal and two close support) and the four tanks at RHQ were normal Churchills.

The other difference was the elimination of 35 3ton 4x4 GS lorries and their replacement with 50 4x4 medium tractors (the Matador Artillery Tractor). These tractors were used to tow the flamethrower trailers when not in use, and for the recovery of damaged trailers. Despite gaining 15 vehicles, the regiment received no additional personnel and thus had to come up with the 15 drivers from their existing resources. The admin troop in the HQ Squadron had five of the medium tractors, to be held in reserve as needed. Each of the three squadrons lost 10 of their 3ton GS lorries (giving them only one), and gained 15 of the medium tractors. The remaining vehicles of all types were identical with the normal tank regiment.

LVT-EQUIPPED ARMOURED REGIMENT

There was no separate war establishment for an armoured regiment converted to the amphibious role. The first such regiment was 11th RTR in October 1944. RHQ did not receive the Buffalo, and probably retained its existing Sherman tanks. The recce troop in the HQ squadron was deleted, but the intercommunications troop retained. There were three squadrons. Squadron HQ had two LVT II; each of the five troops had two LVT II and four LVT IV.[116]

The three regiments of 33rd Armoured Brigade converted in January 1945. They followed the same organization as 11th RTR, but each troop had the same type of vehicle. Squadron HQ had two LVT II, four troops had six LVT IV each, and the fifth had six LVT II. Following the Rhine crossing two of the regiments converted back to Shermans, while 4th RTR remained an LVT regiment. At that point it and 11th RTR were fully equipped with the LVT IV.

CDL-EQUIPPED ARMOURED REGIMENT

War Establishment VIII/451/2, effective February 1944

	Personnel	Equipment
RHQ	5/18	4 cruiser tanks
HQ Squadron	7/158	
▶ Recce Trp	1/19	10 carriers
▶ Intercom Trp	1/17	9 scout cars
Squadron *x3*	10/197	
▶ Sqn HQ	3/14	3 cruiser tanks, 1 scout car
▶ Trp *x3*	2/38	2 cruiser tanks, 6 Grant CDL tanks

This was a large regiment, with 42 officers and 767 other ranks (809 total). There were also the normal attached personnel: RAMC officer, eight REME armourers or mechanics, and 20 ACC cooks. There were 85 tanks: 31 Shermans and 54 Grant CDL tanks.

RHQ had four tanks and a car. The HQ squadron included a HQ and administrative troop in addition to the recce and intercommunications troops. Squadron HQ was two officers and four other ranks in a car and a jeep. The recce troop was an officer and 19 other ranks in the 10 carriers. The intercom troop was two officers and 16 other ranks in the nine scout cars. The admin troop had three officers and 118 other ranks. There were three cars, 19 motorcycles, three halftracks (for the medical officer and casualty evacuation), six 15cwt trucks (four GS, office, and water), ten 3ton lorries (kitchen, petrol, ammunition, and seven for stores, baggage, etc.), a carrier, and starting and charging carrier. Eight of the trucks/lorries carried a Bren LMG on board.

Each squadron had a small HQ—the three tanks, an ARV (REME), and a scout car. It also had an admin troop with an officer and 69 other ranks. It had a car, halftrack, three 15cwt trucks (water and two GS), 13 3ton lorries (seven ammunition, two petrol, one kitchen, and three for stores and baggage), a carrier, and starting and charging carrier.

---

[116] The US LVT 2 and LVT 4 were known as the Buffalo II and Buffalo IV in British service.

Six of the trucks/lorries carried a Bren LMG on board. Each tank troop had two Shermans and six Grant CDL tanks.

ARMOURED PERSONNEL CARRIER REGIMENT

War Establishment XIV/1643/1, effective 1 October 1944

	Personnel	Equipment
RHQ	6/47	1 scout car
Squadron *x2*	7/203	
▶ Sqn HQ	3/23	5 APCs, 1 scout car
▶ Admin Trp	-/68	
▶ Trp *x4*	1/28	12 APCs

When 49th RTR was converted from CDL tanks to Kangaroo APCs, it had only two squadrons (A and C). In February 1945, B Squadron was added to operate 24 CDL tanks (see below). In March 1945, F Squadron was added with APCs; it was identical to A and C Squadrons. The regiment (in October 1944) had 461 personnel: 20 officers and 441 other ranks, along with 15 ACC cooks. There were 106 APCs. According to 21st Army Group, a squadron could carry an infantry battalion: one company in each troop, three APCs for battalion HQ, and two in reserve. This was basically the marching infantry portion of the battalion.

The RHQ was essentially just a command element. It had a car, four jeeps, five motorcycles, four 15cwt trucks (two GS, FFW, water), and five 3ton lorries (four GS, one stores), along with the scout car. There was no HQ squadron for administrative support; since the squadrons normally operated independently, each had a full admin troop. Squadron HQ had two jeeps, six motorcycles, a scout car, and five APCs. The troops had no vehicles beyond their APCs. The admin troop had two halftracks, three 15cwt trucks (two GS, one water), and nine 3ton lorries (eight GS, one stores).

The regiment had an attached signal troop with six other ranks, a jeep, two 15cwt GS trucks with two charging generator trailers. Their LAD REME had a HQ and one section for each squadron. The HQ had an officer and 11 other ranks, with a jeep, 15cwt GS truck, and two 3ton lorries (one binned stores and one machinery). A section had 17 other ranks, with a jeep, motorcycle, 15cwt machinery truck, a 3ton lorry (binned stores) and breakdown tractor with trailer.

War Establishment XIV/1645/1, effective 1 February 1945

Squadron

| ▶ Sqn HQ | 4/49 | 1 scout car, 4 carriers |
| ▶ Trp *x6* | 1/22 | 4 Grant CDL tanks, 1 carrier |

Officially titled 'A Tank Squadron (Type B), 21st Army Group (CDL Tanks)' this was the establishment for the regiment's B Squadron. It had 191 personnel (ten officers and

181 other ranks) and 24 Grant CDL tanks. There were two REME mechanics and four ACC cooks attached. In addition to the scout car and carriers, squadron HQ had a car, a jeep, two motorcycles, a halftrack, two 15cwt GS trucks, eight 3ton lorries (one stores binned, six GS, and one kitchen), and an ARV. A troop simply consisted of the CDL tanks and carrier.

RASC 'FANTAIL' REGIMENT

Created in 1944 from RASC and RAC personnel the intended organization was a RHQ with six LVTs, three squadrons [to lift infantry] each of 38 LVTs, and two squadrons with 62 LVTs between them, one to lift two batteries of 25pdrs and the other to lift vehicles. This would have given a total of 182 LVTs. The LVTs were the Buffalo IV, called 'Fantail' in Italy.

In the event, the regiment was never completed and effectively merged with the US 755th Tank Battalion to create a composite regiment with 185 LVTs, plus another five in reserve. This had two headquarters, two 'infantry' squadrons manned by the British and one by the Americans, an 'artillery' squadron manned by the British, and British support personnel (RE, REME, RAOC).

Reconnaissance Battalions/Regiments

The recce element for infantry divisions evolved from first creation the end of 1940, becoming a mix of armoured and light recce cars and carriers in the scouting/recce troops. There were a few adaptations for special circumstances (mountain warfare, Italy, and Burma). In addition, a special liaison unit (Phantom, or GHQ Liaison Regiment as it became) was part of the Reconnaissance Corps, transferring with it to the RAC in 1944.

RECONNAISSANCE BATTALION 1941

The first war establishment for a divisional reconnaissance battalion was issued almost a month before the Royal Warrant which actually established the Reconnaissance Corps.

War Establishment II/1931/12/I, issued 11 December 1940

	Personnel	Equipment
Bn HQ	4/20	1 carrier
HQ Coy	7/211	
► Coy HQ	1/3	
► Signals Pln	1/62	
► AA Pln	1/18	4 twin Bren on 15cwt trucks
► Mortar Pln	1/19	2x3" mortars
► Atk Pln	1/32	12 Atk rifles
► Admin Pln	2/77	

Recce Coy *x3*	6/166	
▶ Coy HQ	2/19	1 carrier
▶ Recce Pln *x3*	1/36	5 light recce cars, 7 carriers
▶ Infantry Pln	1/39	

The recce battalion showed traces of an infantry battalion (in its HQ company) and the old divisional cavalry regiments, with a mixture of light recce cars and carriers in place of light tanks and carriers. Unlike the cavalry regiment, however, each company included a platoon of infantry.

This new type of battalion had 29 officers and 732 other ranks, for a total of 761 personnel. One officer (RAMC) and 8 other ranks (RAOC) were attached, for a grand total of 770 personnel.

There were 45 light recce cars[117] and 67 carriers (all but one carrier found in the recce squadrons). The unit's anti-tank capability was essentially non-existent: 12 of the .55" anti-tank rifles in an Atk platoon, and another 36 found on the light recce cars and carriers of the recce companies. Anti-aircraft capability was little better: four twin Bren guns in AA mounts on trucks. There were an additional 126 Bren guns, but all other than the 12 in the infantry platoons would have been vehicle mounted as well. There were also 18 2" mortars among the recce companies.

Battalion HQ had a carrier (for the CO) and four-seater car (2nd in command) along with three 15cwt GS trucks and seven motorcycles: one for the provost sergeant and the remainder for an intelligence sergeant and intelligence privates.

The small HQ for the HQ company had four personnel and a four-seater car. The signals platoon had five 15cwt trucks (one GS and four FFW) and 23 motorcycles (19 for orderlies). The admin platoon had 18 15cwt trucks (two for water) and six 3ton lorries, along with three motorcycles.

The AA platoon had four 15cwt trucks with the twin Bren AAMG and three motorcycles.

The mortar platoon had two 15cwt trucks to carry the two 3" mortars and their personnel, along with two more 15cwt trucks (one for a range taker and driver) and two motorcycles.

---

[117] The new battalions began with Beaverettes, possibly surplus to the motor MG regiments and other armoured units finally receiving AFVs; not until January 1942 did a recce unit actually receive a light recce car.

The Atk platoon had a 15cwt truck and three motorcycles, with three more 15 cwt trucks to carry the personnel handling the Atk rifles.

In the recce company, the company HQ had a carrier, four-seater car, and five 15cwt trucks, plus a motorcycle. The recce (also called scout) platoon had a HQ (carrier and two motorcycles), an armoured recce section (five light recce cars), and two carrier sections (each three carriers). The infantry platoon had a HQ (two 15cwt trucks and three motorcycles) and four sections (each a 15cwt truck and eight personnel).

RECONNAISSANCE REGIMENT 1942 (I)

The next war establishment, in March 1942 amounted to little more than a change in unit titles (regiment, squadron, troop instead of battalion, company, platoon), although the Atk troop replaced the completely ineffective Atk rifle with the marginally more effective 2pdr Atk gun.

War Establishment II/12/2, effective 23 March 1942

	Personnel	Equipment
RHQ	6/26	3 light recce cars
HQ Squadron	8/205	
▶ Squadron HQ	2/3	
▶ Signals Trp	1/39	
▶ AA Trp	0/18	4 twin Bren AAMG
▶ Mortar Trp	1/44	6 3" mortars, 7 mortar carriers
▶ Atk Trp	2/46	1 LR car, 6 2pdr Atk guns portée
▶ Admin Trp	2/55	
Recce Squadron x3	9/174	
▶ Squadron HQ	2/26	1 light recce car
▶ Recce Trp x3	2/36	2 armoured cars, 3 LR cars, 7 carriers
▶ Assault Trp	1/40	

The new regiment (due largely to changes in the Atk and mortar troops) was a little larger than the old battalion, with 40 officers and 753 other ranks, an aggregate of 793. Attachments were the expected one RAMC officer and 23 other ranks (RAOC and ACC), for an overall total of 817 personnel.

The recce regiment establishment had 52 light recce cars; however, this seemed to have changed unofficially to 18 armoured cars and 34 light recce cars. There were 63 universal carriers and seven 3" mortar carriers. The number of 3" mortars increased to six, and there were still 18 2" mortars contained in the recce squadrons. The 68 Atk rifles remaining were presumably all vehicle mounted, and of the 133 Bren guns, all but 12 were presumably vehicle mounted as well. AA defence was still the four twin Bren AAMG on trucks. The 2pdr Atk guns were on 30cwt Atk portée lorries.[118]

RHQ now had three light recce cars (CO, 2nd in command, intelligence officer), along with a four-seater car and three 15cwt 4x4 trucks. The seven motorcycles carried the provost sergeant along with the intelligence sergeant and his troopers.

HQ of the HQ squadron had a four-seater car and a motorcycle. The signal troop had six 15cwt trucks (five FFW and one GS), plus 23 motorcycles (21 for orderlies). The admin troop continued to have most of the support vehicles: 20 15cwt trucks (nine 4x4, two personnel, seven GS, and two water trucks), six 3ton GS lorries, and three motorcycles.

The AA troop (no longer containing an officer) still had four 15cwt trucks as mounts for the twin Brens, along with two motorcycles.

The mortar troop now had six 3" mortar carriers to transport the mortars, along with an additional 3" mortar carrier (for the troop commander), three 4x4 15cwt trucks (one for the range taker), and three motorcycles.

The Atk troop had six 30cwt lorries portée, each with a 2pdr Atk gun, along with a light recce car (for the troop commander), two 4x4 15cwt trucks, and four motorcycles.

In the recce squadron, the HQ had a light recce car (squadron commander), four-seater car, five 15cwt trucks (one 4x4, one personnel, three GS), and a motorcycle. The recce troops (also known as scout troops) had a small troop HQ (carrier and two motorcycles), recce section with five light recce cars (later two armoured cars and three light recce cars), and two carrier sections (each three carriers; each section had a 2" mortar). The assault troop was basically an infantry platoon: troop HQ (two 15cwt 4x4 trucks, combination motorcycle and two solo motorcycles) and four sections (each a 15cwt truck and eight men).

RECONNAISSANCE REGIMENT 1942 (II)

A new war establishment for the regiment, II/251/1, became effective 5 August 1942. This was basically similar to the earlier unit, but with more 2pdr Atk guns and some other changes.

---

[118] Portée indicates that the weapon is mounted on the truck, aimed towards the rear. This was a common method of carrying (in lieu of towing) the weapon, and in North Africa it became common to reinforce the truck bed and leave the gun on the truck, with the trail folded down for full traverse.

	Personnel	Equipment
RHQ	5/21	3 light recce cars
HQ Squadron	9/201	
▶ Squadron HQ	2/4	
▶ Signals Trp	1/39	
▶ AA Trp	0/9	2 AAMG
▶ Mortar Trp	1/43	6 3" mortars, 6 mortar carriers
▶ Atk Trp	2/77	12 2pdr Atk guns
▶ Admin Trp	3/37	
Recce Squadron *x3*	9/177	
▶ Squadron HQ	2/34	1 light recce car
▶ Recce Trp *x3*	2/36	2 armoured cars, 3 LR cars, 7 carriers
▶ Assault Trp	1/40	

The revised regiment had the same strength as the earlier one: 40 officers and 753 other ranks, an aggregate of 793. Attached were one officer (RAMC) and 23 other ranks (RAOC, REME, and ACC).[119] The grand total remained at 817 personnel.

The armoured recce component was virtually unchanged: 18 armoured cars (now officially on establishment) and 33 light recce cars. The AA troop was reduced to two twin Brens, slated to change to two 20mm AA guns mounted on trucks. The 2pdr Atk guns were increased to 12, all now towed. While the establishment did not change until the end of 1943, regiments would have begun to introduce 6pdr guns as they became available, probably with some reduction. The mortars (six 3" and 18 2") were unchanged.

RHQ remained unchanged, with three light recce cars (CO, 2nd in command, intelligence officer), along with a 4-seater car and 3 15cwt 4x4 trucks. The seven motorcycles carried the provost sergeant along with the intelligence sergeant and his troopers.

Squadron HQ of the HQ Squadron now had a jeep (5cwt 4x4 car) and a 4-seater car. The signal troop remained unchanged from before: six 15cwt trucks (five FFW and one GS), plus 23 motorcycles (21 for orderlies). The admin troop was reduced in personnel and vehicles. The new one had one jeep, three motorcycles, four 15cwt trucks (one water) and three 3ton lorries.

The reduced AA troop had two 15cwt trucks (each with an AA LMG or 20mm AA gun) and a motorcycle.

---

[119] The new REME took over the armourers and motor vehicle fitters from the RAOC, leaving only the shoemaker from that Corps.

The mortar troop had a jeep for the troop commander and three sections, each with two 3" mortar carriers (and mortars), a 15cwt 4x4 truck and a motorcycle.

The Atk troop had a jeep (troop commander) and two motorcycles, with three sections, each containing four Lloyd carriers to tow the 2pdr Atk guns, a 15cwt 4x4 truck and a motorcycle.[120]

The recce squadron had a somewhat larger squadron HQ. There was still one light recce car (squadron commander), plus a jeep, motorcycle, eight 15cwt trucks, and a 3ton lorry with a water trailer.

The recce troops (also known as scout troops)were the same: a small troop HQ (carrier and two motorcycles), recce section with 2 armoured cars (one with the troop commander) and three light recce cars, and two carrier sections (each three carriers; each section had a 2" mortar).

The assault troop HQ gave up one 15cwt 4x4 truck for a jeep and added a motorcycle; the four sections remained a 15cwt truck and eight men each.

RECONNAISSANCE REGIMENT 1943

The final version of the infantry division recce regiment was issued in December 1943, just before the absorption into the Royal Armoured Corps. The basic structure of the regiment remained unchanged from 1942, although the AA troop disappeared and more modern weapons (6pdr Atk gun and PIATs) were introduced along with some other changes. The recce troops in the recce squadron was now designated as scout troops. There were some changes made in 1944 and 1945. The full version of this war establishment is contained in Appendix 10.

War Establishment II/251/2, effective 17 December 1943

	Personnel	Equipment
RHQ	5/27	1 armoured car, 2 light recce cars
HQ Squadron	9/173	
▶ Squadron HQ	2/8	1 light recce car
▶ Signals Trp	1/23	
▶ Mortar Trp	1/40	6 carriers, 6 3" mortars
▶ Atk Bty	3/64	12 Lloyd carriers, 8 6pdr Atk guns
▶ Admin Trp	2/38	

---

[120] This may reflect North Africa, since David Hughes et al, *The British Armies in World War Two*, Vol Two, p. 122 indicate that the normal organization was two troops in the Atk battery, and that only some regiments in 1942 had a third troop. While they don't specify a location, North Africa is the logical place for a temporary change in 1942, not unlike the change in motor battalions, which replaced one of their motor companies with an Atk company.

Recce Squadron *x3*   9/185
- ▶ Squadron HQ   2/36   1 light recce car
- ▶ Scout Trp *x3*   2/37   3 armoured cars, 2 LR cars, 7 carriers
- ▶ Assault Trp   1/38

The regiment had 41 officers and 755 other ranks, for an aggregate of 796 personnel—an increase of three. Attached were a medical officer RAMC, four armourers REME, a shoemaker RAOC, 15 cooks ACC; these 21brought the aggregate to 817 personnel.

The regiment had 28 armoured cars and 24 light recce cars, an increase in the former and reduction in the latter, and they were rearranged somewhat within the components. Antitank guns were reduced to 8, but these were now 6pdrs, and the regiment gained 36 PIATs. There were still six 3" mortars, and 2" mortars increased to 25.

The PIATs were distributed as follows: two at RHQ, three in the mortar troop, four in the admin troop; two in the HQ of each recce squadron, one in each carrier section of the scout troops, and one in the HQ of the assault troop. For the 2" mortars, there were two with each Atk troop, one in each carrier section of the scout troops, and one in the HQ of the assault troop.

INDEPENDENT RECONNAISSANCE SQUADRON

In 1940, some divisions began to organize provisional brigade recce groups. In many cases, these would be formed from personnel of the brigade Atk company who—if they had served in France—would have lost all of their Atk guns. One example shows a small unit (67 personnel), with four platoons carried in motorcycles with sidecars.[121] An alternative organization was a company with three platoons, which could include some mix of the following: Atk platoon (six carriers and three 2pdr Atk guns), a tank-hunter platoon (three sections on bicycles with Atk rifles and Molotov Cocktails), a recce platoon (three sections in light trucks or carriers), or a motorcycle platoon (three sections each with three combination motorcycles).[122] These units all disappeared in early 1941 as the Recce Corps was established.

---

[121] David Hughes et al, *The British Armies in World War Two*, Vol Two, p. 120 provides the only example I am familiar with, although they use cavalry designations (squadron and troop) which seems unlikely. Richard Doherty's history of the Recce Corps, refers to the 1940 units as 'brigade reconnaissance groups' (*Only the Enemy in Front*, p. 4), the same term used by J.B.M. Frederick in *Lineage Book of British Land Forces*, p. 11.

[122] David Hughes et al, *The British Armies in World War Two*, Vol Two, p. 121. It is not entirely clear how this is distinguished from the unit described on the prior page, although this is explicitly labeled as a recce company formed from a brigade Atk company.

It can be presumed that an independent recce company in 1941 was much like the company in the 1941 recce battalion, with some additional personnel, support weapons, and admin vehicles. War establishment II/251/1 effective 5 August 1942 is for an independent recce squadron.

- ▶ Squadron HQ   5/51   3 light recce cars
- ▶ Support Trp   1/39   2 3" mortars, 4 2pdt Atk guns
- ▶ Scout Trp *x3*   2/36   2 armoured cars, 3 LR cars, 7 carriers
- ▶ Assault Trp   1/38

The independent squadron had 13 officers and 222 other ranks, for an aggregate of 235 personnel. (Compared to 186 in the squadron of a recce regiment.) There were 12 other ranks attached (RAMC, RAOC and ACC), giving a grand total of 247.

There were six armoured cars and 12 light recce cars, along with 21 universal carriers, two mortar carriers (with 3" mortars), and four Lloyd carriers (for towing 2pdr Atk guns). The squadron HQ was similar to the regimental one, albeit with two more light recce cars and additional vehicles and personnel to support the unit. The support troop had a very small HQ (one officer and one other rank, with a jeep), a mortar section (the two 3" mortars) and an Atk section (the four 2pdr Atk guns). The scout troop was identical with that in regimented squadrons (recce section and two carrier sections), as was the assault troop.

MOUNTAIN RECCE REGIMENT

The 52nd (Lowland) Infantry Division was converted in May 1942 as a mountain division. As part of this, its recce regiment was given a special organization.[123]

While the exact date of conversion is unclear, the 52nd Regiment Recce Corps was reorganized as follows:
- HQ Squadron contained a mortar troop (six 3" mortars and three PIAT) and two anti-tank troops (each with four 6pdr Atk guns and four 2" mortars).
- The two (three?) recce squadrons each had a HQ troop (two PIAT), two scout troops (HQ section with a PIAT and 2" mortar and four sections, each nine men in three carriers) and an assault troop (HQ with a 2" mortar and four sections of nine men and a truck each).
- A tank squadron, with HQ troop (four Valentine infantry tanks) and four troops, each of three Valentines.

---

[123] David Hughes et al, *The British Armies in World War Two*, Vol Three, pp 76-77 and 110 show three recce squadrons. The Trux Models Publication 'WE 2110 Reconnaissance Regiment' states that the mountain regiment had only two recce squadrons plus the tank squadron.

Command and support were probably similar to a normal regiment. The tank squadron is striking; as Hughes et al put it, 'Not exactly what one would associate with a mountain division'.

However, there is a 1943 war establishment for a mountain division recce regiment, which may have superseded the earlier organization shown above.

War Establishment VIII/534/1, effective 7 September 1943

	Personnel	Equipment
RHQ	4/31	3 scout cars
HQ Squadron	9/182	
▶ Squadron HQ	2/10	1 scout car
▶ Signals Trp	1/28	
▶ Mortar Trp	1/40	6x3" mortars, 6 mortar carriers
▶ Atk Trp x2	1/31	4x6pdr Atk gun, 6 Loyd carriers
▶ Admin Trp	3/42	
Recce Squadron x3	7/155	
▶ Squadron HQ	2/40	1 scout car
▶ Scout Trp x2	2/37	5 scout cars, 7 carriers
▶ Assault Trp	1/41	

Overall, the regiment had 34 officers and 678 other ranks, for a total of 712 personnel. Attached were a medical officer AMC, three armourers REME, a shoemaker RAOC, six cooks ACC. Transport was restricted to 15cwt GS trucks.

In the recce squadron, the scout troops had a recce section (five scout cars) and two scout sections (each with three carriers). The assault troop had a jeep and two 15cwt 4x4 trucks, and four sections of seven men each in a 15cwt 4x4 truck.

As it happened, the division never led an invasion of Norway. It ceased being a mountain division in June 1944, and trained for airlanding operations in August and September. It finally landed in NW Europe in October 1944, serving as a conventional infantry division.

The recce regiment reorganized in August 1944 when it was made part of 157th Infantry Brigade Group, which went to NW Europe the beginning of September, rejoining the division that October. It lacked both armoured cars and light recce cars and had no halftracks in lieu of any 15cwt 4x4 trucks. The three recce squadrons had three scout troops—each with a HQ (Daimler scout car, universal carrier and two motorcycles with eight personnel); Recce Section (four Daimler scout cars and eight personnel), and two carrier sections (each three carriers and six personnel)—as well as an assault troop (five 15cwt 4x4 trucks and a motorcycle with 39 personnel). The regiment resumed normal organization in February 1945 when it absorbed 61st Recce Regiment RAC.

ITALY

British divisions went to Italy with their recce regiments organized according to the normal 1942 or 1943 war establishments. Hughes et al[124] indicate that a support battery with two troops of T12 halftracks (the M3 variant mounting a 75mm gun) was added by September 1944. They also indicate use of the Greyhound armoured car in lieu of Daimlers or Humbers.

In view of the often mountainous terrain in Italy, some regiments at least reorganized their recce squadrons.[125]

▶ Squadron HQ	42	2 armoured cars
▶ Armoured Car Trp	16	4 armoured cars
▶ Carrier Trp *x2*	12	4 carriers
▶ Jeep Trp	12	
▶ Assault Trp	36	1 carrier, 4 White scout cars

Overall strength of the squadron is 130 personnel. Note the elimination of light recce cars entirely, with armoured cars at squadron HQ (for the CO and 2nd in command) and a separate troop of four vehicles. The total for squadron HQ appears from the detailed diagram to include attached REME/RIEME personnel (seven personnel in an M3 halftrack modified as a recovery vehicle), so the basic squadron may have been only 123 personnel. Other vehicles at HQ include two jeeps, three 15cwt trucks, a water truck, and three 3ton lorries. Both jeeps had Bren guns, and there were one PIAT and two more Bren guns among the support vehicles.

The armoured car troop is unremarkable, as are the carrier troops. Each of the latter included at least one PIAT (Hughes et al) and perhaps two (Platt). The jeep troop was mainly for liaison and communication. The Indian Army version had 12 men and no indication of weapons other than side arms; Hughes et al show 15 men and six jeeps, with three Bren guns. The assault troop is standard, with the troop commander in a carrier (with a PIAT) and four rifle sections, each eight men in a White scout car. Each section included a 2" mortar and a PIAT (per Hughes et al; Platt shows 2" mortars in only two of the vehicles).

---

[124] *The British Armies in World War Two*, Vol Two, p 125.

[125] The basic scheme is set out by Hughes et al (see prior footnote). However, it dovetails almost exactly with a detailed look at the recce squadron of an Indian infantry division in Italy, 1944, so that I have used that as a guide as well. See William E. Platz, 'The Indian Army Reconnaissance Squadron of 1944', *AFV G-2*, Vol 4, No 2 (February 1973), pp. 25-27+. I have not tried to differentiate between officers and other ranks, given the differences between the British and Indian armies.

BURMA

After moving to India the 2nd Infantry Division twice reorganized its recce regiment.[126] In (late?) 1943 the division was supposed to be a tropical assault division. 2nd Recce Regiment's 'B' Squadron was detached to serve a special liaison role (a la Phantom in Europe); 'A' and 'C' Squadrons received Alligator amphibious vehicles;[127] and a new 'D' Squadron was formed from the assault troops of 'A' and 'C' Squadrons and a new troop from personnel of the Atk battery, which was reduced in strength. The regiment never served with this organization.

By April 1944, it had an organization more suitable for combat in Burma.
- The HQ Squadron contained a mortar platoon (six 3" mortars) and only a single troop in the Atk battery (four 6pdr Atk guns).
- Three recce squadrons each had a HQ Troop (with a single light recce car), an infantry troop (carrier section with a 2" mortar and seven carriers, and two infantry sections of eight men each), and an assault troop (three sections of eight men each)
- A fourth recce squadron had a HQ Troop (with a single light recce car) and three assault troops (each with three sections of eight men).

Basically, then, it was an understrength infantry battalion.

PHANTOM (21st ARMY GROUP)

The War Establishment for the GHQ Liaison Regiment was III/253/I with an effective date of 27 August 1943. It was updated and amended at various times but never re-issued. The basic regiment was organized to work with 21st Army Group and its two armies. Two other squadrons were tasked to work with airborne forces (First Allied Airborne Army) and with the SAS. The nominal strength of the regiment (excluding the airborne and SAS squadrons) was 60 officers and 363 other ranks, for an aggregate of 423. In addition, there were 8 officers and 200 other ranks from the Royal Corps of Signals, along with 14 cooks from the ACC. This gave the regiment 645 personnel all told. However, since there was some flexibility in actual organization from time to time, the war establishment should be taken more as suggestive than as fixed.

Regimental Headquarters. This has a HQ element (3 officers and 7 other ranks: 10 personnel), an operations and intelligence troop (5 officers and 18 other ranks: 23 personnel), an administrative troop (27 other ranks), and a signals troop (3 officers and 37 other ranks from the Royal Signals plus 10 extra troopers and an ACC cook: 51

---

[126] The only place I have seen this set out is in David Hughes et al, *The British Armies in World War Two*, Vol Two, pp 71 and 126.

[127] The Alligator was the US LVT 2 or 4, known as Buffalo in NW Europe and Fantail in Italy.

personnel). All told: 11 officers and 100 other ranks; 111 aggregate. There were a variety of motorcycles, cars, jeeps, and trucks/lorries along with two White scout cars in the operations and intelligence troop.

Army Squadron. Each army squadron had an overall command and control organization similar to that of regimental HQ: squadron HQ (11 officers and 83 other ranks: 94 personnel), an operations and intelligence troop (8 officers and 19 other ranks: 27 aggregate), an administrative troop (1 officer, 17 other ranks and a cook: 19aggregate), and a signals troop (2 officers and 54 other ranks from the Royal Signals plus 3 other personnel and 2 cooks: 61 aggregate). This command element had 22 officers and 179 other ranks all told, for a grand aggregate of 201. It had motorcycles, jeeps, cars, and a variety of trucks/lorries.

The operating element of the squadron were its patrols, which came in three types. A *captain's patrol* had 2 officers and 10 other ranks, mounted in a jeep, 15cwt 4x4 armoured truck (the White scout car), a 15cwt FFW truck, and 2 motorcycles. A captain's patrol was assigned to a corps headquarters. Assigned to a divisional headquarters (as needed) was a *subaltern's patrol*.[128] This had an officer and 6 other ranks, in a jeep, White scout car, and 2 motorcycles. Finally there were *J patrols*, assigned to armoured divisions. Each of these had 3 officers and 42 other ranks (including 12 from the Royal Signals and a cook). This patrol had 3 cars, 3 jeeps, 3 15cwt 4x4 trucks (Whites?), 5 15cwt FFW trucks, 3 3ton Wireless I lorries and 6 motorcycles.

The number of patrols per squadron was variable. The normal number was nine plus two J patrols, but additional patrols could be formed as needed from headquarters and depot personnel, or borrowed from the other army squadron.

Army Group Squadron. One squadron kept its headquarters with HQ 21st Army Group, keeping track of confirmed information forwarded by other Phantom units. Its patrols were initially with each US corps under the army group's command, with a captain's patrol at First US Army's HQ. Its squadron HQ had 2 officers and 49 other ranks, plus 3 ACC cooks, and one officer and 22 other ranks from the Royal Signals; an aggregate of 3 officers and 74 other ranks (77 personnel). As with similar units, it had a jeep and a variety of 15cwt and 3ton vehicles, including one White scout car.

First Allied Airborne Army squadron. This squadron had a very small HQ of 2 officers and 6 other ranks. Each airborne division had a patrol of 6 other ranks with an airborne signals jeep, lightweight trailer, and lightweight motorcycle.[129]

---

[128] Subaltern's and J patrols worked with divisions in action and did not need to be with a division in reserve, so they were shifted as needed and not permanently attached to a particular division.
[129] When formed, the squadron had patrols with 1st Airborne Division, 82nd and 101st US Airborne Divisions, and 52nd (Lowland) Infantry Division which was changing from mountain to

I have seen no details for F Squadron (SAS liaison). At least initially its patrols were intended to operate on foot, with a jeep patrol landed as soon as possible. These went into France beginning on D+2.

Airborne Reconnaissance Units

Until January 1944, there were no airborne recce units larger than a squadron. In that month, a regiment was formed for 6th Airborne Division. However, the other (1st) airborne division never had more than a squadron assigned.

AIRBORNE RECONNAISSANCE SQUADRONS

The first unit was the 1942 **airlanding reconnaissance squadron**, a lightly armed organization mounted on motorcycles and jeeps.

War Establishment XI/151/I, effective 13 May 1942

	Personnel	Equipment
Sqn HQ	6/34	5 Jeeps with MMG
Scout Trp *x4*	4/48	8 Jeeps with MMG, 3" mortar
Admin Section	-/10	2 unarmed Jeeps

The squadron had 199 personnel (22 officers and 177 other ranks). Of these, 15 were glider pilots carried in the HQ strength. There were also a sergeant armourer REME, corporal medical orderly and three nursing orderlies RAMC, and six cooks ACC attached to the admin section. Except for the two in the admin section, every jeep had a MMG mounted on it.[130] The jeeps in squadron HQ also carried two Bren LMG and two Atk rifles. There were 11 combination and 15 solo motorcycles. The admin section had five motorcycles in addition to its jeeps.

The scout troops had a small HQ (officer and nine other ranks), mortar detachment (five other ranks), and three scout sections (each an officer and eight other ranks). In addition to the jeeps, there were one combination and five solo motorcycles in HQ, one in the mortar detachment, and three in each scout section. The mortar detachment also had an Atk rifle. The jeeps in the scout sections each had a Bren LMG and one carried an Atk rifle.

---

an airportable role. It appears to have later created a patrol of 17th US Airborne Division as well. (possibly by using that from the 52nd when it resumed its role as a conventional infantry division).

[130] The medium MGs, all jeep-mounted, were (or soon became) Vickers 'K' guns. These were originally weapons for open cockpit aircraft, and had a top-mounted 96-round magazine. They were not the Vickers .303 Mk I medium MG.

The 1943 **airlanding reconnaissance squadron** was a revised but similar version of the earlier unit. A major change was the elimination of glider pilots and motorcycles for their use. In addition, all jeeps now were now armed with the Vickers MMG.[131]

War Establishment I/261/2, effective 10 March 1943

	Personnel	Equipment
Sqn HQ	7/39	11 jeeps
Scout Trp *x4*	4/42	5 jeeps, 3" mortar

The new squadron had 35 officers and 207 other ranks (242 personnel). The sergeant armourer REME, corporal medical orderly and three nursing orderlies RAMC, and six cooks ACC were still attached. Squadron HQ incorporated the former admin section. In addition to the jeeps, there were two combination and 21 solo motorcycles. The jeeps also carried two Bren LMGs and two Atk rifles.

The four scout troops had a small HQ (officer and 15 other ranks, with two jeeps, a combination motorcycle and six solo motorcycles) and four sections (each officer, nine other ranks, single jeep, and six motorcycles). Troop HQ had a Bren LMG and Atk rifle in one jeep, and a Bren LMG and 3" mortar in the other. The jeep in each section also carried a Bren LMG and Atk rifle.

The next version was the 1944 **airborne reconnaissance squadron**. This was found only in 1st Airborne Division.

War Establishment I/261/3, effective 15 March 1944

	Personnel	Equipment
Sqn HQ	6/15	3 jeeps
HQ Trp	2/38	9 jeeps
Recce Trp *x3*	4/34	8 jeeps, 3x2" mortars
Support Trp	1/25	5 jeeps, 4x3" mortars

The squadron had 201 personnel (21 officers and 180 other ranks). There were also 11 attached personnel: medical and three nursing orderlies RAMC, one armourer REME, and six ACC cooks. All of the 41 jeeps were shown with the Vickers MMG.

Squadron HQ was now purely a command element, with its three jeeps and nine solo motorcycles. Each jeep also had a Bren LMG.

The new HQ troop had a small command element (officer and three other ranks in a jeep). There was an intercommunications section with six motorcyclists. The admin section had an airborne portion (officer and 20 other ranks, eight jeeps) and a non-

---

[131] Actually, the version of the war establishment available does not show any MMGs at all, but it is impossible to believe that the unit simply removed all of the 'K' guns and had unarmed jeeps.

airborne portion (nine personnel, four-seater 4x2 car and two 3ton 4x4 GS lorries). The RAMC personnel were attached to the airborne portion, the cooks to the non-airborne. There were two Bren LMGs in the airborne portion and a PIAT in the HQ.

There were now three recce troops. Each had a HQ (officer and seven other ranks) with two jeeps and three sections (each an officer and nine other ranks) with two jeeps. The HQ jeeps had two Bren LMGs and a PIAT. Each section had four Bren LMGs and a 2" mortar.

The support troop was a new unit. Troop HQ (one officer and four other ranks) had two motorcycles and a jeep. The jeep carried a Bren LMG and PIAT. There were four sections, each five other ranks with a jeep and a mortar trailer. Each section had a Bren LMG and a 3" mortar.

Overall, this squadron had 53 Bren LMG and 41 Vickers ['K'] MMGs, along with five PIATs, nine 2" mortars and four 3" mortars. Unlike the earlier variants, motorcycles had virtually disappeared and this was now a jeep-mounted force.

The final version was the 1945 **airborne reconnaissance squadron** (War Establishment I/261/4, effective 15 March 1945) still found only in the rebuilding 1st Airborne Division. There does not appear to be any difference at all in the organization, strength or armament between this and the 1944 establishment.

While not strictly speaking recce, this is a logical place for the **Airborne Light Tank Squadron**. The first war establishment was in 1942.

War Establishment X/26/1, effective 13 April 1942

	Personnel	Equipment
Sqn HQ	4/8	4 light tanks
Intercomm Trp	1/8	
Admin Trp—Abn	-/19	
--Non Abn	-/9	
Tank Trp *x5*	1/8	3 light tanks

The squadron had 94 personnel (ten officers and 84 other ranks), along with a medical officer RAMC and four cooks ACC. It also operated with three signalmen attached from airborne divisional signals. There were 19 light tanks. The only weapons in the unit were small arms (rifles, pistols, machine carbines).

The intercommunications troop had a 5cwt FWD car and seven motorcycles. The airborne portion of the admin troop had 11 5cwt FWD cars. The non-airborne portion lacked any vehicles. The medical officer and attached signalers were with the airborne portion, the cooks with non-airborne.

This was followed by a 1943 war establishment, with the same basic structure and still 19 light tanks.

War Establishment I/136/2, effective 17 March 1943

	Personnel	Equipment
Sqn HQ	4/7	4 light tanks
Intercomm Trp	1/8	
Admin Trp—Abn	-/49	
--Non Abn	-/18	
Tank Trp *x5*	1/8	3 light tanks

The revised squadron was larger: ten officers and 122 other ranks (132 total). The medical officer and now five cooks are attached; no attached signalmen are in the establishment.

The intercommunications troop had seven motorcycles and a jeep (or car, 5cwt, 4x4). The airborne portion of the admin troop had 11 jeeps. The non-airborne portion now came with a two-seater 4x2 car, two 15cwt 4x2 GS trucks, two 3ton 4x2 GS lorries, and a 3ton 4x2 breakdown lorry. The admin troop had three Bren LMGs (one in the non-airborne portion) and an Atk rifle.

AIRBORNE ARMOURED RECONNAISSANCE REGIMENT

When the airborne armoured reconnaissance regiment was created in January 1944, it was little more than a combination of 6th Airborne Division's airlanding recce squadron and the airborne light tank squadron.[132] Total strength was only 355 (38 officers and 317 other ranks).

Regimental HQ had two of the CS Tetrarch light tanks. HQ Squadron included medical, signals and administrative detachments. In addition, there were two MG troops (each of four Vickers medium MGs on jeeps) and a troop of two 3" mortars mounted on universal carriers. Finally, there was an assault troop of around 20 men on motorcycles.

The light tank ('A') squadron had four Tetrarchs (two CS) at HQ and five troops of three (possibly four) Tetrarchs. The recce ('B') squadron had five troops, each with 11 men, a jeep, a universal carrier, and five or six motorcycles. Squadron HQ probably had a jeep and universal carrier as well as motorcycles.

There was a major reorganization in October 1944 and a very different type of airborne armoured recce regiment emerged, eliminating separate tank and recce squadrons among other changes. The complete war establishment is given in Appendix 11.

---

[132] Here again, I am following Flint (p 88) in the absence of a copy of the actual war establishment.

War Establishment I/138/I, effective 18 October 1944

	Personnel		Equipment
RHQ	6/15		2 scout cars
HQ Sqn	7/111		
▶ Sqn HQ		1/2	
▶ Intercomm Trp		-/10	
▶ Admin Trp		3/34	
▶ Seaborne party		3/65	8 cruiser tanks
Squadron x2	6/58		
▶ Sqn HQ		1/14	2 scout cars
▶ Heavy Trp		1/11	4 light tanks
▶ Trp x3		1/11	2 scout cars, 2 carriers, 2 2" mortars
Support Sqn	6/74		
▶ Sqn HQ		2/7	1 scout car
▶ MMG Trp x2		1/15	4 MG carriers, 4 MMG
▶ Mortar Trp		1/18	4 4.2" mortars
▶ Infantry Spt Trp		1/19	1 scout car

The regiment had 31 officers and 316 other ranks (347 aggregate). The 11 attached personnel (RAMC officer, two REME armourers and eight ACC cooks) brought overall strength to 358.

The number of tanks was greatly reduced, with a single troop of four Locust tanks in each of the recce squadrons. The MG-armed jeeps were gone as well, with the personnel now mounted in scout cars and carriers. A new support squadron was assigned with eight actual MMGs mounted on carriers, and four 4.2" mortars carried in trailers behind jeeps. The so-termed 'seaborne party' had two elements. The first was the lorries and personnel to support operations on land. The second was eight Cromwell tanks. The Locust tanks would be delivered by glider in airborne operations. Once there was a ground route to the division, the Locusts would be turned over to the REME and the Cromwells substituted in the recce squadrons.

Armoured Replacement/Refitting Units

The information in this section is specific to 21st Army Group, but should be roughly typical for Italy during the same time period.

Armoured Replacement Group RAC   This was basically a small HQ, which coordinated the work of armoured delivery, armoured refitting and armoured reinforcement units. There were a total of 66 personnel, headed by a colonel. There were seven cars, seven jeeps, three motorcycles, three 15cwt trucks (two GS, one water), and three three-ton 4x2 GS lorries.

Armoured Reinforcement Unit   This was created in early 1944 to separate the role of providing RAC reinforcement personnel from that of replacement vehicles; both tasks originally assigned to delivery squadrons. The unit could train and administer up to 600 personnel.

There was a small HQ (commanded by a lieutenant colonel) and two squadrons, one devoted to cruiser tanks (Sherman and Cromwell) and one to infantry tanks (Churchill). Altogether there were 151 personnel, along with attached ACC cooks (nine). Administrative vehicles included seven cars, two motorcycles, five 15cwt trucks (two GS, one office, two water), and seven 3ton lorries (five GS, one store, and one mobile kitchen). For training purposes, the unit had five scout and two armoured cars, 11 cruiser tanks, two AA tanks,[133] 15 infantry tanks, and five light tanks.

Armoured Delivery Regiment   This grew to be a very large 'regiment' in 21st Army Group: 21 squadrons—one army delivery squadron, four corps delivery squadrons, and sixteen forward delivery squadrons (one for each armoured brigade). It took vehicles from the armoured refitting unit or from RAOC armoured vehicle parks, and delivering them to fighting units. Personnel for the vehicles came from tank crews who had lost their vehicles or from the armoured reinforcement unit.

RHQ was relatively small, with 30 personnel plus two ACC cooks. Despite the size of the unit, it was commanded by a lieutenant colonel. There were two cars, a jeep, two motorcycles, a 15cwt office truck, and two 3ton GS lorries.

An army or corps delivery squadron had 64 personnel, along with attachments (one REME, one ROAC, and six ACC cooks). There were two jeeps, five motorcycles, three 15cwt trucks (office, personnel, and water), and seven 3ton lorries (five GS, one stores, one kitchen). The unit also had a starting and charging carrier (usually called a carrier slave battery) and five trailers.

Provision was also made for the organization to handle replacement vehicles for the RA: SP guns, OP tanks, and tanks used as gun towers. An army delivery squadron had an additional increment of 17 personnel, with a motorcycle, two 15cwt personnel trucks and a 3ton GS lorry. A corps delivery squadron had an increment of 18 personnel with one additional 15cwt personnel truck.

The forward delivery squadrons had 42 personnel, plus one REME and six ACC cooks. They had two jeeps, four motorcycles, three 15cwt trucks (office, GS or personnel, and water), a carrier slave battery, and four 3ton lorries (two GS, stores, and mobile kitchen) along with three trailers.

---

[133] These can be presumed to disappear when the AA troops in regiments were disbanded after Normandy.

Royal Marines

The Royal Marine Armoured Support Group of 1943-44:

	Personnel		Equipment
Group HQ	30		
HQ Wing & Holding Bty	132		
Armoured Spt Regiment *x2*	373		
► RHQ		39	
► Armoured Spt Bty *x2*		167	4 Sherman IV, 16 Centaur IV
Independent Armoured Spt Bty	167		4 Sherman IV, 16 Centaur IV

The entire Group had 1,075 personnel, with 100 tanks (20 Sherman IV and 80 Centaur IV). Each battery was composed of four troops (troop commander in Sherman IV, and four Centaur IV tanks). Two LCT(A) [Landing Craft Tank (Armoured)] were used for each troop, with the Centaurs in pairs towards the front (where they could fire over the bow); one LCT(A) also had the troop commander's Sherman.

In their original incarnation as the Support Craft Regiment, they would be static, sea-borne artillery with the tank engines removed. Most of their crews came from the artillery of the former Royal Marine Division. Following initial exercises, the tank engines were re-installed and the plan was that the vehicles would provide fire support from the LCTs on the run into shore, and then land. Following redesignation in March 1944 as the RM Armoured Support Regiment, the Marines were joined by personnel from the Royal Armoured Corps (officers and gunner-drivers) and REME (fitters and mechanics).[134] The Shermans were added at this time for the troop commanders.

The 34th Amphibian Support Regiment had an establishment of 43 officers and 725 other ranks (768 total), mainly RM but with some Army personnel. It operated a variety of LVTs (armoured, rocket and flamethrower) but I have not seen any details of battery strength or LVT numbers.

---

[134] Ladd, in both his earlier article and later published history of the RM speaks of officers and drivers from the Royal Artillery and fitters and mechanics from the Royal Armoured Corps. While the unit was commanded by a brigadier from the RA, it is hard to see how that arm could have provided drivers for a Centaur tank, although they did use some for OP duties. Fitters and mechanics would seem to describe REME and not RA personnel.

Royal Engineers

The bulk of the assault (later armoured) engineers belonged to 79th Armoured Division and its 1st Assault Brigade RE (later 1st Armoured Engineer Brigade). These were the pioneers of the type, although some of them converted from AVREs to LVTs and then back again during the campaign in NW Europe.

ARMOURED ENGINEERS IN NW EUROPE

Detailed war establishments are contained in Appendix 12.

Headquarters, Assault Regiment RE (Armoured Engineer Regiment)

From May 1944 to January 1945 the RHQ and assault park squadron were combined into a single unit. This war establishment may be from January 1945, although it is unlikely that the 'RHQ' itself was much different even before. It was intended to be self-contained, so that it could operate apart from brigade HQ. Neither the parent brigade nor the threeregiments ever actually operated as a tactical headquarters—the various squadrons commonly operated apart in support of particular formations or units.

RHQ had seven officers and 52 other ranks for an aggregate of 58. Other than two scout cars, its vehicles were the assortment of motorcycles, jeeps, 15cwt trucks and 3ton lorries normally found at a headquarters. The regiment was supported by an attached signals section and a large light aid detachment REME.

A regiment originally commanded four squadrons. This was officially reduced to three in December 1944, although most were effectively reduced before then.

Assault Squadron RE (Armoured Engineer Squadron)

These were changed July 1944 from the D-Day organization by withdrawing one troop per squadron to form a training regiment.

The revised squadron had 9 officers and 230 other ranks for an aggregate of 239 personnel. Squadron HQ included two AVREs and a Churchill ARV Mk I along with its supporting vehicles.

Each troop had a small HQ element (officer and two other ranks) with a Humber scout car and motorcycle. There was an admin element with supporting vehicles. Finally, there were two sections, each with three AVREs. Overall troop strength was two officers and 61 other ranks. The troop had sufficient personnel and equipment to operate apart from the squadron for short periods.

Overall the squadron had 20 AVRE, five scout cars, a Churchill ARV, and the assorted jeeps, car, trucks and lorries and motorcycles.

If the only change from the D-Day squadron was the loss of a troop, that squadron would have had 302 personnel and 26 AVRE.

Assault Squadron RE (Armoured Engineer Squadron) [Buffalo]

The war establishment above remained in effect for these units, although the equipment was modified. There may have been some personnel changes as well. All but one of these squadrons changed back to AVRE in 1945. All of the AVREs (two at HQ and six in each troop) was replaced by an LVT, and the scout car in each troop was replaced by a Weasel.

Assault Squadron RE (Armoured Engineer Squadron) [Terrapin]

There is no known separate war establishment for the single squadron that converted to operating the Terrapin, although it is known it had 40 of those vehicles and was still organized in three troops. Squadron HQ had four Terrapins, and there were 12 of them in each of the three troops. As with the Buffalo squadrons, the scout cars in the troops were replaced by Weasels.

Assault Park Squadron RE (Armoured Engineer Park Squadron)

In May 1944, 149th Assault Park Squadron RE was combined with HQ 1st Assault Brigade RE. The two were made separate again in January 1945. While the available war establishment is from January 1945, the unit was probably effectively the same while combined with brigade HQ.
The squadron had five officers and 282 other ranks, for an aggregate of 287, plus nine ACC cooks. It did not have sufficient vehicles to move all of its personnel and equipment in one lift. Aside from various trucks and related vehicles, the squadron had 12 lightly armoured Caterpillar D7 Angledozers [US bulldozers], also known as a Tractor, crawler, Class II. These could be leant to squadrons on an as-needed basis.

Squadron HQ had two officers and 45 other ranks (47 aggregate) plus three of the ACC cooks. In addition to the normal support vehicles, there were two different machinery trucks.

The squadron had three identical park troops, allowing one per regiment, each with an officer and 79 other ranks (80 personnel) plus two ACC cooks. In addition to the four angledozers, there were the normal support vehicles, alone with a 3ton 6x4 Coles Crane Mk IV. The troop also had two 6ton tractors (such as AEC Matador) with 18ton multiwheel trailers, allowing it to carry two of the four dozers at a time to a work site. These were replaced where possible with Scammel Artillery Tractors and 20ton trailers.

Assault Dozer Squadron

The Centaur Assault Dozer was created to improve capabilities above what the Caterpillar dozers could provide. Based on a tank chassis, it was better armoured and had the same road speed as a tank, allowing it to travel on its own instead of being towed. These were provided to one squadron around November 1944 The squadron had six officers and 225 other ranks; 231 aggregate. There were four scout cars and 36 tank dozers, along with an ARV.

Headquarters (three officers and 57 other ranks—60 total) and a scout car, supporting vehicles, and an ARV. Each of the three troops had an officer and 56 other ranks (57 total) with a scout car, 12 tank dozers, and supporting vehicles.

Assault Training Regiment

One squadron was withdrawn from a regiment following D-Day for training and replacement duties, since there was no depot system for replacing the trained engineers in the brigade. Each of the other squadrons contributed a troop, and the new regiment was in place by September 1944. In December 1944 it also took over the experimental unit (F Wing) and ended up designated as 557 Assault Training and Experimental Establishment.

War Establishment XIV/951/1 (effective July 1944)

	Personnel	Equipment
RHQ	4/20	
HQ Sqn	5/119	2 scout cars, 2 ARK, 1 ARV
Sqn *x3*	6/20	26 AVRE, 1 ARK

Total assigned personnel were 27 officers and 199 other ranks (226 in total), along with a medical officer RAMC and 27 ACC cooks. Of the 78 AVREs and 3 ARKs, half were operational replacements and half training vehicles.

The small RHQ had only four motorcycles as assigned vehicles. The HQ squadron had an admin troop and a park troop, and most of the vehicles; there was no separate squadron HQ. The training squadrons had only a motorcycle and car (FFW) in addition to the armoured vehicles. Each troop had a single motorcycle in addition to the AVREs. Basically, the regiment was immobile and dependant on outside support.

ARMOURED ENGINEERS IN ITALY

An assault regiment RE (later armoured engineer regiment) had an RHQ, assault (later armoured) park squadron, and three assault (later armoured engineer) squadrons. Squadron HQ had a Churchill control tank; there were two armoured troops, each with a Churchill control tank, three AVREs, and three ARKS; and two dozer troops, each with three Sherman tank dozers. This gave the regiment nine regular Churchill tanks for control, 18 AVREs, 18 ARKs, and 18 tank dozers.[135]

Miscellaneous Units

HORSED CAVALRY REGIMENT

War Establishment I/1931/4/3 (effective 8 November 1939)

	Personnel		Equipment
RHQ	18		
HQ Sqn	183*		9 MMG, 9 Atk rifles**
Sabre Sqn *x3*	170		
▶ Sqn HQ		19	
▶ Trp *x3*		37	1 Atk rifle, 2 LMG

* Includes 5 attached (1 RAMC, 4 RAOC); should also receive 1 RAVC from brigade.
** Five of each are carried in trucks.

The overall strength was 711 personnel including the five attached. The original horsed cavalry regiments included a HQ squadron with machine gun and antitank rifle troops (four weapons each), signal troop, administrative group and motor transport group; and three sabre squadrons. The sabre squadrons had three troops, each with four rifle sections (eight men each), a LMG section (six men and two Lewis LMGs) and an Atk rifle section (three men with an Atk rifle). With squadron HQ, this would make a cavalry troop somewhat larger than an infantry rifle platoon, and the squadron similar to a rifle company.[136]

---

[135] I have followed Maj Gen R P Pakenham-Walsh, *History of the Corps of Royal Engineers*, Vol VIII, p 196. David Hughes et al, *The British Armies in World War II*, Vol Four, p 57, shows each regiment with three distinct squadrons (AVRE, ARK, and dozers) with 36 vehicles in each squadron. That would have made them significantly larger than the squadrons in 1st Assault Brigade RE (later 1st Armoured Engineer Brigade) which seems unlikely. In addition, since armoured engineers usually operated by squadron, a mixed squadron is more likely.

[136] However, the cavalry did not have the firepower of an infantry company or battalion. In 1940, a rifle company had 10 LMG, one Atk rifle, and a 2" mortar; the battalion had an additional two 3" mortars, four twin AAMG, and a carrier platoon (10 carriers, each with a LMG and Atk rifle). By June 1941, a rifle company (four per battalion) was about the same, but the battalion had six 3" mortars, 2pdr Atk guns, and the carrier platoon had 13 carriers (each still with a Bren LMG and Atk rifle, as well as 4 2" mortars).

The regiment had 617 riding horses and 45 pack horses, for a total of 662. Motor transport was fairly limited. RHQ had a single 8cwt truck; all of the other trucks were in the HQ squadron: two 8cwt GS; six 8cwt FFW; six 15cwt for cooks (four) and water (two); ten 30cwt 4-wheel lorries (medical stores, veterinary stores, ammunition, dismounted personnel, officers' mess, and baggage); and six 3ton 4-wheeled lorries (petrol, anti-gas capes, MT stores and fitters tools, and three for tools, stores and reserve pack equipment). The only other vehicles were 19 motorcycles (including two in each sabre squadron).

After arrival in Palestine, the regiments were reduced somewhat. The MG and Atk rifle troops in HQ Squadron were consolidated into a single troop, which also pulled in the squadron Atk rifles; the resulting unit had four Vickers MMG and eight Atk rifles. A sabre squadron still had three troops, but a troop now had three rifle sections (six men each) and a LMG section (five men and two LMG). Those surviving into early 1942 gained a mortar troop (four 3" mortars).

In addition to these changes, regiments generally converted one squadron from horses to 15cwt trucks. There was no real difference between a horsed or truck-borne squadron. Regiments also had a scout troop (nine regular cars) and some at least added 2pdr Atk guns (two truck-drawn guns in 1940, four by 1941). Most transport was motor vehicles, even where all of the troopers were horsed.

SCOUT REGIMENT

War Establishment III/1931/8B 1 (effective 3 June 1936)

	Personnel	Equipment
RHQ	64	
Sabre Sqn *x3*	170	
▶ Sqn HQ		38
▶ Trp *x4*		33

There were two TA scout regiments (horsed recce), both based in Scotland.[137] The regiment totaled 574 personnel, including the two attached (RAMC and RAOC) at RHQ. RHQ comprised No 1 Group (command element) and No 2 Group (signal troop). The available copy of the war establishment does not show any weapons. Troops had a small HQ (including an LMG detachment) and three sections of eight men each.

Overall the regiment had 56 riding horses, 433 riding ponies, and 12 pack ponies; 501 animals overall. There were nine cars, 38 other motor vehicles, and 26 motorcycles: six at RHQ and seven in each squadron). All cars were at RHQ: four 2-seater and five 2-

---

[137] These were originally formed with about ¾ of the troopers on bicycles and the rest on small ponies.

seater FFW. RHQ also had three 12cwt GS motor vans (medical equipment, veterinary equipment, officers' mess) and five 15cwt GS trucks (dismounted personnel and equipment [two], cooks and cooking sets, fitters, and baggage and blankets). Each squadron had eight 15cwt GS trucks (SAA, dismounted personnel and equipment [four], cooks and cooking sets, water tanks, baggage and blankets).

DIVISIONAL CAVALRY REGIMENT

The war establishment for recce regiments for infantry divisions was established in May 1938. However, those regiments serving in the BEF were officially grouped May 1940 into armoured recce brigades. Since the only fully equipped regiments lost all their vehicles in combat or at Dunkirk, this type of unit actually disappeared in May 1940.

War Establishment II/1931/12D/1, effective 25 May 1938

	Officers/Men	Equipment
RHQ	5/15	4 light tanks, 2 scout carriers
HQ Squadron	4/91	
▶ Squadron HQ	1/5	
▶ Motorcycle Trp	1/40	[41 motorcycles]
▶ Admin Trp	2/46	
Squadron x3	4/88	
▶ Squadron HQ	2/39	2 light tanks, 2 scout carriers
▶ Light Tk Trp x2	1(0)/8(9)	3 light tanks
▶ Carrier Trp x4	1(0)/10(11)	3 scout carriers

The regiment itself had 21 officers and 415 other ranks, for a total strength of 436. There were an additional 29 personnel attached (one RAMC officer; 11 personnel from the Royal Signals, four RASC drivers, and 13 RAOC personnel in a light aid detachment). The regiment had 28 light tanks and 44 armoured scout carriers. The tanks only had machine guns for armament, and the scout carriers came with a Boys anti-tank rifle in front and a Bren light machine gun on an AA pintle mount. Other than side arms, these were probably the only weapons in the regiment.

RHQ had only a single 8cw truck in addition to its light tanks and carriers. Squadron HQ of the HQ Squadron likewise had an 8cwt truck. The admin troop had three 8cwt and six 15cwt trucks along with eight 30cwt lorries.

The motorcycle troop (41 solo motorcycles) was intended mainly for communications and liaison. The only identified positions are a transport officer and sergeant, and the provost sergeant and two regimental police. The remaining personnel were one corporal and 35 privates.

In the three fighting squadrons, squadron HQ had was divided into a fighting element (the two tanks and scout carriers) and a small administrative element (three 15cwt trucks and three 30cwt lorries). In the light tank and carrier troops, the first of each was led by a subaltern, the others by a WO III.

The attached signals section added a 15cwt truck and a 3ton lorry (battery charger). The ROAC LAD had a 2-seater car, a motorcycle, a 3ton stores lorry and a 3ton breakdown lorry.[138]

A new war establishment was published in late 1940.

War Establishment II/1931/6/3, effective 9 October 1940

	Officers/Men	Equipment
RHQ	5/21	4 light tanks, 2 scout carriers
HQ Squadron	4/105	
▶ Squadron HQ	1/3	
▶ Intercomm Trp	1/41	[41 motorcycles]
▶ Admin Trp	2/62	
Squadron *x3*	8/109	
▶ Squadron HQ	2/45	2 light tanks, 2 scout carriers
▶ Light Tk Trp *x2*	1/13	3 light tanks
▶ Carrier Trp *x4*	1/10	3 scout carriers

This regiment had 33 officers and 453 other ranks (486 total), with three attached personnel (medical officer RAMC, two RAOC armourers), for an aggregate of 489. There were still 28 light tanks and 44 scout carriers. Supporting vehicles were similar, although there were now six 3ton, 4-wheeled GS lorries among them. It is not clear if any regiments were actually organized at strength under this establishment; the four Regular and two of the TA regiments were motor MG units, and it is unlikely that the remainder were at strength. The role served by divisional cavalry regiments would be assumed the next year by the Reconnaissance Corps.

MOTOR MACHINE GUN REGIMENT

Two of the motor MG brigades were formed of former divisional cavalry regiments, while the remaining one was an erstwhile army tank brigade lacking tanks or other armoured vehicles. At first, the units were outfitted with a variety of cars and trucks given some armament and mild steel and wood 'armouring'. Vehicles in motor troops might have a medium or light MG or an Atk rifle, and there were also infantry troops in vehicles. However, a formal war establishment was issued in October 1940, on the same date as the divisional cavalry establishment above.

---

[138] This appears to be a rare establishment, including personnel and vehicle details of the attached Royal Signals section and ROAC LAD.

War Establishment I/1931/6/4A/1, effective 9 October 1940

	Officers/Men	Equipment
RHQ	4/28	
HQ Squadron	5/105	
▶ Squadron HQ	1/3	
▶ Intercomm Trp	2/39	[41 motorcycles]
▶ Admin Trp	2/63	
Squadron *x3*	8/126	
▶ Squadron HQ	2/66	
▶ Troop *x3*	2/20	2 LMG, 2 MMG, 2 Atk rifles, [6 cars]

This regiment had 544 personnel (33 officers and 511 other ranks) plus three attached (medical officer RAMC and two RAOC armourers), for a grand total of 547. There were no armoured vehicles of any kind. In addition to small arms, the regiment had 31 LMGs, 31 Atk rifles, and 15 Vickers MMGs.

RHQ had seven utility cars: one 4-seater 4-wheeled, six 2-seater 4-wheeled, and three 6-seater 4-wheeled. The HQ squadron, in addition to the motorcycles of the intercommunications troop, had four 8cwt 4-wheeled GS trucks, seven 15cwt trucks (six 4-wheeled GS and one water), and eight 3ton 4-wheeled GS lorries.

Squadron HQ (with fighting and admin elements) had five utility cars (four 2-seater 4-wheeled and one 6-seater 4-wheeled), three 15 cwt 4-wheeled GS trucks, three 3ton 4-wheeled lorries, and a 28-seater coach. A troop had six 2-seater 4-wheeled cars and a motorcycle. There was a LMG section (two cars and two LMG), Vickers MG section (two cars and two MMG), and an antitank section (two cars and two Atk rifles). Interestingly, the details show three people for each 2-seater car.

Two months after this war establishment was issued, all of the motor MG regiments were converted: six became armoured regiments (without tanks) of the new 9th Armoured Division and the other three resumed their status of army tank battalions without tanks.

MOTORCYCLE BATTALION

These units were first formed in 1939. They were the recce unit for motor divisions; after the summer of 1940 they survived as GHQ units until converted between that autumn and April 1941 to other roles.

Total personnel for the battalion was 23 officers and 545 other ranks (568 aggregate). Attachments included one officer RAMC and three RAOC other ranks for a grand total of 572.

War Establishment II/1931/12D/1, effective 29 November 1939

	Officers/Men	Equipment
Bn HQ	5/20	
HQ Coy	6/153	
▶ Coy HQ	1/5	
▶ Signals Pln	1/26	
▶ Scout Pln *x2*	1/23	11 scout cars
▶ Admin Pln	2/76	
M/C Coy *x3*	4/125	
▶ Coy HQ	2/32	
▶ M/C Pln *x3*	1(0)/31(32)[139]	[11 combo, 2 solo motorcycles]

The scout platoons in HQ Company were organized with a platoon HQ (two scout cars) and three sections of three scout cars each. Not all of the battalions had the full complement of these (22) in 1939, with light trucks substituting for missing scout cars.

Combination motorcycles (99) were all in the motorcycle platoons (three in each of the three sections, with two more and two solo motorcycles at platoon HQ). Solo motorcycles were found throughout the battalion (43 all told), which also had one car, 24 8cwt trucks (eight GS and 16 wireless), 28 15cwt GS trucks and another water truck, and 12 30cwt lorries.

Weapons included nine 2" mortars (presumably three with each motorcycle company, or one per platoon). Each motorcycle platoon had nine Bren guns and the scout platoons 16 more;[140] along with 5 marked 'A.A. defence' this gave the battalion 48 light machine guns. The only other weapons besides side arms were 23 of the .55" Atk rifles.

SPECIAL SERVICE SQUADRONS RAC

These existed between 1941 and 1942. 'A' and 'B' Special Service Squadrons RAC had essentially the same organization: eight officers and 97 other ranks for 'A'; eight officers and 96 other ranks for 'B'. Each had eight Valentine infantry tanks (two at squadron HQ and two troops of three each) along with six Mk VI Light tanks (two troops of three each).

'C' Special Service Squadron (Light) RAC was equipped with the Tetrarch light tank (three troops of three tanks each and three more at squadron HQ). Strength was probably similar to the other two squadrons. Elements went to Madagascar with 'B' Special Service Squadron RAC. At the time of conversion to the Airlanding Light Tank Squadron RAC in June 1942, the remainder of the squadron had seven Tetrarchs, four

---

[139] One platoon in each company was led by a WO III instead of a subaltern.

[140] Clearly indicating that not all scout cars had a machine gun.

scout cars and three tracked carriers along with 84 personnel. Presumably the other two squadrons had scout cars and carriers as well.

Signalers and Fitters

While a unit's war establishment always had some attached personnel—a medical officer from the RAMC, armourers and fitters from the RAOC (later REME) and, from 1941, cooks from the ACC—these were insufficient to keep the unit operational. Ultimately regiments operated with attached Royal Signals personnel and with a light aid detachment REME. While essential, these are not always detailed in sources looking at the armoured or recce units themselves.

ROYAL CORPS OF SIGNALS

Each regiment had a small group of personnel and vehicles to augment the signals capability of the regiment. These are variously termed troops or sections.

Armoured Regiment 1944. No. 4 Squadron of armoured division signals supported the armoured brigade, including X, Y and Z Troops (each 14 other ranks) parceled out one to each of the three armoured regiments. Each troop had a jeep, a 15cwt GS truck, a 15cwt FFW truck and two 3ton 4x4 GS lorries. (The 15cwt GS truck and one 3ton 4x4 GS lorry each carried a Bren LMG.) The 15cwt vehicles could be replaced by White scout cars or even halftracks. The Royal Signals operator in one of the RHQ tanks came from here.

Armoured Recce Regiment 1944: R Troop of No. 3 Squadron of armoured division signals (21 other ranks) supported the armoured recce regiment. It had a jeep, motorcycle, three 15cwt GS trucks, one 15cwt FFW truck (carries a Bren LMG), one 15cwt armoured vehicle (either White scout car or halftrack; carries a Bren LMG), and two 3ton 4x4 GS lorries (one carries a Bren LMG). A Royal Signals operator from here was at RHQ.

Tank Regiment 1944: the troop supporting a regiment in a tank brigade had 18 personnel. It had a jeep, two 15cwt GS trucks, a 15cwt FFW truck and one 3ton 4x4 lorry (which carried a Bren gun).

Recce Regiment 1944: R Section of 3 Company of infantry division signals (19 other ranks) supported the recce regiment. There was a motorcycle, six 15cwt 4x4 trucks (three GS, one wireless house, two personnel), and a 3ton 4x4 GS lorry. The lorry carried a Bren gun.

Armoured Car Regiment signal section from Corps Troops Signals. This section had 24 personnel (led by a sergeant), with motorcycle, three 15cwt trucks (GS, wireless house, personnel), five 3ton GS lorries, and a lorry command vehicle. It may be that one of the operators was with the armoured car RHQ.

Each *assault regiment RE* (later armoured engineer regiment) had a section from the signal squadron at brigade. This unit had 17 other ranks, a jeep, two 15cwt GS trucks, two 15cwt FFW trucks, and a 3ton 4x4 GS lorry. (A Bren LMG was carried in the lorry.)

The *Armoured Replacement Group* in 21st Army Group had a strong signal squadron, with 71 personnel and two attached cooks. There were three cars, two jeeps, and five motorcycles, along with eight 15cwt trucks (seven wireless house and one signal office) and five 3ton GS lorries. The assigned *armoured delivery regiment* had a signal section with 33 personnel and two cooks. It had a car, two motorcycles, six 15cwt trucks (four wireless house, one signal office, and one GS) and one 3ton GS lorry. The *corps delivery squadron* had a signal troop, with 39 personnel. They had a jeep, motorcycle, eight 15cwt trucks (GS, office, and six wireless house) along with a 3ton GS lorry. An *armoured delivery squadron* had a signal detachment 22 personnel (no officers) and an attached cook. They had a motorcycle, three 15cwt wireless house trucks, and a 3ton GS lorry.

Light Aid Detachment REME

The light aid detachment (LAD) had become a standard attachment even before the REME was split off from the RAOC in October 1942. These served as small repair and recovery workshops. The LAD with the 9th Royal Tank Regiment described their activities as:[141]

> …front line repairs, changing engines and gearboxes, maintaining electrical equipment, and recovering vehicles under all kinds of conditions. We carried a large range of spares and also we had electric welding equipment.

There were a variety of light aid detachments ('A' to 'D') and some could exist in armoured or non-armoured varieties.

Light Aid Detachment, Type 'A'. The final war establishment was II/325/3 (December 1943). These were for units with more than the normal amount of wheeled transport.

> LAD Type 'A' (Armoured) for GHQ Liaison Regiment (Phantom). Officer and 15 other ranks (16 aggregate). Motorcycle, 2-seater car, two 3ton stores lorries, one 3ton 6x4 breakdown gantry lorry.

---

[141] *Tank Tracks*, Appendix VI, online at 9th RTR web site, www.9thrtr.com/.

LAD Type 'A' (Armoured) for an armoured car regiment. Officer and 15 other ranks (16 aggregate). Motorcycle, 2-seater car, two 3ton stores lorries, one 6x4 recovery tractor.

LAD Type 'A' (Armoured) for a recce regiment. Officer and 15 other ranks (16 aggregate). Motorcycle, 2-seater car, two 3ton stores lorries, one 3ton 6x4 breakdown gantry lorry, one 7½ton recovery trailer.

There were also a variety of LADs Type 'A' (Unarmoured); a light aid detachment type 'B' was a smaller version of type 'A', and also came in (Armoured) and (Unarmoured) variants; neither of these were attached to any armoured or recce units.

Light Aid Detachment, Type 'C' was intended for units with tracked armoured vehicles. The war establishment shown here is III/100/3 (December 1943). It may have been changed as there was a III/100/4 but no details of that one are known. These were normally commanded by a captain rather than a subaltern.

LAD Type 'C' for armoured or tank regiments. Officer and 24 other ranks (25 aggregate). Two motorcycles, one 15cwt GS truck, one 15cwt Machinery KL truck, one 15cwt FFW truck, two 3ton stores lorries, two 6x4 breakdown tractors.

LAD Type 'C' for armoured recce regiments. Officer and 24 other ranks (25 aggregate). Two motorcycles, one 15cwt GS truck, one 15cwt Machinery KL truck, one 15cwt FFW truck, one 3ton stores lorry, two 6x4 breakdown tractors.

Light Aid Detachment, Type 'D' was for use in 79th Armoured Division. Its war establishment was II/420. It was larger than other LADs, with a small HQ and a section to be allocated to each squadron of the regiment being supported. However, there were varieties of these LADs.

LAD (Special) for armoured engineer regiments and flail tank regiments of 30th Brigade: War Establishment VIII/707/1 effective April 1944; later War Establishment XIV/1685/1 effective May 1945
- HQ had an officer and ten other ranks (11 aggregate). Two motorcycles, one 15cwt KL truck, one 3ton 4x4 GS lorry, and one heavy recovery tractor or ARV.
- Three sections (one per squadron supported), each nine other ranks. One jeep, one 15cwt GS truck, one 15cwt machinery KL truck, one 3ton stores lorry, and one heavy recovery tractor, along with a 10cwt trailer and 10cwt welding trailer.

LAD (Armoured Personnel Carrier), War Establishment XIV/1683/1, effective March 1945. (LAD (Special) used prior to March 1945.)

- HQ had an officer and 12 other ranks (13 aggregate). One jeep, one 15cwt GS truck, one 3ton 4x4 stores binned lorry, and one 3ton 4x4 machinery M lorry, along with a 1-ton trailer.
- Three sections (one per squadron supported), each 17 other ranks. One motorcycle, one jeep, one 15cwt KL truck, one 3ton stores binned lorry, and one 3ton 6x4 breakdown lorry, along with a single 1ton trailer.

Vehicle notes. The 15cwt Machinery KL was a modified 15cwt GS truck with welding equipment for light repairs on site. A 3ton Machinery M lorry was a 6x4 or 4x4 vehicle with equipment for motor maintenance and battery charging. Breakdown gantry vehicles (at least in 21st Army Group) were generally a Leyland Retriever or modified Austin K6. The heavy breakdown tractor was a Scammel Pioneer, which could recover and tow most vehicles including tanks. If the Scammel could not manage a recovery, a Caterpillar D8 tractor with winch could be used instead if available; it had to be carried on an 18ton trailer towed by a Scammel. Where an LAD had an armoured recovery vehicle, the intended version was ARV Mk II, with a full range of towing, recovery and lifting equipment as well as a winch and heavy spade anchor. However, most units actually had an ARV Mk I until late in the war.

Part 3: Armoured Fighting Vehicles

Introduction to AFVs

This chapter covers the tanks and other principal armoured fighting vehicles used by the British armoured and recce units in the Second World War. The intent is to give summary information on the characteristics and production for each vehicle covered, along with information on use where applicable. Self-propelled antitank guns (or tank destroyers) are not included, since they were issued to antitank regiments of the Royal Artillery.

TANK PRODUCTION AND DESIGN

The British actually had almost no modern tanks on hand when the war began. As of mobilization in September 1939, only 79 cruiser tanks (Marks I and III, or the A9 and A13) had been produced, and 77 were in service. The first Cruiser Mark II (the A10) did not even appear until December 1939. Only 67 infantry tanks had been produced, 65 being the machine-gun armed Mark I and only two of the Mark II, Matilda. There were about 1,000 light tanks, several hundred being the most recent version, the Mark VIA or VIB. From September 1939 through the end of June 1940, the British produced 320 light tanks (Marks VIB and VIC), 322 cruisers, and 230 infantry tanks. Production increased from that point, although the output of cruisers would lag behind that of infantry tanks: about two cruisers to three infantry tanks considering only British output. Few light tanks were manufactured after 1940.[142] From 1941, British tank production was supplemented by the purchase or Lend-Lease acquisition of US tanks.

It breaks no new ground to say that most British tanks of the Second World War were not well regarded. One historian summed up his views of tank development as follows:[143]

> The categories of tanks required at different times before and during WWII included: light, medium, cruiser, infantry, assault, and ultra-heavy. The result of this large number of categories was a dispersion of design and manufacturing resources such that over the years 57 different designs were commenced, of which 38 were cancelled either at the paper stage or at the prototype stage. Of the 19 that became production models, eight were moderately battle-worthy. The rest were either useless or close to it, and included the Covenanter, Crusader, Centaur, Cavalier, Challenger, and Matilda

---

[142] Duncan Crow, *British and Commonwealth Armoured Formations*, pp 81ff.
[143] Peter Beale, 'Be Unprepared'.

Mark I. The problems with these tanks included mechanical unreliability, insufficient armour, and under-gunning.

In fact, it was necessary in 1944 for the Secretary of State for War, Sir P. J. Grigg, to deny in the House of Commons 'that British tanks were not up to their German counterparts, but such criticisms have been continued to be repeated by modern authors'.[144] It says much for the courage and dedication of the RAC that their officers and troopers persevered in combat despite the often poor quality of their tanks.

While the US-built Sherman, which became the main equipment for armoured regiments from 1942 onwards was well-regarded in terms of mechanical reliability and its dual-purpose 75mm gun (compared to the 6pdr [57mm] gun on British tanks at the time) it was an imperfect tank as well. Its design flaws let at least earlier models catch fire easily when hit, and it ended up under-gunned and under-armoured compared to German tanks of 1944-45. Worse, perhaps, continuing reliance on production of the Sherman delayed production of a better tank, the M26 Pershing.[145] The rough British equivalent, the Cromwell, also had problems dealing with German tanks.[146]

---

[144] David French, *Raising Churchill's Army*, pp. 96-97. Both French and Beale note that Field Marshal Montgomery was so concerned about reports in 1944 comparing (unfavorably) British and German tanks that he kept them from being circulated. French has a nice summary of all of the problems and decisions that hampered production of better British tanks at pp 96-106.

[145] While these flaws are often more or less acknowledged in various works on World War II tanks, there is probably no more savage an indictment than Belton Y. Cooper, *Death Traps: The Survival of an American Armored Division in World War II.* (Novato, California: Presidio Press, Inc., 1998). Cooper was an officer in the 3d Armored Division's maintenance battalion, with the duty of trying to recover and repair damaged tanks. 3d Armored Division had 648 Shermans destroyed completely and another 700 hit, repaired and returned to action; this amounted to losses of 580% against their establishment of 232. In his preface he states that the Sherman 'was decidedly inferior to the superior German tanks it encountered' in firepower, armor and mobility, with a resulting losses in personnel and even a delay in winning the war' (p vii). Cooper is especially critical of the decision to delay production and deployment of the M26 Pershing, which had better armour, a 90mm gun, and a better horsepower ratio than the M4 Sherman, making it a more agile tank. He calls it one of 'the most disastrous decisions of World War II' (p 28). This delay is also noted critically by Peter Chamberlain and Chris Ellis, *British and American Tanks of World War Two*, p 12. The first 20 of the M26 entered service in February 1945 (full production was only ordered the month before). Some authors have later suggested that Cooper overstates his case. A good recent overview of the Sherman and all of the issues around it –including failure to pursue the M26—is Steven J. Zaloga, *Sherman Medium Tank.*

[146] The worst example of this being the debacle at Villers Bocage in June 1944 where a single Tiger tank, with marginal assistance from four others, halted the 22nd Armoured Brigade. The brigade lost 20 Cromwells, four Sherman Fireflies, three Stuarts, three artillery Shermans, 16 carriers, 14 halftracks, and two 6pdr Atk guns in addition to around 160 prisoners. See the summary in Michael Reynolds, *Steel Inferno: I SS Panzer Corps in Normandy* (New York: Dell Publishing, 1997), pp 124-139. While problems of terrain (the Normandy bocage) are often mentioned in other accounts, Reynolds (a retired British major general) states flatly that the real

The last of the British wartime tanks was the Comet, used only briefly in the final campaigns in Germany. The historian of the 15th/19th The King's Royal Hussars commented (circa 1946) as follows:[147]

> The Comet, unlike many previous British Cruiser tanks, was reliable and battleworthy from the first—a statement that bodes well for the future but provides a sorry epitaph on British tank provision before and during the war.

While the first prototypes of the Centurion—the main battle tank of the 1950s—reached Europe in May 1945, the Comet remained in use in Berlin to 1957 and in Hong Kong through late 1959.

TANK ARMAMENT

From the pre-war years until March 1942, British tanks were limited to a width of no more than nine feet in order to allow movement by rail, a necessity given their mechanical unreliability and the resultant impracticality of long road movements. This limited turret size as well, making it difficult to up-gun an existing tank even where newer and larger guns might become available.[148] This contrasts markedly with German pre-war tank design. For example, the first version of the PzKpfw IV appearing in 1936 had virtually the same design as the last model of the tank, appearing in 1944.[149] The initial PzKpfw IV was a close support tank with a short barreled (L/24) 75mm howitzer. This went through a number of revisions until 1942 when the howitzer was replaced by a high velocity anti-tank gun (75mm L/43), and an improved version (75mm L/48) was introduced in 1943. Despite the fame of the Panthers and Tigers, the PzKpfw IV still constituted half of a panzer division's tank strength in 1944-45 (10 years after the 1935 prototype). No pre-war British or American tank could (or did) soldier on that long.[150]

The first gun mounted on cruisers and infantry tanks was the *2pdr Ordnance Quick Firing Mks 9, 10 and 10A*, identical to the towed 2pdr anti tank gun. These were, in

reason for the defeat 'is clear—the incompetence of .the senior commanders'. He faults both the planning and execution. Thus, while this battle is often portrayed as an extreme example of the inferiority of Allied armour, it may rather reflect tactical incompetence.

[147] Quoted in Maj James Bingham, *Cromwell and Comet*, p 44.

[148] David French, *Raising Churchill's Army*, p 99.

[149] Panzerkampfwagen [armoured battle wagon], or tank. The first four tanks are sometimes shown as Marks I to IV in English in lieu of PzKpfw I to IV.

[150] There are any number of books on German tanks. An example for this one in particular is Bruce Culver, *PzKpfw IV in Action* (Carrollton, TX: Squadron/Signal Publications, Inc., 1975). From p 4: 'As mentioned, the basic structure and design of the PzKpfw IV ausf A [version, or mark A] (Vers. Kfz 622) [experimental vehicle 622] was virtually the same as that of the last PzKpfw IV J. The improvements made in the tank were almost entirely in the nature of increasing armor protection, mounting heavier weapons, improving vision devices and the like – upgrading the combat capabilities of the tank'.

1939, better than the 37mm anti tank gun or the cannon on the German PzKpfw III. (For comparative armour penetration of this and other tank guns, see the table on p 175.) However, it remained in use far too long, becoming outranged by German tank and anti tank guns. In addition, it had no ability to fire a high explosive (HE) shell at other targets, such as anti-tank guns. Hence, creation of close support (CS) versions of cruisers, armed either with the *3.7" Howitzer Ordnance Quick Firing* or (later) the *3" Howitzer Ordnance Quick Firing*. In both cases, the main role was to fire smoke shells: the 3.7" could only fire smoke but the 3" howitzer could fire HE as well. Since the 3.7" howitzer was on the CS versions of the first three cruisers in use (A9, A10 and A13), those regiments had no HE capability at all.[151] The 2pdr had two different types of an armour piercing (AP) shot.[152]

The next weapon, again intended both as an anti tank gun and tank gun, was the *6pdr Ordnance Quick Firing Mks 3 and 5*.[153] Development of this weapon (57mm) had been given low priority, and it did not enter mass production until November 1941; as with the 2pdr, it was intended both as a towed anti tank weapon and a tank gun.[154] Before any of the tanks were up-gunned to the 6pdr the PzKpfw III had a 50mm weapon and the PzKpfwIV had begun changing to a 75mm gun. Again, the 6pdr could only fire shots intended to fight tanks, it was not until 1944 that a small HE shell was finally developed and issued for this weapon. There were still many tanks armed with 6pdrs (Churchills) in use in 1944. The 6pdr had AP, armour piercing capped (APC), and armour piercing discarding sabot (APDC) shots developed over the years.

While the US M3 Light (Stuart) was mechanically reliable, its *37mm Gun M6* was inferior in armoured penetration to the 2dpr. As with the British, this had been developed as both an anti tank gun and tank weapon. It was also the turret-mounted gun on the US M3 Medium (Grant/Lee) series. The 37mm gun had AP and APC shots, an HE shell, and a canister round for use against exposed troops.

The US M3 Medium (Grant or Lee) was designed around a 75mm gun, but it was mounted in a hull sponson. This meant you had to aim the tank to aim the gun, and it was mounted so low in the hull that most of the tank had to be exposed to fire. However, the *US 75mm Gun M2* had several advantages over previous weapons. Not only did it have an increased range, it could fire both AP and HE shells. In addition, a gyrostabilizer

---

[151] According to Ian V. Hogg, *British & American Artillery of World War 2*, there actually was an HE shell for the 2pdr anti tank gun, 'though it appears not to have been issued to tanks' (p 75). It appears that the HE shell became available ca 1941.

[152] See the discussion of different types of shells below, p 185.

[153] Mk 3 was a Mk 2 intended for tanks; Mk 5 was a variant of the Mk 4 (longer barrel and muzzle counterweight).

[154] One problem was that so many anti tank guns were lost in France, and the British had the choice of continuing to produce the 2pdr or retooling for the larger gun and having no anti tank guns at all until the factories retooled.

meant that the tank could maintain its aim even when moving, giving American tanks a tactical advantage.

Only with the M4 Sherman and a turret-mounted 75mm weapon was there a tank that could easily use its main armament to engage tanks or other targets. At first the Sherman had the 75mm M2, but most ended up armed with the *75mm Gun M3*. Note that both versions of the US 75mm gun were inferior in armour penetration to the British 6pdr. However, gyrostabilization, increased range, and the ability to fire HE made it a more versatile gun. Still, it was a relatively low muzzle velocity weapon (especially the M2) and inferior to German 75mm tank guns. The 75mm gun had AP and APC shots, along with HE and smoke shells.

In December 1942 the British began to develop a 75mm gun similar to that on the US Sherman. It had to fit on the existing 6pdr gun mount in tanks and fire US 75mm ammunition. The result was the *75mm Ordnance Quick Firing Mks V and VA*, which first appeared on a tank in October 1943. This had superior armour penetration to the original US 75mm M2 and was almost the same as the final M3 version of the US tank gun. It was also the first British tank gun that had HE as well as armour piercing capability from the start.

By the end of 1942, the US was looking for a weapon superior to the 75mm guns used on the Grants and Shermans. From 1944, it began to mount the *76mm Gun M1* (with various later marks) on the Shermans. It had better armour penetration than any of the 75mm variants, and almost twice the rate of fire of the British 17pdr. This gun had AP and APC shots, HVAP shots, HE shells, smoke and white phosphorous shells, and an illuminating round.

The final evolution of the British anti-tank gun was a 76.2mm weapon the *17pdr Ordnance Quick Firing Mks 2, 4, 6 and 7*.[155] Through some clever adaptation (turning the gun on its side, extending the turret, and modifying it for left-hand loading) it proved possible to mount this in a Sherman, as the Sherman Firefly. These were used to stiffen Sherman- and Cromwell-equipped armoured regiments, mainly in 21st Army Group. It also ended up mounted on a variety of SP anti-tank weapons, and was the main armament of the Challenger (intended to replace Fireflys in Cromwell regiments). The Centurion—the first prototypes of which appeared in June 1945—was the first tank to be designed around the 17pdr. There were a variety of shots for this weapon: AP, APC, APCBC (armour piercing capped, ballistic capped), and APDS (armour piercing discarding sabot). There were also regular and high capacity HE shells.

---

[155] Mk 2 was the Mk 1 with a muzzle counterweight for use in tanks; Mk 4 was a tank version of the Mk 1 with a new breech ring; the Mks 6 and 7 were further adaptations of the Mk 4.

The final British tank gun of the war was the *77mm Ordnance Quick Firing Mk II*. This was a 17pdr shortened and somewhat altered to fit the Comet tank turret. Although actually the same 76.2mm as the 17pdr, it was called 77mm to distinguish it from the US 76mm guns. Its armour penetration was better than most other tank guns of the time. This gun had APCBC and APDS shots, two versions of HE shells, and a smoke round.

Close Support Weapons

The *3.7" Mortar (Howitzer) Ordnance Quick Firing Mk I* on the original CS cruisers was only capable of firing smoke shells. It was replaced by the *3" Howitzer Ordnance Quick Firing Mks I and IA*, which had a range of 2,000-2,500 yards. While its main role continued to be firing smoke shells, it did have an HE round. The final weapon in this category was the *95mm Tank Howitzer Ordnance Quick Firing Mks 1 and 4*.[156] This had a maximum range of 6,000 yards. In addition to smoke and HE shells, it had an HEAT (high explosive anti-tank) round.

Some US Shermans mounted the *105mm Howitzer M2A1*. This had a maximum range of 12,205 yards firing HE or 8,590 yards firing HEAT. It also had a white phosphorous smoke shell. Used on the CS version of the Sherman, these were only issued to British regiments in Italy.

The Petard (officially, *Mortar, Recoiling Spigot*) on the AVRE was a 290mm weapon with an effective range of only 80 yards. Its 40lb demolition bomb was known as the 'Flying Dustbin'.

Note

Armour piercing (AP) shells have a hardened nose to punch through armour plate. If capped, (APC), there is soft metal cap to absorb some shock that might otherwise shatter the round. A refinement for better aerodynamics is to add a further hollow [ballistic] cap (APCBC). The British developed the APDS round, introduced 1944; this has a lightweight outer carrier (the sabot, French for 'shoe') which fits the barrel diameter and falls away on firing; the actual shot (with a tungsten core) is smaller but heavier.

---

[156] This began development in 1942, both for tanks and as a towed weapon for the infantry. Mk 1 was the original tank howitzer; Mk 4 a conversion of the Mk 1 with a horizontal breech block and semi-automatic operation.

Comparative Armour Penetration

The penetration represents the thickness (in mm) that can be penetrated
at a range of 500 yards and with the armour angled at 30°.

Allied Tank Guns	Penetration
2pdr OQF (AP)	57
2pdr OQF (APCBC)	57.5
37mm M6	48
6pdr OQF Mk 3	81
6pdr OQF Mk 5	83
75mm M2	60
75mm M3	70
75mm OQF	68
76mm (APC)	88
76mm (HVAP)	133*
17pdr OQF	120
17pdr OQF using APDS	186
77mm OQF	109

*Penetration at 1000 yards instead of at 500 yards.

German Tank Guns	Penetration
5cm KwkK* 38 L/42 (APCBC) PzKpfw III	46
5cm KwkK 38 L/42 (APCR) PzKpfw III	58
5cm KwkK 39 L/60 (APCBC) PzKpfw III	57
5cm KwkK 39 L/60 (APCR) PzKpfw III	72
7.5cm KwK 40 L/43 (APCBC) PzKpfw IV	91
7.5cm KwK 40 L/43 (APCR) PzKpfw IV	108
7.5cm KwK 40 L/48 (APCBC) PzKpfw IV	96
7.5cm KwK 40 L/48 (APCR) PzKpfw IV	120
7.5cm KwK 42 L/70 (APCBC) Panther	124
7.5cm KwK 42 L/70 (APCR) Panther	174
8.8cm KwK 36 L/56 (APCBC) Tiger I	110
8.8cm KwK 36 L/56 (APCR) Tiger I	156
8.8cm KwK 43 L/71 (APCBC) Tiger II	185
8.8cm KwK 43 L/71 (APCR) Tiger II	217

* Kampfwagenkannone (tank gun)

Where shell type is indicated: AP (Armour Piercing), APC (Armour Piercing Capped), APCBC (Armour Piercing Capped, Ballistic Capped), HVAP (High Velocity Armour Piercing), APDS (Armour Piercing Discarding Sabot); APCR (armor piercing composite rigid, tungsten core).

'A' NUMBERS.

From 1926, all tank prototypes received an 'A' designation. At the beginning of the war, cruiser and infantry tanks were generally known only by their A number, but from 1940 most tanks were better known by their names or, just to be confusing, their marks in the cruiser or infantry tank series. Beginning with the first cruiser, the Second World War A numbers are given below (the date of the first pilot is given in parentheses):

A9	Cruiser Mark I (1936)
A10	Cruiser Mark II and IIA (1938)
A11	Infantry Mark I (1937)
A12	Infantry Mark II, Matilda (1938)[157]
A13 Mk I	Cruiser Mark III (1937?)
A13 Mk II	Cruiser Mark IV and IVA (1938?)
A13 Mk III	Cruiser Mark V, Covenanter (1939?)
A14	Cruiser tank [experimental, 1938, did not enter production]
A15	Cruiser Mark VI, Crusader (1939)
A16	Cruiser tank [experimental, 1938, did not enter production]
A17	Light Mark VII, Tetrarch (December 1937)
A20	Infantry tank [only four prototypes, ca 1939]
A22	Infantry Mark IV, Churchill (1940)
A24	Cruiser Mark VII, Cavalier (1942)
A25	Light Mark VIII, Harry Hopkins (1942?)
A27L	Cruiser, Centaur (1941 or 1942)
A27M	Cruiser, Cromwell (1942)
A30	Cruiser, Challenger (1944)
A33	Heavy Assault Tank [only two prototypes 1943]
A34	Cruiser, Comet (1944)
A38	Infantry, Valiant [one prototype 1944]
A39	Heavy Assault Tank, Tortoise [design began 1942 but the six prototypes were not completed until 1947]
A41	Cruiser, Centurion (1945)
A42	Infantry, Churchill VII (1942?)
A43	Infantry, Black Prince [six prototypes completed by May 1945; basically an improved Churchill with 17pdr gun]

The light tanks before Mark VII did not have 'A' numbers, although A4 was the prototype for the Light Marks I to IV. Also missing from the list is the Infantry Mark III, Valentine, which had no 'A' number since it was developed by Vickers-Armstrong on their own and not the result of a War Office specification.

---

[157] Infantry Mark I also unofficially known as Matilda; the name officially given to Infantry Mark II, but the two are sometimes referred to as Matilda I and Matilda II.

VEHICLE MARKINGS

British tanks and other AFVs and vehicles had a comprehensive and formalized system of vehicle markings during the Second World War. This began with formation signs, which were created for vehicles before they became the now-familiar cloth emblems worn on sleeves. Then there were arm of service marks: squares showing by various colours either the arm of service or the brigade within a division to which the unit was assigned. Numbers on the arm of service marks distinguished the various regiments or other units. Within a regiment, squadrons were distinguished by outline markings: diamond for HQ Squadron, and triangle, square, and circle for 'A', 'B' and 'C' Squadrons. Where a 'D' Squadron existed, it had a filled rectangle standing on the narrow end. These could appear on the hull front and rear and the turret sides. Officially, colours indicated the seniority of the regiment within the brigade, but in practice regiments or brigades apparently did pretty much what they wanted to. Vehicles had bridging classification marks (a number in a circle). Many regiments had names painted on tanks or other vehicles. Vehicles could also have air recognition signs: RAF-style roundels of red, white and blue in North Africa or Italy, white stars (sometimes within a white circle) in North West Europe and later in Italy.[158]

Cruiser/US Medium Tanks

The cruiser was one of two tank types decided on in the 1930s, a replacement for the medium tanks of the post-war era. They were to be highly mobile, used in armoured brigades and divisions to defeat enemy tanks and then romp through their headquarters and rear areas. Despite the latter role, their main armament was designed only to fight tanks. Hastily developed and issued mainly in 1939 for the first time, the early cruisers were mechanically unreliable, and proved difficult to up-armour or up-gun. One result was that, from 1942 to 1944, armoured regiments became dependent on US medium tanks, and the Sherman remained the main tank in armoured regiments through the end of the war.

EARLY CRUISER TANKS

The British began the war with small numbers of a variety of cruiser tanks.

A9 (or Cruiser Mark I) had a crew of six (commander, gunner, loader, driver, two MG gunners), 2pdr gun (3.7" howitzer in CS versions), and three Vickers MGs: one coaxial and two in small turrets on the hull front. (Sometimes the two small turrets were unmanned, reducing the crew to four and increasing available space.)

---

[158] This subject is covered in great detail in Peter Hodges and Michael D. Taylor. *British Military Markings 1939-1945*. [revised and expanded edition]. The white Allied recognition stars quickly disappeared from vehicle sides in British units, but could still be found on the roof. A more recent work is Dick Taylor, *Warpaint: Colours and Markings of British Army Vehicles 1903-2003*, especially Vol III.

Maximum armour was only 14mm (same as on the light tanks) and maximum road speed only 25mph (15mph cross-country). The tank weighed 28,728lbs.

The first prototype appeared in 1936 and the first deliveries were made in January 1939; 125 were built. These were used in France 1940 and the Western Desert into 1941.

A10 (Cruiser Mark II) had a crew of four with a 2pdr gun, coaxial Vickers MG, and (added 1940) a Besa MG in the hull (Mark II); or a crew of five (commander, loader, gunner, driver, hull machine gunner) and a 2pdr gun with two Besa MGs (one coaxial and one in the hull) (Mark IIA). The IIA also had a CS version with the 3.7" howitzer. Armour was a maximum of 30mm and maximum road speed only 16mph (8mph cross-country).[159] The tank weighed 31,696lbs.

The first prototype appeared in 1936 but the first deliveries were in December 1939 and 170 (13 Mk II and the rest Mk IIA, including 30 IIA CS) were built; production was completed by September 1940. These were also used in France 1940 and the Western Desert until late 1941. The A10 actually began its design life intended to be an infantry tank, hence the low speed, but was produced as an interim 'heavy' cruiser.

A13 (Cruiser Mark III) was the first to use a Christie suspension. Production began in January 1938 and the first deliveries were that December; production ended summer 1939. It had a 2pdr gun, Vickers MG, and crew of four (commander, gunner, loader, driver). Maximum armour was only 14mm and maximum road speed 30mph (24mph cross-country). It weighed 31,360lbs. Only 65 of these were built. It was used by 1st Armoured Division in 1940; a few also went to 7th Armoured Division in Egypt.

The **A13 Mark II (Cruiser Mark IV)** was the last pre-war cruiser and similar to the earlier vehicle. However, like the A10, its maximum armour was increased to 30mm; despite the increase in armour its road speed was still 30mph (however, cross-country speed was only 14mph). Crew of four (commander, gunner, loader, driver).It weighed 33,040 lbs. A few of the Cruiser Mark IV were built in the CS version with a 3.7" howitzer. The normal armament was a 2pdr gun with either Vickers MG (Mark IV) or Besa MG (Mark IVA).

It was used in France in 1940 and the Western Desert into 1941, as well as for training in the UK. When production ceased in 1941, about 655 of the two marks of the A13 Mk II had been delivered.

---

[159] By comparison, the Infantry Tank Mk II (Matilda) had a road speed of 15mph.

COVENANTER

The Cruiser Tank, Mark V Covenanter [also known as A13, Mark III] had many mechanical problems and was never used in battle. It was a 40,320lb vehicle with a crew of four (commander, gunner, loader, driver) and a 2pdr gun and Besa MG. The CS version was the first to mount the 3" howitzer (with HE capability) as opposed to the smoke-only 3.7" howitzer in earlier CS cruisers. Maximum armour was increased to 40mm and the road speed was 31mph (25mph cross-country).

Some 1,771 of these were built, with deliveries beginning in summer 1940. There were four marks, and a small proportion were the CS version. The Covenanter equipped armoured divisions in Home Forces and some were sent to the Middle East for training. This tank was regarded by one author as 'one of the worst tanks ever produced'.[160] There were actually four different marks, with various differences, and each mark had a CS version. The tank was withdrawn from Home Forces units in late 1943. A few were converted to command, OP and ARV roles, and Covenanters were the first to mount a scissors bridge, used mainly for development of the bridgelayer role.

CRUSADER

The first pilot model of the Cruiser Tank, Mark VI Crusader [or A15] was completed in March 1940 and the tank was first used in action June 1941 in the Western Desert. Crusader I [Cruiser Mk VI] had a 2pdr gun, coaxial Besa MG, and another Besa in a small auxiliary turret. Crusader II [Cruiser Mk VIA] was similar but eliminated the machine gun turret. Both also came in a CS version with a 3" howitzer. The tank had a crew of five (commander, gunner, driver, loader, hull gunner) and weighed 42,560 lbs, had maximum armour of 40mm (Mk I) or 49mm (Mk II), and a road speed of 27mph (15mph cross-country).

The Crusader III, in production from May 1942, was the first cruiser with a 6pdr gun, along with the coaxial Besa MG. Its crew was only three (commander, gunner, driver). Armour increased to 51mm maximum, and the weight went up to 44,240 lbs; road speed was still 27mph.

Production totaled 4,350 gun tanks and 1,373 in special roles.

Inheriting mechanical troubles from both the A13 and the Covenanter, the Crusader also suffered from being clearly under-gunned for most of its operational use in North Africa.

---

[160] Peter Beale, 'Be Unprepared'. His quote in full runs: 'The Covenanter, or A13 Mk III, was one of the worst tanks ever produced, and represented an enormous waste of human, material, and financial resources. It looked sleek and powerful, but it was a mechanical disaster and never saw fighting in any theatre of war'. The many failings are well covered in David Fletcher, *Crusader and Covenanter Cruiser Tanks*.

From 1942 it was generally mixed with the Grant in armoured regiments, and the Crusader went out of service as a combat tank following the end of the Tunisian campaign in May 1943.

Crusaders were later adapted as AA tanks, command tanks (armament removed), OP tanks in artillery regiments (6pdr removed and replaced by a dummy), and as armoured tractors (Gun Tractor Mk I) for 17pdr Atk guns. There was a Crusader ARV and the RE had a Crusader Dozer. The ARV was a standard vehicle with the turret removed, and a demountable jib and winch in that space. The dozer version also had the turret removed, with a dozer fitted in front with a winch and jib to operate it.

CAVALIER

A few hundred of the Cruiser Tank, Mark VII Cavalier [A24] were built from January 1942; the 1941 production order was for 500. The tank had a crew of five (commander, gunner, loader, driver, co-driver), 6pdr gun and one or two Besa MGs. It weighed 59,360 lbs, had maximum armour of 76mm and maximum road speed of 24mph (14mph cross-country). With the extra weight and no improvement in engine, the Cavalier was even more likely than the Crusader to break down and had worse performance all around.

It was never used in battle as a gun tank, but half of them were modified as an OP tank (with a dummy gun barrel) and used by the Royal Artillery in NW Europe. A few were converted to the ARV role (turret removed and winch fitted in the former turret space).

CENTAUR

Similar to the Cavalier, the Cruiser Tank Mark VIII Centaur [A27L] also began appearing from 1942: pilot model in June 1942 and production versions from the end of the year. Total production was 950. The first, Centaur I, had a 6pdr gun. Centaur III was armed with a 75mm gun. (There was no Centaur II.) The final version (80 built) was Centaur IV, a CS model with a 95mm howitzer and improved engine.

Generally, production vehicles were used for training, although some of the Centaur III were converted to Cromwells by changing to that tank's Merlin engine. The Centaur IVs were used at Normandy by the RM Armoured Support Group. The Centaur was also used as the basis for an AA tank, while others were converted as ARVs, OP tanks, and as dozers. One Centaur Dozer was issued to each Cromwell squadron, and some were also used by the RE.

The tank weighed 63,600 lbs, had maximum armour of 76mm, a crew of five (commander, gunner, loader, driver, co-driver), and road speed of 27mph (16mph cross-country).

GRANT

The Grant Medium Tank was a variant of the US M3 Medium Tank, built specifically for the British and modified slightly to suit British requirements: the turret was lower and able to accommodate British radio equipment, and a machine gun cupola on top eliminated. The Grants were available from early 1942 and first used in the Western Desert in May.[161]

The British variants were known as:
- Grant Mk I   M3 variant: 1,685 received[162]
- Grant Mk II   M3A5 variant: 185 received

The tank had a crew of six (commander, driver, two loaders, two gunners) and weighed 60,000 lbs (Mk I) or 64,000 lbs (Mk II). The tank came with a 75mm gun mounted in the hull and a turret with a 37mm gun and coaxial .30 MG. It could also have a MG in the hull and another on the turret. Maximum road speed was 26mph (Mk I) or 29mph (Mk II), and maximum armour was 37mm. (Cross country speed was around 16 mph.) These were tall tanks, although the Grant (9'4") was nearly a foot lower than the standard US M3 (10'3").

Contracts were placed in October 1940, and the tanks began shipping to Eighth Army in early 1942. Grant squadrons were placed in armoured regiments along with Crusader squadrons. Other than specialized types, the Grants were all replaced by Shermans by 1943 and the surviving tanks sent to Australia and India, where they remained in use.

The chassis was used for a tank recovery vehicle (US T2, later M31; British Grant ARV I); this had the turret and guns removed and a rear mounted boom and winch, along with tool boxes. In 1943 the British converted some obsolete Grants as the Grant ARV; these had a towing winch and limited recovery equipment. A few kept the turret (dummy gun) but in most cases the turret was removed and replaced with a hatch and twin Bren LAA MG mount. The Grant CDL was created by replacing the original turret with an armoured searchlight turret; the hull-mounted 75mm gun could remain. Finally, some Grants were converted as Scorpions (or flail tanks) for mine-clearing, with limited use in Tunisia, Sicily and Italy.

---

[161] Despite their faults—height and a hull-mounted main gun—the tanks were welcomed in the Desert. 'In them [Grants] at last we felt we had a tank, which if not the superior, was at least able to take on a German tank on more or less equal terms'. Brig R. M. P. Carver, *A Short History of the 4th Armoured Brigade*, Ch. II.

[162] Totals in both cases are for Great Britain and the Commonwealth.

LEE

The Lee was the standard U.S. M3 Medium Tank, provided under the Lend-Lease Act. The US began building the M3 in mid 1941, with production of the last model (M3A4) ending in December 1942. The biggest difference was the MG cupola on top of the turret.

The variants were designated as:[163]

- Lee Mk I   M3 (riveted hull)
- Lee Mk II   M3A1 (cast hull)
- Lee Mk III   M3A2 (all-welded hull)
- Lee Mk IV   M3A3(all-welded hull, new diesel engines)
- Lee Mk V   M3A4 (as M3A3 but gasoline engines)
- Lee Mk VI   M3A5 (riveted hull)

Britain and the Commonwealth received 968 Lee III and 49 Lee V. The Lees in particular went to India, and remained in use to the end of the war. Armament, weight and other characteristics were similar to the Grant.

SHERMAN

The U.S. M4 Sherman Medium Tank became, from 1943, the most widely-used tank in British and Commonwealth armoured formations.

The various Shermans were designated as:[164]

- Sherman Mk I   M4: 2,096 received
- Sherman Mk IB   M4 with 105mm gun 593 received
- Sherman Mk II   M4A1: 942 received :
- Sherman Mk IIA   M4A1 with 76mm gun:1,330 received
- Sherman Mk III   M4A2: 5,041 received
- Sherman Mk IIIA   M4A2 with 76mm gun: 5 received
- Sherman Mk IV   M4A3: 7 received
- Sherman Mk V   M4A4: 7,041 received
- Sherman Mk VII   M4A6[165]

---

[163] For whatever reason, most versions of the Lee received a British designation even though only two variants were actually supplied. The final version, M3A5, did not receive a British designation, although some were built to Grant specifications as the Grant II.

[164] Totals include Great Britain and the Commonwealth.

[165] Although given a designation by the British, it was unlikely any were received since the M4A6 was cancelled after only 75 were produced due to problems with the engine. M4A5 was the American designation allocated for the Canadian-built Ram tank.

The Sherman IIAs were largely sent to Italy due to the availability of the Firefly in 21st Army Group.

The Sherman I and II weighed 66,500lbs, the Sherman III and IV 69,000lbs, and later marks 68,500lbs. The tank was originally armed with a 75mm gun, replaced from 1944 by a 76mm gun, along with two .30 caliber MGs (one coaxial and one in the hull) and a .50 caliber AAMG on the turret. The close support versions had a 105mm howitzer. The crew was five (commander, gunner, loader, driver, co-driver-hull gunner). Maximum armour was 75mm (turret) or 50mm (hull) and maximum road speed 24-30mph (cross-country about 15-20mph). The various marks differed in terms of suspension, engines, and whether they had a cast or welded hull.[166] In addition, all 76mm models and later 75mm models had a 'wet storage' system for the ammunition to try and reduce the incidence of catching on fire after a hit.

US production began in March 1941. The tank was first used by the British autumn 1942 at El Alamein, and from 1943 was the main tank for all armoured regiments. Even tank regiments in Italy received Shermans in place of some Churchills until the Churchill NA75 (armed with the Sherman's main gun) was received. The command or OP version of the Sherman would have a dummy gun and additional radio equipment.

There were any number of variants derived from the Sherman. It became the main duplex drive (DD) tank used in operations, as the Sherman III or V DD, later improved as DD Mk I or DD Mk II. The Sherman was also the basis for the final mine-clearing tanks. While the US developed a flamethrower variant, the British used the Churchill flamethrower (Crocodile) for that role. The Cullin Hedgerow Cutting Device was fitted in the June-August 1944 period in the Normandy bocage country but (unlike with the Cromwell) there was no special nickname.

The British developed armoured recovery variants of the Sherman III and V (Mk I for the Sherman III; Mks I and II for the Sherman V: Mk II had a dummy gun, earth spade, and other improvements over the ARV Mk I). The standard US ARV version was designated the M32 Tank Recovery Vehicle, and this became the Sherman II ARV Mk III in British service. A few (60 Sherman ARV I) vehicles were outfitted for recovery work on landings as the Sherman BARV (Beach Armoured Recovery Vehicle). Since winches were omitted on the BARV, they were towing vehicles only.

---

[166] The major versions, such as M4A3, could have subvariants as well, with differences. In the US Army, these were designated by 'E' and a number: e.g., the M4A3E2, an up-armoured Sherman with a new and heavier turret produced in limited numbers and sent to France in 1944; nicknamed the 'Jumbo'.

SHERMAN FIREFLY

From November 1943 the British began to convert a number of Sherman tanks to carry the 17pdr gun, in case the Challenger program did not prove successful. Fireflys were identified by a C following the Mark number: thus Sherman VC was a Sherman V [M4A4] with the 17pdr gun. These were issued on the scale of one per tank troop in North-West Europe, increased later where possible. About 600 Shermans were converted, mainly the Mk V to VC. The hull MG (and gunner) were deleted as part of the conversion, reducing the crew to four.

While almost all went to 21st Army Group, at least 100 of the Sherman IC were in the Mediterranean by December 1944, issued to the 2nd and 7th Armoured Brigades and 5th Canadian and 4th New Zealand Armoured Brigades.[167]

CROMWELL

Production of the Cruiser Tank, Cromwell [A27M] began January 1943. Early Centaurs—A27L—and Cromwells were externally indistinguishable, since they were essentially the same tank with different engines. The Cromwell used the Meteor engine, derived form the Rolls-Royce Merlin engine used in aircraft. With a rated speed of 40mph (later geared down to 32mph; 18mph cross-country) it was one of the faster medium tanks in World War II. The vehicle grew about half a ton from earlier marks to 61,600 lbs and had a crew of five (commander, gunner, loader, driver, co-driver). Maximum armour was 76mm, increased to 101mm with appliqué armour.

The Cromwell I had a 6pdr gun and two Besa MGs (one coaxial and one in the hull). Cromwell II was essentially the same, with the hull MG removed and wider tracks. Cromwell III was a Centaur I changed over to the Meteor engine; it was originally designated Cromwell X. From Cromwell III on, all of the marks had the hull Besa MG.

Cromwell IV was actually the Centaur III, with the engine changed. This tank had a 75mm gun. Cromwell IVw was built initially with the Meteor engine and had a welded hull, and Cromwell Vw was the same.

Cromwell VI was the CS version, a Mk IV with a 95mm howitzer in place of the 6pdr gun.

Cromwell VII was a Cromwell IV, with appliquéd armour in the front, improved suspension and wider tracks; this was the first version geared down to a maximum speed

---

[167] Middle East AFV Technical Liaison Letter 25, 16 December 1944, posted online [2005] at http://web.inter.nl.net/users/spoelstra/g104/firefly-i.htm.

of 32mph (about 18mph cross-country). Cromwell VIIw was a Cromwell Vw similarly modified. Finally, Cromwell VIII was the CS Cromwell VI reworked.

The armoured recce regiments in North-West Europe were equipped with Cromwells, as was the 22nd Armoured Brigade of 7th Armoured Division. When regiments began to change to the Comet, the Cromwell CS remained in use since there was no close support version of the Comet.

Some Cromwells had the turret removed and were converted as ARVs, with a jib crane, winch, drawbars, etc. The hull MG was retained, and twin Bren AAMG were mounted in the former fighting compartment. Some were also converted for the command and OP roles, with dummy guns, additional wireless sets and some other internal modifications. A Cromwell Prong had the Cullin Hedgerow Cutting Device fitted in the June-August 1944 period in the Normandy hedgerows. As with Sherman regiments, these were all discarded after the breakout.

CHALLENGER

The Cruiser Tank, Challenger [A30] was a modification of the Cromwell, weighing 72,800 lbs. It had a 17pdr gun and a coaxial .30 Browning MG, in a very high turret. The tank had a crew of five (commander, driver, gunner, two loaders), maximum armour of 101mm and a road speed of 32 mph (about 15 mph cross-country).

The tank was built in small numbers (about 200 during 1944; first production that March) to stiffen Cromwell-equipped units, performing the same role as Sherman Fireflys. Various troubles (the vehicle was longer and heavier than the Cromwell) delayed introduction of the Challenger, and very few seem to have actually reached 21st Army Group.[168] Even though the chassis was lengthened, the 17pdr was too big for a tank initially designed to use the 6pdr.

A variant, the SP Gun Avenger, also used the A30 designation. This was intended for the tank destroyer (SP Atk gun) role in the Royal Artillery.

COMET

The prototype for the Cruiser Tank, Comet [A34] was ready in February 1944 and production began in September. The tank weighed 78,800 lbs, had a crew of five (commander, gunner, loader, driver, co-driver), and was armed with the new 77mm gun (derived from the 17pdr) and two Besa MGs (coaxial and hull). It had maximum armour

---

[168] In June 1944 21st Army Group had 18 Challengers in reserve equipment and none issued to units. In December 1944, there were only 21 Challengers in 21st Army Group divisions (10 with 11th Armoured Division and 11 with Guards Armoured Division) and a further 11 with the armoured replacement groups.

of 101mm and a road speed of 29 mph (16 mph cross-country). No close support version of the Comet was designed. The Comet has been described as 'essentially an up-gunned, up-armoured Cromwell' with the same lay-out although the exterior look (especially the turret) was very different.[169] It has been termed 'a fast and reliable tank, the first British AFV to come near matching the German Panther in performance and gun power…[but it] appeared too late to play any prominent part in British tank combat in World War II.'[170]

29th Armoured Brigade of 11th Armoured Division was withdrawn in December 1944 to convert; this was delayed until February-March 1945 by service in the Ardennes after reclaiming their Shermans. The armoured recce regiment of the division was also converted in April 1945. The tank was first used in action after the Rhine crossing in early 1945. 7th Armoured Division converted to Comets in June 1945, after the war in Europe ended, and this became the tank for surviving armoured units in the early post-war years.

Medium Tanks

About 160 of the Medium, Marks I and II were delivered 1923-1928 while three Mark III mediums were produced 1929-1937. The Medium formed the backbone of the RTC during the inter-war years. Long obsolete, some remained in service in the UK until 1941 and a few were used in the Western Desert 1940-41. These were the first British tank with a revolving turret, and had a 3pdr gun and three Vickers MGs. The crew was five (commander, driver, wireless operator, two gunners). The Mk II weighted 30,240lbs, had maximum armour of 8mm (even less than the light tanks), and a road speed of 18 mph.

Light Tanks

The British had more light tanks than any other type in 1939, although their tactical value was slight. Due to limited numbers of cruisers available, former cavalry regiments were all-light tank, and even the 'heavy' regiments of the RTR were a mix of cruisers and light tanks. Light tanks were largely abandoned for active use after 1940, although the US Stuart was pressed into use as a substitute for cruisers in North Africa 1941-42, after which it was relegated for use in recce units.

LIGHT TANK, MARKS II-V

Pre-war vehicles (production ending around 1935), with two- (Marks II-IV) or three-man (Mark V) crews (commander and driver; commander, gunner driver) . Marks II-IV had a

---

[169] Maj James Bingham, *Cromwell and Comet*, p. 39.
[170] Peter Chamberlain and Chris Ellis, *British and American Tanks of World War Two*, p 50.

single Vickers MG (.303 or .5 inch), the Mark V had two Vickers MGs (.5 and .303 inch). Weight ranged from 9,520lb to 10,080lb (Mk III), up to 10,740lb (Mk V), maximum armour was 10mm (12mm Mks III and later), and maximum road speed 30mph (Mks I-III) or 32.5mph (25mph cross-country) (Mks IV and V).

By 1939 these were primarily used for training, although a small number of Marks IIA and IIB were used in the Western Desert 1940 and IIAs and IIIs by the South African Tank Corps in the 1941 Abyssinian campaign. A few Mks IV and V could still be found in units with the Mk VI at the beginning of the war.

LIGHT TANK, MARK VI

Entering service 1936, this was the main British tank type at the beginning of the war. It had a three-man crew (commander, gunner, driver) and two machine guns (Vickers .303 and Vickers .5 inch in Mark VI, VIA and VIB, Besa 15mm and Besa 7.92mm in Mark VIC). The tank grew from 10,800lbs (Mark VI) to 11,740lbs (Mark VIC); maximum armour was 14mm and maximum road speed 35mph (25mph cross-country). These were produced through the end of 1940, although in very small numbers after June 1940. The only variant was the light AA tank.

LIGHT TANK, MARK VII TETRARCH

The prototype was completed in December 1937, but production did not begin until November 1940 and only 171 were completed by 1942. The tank weighed 16,800lbs, had a crew of three (commander, gunner, driver), and was armed with a 2pdr gun and Besa MG. The close support version had a 3" howitzer in place of the 2pdr. (There was only a single mark, so the basic tank was a Tetrarch I and the close support version the Tetrarch I CS.) Maximum armour remained as for the Light Mark VI at 14mm, and the maximum road speed was 40mph (28mph cross-country).

These were used in the Madagascar campaign and then held for airborne operations; the Hamilcar glider was specially designed to carry a Tetrarch.

LIGHT TANK, MARK VIII HARRY HOPKINS

A development of the Tetrarch, with production of 102 by 1944. The vehicle weighed 19,040lbs and had a maximum road speed of 30mph (20mph cross-country). It had a crew of three (commander, gunner, driver) and was armed with a 2pdr gun and Besa MG. Maximum armour was 38mm. The tank never entered service since there was no role for it; by that point light tanks were limited to the airborne role. The chassis was the basis for the Alecto, with turret removed and a 95mm howitzer or 6pdr gun mounted low in the hull, intended for recce vehicles. (These added a loader to the normal crew of three.) A small number in 1945 were converted to Alecto Dozers.

STUART

This was the US *M3 Light Tank*, provided under Lend Lease. The name also referred to the later development, the US *M5 Light Tank*. The various designations used were:

- Stuart Mk I   M3
- Stuart Mk II   M3 (diesel; about 10% of M3 production)
- Stuart Mk III   M3A1
- Stuart Mk IV   M3A1 (diesel; under 5% of M3A1 production)
- Stuart Mk V   M3A3
- Stuart Mk VI   M5
- Stuart Mk VII   M5A1

Production of the M3 ended in August 1942, with the M3A1 in production April 1942 to January 1943, and the M3A3 December 1942 to August 1943. (The British also received some of the earlier M2A4 light tanks in the UK and Middle East for use as training vehicles along with the first shipments of the M3.) Production of an improved variant, the M5, began in 1942.[171] Its final version, the M5A1 (produced 1942 to June 1944) was the most widely-produced of the US light tanks. The British only received small numbers of the M5/M5A1 tank, all of which were used in NW Europe.

The M3 had a crew of four (commander, gunner, driver, co-driver), and weighed 27,400 lbs (M3) rising to 31,752 lbs (M3A3). Road speed was 36mph (20mph cross-country) and maximum armour 51mm. The tank had a 37mm gun (with APC, HE or canister rounds) and a coaxial .30 MG. The original M3 had two additional .30 MGs in hull sponsons;[172] these were eliminated on the M3A1. That tank and later M3 variants had two .30 MGs, one in a bow mount and the other on a turret pintle. The M5 was somewhat heavier—33,000 lbs (M5) and 33,907 lbs (M5A1). It had the same main gun and two .30 caliber MGs, and could have a .50 caliber AAMG. Maximum armour was increased to 67mm but the road speed remained at 36mph (cross-country speed, however, was improved at 24mph).

The M3 was first used from July 1941 to replace older British cruiser tanks in North Africa, and saw action in November 1941. They were used in the Desert with armoured regiments through 1943, but in Europe limited to armoured recce regiments or as the recce troop in armoured regiments. Stuarts were used with armoured regiments in Burma until the end of the war. The tank was first popularly known as the 'Honey' from its performance and layout, a nickname that remained in use to the end of the war alongside the official Stuart..

---

[171] There was no US M4 light tank; the M5 (light) was at first to be the M4 light, but changed to avoid confusion with the M4 medium, the Sherman.

[172] Generally removed by the British.

In some cases, the turret was removed and replaced with machine guns fitted on pintles. This was known unofficially as a 'sawn-off Honey' or more officially as the Stuart Recce. Armoured recce units did this to reduce the height of the vehicle, figuring that its 37mm gun was of little practical value in the field.[173] At least a few were used as APCs (turret removed and seats added), and these Stuart Kangaroos could also be used (with additional radio equipment) as a command vehicle.

LOCUST

The US M22 Light Tank, developed to be an airborne tank and thus lighter and smaller than the M3/M5 series. Several hundred were sent to Britain for use by US and British troops. The tank weighed 16,400 lbs, had a crew of three (commander, gunner, driver), and was armed with a 37mm gun and coaxial .30 MG. Maximum armour was 25mm and road speed was 40mph (30mph cross-country). With a single exception, the tank was used solely for training or other purposes. 6th Airborne Division utilized 12 of them (carried in Hamilcar gliders) for the March 1945 airborne operations.[174]

CHAFFEE

The US M24 Light Tank, provided under Lend Lease in 1945. The tank had a crew of five (commander, gunner, loader, driver, co-driver/radio operator) and weighed 40,500 lbs. Maximum armour was 25mm and maximum road speed was 35mph (25mph cross-country). It was armed with a 75mm gun,[175] coaxial .30 MG, bow-mounted .30 MG, and turret-mounted .50 AA MG. A small number were supplied to the British in 1945; US units had begun to receive it in late 1944 and were supplanting the M5 series by the war's end.

Infantry Tanks

These were the other major type of tank decided on in the 1930s. While cruisers would roam the battlefield, infantry tanks were intended to be heavily armoured vehicles which could support the infantry in attacks on prepared positions. Their heavy armour made them especially valuable in the early years, since most German tank and anti-tank guns had trouble penetrating them. Shortages of cruisers meant that some were pressed into use in armoured brigades for a period, although mainly they were found in separate tank

---

[173] Even in 1942, US tankers referred to the M3 light's main armament as a 'squirrel rifle' and thought the tank somewhat top-heavy due to its height. Rick Atkinson, *An Army at Dawn: The War in North Africa, 1942-1943* (New York: Henry Hold and Co, LLC, 2002), p 187.

[174] At one point these had replaced the Tetrarchs in the armoured squadron of the airborne armoured recce regiment, but the Tetrarchs returned prior to Normandy. When the regiment reorganized later in 1944, the Tetrarchs were replaced by the Locust.

[175] Its 75mm gun M6 was derived from the cannon used in the Mitchell bomber, and was not the 75mm M2 or M3 found on Sherman tanks.

brigades. Their slow speed made it hard for them to keep up in any kind of mobile operations, such as in the western desert or the breakout from Normandy in 1944. Creation of infantry tanks was regarded by many as a mistake, and the type was abandoned at the end of the war.

INFANTRY TANK, MARK I

The A11 was the first of the infantry tanks, with 140 completed by August 1940. This was a two-man tank (commander-gunner, driver) with a single MG (.303 or .5 Vickers). The vehicle weighed 24,640 lbs, had maximum armour of 60mm, and a road speed of just 8mph (cross-country was 5-6mph). Sometimes called the Matilda I. Used in France 1940, after which the remaining vehicles were utilized for training only.

MATILDA

Infantry Tank Mk II (A12) was sometimes called 'Matilda Senior' until the Infantry Tank Mk I disappeared; after that simply the Matilda. Only a few were available in September 1939; total production was 2,987 through August 1943. The vehicle weighed 59,360 lbs, had maximum armour of 78mm, and a road speed of 15mph (8mph cross-country). The Matilda's armour made it impervious to virtually any German tank or anti-tank weapon through 1942 except the 88mm AA gun. The crew was four (commander, gunner, loader, driver), and the armament was a 2pdr gun and Vickers MG (Mk I) or Besa MG (Mks II, III, IV and V). The III and IV CS versions had a 3" howitzer in place of the gun. The small size of the turret ring made it impossible to up-gun to the 6pdr, leading to the end of production.[176]

The first version was Matilda Mk I, then II, III (which had a CS version), IV (also with a CS version), and V. Variations were known officially as the Infantry Tank Mk IIA [Matilda II], then IIA* [Matilda III] and IIA** [Matilda IV]. The major changes were in the engine. Matilda V was simply a IV with improvements to the gear box and gear shift; there was no V CS.

Small numbers were available in France 1940, and the tank was later used in the Western Desert until July 1942, as well as equipping tank brigades in the UK. It was the basis for early mine-clearing and CDL tanks.

---

[176] As David Fletcher notes, with some irony, in *Matilda Infantry Tank*, the tank had no HE shell for its 2pdr gun, making it impossible to engage enemy infantry, despite the presumed mission of infantry tanks to help their own infantry break through positions (p. 17).

VALENTINE

Officially the Infantry Tank, Mark III, the Valentine was a private venture begun in 1938 by Vickers, derived in part from their work on the A9 and A10 cruisers. (As a private venture it had no 'A' number.) The first production tanks were delivered in 1940 (10 by June). Over 8,200 of the Infantry Tank, Mark III Valentine were built from 1940 to 1944 in the UK and Canada.[177] Even though an infantry tank, the armoured brigades of new armoured divisions from 1940 were often equipped with it. Unlike some of its contemporaries (especially cruisers), the Valentine was mechanically reliable, albeit slow (top road speed of 15mph; 8mph cross-country).

The tank began at 39,000lb, increasing to 41,000lb in Marks VIII-XI. Maximum armour was 65mm. Maxim road speed was 15mph (8mph cross-country).

Marks I and II had a crew of three (commander, gunner, driver) and were armed with a 2pdr gun and coaxial Besa MG. Marks III, IV and V had a new turret and the crew increased to four (adding a loader). Other differences among the early marks related to the engine. Marks VI, VII and VIIA were built in Canada, with a Browning .30 MG in lieu of the Besa.

Mark VIII was a Mark III up-gunned; it reduced the crew back to three, but mounted a 6pdr gun and eliminated the coaxial MG. Mark IX was an up-gunned Mark V. Mark X, in production 1943, was built with the 6pdr gun, and had a coaxial Besa MG.

Mark XI was built beginning late 1943, and mounted a 75mm gun.

There was no close support version of the Valentine. However, it was the basis for a number of variants and adaptations. The first DD tank was a Valentine (utilizing Mks V, IX and XI): 625 Valentines were converted March 1943 to 1944. These were used for training in the UK, Italy and India, with their only operational use in Italy in 1945, and that in small numbers. An armoured bridgelayer (scissors bridge) was developed, with an establishment of six for each armoured brigade. Some 150 were converted 1943-44 as the 'UK Scorpion Mk III' and used to train flail regiments. There were dozer and OP variants, and the Valentine was the basis for the Bishop SP 25pdr and Archer SP 17pdr tank destroyer. Some of the tanks were used as battery commander vehicles in the Archer regiments.

---

[177] Of the 1,420 built in Canada, all but 30 went to the USSR, along with about 1,300 of the Valentines built in the UK, leaving about 5,500 for UK use.

CHURCHILL

Built from 1941 (the first 14 production models delivered that June), some 5,640 of the Infantry Tank, Mark IV Churchill [A22] were manufactured during the war.[178]

The tank grew from 87,360lb (Mks III-VI) to 89,600lb (Mks VII-VIII). It had a crew of five (commander, gunner, loader, co-driver/hull gunner). The original maximum armour was 102mm, increasing to 152mm for Mks VII and VIII. Maximum road speed was 15½mph in the early marks, reduced to 12½mph in the heavier Mks VII and VIII (cross-country around 8mph in either case).

Churchill I had a 2pdr gun and coaxial Besa MG, plus a 3" howitzer mounted in the nose. Churchill II was similar, but dropped the hull howitzer and replaced it with another Besa MG. The Churchill II CS (built in small numbers) was the reverse of Churchill I: the 3" howitzer was in the turret and the 2pdr was in the nose.

Churchill III (appearing March 1942) was the first to mount the 6pdr gun, also having a redesigned turret. Many of the earlier marks were given the new turret and gun, bringing them up to Mk III standards. Churchill IV was similar, but with a cast turret. Both these and later marks had two Besa MGs (coaxial and hull).

In 1943, an REME captain in Tunisia suggested fitting the 75mm gun and mantlet (including coaxial .30 caliber MG) from wrecked Sherman tanks to the Churchill Mark IV. After experiments with a prototype, about 200 were converted in the beginning of 1944, known as the Churchill IV (NA 75), or simply Churchill NA75. The hull Besa was also replaced by the US 30 caliber MG to standardize ammunition for the tank. These began to be issued to the 21st and 25th Tank Brigades in Italy, replacing the Sherman tanks that had been issued to two troops in each squadron. They remained in use in Italy to the end of the war.[179]

Churchill V was the CS version, with a 95mm howitzer in place of the 6pdr gun. Ten percent of the Churchills (Mks V and VIII) were the CS version.

The Churchill VI was a reworked Mk IV with the new British 75mm tank gun. These conversions began in November 1943. Because work on this started so late, along with the new Churchill VII, fully 73% of the gun-armed Churchill tanks with 21st Army Group in June 1944 were still armed with the 6pdr gun.

---

[178] Churchill VII was originally the A22F, changed to A42 in 1945.
[179] The officer was Captain P. H. Morrell. The full story of the conversions is contained in Chris Shillito, 'The Churchill N.A. 75'.

Churchill VII was a larger and redesigned tank, built from the start to mount the 75mm gun. It had heavier armour, a heavier suspension, and other improvements. Churchill VIII was the CS version of this mark, with the 95mm howitzer.

Churchill IX was a III or IV reworked in part; it gained the turret from the VII but retained a 6pdr gun. The IX LT retained the original turret (LT='light turret'). Churchill X was a reworked VI with the new turret, retaining its 75mm gun; a reworked version with the original turret was a X LT. Churchill XI was a reworked V (CS) with the turret from the VIII; XI LT was a reworked V but with the original turret.

The Churchill was also the basis for a wide variety of specialized armour, including the AVRE, flamethrower tanks, and bridgelayers. The Churchill ARV Mk I was a Churchill I or II with the turret removed and other changes made; it had a mount for a twin Bren LMG; and was produced from February 1942. Churchill ARV Mk II was a converted III or IV, produced beginning 1944. In addition to the front and rear demountable jibs of the Mk I, it had an earth spade at the rear and a winch. A very small number of vehicles were converted to the Churchill BARV [Beach ARV]; these were the ARV Mk I standard with deep wading gear and were for recovering tanks on beaches.

Miscellaneous Tanks

The Centurion appeared just as the war ended in Europe; it would go on to be the first major British tank of the post-war era, with 13 marks and a production run that only ended in 1962. With that exception, the vehicles in this section reflected dead ends or a waste of resources.

CENTURION

The Centurion [A41] was designed to be a heavy cruiser, although it would later become the first 'universal tank': a replacement for both cruisers and infantry tanks. Development was approved in July 1943. The tank was to have the 17pdr gun and either a 20mm Polsten cannon or 7.92mm Besa MG in the turret front; there was no hull MG. Centurion Mk I weighed 107,520 pounds, had a crew of four, and a maximum road speed of 21.4mph (15mph cross-country). Twenty pilots were ordered, with varying combinations of Polsten or Besa. The first six completed went to 22nd Armoured Brigade in May 1945 in the hopes of combat testing, but the war ended before they arrived. A prototype of Centurion Mk II was approved in January 1945, and that would be the first production vehicle (as Centurion Mk 2).

BLACK PRINCE

The Black Prince [A43] was intended to be an infantry tank armed with the 17pdr gun. It was a larger and heavier derivative of the Churchill VII. The tank had a crew of five, weighed 112,000 lbs, and had road speed of only 11mph (about 7mph cross-country). It was armed with a 17pdr gun and two 7.92mm Besa MGs (coaxial and hull). Six prototypes were delivered in May 1945 and tested, but the tank never entered production due to the superiority of the Centurion.

HEAVY TANK TOG

A committee began to design a heavy tank in 1939, and construction on TOG I ['The Old Group' Mk I, a reference to the committee] began in February 1940, with the prototype ready that October. The vehicle weighed 142,320 lbs, with a crew of eight and a maximum road speed of 5-8mph (perhaps 4mph cross-country). It had a French 75mm gun fitted in the nose and a Matilda turret with 2pdr gun. No MGs were fitted. An improved version, TOG 2, had its only prototype built in March 191. This vehicle would have been 179,200 lbs with a crew of six. It was first completed with a mock-up turret and 6pdr gun, later replaced by a different turret with the intended 17pdr gun.

HEAVY ASSAULT TANK A33

The A33 was intended to use the Cromwell chassis as the basis for a heavier infantry tank to replace the Churchill. Two pilots were built in 1943, but the Churchill had proven itself in combat and the tank was never produced. It weighed 100,800 lbs with a road speed of 24mph (12mph cross-country). There was a crew of five; the pilot was built with a 6pdr gun although the design was for a 75mm gun.

VALIANT INFANTRY TANK

The A38 Valiant was to be an improved Valentine. A pilot appeared in mid 1944, and a second pilot with different engine was produced later. The tank weighed 60,480 lbs, with a road speed of 12mph (7mph cross-country). It had a crew of four and was armed with a 75mm gun and two Besa MGs. Note that work on an improved Valentine was going on at the same time as the Black Prince, an improved Churchill.

Specialized Armour

ASSAULT VEHICLE RE [AVRE]

 The AVRE was developed from 1942 on the Churchill III or IV infantry tank chassis. There were 180 converted by D-Day (6 June 1944) and another 574 converted later. The basic vehicle had a Petard spigot mortar, which could fire a 26-pound charge 80 yards or so. The idea was to use this to destroy obstacles, especially on beaches. Each vehicle carried 14 Petard bombs and 18

General Wade charges.[180] Two of the lorries in each troop carried an additional 84 Petard bombs and 108 General Wade charges, along with other explosives. The vehicle had a crew of six (commander, corporal demolition NCO, driver, co-driver/loader, mortar man, operator).

The AVRE could also carry a Small Box Girder [SBG] bridge (30' span), carry fascines (a brushwood bundle 8' in diameter and 12-14' wide for crossing trenches), or operate a wide variety of attachments.[181] An AVRE could be used to push Bailey Bridges on skids into position. For the Rhine crossings in 1945, most were used with Class 50/60 Rafts.[182]

MINE-CLEARING TANKS

A device with rows of chains attached to a power-driven revolving drum was fitted to the front of tanks to use in clearing minefields. In the Middle East, these were known as **Scorpions**. The first version was fitted to a Matilda Infantry Tank (Scorpion Mark I, the first 32 were used October 1942 at El Alamein). Fitted to a Valentine with turret removed, this became the Scorpion II, which was never used operationally. The device was also fitted to the Grant tank, as Scorpion Mark III; only a few were built, and used in Sicily. This equipment was later fitted to the Sherman tank, which could retain its turret armament; these were known as Sherman Scorpion IV. Scorpions were the flail type used in Italy.

There was a separate development of flail tanks in the UK, beginning in December 1941 and also using a Matilda. These were known as the **Baron**, with Marks I, II, III and IIIA depending on attachments and mechanism from 1941-43. However, the Middle East design proved better, and a modification of it was fitted to Valentine tanks as Scorpion Mark III [duplicating the designation given the Grants] or as Valentine Scorpion. Barons were used only for training.

From 1943, a design was also built for a Sherman; called the **Marquis**, the turret was replaced by an armoured housing to power the flail. This was abandoned in favor of the **Crab**. In the Scorpions (and other early flail tanks), the power came from auxiliary engines in the equipment. For Crabs, the power was drawn from the tank's own engine. In addition, the tank could retain its turret and armament. The Sherman V was selected in June 1943 for production in quantity for use in NW Europe as the Sherman Crab,

---

[180] These were a shaped charge with 26 pounds of explosives, fitted to collapsible frames and placed on concrete obstacles by dismounted crewmen.

[181] These included folding and towed SBG assault bridges, a Bailey bridge on skids (which could be pushed by the AVRE), carpet layers to cross clay and later log carpet layers to cross waterlogged ground, and some mine clearing attachments.

[182] The Class 50/60 Raft was first delivered in August 1944, and operated as a ferry to carry heavy vehicles across rivers. Bridge panels were 8'6" long, plus ramps; five pontoons formed a Class 60 Raft and four a Class 50. They were towed on trailers.

Marks I and II. (Mark II had a contouring device for better coverage on rough ground, but was not available in quantity before the war ended.) 689 Shermans were modified as Crabs between November 1943 and December 1944. A Crab squadron was responsible for clearing three 24-foot paths through a minefield, with each of its three troops deploying three Crabs for clearing; the other two provided fire support or replacements.

FLAMETHROWER TANKS

Work on flamethrower tanks began in late 1940, and two early designs were built around the Valentine. While these were being evaluated in 1942, work also started using the Churchill as the basis. These became known as **Crocodiles**. The Churchill IV was the basis for the first Crocodiles, although production Crocodiles were based on the Mk VII. The vehicle had an armoured trailer with 400 gallons of flame fuel. The flame projector was mounted in the hull, in place of the machine gun in the front, allowing the tank to retain its main armament of a 75mm gun and coaxial Besa MG. The flamethrower had a range of 80-120 yards. A total of 800 Crocodiles were produced by May 1945, with 250 earmarked for the far east.

SEARCHLIGHT [CDL] TANKS

These began production in 1941, on the Matilda chassis, and were known for secrecy as 'Canal Defence Lights' (CDL), the reference being to the Suez Canal. The Matilda II and Matilda V were first used for this role, with an order of 300 armoured housings with a high intensity arc lamp which could project a beam. Final development of the CDL was on a Grant chassis, which could retain the hull 75mm gun when the turret was removed and replaced by the special armoured searchlight turret. There was a MG mounted in the turret front.

DUPLEX DRIVE (DD) TANKS

Duplex Drive (DD) tanks were simply standard vehicles given limited amphibious capability via canvas flotation screens and a propeller/rudder assembly. Once on land the DD attachments could be removed and the tank functioned normally. The first DD tank was a single Tetrarch light tank, used to test the equipment in 1941; production DDs 1942-43 (650) were the Valentine (Marks III and VIII). The Valentine DD was largely used for training crews, although a few were also used in Italy late in the war. From late 1943, the standard DD tank was the Sherman, which had twin screws on the equipment. Once ashore (D-Day) or across the river (Rhine 1945) the DD equipment was jettisoned and the Shermans operated normally. The first version were Sherman III and V, using essentially the same equipment as the Valentine. Improved conversion kits led to the Sherman III and V DD Mk I and Sherman III DD Mk II. An American conversion to

British vehicles with detail changes led to the Sherman III and IIIAY DD Mk III, but these were not available until late 1945.

BRIDGELAYER TANKS

There were a variety of bridgelayer tanks. A 30' scissors bridge, which could support vehicles up to 30 tons, was fitted to Covenanter or Valentine tanks. The bridge was later modified to take up to 80 tons and carried on the Churchill. The Churchill Bridgelayer was originally on a Mk III or IV; from 1945 conversions were based on the Mk VII chassis. Generally, Valentine Bridgelayers were issued to armoured brigades and Churchill Bridgelayers to tank brigades.

Vehicles with a rigid ramp bridge were known as **Arks**.[183] A small number of Shermans were used in Italy, but the basic Ark was a Churchill. Churchill Ark Mk I was built on the chassis of a II or IV; 50 were ordered in February 1944 following initial tests. Its bridge could cover 28'.

The Churchill Ark Mk II came in two different versions, the UK Pattern used by 79th Armoured Division and the Italian Pattern used in Italy. Following testing in July 1944, all 79th Armoured Division Ark Mk Is were converted to Mk II. In Italy the Churchill III chassis was used for conversion; this utilized US made ramps which came in somewhat different lengths than the British. The Ark Mk II could span 47'6" to 54'4" depending on variant. With an Ark, the vehicle drove into the ditch and then dropped the ramps to create a bridge.

Anti-Aircraft Tanks

AA tanks began to appear on war establishments in the UK 26 August 1942 when eight AA tanks were added to the RHQ of an armoured regiment. On 30 November 1943 this was changed to an AA troop (six AA tanks) in the HQ squadron.

For tank regiments, the eight AA tanks at RHQ were added 16 August 1942. As with armoured regiments, this was changed 30 November 1943 to a troop of six AA tanks in the HQ squadron.

The AA troops were all disbanded during the summer of 1944, given the lack of any serious German air threat and the need for personnel. Despite that, they remained part of the armoured regiment May 1945 war establishment.

---

[183] Shorthand for 'Armoured Ramp Carriers'. Shown as Ark or ARK in different publications; the shorthand appears to mimic the pronunciation rather than the spelling of the full title.

LIGHT AA TANKS

Light Tanks Mark VI were modified from 1940 to take a special turret with four Besa 7.92mm MGs. There was a Light AA Tank Mark I (built on the Mk VIA chassis) and then a Mark II (built on the Mk VIB chassis) with improvements to the turret and sights.

CRUISER AA TANKS

Two versions of AA tank on the Crusader III were built: one with a 40mm gun (Crusader AA Mk I) and another (Crusader AA Mk II, appearing summer 1943) with twin 20mm Oerlikon cannon in a turret. There was also a Crusader AA Mk III which was the Mk II with a redesigned turret and radio equipment moved to the hull. The original version of the Crusader AA Mk I simply had the 40mm gun with a front shield, but this was later replaced by an all-around open-topped shield. There were orders for 215 of the Crusader AA I, but actual production is unclear and the vehicle appears not to have been used. About 600 of the Crusader AA II and III were produced.

Centaur AA tanks were built on the Centaur III or IV chassis. Centaur AA Mk I had the same turret as the Crusader AA Mk II, but with Polsten 20mm cannons in place of the Oerlikons. Centaur AA Mk II had turret of the Crusader AA Mk III, again substituting Polstens for Oerlikons.

Armoured Cars

As with tanks, armoured cars were originally part of the RTC. Several regular armoured car companies survived into the post-war years, and a number were formed in the TA from former Yeomanry regiments. In 1928, two regular cavalry regiments converted to armoured cars, and the regular RTC companies were gradually disbanded or converted over to light tanks. When the TF companies resumed their former identities in 1939, the RTR no longer had any connection with armoured cars. For a period mainly in 1940, armoured cars were officially designated light tanks (wheeled); the designation armoured car returned by 1941.

ROLLS-ROYCE, 1920 OR 1924 PATTERN ARMOURED CAR

These were old vehicles, 70 of which were still in service at the beginning of the war. Mostly used in the UK for training, the 11th Hussars took them into action 1940-41 in the Desert. Originally armed with a Vickers MG, the 11th Hussars variant had an open-topped turret with Boys Atk rifle, Bren LMG, and smoke discharger. The cars had a maximum of 9mm of armour and a road speed of 45mph; the 1920 Pattern weighed 3.8 tons and the 1924 Pattern 4.15 tons. Both vehicles had a crew of three.

MORRIS ARMOURED CAR

Built 1935-36 (99 vehicles) and used by 12th Lancers in France 1940 and 11th Hussars in the Desert to spring 1941. Also known as Morris CS9/LAC. More properly a light recce car than an armoured car, this 4x2 vehicle had a crew of four and an open-top turret with Boys Atk rifle, Bren LMG, and smoke discharger. It weighed 4.2 tons, had maximum armour of 7mm, and a road speed of 45mph.

GUY ARMOURED CAR

The first 4x4 all-welded AFV to go into production for the British Army, developed on the chassis of the Guy Quad-Ant field artillery tractor. The vehicle weighed 5.2 tons, could travel 40mph. It had a crew of three and was armed with a Vickers .50 MG and either a Vickers .303 (Mark I) or Besa 7.92mm MG (Mark IA). Production only began in 1939, and 101 were built (50 Mk I and 51 Mk IA). A few were used in France 1940 with the unit that would become the GHQ Liaison Regiment ('Phantom'), the others going to regiments in the UK.

HUMBER ARMOURED CAR

The chassis of this vehicle was based on a 4x4 field artillery tractor; the hull and turret of the Humber Mark I were identical with the Guy IA. Later marks changed the hull, turret and armament. Marks I and II had a crew of three, maximum armour was 15mm and were armed with two MGs (Besa 15mm and Besa 7.92mm). Road speed was 45mph, and weight went from 6.85 tons (Mark I) to 7.1 tons (Mark II).

Marks III and IV also weighed 7.1 tons, but had different turrets and a crew of four. Mark III (in production 1942) retained the armament of two MGs, but the Mark IV had the US 37mm gun and a Besa 7.92mm MG. Maximum armour remained at 15mm and road speed at 45mph. Production, which ended in mid 1944, totaled about 5,400 vehicles (500 were the original Mark I).

The Humber was first issued to units in the UK about June 1941 and in the Middle East September 1941. While the Daimler became the preferred vehicle in armoured car regiments from 1943, Humbers were still used (often for command purposes, because of their greater roominess). They were also the basic vehicle in [infantry division] reconnaissance regiments. General Motors built a variant in Canada, designated the Fox Mark I (similar to Humber Mark III, but with .50 and .30 Browning MGs and a different engine; 200 were built). The Humber also provided the basis for an AA variant.

DAIMLER ARMOURED CAR

This 4x4 car was designed in 1939 and in service from 1941. The vehicle weighed 7.5 tons, had a crew of three, maximum armour of 16mm, and a road speed of 50mph. Armament was a 2pdr gun and Besa MG. The vehicle was built in two marks (Mark II entering production in 1944). Some cars used as regimental command vehicles had the turret removed. Production totaled 2,694 vehicles (some 1,900 being Mark I).

First received in the Middle East about July 1942. From 1943 the Daimler became the preferred basic vehicle in armoured car regiments. Some recce regiments replaced their Humber armoured cars with Daimlers beginning August 1944.

MARMON-HARRINGTON ARMOURED CAR

Built in South Africa and known to the Union Defence Force (UDF) [184] as South African Reconnaissance Car. These were used by South African and other units, especially in the Desert during 1941. Mark I was used only by the UDF. Mark II weighed 6 tons, maximum armour of 12mm, road speed of 50mph, a crew of four, and was armed with a Boys Atk Rifle and Bren LMG. Mark III was similar, but with a crew of three. These were often modified in the Desert, and could be found with Italian 47mm or French 25mm anti-tank guns, the German 37mm anti-tank gun, or a 20mm Breda AA/Atk gun.

The Mark IV was a new design, appearing January 1943, with a 2pdr gun and .30 MG; the IVF was the same vehicle on a Ford F60L lorry chassis instead of the Marmon-Herrington. Weight, armour and road speed were the same as earlier marks. The IV and IVF were used in the Mediterranean. Altogether, 5,746 were built.

AEC ARMOURED CAR

Begun as a private venture and prototyped in 1941, based on their Matador heavy truck, the AEC [Associated Equipment Company] Mk I saw action from 1942. It weighed 11 tons, had a road speed of 36mph, double the armour of earlier armoured cars (30mm), a crew of three, and armament of a 2pdr gun and Besa MG.

The Mk II was increased to 12.7 tons, a crew of four, and armed with a 6pdr gun and Besa MG. It also had 30mm of armour and a road speed of 41mph.

Mk III was similar in weight and other characteristics, but armed with a 75mm gun and Besa MG. These last were employed in the heavy troops of armoured car regiments (in

---

[184] Union Defence Force: the South African military.

21st Army Group) from 1944 on.[185] Production of the AEC totaled 629 (120 were Mark I and 200 Mark III).

COVENTRY ARMOURED CAR

The Mark I weighed 11.5 tons, had maximum armour of 14mm, road speed of 41 mph, and a crew of four. It was armed with a 2pdr gun and Besa MG. It was a joint effort by Humber and Daimler, with the first prototypes read in 1944. The planned Mark II would have had a 75mm gun and a crew of three.

This was intended to replace the US-built Staghound at regimental and squadron headquarters in armoured car regiments. The order for Mark I was 300, with production beginning in 1944 (68 built by December, and perhaps 175 by June 1945). The Mark II was cancelled without being produced. Of the 300 to be built, 280 ended up allocated to the French Army who used them in Indo China after the war.

U.S.-BUILT ARMOURED CARS

The M8 Armored Car was known to the British as **Greyhound** (six-wheeled vehicle, weighing 17,200 lbs, and armed in a turret with 37mm gun and 0.30 cal MG). The order was for 496 vehicles, which were used almost entirely in the Central Mediterranean Force (Italy, North Africa, the Middle East). Deliveries began in 1944.

The M6 Armored Car was known as **Staghound** and was used mainly by the British as opposed to the US itself (four-wheeled vehicle, 29,100 lbs, and armed with a 37mm gun and three 0.30 cal MGs). The crew was five and maximum road speed 55mph. The original M6 was T17E1; the similar T17E2 was originally fitted with twin 0.50-cal AAMG. The British also equipped Staghounds with a 3" howitzer and then with a Crusader-type tank turret with a 75mm gun. Some 3,844 of the T17E1 and T17E2 were produced, of which 2,844 went to the British Army. The Staghound with a 37mm gun (Staghound I) was used at regimental, and sometimes squadron, headquarters in armoured car regiments. Staghound II was a field conversion with the 3" howitzer in place of the 37mm gun. The Staghound III (the turret of Crusader tank with 6pdr gun, and some were refitted with the 75mm gun) was limited to an order of 100; possibly reduced later to 50, with at least 32 produced. A Staghound Command variant (turret removed and extra wireless equipment) existed. The Staghound AA (789 produced 1943-44) had a crew of three.

---

[185] The earlier, and alternative vehicle for this role, was the US M3 75mm GMC (a modification of the M3 halftrack with a 75mm gun). Heavy troops in the Mediterranean usually had the halftrack in lieu of the AEC III, and regiments from that theatre brought the vehicle with them to NW Europe.

The T18E2 was known as the **Boarhound**. Designed for the British Army in North Africa, but only a few (30) were produced and delivered. The vehicle was eight-wheeled, weighed 53,000 lbs, and armed with a 6pdr gun in a turret. Crew was five and maximum road speed 50mph.

The M38 Armored Car was known as **Wolfhound**. Although standardized, there was no series production.

COVENTRY ARMOURED CAR

Begun late in the war, designed to replace Humber and Daimler armoured cars and involving both companies. Mk I had a 2pdr gun and Mk II a 75mm gun, but few were produced before the war ended.

ANTI-AIRCRAFT ARMOURED CARS

A version of the Humber Mk I appeared in 1942, with a special turret mounting four Besa MGs and an AA sight. It appears that only 91 were built. Some Marmon-Harringtons and Daimlers were fitted for AA work, and a prototype of the AEC with twin 20mm Oerlikon cannon or US .50-caliber MGs was produced in 1944. There apparently at one time an intent to order 1,000 of these, but it is unclear how many were built, and some of those were used for command rather than AA purposes.

Scout and Light Reconnaissance Cars

SCOUT CARS

The Scout Car was a small, two-person armoured vehicle for liaison and reconnaissance work. The first version were made by **Daimler**. These were 2.8 tons (Mk I), growing to 3 tons (Mks II and III). Road speed was 55mph, and armament a single Bren LMG. A total of 6,626 were produced (1,659 Mk I, 4,527 Mk II and 199 Mk III). These had folding or sliding roofs.

Ford Motor of Canada produced a similar vehicle for Canadian units, the **Lynx** (Mks I and II), which was slightly heavier at 4 tons; 3255 were built. The British used some of these in North Africa and in India.

Finally, **Humber** produced 4,300 scout cars (also in two Mks; 1,698 Mk I). These weighed 3.39 tons and had a road speed of 60mph. The crew was two, but there was emergency seating for a third.

Daimlers were used throughout the world, Lynxes in South-East Asia and with Canadian formations, and the Humbers mainly with 21st Army Group.

LIGHT RECONNAISSANCE CARS

The first vehicles in this category were simply improvised 4x2 vehicles and intended for home defence. The Beaverette (Mks I to IV, 2,800 built) was ultimately used by the RAF for airfield protection as well as by the Army. All came with a Bren LMG, in an open compartment on Marks I and II and a small turret in Mks III and IV. When used by the RAF, Mks III and IV could be re-armed with twin Vickers 'K' aircraft MGs. Armor was basically mild steel (less than ½") on front and sides with 3" oak slabs in the front. The Beaverette III was fully enclosed and had proper armour plate. The name derived from Lord Beaverbrook, who intended it for the defense of factories. It was also known as the Humberette, since these were built on Humber Super Snipe or Standard car chassis.

Humber cars began with the Mk I (2.8 tons, 45mph road speed, and crew of three), with a Bren LMG and Boys Atk Rifle The Humber II came with a small turret, and was only marginally heavier (2.98 tons). Final production was Mk III and IIIA, at 3.5 tons and a road speed of 50mph. The II was still 4.x2, while the III and IIIA were 4x4. 3,599 Humbers of all marks were built; they were used by the recce regiments in infantry divisions and by the RAF Regiment for airfield protection.

Canadians used the **Otter** Mk I, which was similar to the Humber III; 1,761 were built and some also used by British units.

The final vehicle of this type was the **Morris**, with about 2,200 built; Mk I was 4.x2 and Mk II 4x4. By 1944 it was the only one still in production.

Armoured Personnel Carriers

There was no purpose-built APC in the Second World War. However, beginning in 1944 surplus SP gun and tank chassis were converted for the role.

MODIFIED PRIEST

In summer 1944, II Canadian Corps oversaw the conversion of US-built SP 105mm Howitzers ('Priests', leading to the APC being dubbed an 'unfrocked Priest') into APCs.[186] The howitzer was removed and the openings plated over. These could carry 12 men (crew and 10 infantry), and were first used on 7 August 1944. (Those in 21st Army Group were withdrawn once the Ram Kangaroo became available.) A similar conversion was carried out in Italy between October 1944 and April 1945, with 102 Priests converted to APCs. These had new front armour protection added.

---

[186] The three Normandy assault divisions—3rd Infantry, 50th (Northumbrian) Infantry and 3rd Canadian Infantry—had their towed 25pdr guns replaced by the Priest for the landings. The SP vehicles were withdrawn by August 1944 due to ammunition shortages; the regiments re-equipped with the 25pdr and the Priests were thus available for other purposes.

KANGAROO

Turretless Canadian Ram chassis were converted by 21st Army Group into an APC, with about 300 vehicles available by December 1944.[187] The turret and ammunition stowage were removed, the transmission shaft boxed in, and fittings for a wireless set were installed in the front near side. (One vehicle in each section had wireless set installed.) The hull machine gun was retained. There were no seats, and the vehicle had no overhead cover for the passengers. Each could carry crew (two) and 8-10 infantry.

In Italy, 75 Sherman IIIs were converted to Sherman Kangaroos between October 1944 and April 1945. Similar to the Ram Kangaroos, the turret was removed and the interior cleaned out, allowing a crew of two and 10 infantry.

ARMOURED COMMAND VEHICLES

The first of these, produced in 1937, was an armoured office body on a Morris 4x2 15cwt truck. Some Morris armoured cars were also later converted to an ACV configuration. Larger vehicles, on a 4x4 chassis became available from late 1941. The standardized version of this, somewhat later, was the Armoured Command Vehicle (AEC), 4x4, Mk I, built on the AEC Matador chassis. The two variants were HP (High Power) and LP (Low Power), depending on the installed radio equipment. An AEC 6x6 chassis was used, towards the end of the war, for a larger ACV, the Armoured Command Vehicle (AEC), 6x6, Mk I; this also came in HP and LP versions. ACVs were used by armoured formation headquarters. The basic crew was a driver, two radio operators, and four officers.

Carriers and Halftracks

Carriers were unique to the British and Commonwealth armies, found throughout the combat arms.

EARLY CARRIERS

The carrier was a small, lightly-armoured and fully-tracked vehicle, developed in 1935 and placed into service from 1936. The first were intended to carry the Vickers MG, and known as *Carrier MG*. Three more types were ordered after 1936: Cavalry, Bren, and Scout. The *Cavalry Carrier* was intended for mechanized cavalry units and could carry four-six men and their weapons. By 1939, there was no actual requirement for this vehicle, since cavalry regiments were not used as mechanized infantry. The *Scout Carrier* was also for the cavalry (divisional cavalry regiments with infantry divisions),

---

[187] The Ram was a tank built in Canada, utilizing mechanical components of the US M3 medium tank, but with a hull and turret. Used in the end only for training, Ram I had a 2pdr gun and Ram II a 6pdr gun.

and armed with a Bren LMG and Boys Atk Rifle along with a 3" smoke discharger and a wireless set. It was used in France 1940 and early desert campaigns. The *Bren Carrier* was intended as a vehicle for carrying the Bren LMG into action, with the gun used mounted or dismounted.

UNIVERSAL CARRIERS

In April 1939, the Army standardized on a vehicle with a new hull to replace the four different hulls then in production. These are often called 'Bren Carriers' even though the original Bren Carrier went out of production by 1940 and the 35,000 or more Carriers produced were actually the Universal version. Mark II weighed 3.95 tons, had a road speed of 32mph, and could carry four-five men. Normal armament carried was a Bren LMG, a Boys Atk Rifle, or both. (The Atk Rifle was discarded later in the war.) Universal Carriers filled a variety of roles, carrying personnel in motor and reconnaissance units as well as serving as liaison vehicles and towing vehicles for 6pdr Atk guns in infantry battalions.

Specialized variants included Carrier AOP [Armoured Observation Post] for artillery units, Carrier 3" Mortar, and Carrier MMG (built from 1943 and intended for the Vickers MG, mounted on a pedestal in the center of the vehicle). A flamethrower version was developed for the infantry.

Larger variants of the Universal Carrier were built: the T16 (4.25 tons) and Windsor (5.35 tons). The latter was built in Canada and placed in use from 1945 in 21st Army Group as a towing vehicle for 6pdr Atk guns and a method of carrying the 4.2" mortar. The Universal Carrier T16 was manufactured in the US (13,893 manufactured), and used primarily in the Far East at the end of the war.

The *Lloyd Carrier* was a larger but unarmoured carrier variant. These filled a variety of roles, including cable-laying for the Royal Signals or slave battery carriers as mobile charging units. They were also used as tractors, especially for the 6pdr Atk gun or the trailer carrying the 4.2" mortar or its shells.

WHITE HALFTRACKS

This was the U.S.-built M5 and M5A1 half-tracked personnel carrier. It weighed just over 7 tons (depending on the version and whether or not a winch was fitted) and could carry 13 men (3 in front and 10 in the rear). The M5A1 variant differed in part by having a ring mount for an AA MG. They could be built by White or International Harvester, although the latter may have built most. The original, and identical, US vehicle was the M3/M3A1, but it appears that few were supplied to other armies. The M5/M5A1 were built solely for Lend Lease. In some cases, the halftracks ended up replacing smaller White scout cars. There were FFW and Wireless versions, the latter for the Royal Signals.

International Harvester also built a variant of the earlier and smaller M2/M2A1,[188] as the M9/M9A1 and these were also supplied to other armies. Beginning in 1943, Great Britain received 4,296 M5/M5A1 halftracks and 1,419 of the M9A1. The latter could be converted to M5A1 specifications although the shorter hull still limited seating to seven instead of 10 in the rear and two rather than three upfront. The vehicle was also used as a tractor for the 17pdr Atk gun and as an ambulance.

The T48 57mm Gun Motor Carriage was designed to a British specification for a self-propelled tank destroyer with the 57mm anti-tank gun (US version of the British 6pdr). Only 30 were provided in 1943; no longer desired for the original role, they were converted back to the basic M3 vehicle.

Some 1,600-1,800 of the M14 multiple gun carriage (M5 variant with quad .50 caliber machine guns and no rear door) were supplied under Lend-Lease. However, the British did not take them into use in the AA role. They removed the guns from these and converted them to other uses.[189] Unlike the standard vehicle, there was no rear door but the top of the sides and rear could be folded down. Common uses were as a replacement for the Loyd Carrier or as a ammunition carrier. There was a FFW command variant.

M3 GUN MOTOR CARRIAGE, 75MM GUN

An M3 halftrack modified with the M1897A4 75mm gun[190] mounted in the rear compartment, facing forward. Developed in 1941 as the first US self-propelled tank destroyer, it was later supplanted in that role. About 170 (possibly all used vehicles in NW Africa) were taken over by the British Army and used in the heavy troop of armoured car regiments serving in Italy and the Mediterranean. The vehicle was officially declared obsolete by the US in September 1944. British armoured car regiments in Italy appear to have kept it in use until the gun barrels wore out, at which time they would have switched to the AEC Mk III armoured car.

---

[188] At least in the US Army, the M2 series was initially used as a prime mover for the 105mm howitzer and replaced by other vehicles from 1943.

[189] Given that the entire production run of the M14 was for the British—the US Army used the M13 (built on the M3 chassis)—it is not clear how so many unwanted vehicles ended up produced and transported across the Atlantic. The US Army used the M13 (and the M16, a variant with a different mount for the quad 50s) in anti-aircraft artillery battalions.

[190] The 'French 75' of World War I, adopted by the US Army in 1917 and modified. Some had been supplied to the British, who termed it the Ordnance QF 75mm Mk 1.

White Scout Cars

The U.S.-built 4x4 M3 and M3A1 Scout Car, classified by the British as Truck, 15-cwt 4x4. A lightly-armoured vehicle used in various roles, including APC, command, and ambulance. The personnel variant could carry eight men. There was a FFW variant, but it was cramped due to the small size of the vehicle. The Royal Signals had a wireless version that was even more cramped, due to the greater variety of equipment on board.

Amphibians

Terrapin

Officially, Amphibian, 4-ton, 8x8. The Mark I reached series production (500 built). Like the American DUKW ('Duck'), the Terrapin was intended mainly for ship-to-shore movement of supplies. It weighed 6 tons 16 cwt. There was also a larger Mark II (5-ton payload, 11 ton 8 cwt overall weight). With the engines and driving positions in the center, there were two cargo holds (forward and aft); capacity was four tons. Only the center four wheels were actually powered; the rear two made contact only in soft going, and the front two were set higher for use when climbing banks.

Neptune

A fully-tracked, lightly-armoured vehicle similar to the U.S. LVT 4 (Buffalo IV) and developed so as not to be entirely dependant on US Lend Lease. Payload was 4-5 tons, making it larger than the American vehicle. Only a few of the 2,000 ordered were actually built and delivered before the end of the war.

Water Weasel

The U.S.-built M29C Cargo Carrier, Amphibian; a fully-tracked vehicle known to the British as Amphibian, 10-cwt, Tracked, GS. This also existed as a non-amphibious tracked cargo carrier (M29, US 'Weasel', British Truck, 10-cwt, Tracked, GS).[191] In either form, the vehicle was intended for use over snow or swamp and had a very low ground pressure. It could have one seat with a cargo compartment or three seats. As an amphibian the vehicle was only suitable for use in calm or slow moving water.

---

[191] The basic vehicle had some amphibious capability, but with a very low freeboard.

GMC DUKW 353

A 6x6 amphibious truck, the 'Duck'[192] was basically a boat body built around the standard 2½ton truck chassis. The vehicle had the same 2½ton capacity as the truck. These were mainly in RASC transport companies, but later DD regiments added them in 1945. This was generally regarded as a better vehicle than the British Terrapin, 'very handy and seaworthy afloat'.[193]

BUFFALO

The US-built Landing Vehicle, Tracked LVT 2 and LVT 4 were provided and known in British service as Buffalo II and Buffalo IV.[194] (In Italy, the vehicle was known as a Fantail, and in the Far East as an Alligator.[195]) The British received 100 of the LVT2 and larger numbers of the LVT4. The latter at least had light armour, but was not the US armoured variant, the LVT(A)4.

The LVT 2 had the engine at the rear (dismount was over the sides). It could carry 30 troops or 6,000lbs of cargo. The LVT4 had the engine behind the driving compartment, giving it a hinged ramp at the rear for loading/unloading. The vehicle had a 6,000-lb payload. Cargo could be 30 men, or a jeep or carrier or scout car or 6pdr Atk gun. Armament fitted by the British (at least in NW Europe) to either type was a 20mm Polsten cannon and two machineguns with armoured shields (one .50 caliber and one .30 caliber). The vehicles could do 25 mph on land and 5.4 knots in the water.

Variations developed for use in the war against Japan included an armoured Buffalo IV with two small turrets, each mounting a Wasp flamethrower (LVT(F) or 'Sea Serpent'), a Buffalo IV with rocket projectors (LVT(R); could fire 72 rockets in three minutes), and a Buffalo IV with a 3.7" howitzer fitted in the cargo compartment. These were the equipment intended for the four batteries in the 34th RM Amphibious Support Regiment.

---

[192] DUKW was from a model naming system used by GMC, the builder: D (vehicle designed in 1942), U (utility), K (driven front wheels), W (two powered rear axles).
[193] Maj Gen J. L. Moulton, *Battle for Antwerp: The Liberation of the City and the Opening of the Scheldt 1944* (New York: Hippocrene Books, Inc., 1978), pp 254-255.
[194] 'Buffalo' is a shortened version of the original US nickname 'Water Buffalo'.
[195] Alligator also happened to be the name of the original US LVT, whose design led to the later LVT 2 and 4 supplied to the British.

Appendix 1: The Regiments Depart

A person looking at a roll of the regiments of the British Army today would find virtually none of the 1939-1945 regiments. The end of the Second World War and then the withdrawal from the Indian subcontinent led to an initial round of reductions, with all of the wartime regiments disbanded. From 1958, with the pending elimination of National Service and reduced commitments outside Europe, the Army began a series of reductions. These involved in part the amalgamation of various cavalry and RTR regiments. Further reductions led to even more amalgamations, or the outright disbanding of regiments. The entire Territorial Army itself disappeared in 1967, with all sorts of new units in the Territorial and Army Volunteer Reserve (TAVR); that awkward title itself went away in 1979 as the reserves again became the Territorial Army. Other changes came with Options for Change (1991-93) and the Strategic Defense Review (1998); with the full implementation of the Future Army Structure (2004-6) there would be virtually no units at all surviving with their Second World War titles, and this was followed by the Strategic Defense and Security Review of 2010 and the more draconian, budget-driven Army 2020 plan of 2012.

This Appendix traces the evolution of armoured units from World War II down to the present. It does not include changes to any infantry regiments who had some units serving as armoured in the war.

A title in plain type indicates the Second World War designation. A title in italics indicates amalgamation in one round or another. An asterisk in front of an italic designation indicates an amalgamation under Options for Change.

Household Cavalry

Life Guards
The Blues and Royals (Royal Horse Guards and 1st Dragoons)
> Formed 23 March 1969 by amalgamation of:
> > • Royal Horse Guards (The Blues)
> > • The Royal Dragoons (1st Dragoons)

In 1992, both regiments were amalgamated in effect, each being reduced to two squadrons and a mounted ceremonial squadron. Thus, under Options for Change the World War II title—The Household Cavalry Regiment—came back into use for the surviving units of the two regiments as a tactical unit; their mounted squadrons were grouped as The Household Cavalry Mounted Regiment.

Cavalry

1st The Queen's Dragoon Guards
> Formed 1 January 1959 by amalgamation of:
> > • 1st King's Dragoon Guards
> > • The Queen's Bays (2nd Dragoon Guards)

The Royal Scots Dragoon Guards (Carabiniers and Greys)
> Formed 2 July 1971 by amalgamation of:
> > • 3rd Carabiniers (Prince of Wales's Dragoon Guards)
> > • The Royal Scots Greys (2nd Dragoons)

*The Royal Dragoon Guards
> Formed 1 August 1992 by amalgamation of:
> > • 4th/7th Royal Dragoon Guards
> > • 5th Royal Inniskilling Dragoon Guards

*The Queen's Royal Hussars (The Queen's Own and Royal Irish)
> Formed 1 September 1993 by amalgamation of:
> > *The Queen's Own Hussars*
> > > Formed 3 November 1958 by amalgamation of:
> > > > • 3rd The King's Own Hussars
> > > > • 7th Queen's Own Hussars
> > *The Queen's Royal Irish Hussars*
> > > Formed 24 October 1958 by amalgamation of:
> > > > • 4th Queen's Own Hussars
> > > > • 8th King's Royal Irish Hussars

9th/12th Royal Lancers (Prince of Wales's)
> Formed 11 September 1960 by amalgamation of:
> > • 9th Queen's Royal Lancers
> > • 12th Royal Lancers (Prince of Wales's)

*The King's Royal Hussars
> Formed 4 December 1992 by amalgamation of:
> > *The Royal Hussars (Prince of Wales's Own)*
> > > Formed 25 October 1969 by amalgamation of:
> > > > • 10th Royal Hussars (Prince of Wales's Own)
> > > > • 11th Hussars (Prince Albert's Own)
> > • 14th/20th King's Hussars

*The Light Dragoons
> Formed 1 December 1992 by amalgamation of:
> > • 13th/18th Royal Hussars (Queen Mary's Own)
> > • 15th/19th The King's Royal Hussars

*The Queen's Royal Lancers
> Formed 25 June 1993 by amalgamation of:
> > • 16th/5th The Queen's Royal Lancers
> > • 17th/21st Lancers

In July 2012, the Ministry of Defence announced further reductions under the rubric of 'Army 2020'. Under this scheme, The Queens Royal Lancers will amalgamate with 9th/12th Royal Lancers (Prince of Wales's) upon completion of scheduled operational commitments but not before October 2014.

The wartime regiments (22nd Dragoons, 23rd Hussars, 24th Lancers, 25th Dragoons, 26th Hussars and 27th Lancers) were officially disbanded June 1948, but all had gone into suspended animation or been disbanded before then.

Royal Tank Regiment

The old eight regular regiments (1st to 8th) continued until 1959-60 when the 6th, 7th and 8th were amalgamated with the 3rd, 4th and 5th RTRs, respectively. The 5th RTR was subsequently disbanded in 1969, leaving only four active regiments. In September 1992, 2nd and 3rd RTR were amalgamated as 2nd Royal Tank Regiment.[196] On 30 April 1993 1st RTR absorbed the 4th RTR. In 1999, 1st RTR itself effectively disappeared, forming the RHQ and one squadron of the new Joint Nuclear, Biological and Chemical Reconnaissance Regiment (JNBCR), along with a separate tank squadron.[197]

In July 2012, the Ministry of Defence announced further reductions under the rubric of 'Army 2020'. Under this scheme, the 1st Royal Tank Regiment and the 2nd Royal Tank Regiment will merge upon completion of scheduled operational commitments but not before April 2014.

The original Territorial Army regiments (40th to 45th) were all reformed in 1947; their duplicate units were disbanded (47th, 48th and 49th), converted to other arms (46th), or amalgamated with the parent unit (50th and 51st). With the reductions in 1956, the 40th (King's) and 41st (Oldham) RTR were amalgamated as 40th/41st RTR. The 42nd, 43rd and 45th were converted back to infantry as 23rd London Regiment [part of the corps of The East Surrey Regiment], 6th (City) Bn The Royal Northumberland Fusiliers, and 7th (Leeds Rifles) Bn The West Yorkshire Regiment (The Prince of Wales's). The 44th RTR was amalgamated with The North Somerset Yeomanry. 40th/41st RTR finally disappeared in 1967.

The wartime regiments (9th to 12th RTR) were all disbanded during the war or by 1946.

Yeomanry (I)

All of the Yeomanry regiments disappeared in April 1967, with a few becoming squadrons of the new Royal Yeomanry Regiment. Later, some reappeared as squadrons

---

[196] The regiment was sometimes shown as Second Royal Tank Regiment.

[197] 'A' Squadron, posted to Warminster (part of Combined Arms Training Centre), remaining a tank unit; 'D' and 'H' Squadrons amalgamated as 'G' Squadron of the new regiment and former 'G' Squadron disbanded. RHQ 1st RTR became RHQ JNBCR.

of additional Yeomanry regiments formed, and some survived in other arms, especially the Royal Signals. However, continued reorganizations and other changes left a confusing paper trail. This section lists the Yeomanry serving as cavalry or armour in the Second World War and their fates through 1967.

The Cheshire Yeomanry (Earl of Chester's), reformed in the RAC, survived to 1967.

The Derbyshire Yeomanry amalgamated 9 February 1957 with The Leicestershire Yeomanry (Prince Albert's Own) [RA World War II and RAC after] to form *The Leicestershire and Derbyshire (Prince Albert's Own) Yeomanry.*

The Fife and Forfar Yeomanry amalgamated 31 October 1956 with The Scottish Horse [wartime RA unit, reformed in the RAC] to form *The Fife and Forfar Yeomanry/Scottish Horse.*

The Royal Gloucestershire Hussars survived to 1967.

The Inns of Court Regiment amalgamated 1 May 1961 with The City of London Yeomanry (Rough Riders) [World War II RA, RAC 1947, then an infantry battalion from 1956] to form *The Inns of Court and City Yeomanry.*

North Irish Horse[198] survived to 1967.

The Duke of Lancaster's Own Yeomanry survived to 1967.

The 2nd County of London Yeomanry (Westminster Dragoons) inverted their title 1 September 1951 to become The Westminster Dragoons (2nd County of London Yeomanry); they were amalgamated 1 May 1961 with 'R' (Berkshire Yeomanry) Battery, 299 Field Regiment RA to form *The Berkshire and Westminster Dragoons.*

3rd/4th County of London Yeomanry (Sharpshooters) amalgamated 1 May 1961 with 297 Light AA Regiment RA (Kent Yeomanry) to form *Kent and County of London Yeomanry (Sharpshooters).*

1st/2nd Lothians and Border Horse amalgamated 20 October 1956 with two Yeomanry regiments that were RA in the war and RAC after—The Lanarkshire Yeomanry and The Queen's Own Royal Glasgow Yeomanry—to form *The Queen's Own Lowland Yeomanry.*

The Northamptonshire Yeomanry was reduced 31 October 1956 to 'D' (NY) Squadron, The Inns of Court Regiment; then withdrawn 1 May 1961 and converted as 250 (NY) Field Squadron RE.

The Northumberland Hussars, wartime RA, reformed 1947 in the RAC and survived to 1967.

The Nottinghamshire Yeomanry (Sherwood Rangers) was retitled 1 September 1951 as The Sherwood Rangers Yeomanry, and survived to 1967.

The Shropshire Yeomanry, wartime RA, reformed in the RAC and survived to 1967.

---

[198] Special Reserve in the Second World War, reformed in the TA when it was finally extended to Northern Ireland in 1947.

The North Somerset Yeomanry amalgamated 31 October 1956 with 44th RTR to form *The North Somerset Yeomanry/44th Royal Tank Regiment*, which was renamed April 1965 as *The North Somerset and Bristol Yeomanry* and then disappeared in 1967.

The Staffordshire Yeomanry (Queen's Own Royal Regiment) survived to 1967.

The Warwickshire Yeomanry was amalgamated 1 October 1956 with The Queen's Own Worcestershire Hussars [RA since the 1920s but RAC after the war] to form *The Queen's Own Warwickshire and Worcestershire Yeomanry*.

The Royal Wiltshire Yeomanry (Prince of Wale's Own) survived to 1967.

The East Riding Yeomanry,[199] The Yorkshire Hussars (Alexandra, Princess of Wales's Own) and The Queen's Own Yorkshire Dragoons [RAC after World War II] were amalgamated 1 November 1956 as *The Queen's Own Yorkshire Yeomanry*.

The Lovat Scouts were reformed as a squadron in The Scottish Horse, but from 1949 were withdrawn and became part of the Royal Artillery.

Yeomanry (II)[200]

In April 1967 the Territorial Army and the Army Emergency Reserve were merged and much reduced as the Territorial Army and Volunteer Reserve (TAVR). The TAVR had three parts: I (essentially the old AER), II (formed units with a NATO mission, such as the new Royal Yeomanry regiment), and III (home defense, with a secondary role of preserving old units titles).[201]

TAVR II units contained '(Volunteers)'—often shown just as '(V)'—in their unit titles, while TAVR III were 'Territorials', or '(T)'. Lineages can be rather complex, given the creation, expansion, contraction, and reassignments over time. The old Yeomanry regiments all had a TAVR III successor. These were disbanded in 1969 and reduced to a cadre of eight men by the end of March;[202] however, some of the disbanded units formed new TAVR II units, and some cadres were expanded later to form new units as well.

In April 1967, five of the old Yeomanry regiments survived as squadrons of a new regiment, The Royal Yeomanry (V). This was joined in 1971 by The Queen's Own Yeomanry (V), formed in part by reconstituting squadrons from units reduced to cadre in 1969. Other regiments came later, and then in 1999 the Yeomanry were reduced to four regiments. Squadrons came and went and were shuffled around during this time, and some old RAC Yeomanry spent time in other roles, such as home defense infantry or squadrons of the Royal Signals or Royal Corps of Transport. Some Yeomanry titles

---

[199] The regiment dropped 'of Yorkshire' from the end of their title in 1951.

[200] Information in this section is largely drawn from Wienand Drenth's extensive work at Lineage of British Army Regiments, 1967-2000, online [2012] at www.win.tue.nl/~drenth/BritArmy/Lineage/.

[201] On 7 August 1979 the old title Territorial Army replaced TAVR.

[202] The cadres generally resumed their former titles, and '(Territorial)' disappeared.

reappeared in these changes, but those units are not in this section since they were other arms in 1967.

The existing Yeomanry regiments are The Royal Yeomanry (V) (formed 1 April 1967),[203] The Queen's Own Yeomanry (V) (formed 1 April 1971), The Royal Mercian and Lancastrian Yeomanry (V) (formed 1 November 1992),[204] and The Royal Wessex Yeomanry (V).[205]

The Ayrshire (Earl of Carrick's Own) Yeomanry
- 1 April 1967 formed TAVR III units as The Ayrshire (Earl of Carrick's Own) Yeomanry (T), which became a cadre 1 April 1969 and dropped (T)
- 1 April 1971 B Sqn, The Queen's Own Yeomanry (V) formed from the cadre; redesignated November 1972 as A (Ayrshire Yeomanry) Sqn of regiment
- 1 November 1992 transferred as A (Ayrshire Yeomanry) Sqn, The Scottish Yeomanry (V)
- 1 July 1999 transferred as A (Ayrshire (Earl of Carrick's Own) Yeomanry) Sqn,, The Queen's Own Yeomanry (V)

The Berkshire and Westminster Dragoons
[I]
- 1 April 1967 became HQ (Berkshire & Westminster Dragoons) Sqn, The Royal Yeomanry (V); changed 8 October 1973 '(Berkshire and Westminster Dragoons)'; 1984 rebadged and redesignated as '(Westminster Dragoons)'[206]
- 1 July 1999 merged with D (Berkshire Yeomanry) Sqn of regiment to form a sabre squadron, W (Berkshire and Westminster Dragoons) Sqn
[II}
- 1 April 1967 formed TAVR III A Coy (Berkshire Yeomanry), The Royal Berkshire Territorials; that unit reduced to cadre 1 April 1969, with A Coy becoming 94 (Berkshire Yeomanry) Signal Sqn, 71 (Yeomanry) Signal Regiment (V)

---

[203] In September 2008 the regiment adopted a single capbadge; prior to that each squadron had its own capbadge.

[204] The Mercian Yeomanry (V) was formed 1 April 1971 as a home defense infantry battalion; redesignated 25 May 1973 as The Queen's Own Mercian Yeomanry (V); on 1 April 1983 it was made part of the RAC as a home defense recce regiment. On 1 November 1992 part of the regiment was disbanded and the rest amalgamated with a surviving squadron from The Duke of Lancaster's Own Yeomanry (V) to form The Royal Mercian and Lancastrian Yeomanry (V).

[205] Formed as The Wessex Yeomanry (V) (a home defense infantry battalion) 1 April 1971; retitled The Royal Wessex Yeomanr (V)y 8 June 1979; re-roled as a home defense recce regiment and made part of the RAC 1 April 1983.

[206] The Berkshire Yeomanry title was revived 1 April 1992 by organization of D (Berkshire Yeomanry) Sqn, The Royal Yeomanry from personnel of The Wessex Regiment; this was not considered a successor to the disbanded unit.

- 1 April 1996 squadron became independent
- 1 July 1999 assigned to new 72 Signal Regiment(V)

The Cheshire Yeomanry (Earl of Chester's)[207]

- TAVR III units formed 1 April 1967 as The Cheshire Yeomanry (Earl of Chester's Territorials); became a cadre as The Cheshire Yeomanry (Earl of Chester's)
- 1 April 1971 C Sqn The Queen's Own Yeomanry (V)formed from cadre; redesignated November 1972 as C (Cheshire Yeomanry) Sqn
- 1 July 1999 transferred as C (Cheshire Yeomanry) Sqn, The Royal Mercian and Lancastrian Yeomanry (V)

The Fife and Forfar Yeomanry/Scottish Horse

- 1 April 1967 formed TAVR III units as The Fife and Forfar Yeomanry/Scottish Horse (T)
- 1969 reduced to cadre and also used to form 239 (Highland Yeomanry) Sqn, 153 (Highland) Regiment RCT (V)
- 1 April 1975 cadre disbanded
- 1 Nov 1992 239 (Highland Yeomanry) Sqn RCT transferred as C (Fife and Forfar Yeomanry/Scottish Horse) Sqn, The Scottish Yeomanry (V)
- 1 July 1999 transferred as C (Fife and Forfar Yeomanry/Scottish Horse) Sqn, The Queen's Own Yeomanry

The Royal Gloucestershire Hussars

- 1 April 1967 amalgamated with other units to form TAVR III units as The Royal Gloucestershire Hussars (T); educed to cadre 1 April 1969 and dropped (T)
- 1 April 1971 cadre used to form RHQ, A (Royal Gloucestershire Hussars) Sqn, and C (Royal Gloucestershire Hussars) Sqn, The Wessex Yeomanry (V) [HD infantry battalion]; The Royal Wessex Yeomanry (V) 8 June 1979; 1 Apr 1983 reroled as HD recce regiment in RAC
- 1992 C Sqn disbanded and HQ (Royal Gloucestershire Hussars) Sqn formed
- 1 July 1999 A and HQ Sqns merged as C (Royal Gloucestershire Hussars) Sqn

The Inns of Court and City Yeomanry

- 1 April 1967 merged into the TAVR III London Yeomanry and Territorials
- 1 April 1969 separated from London Yeomanry and Territorials and formed a cadre under former title; also formed 68 (Inns of Court and City Yeomanry) Sqn, 71 (Yeomanry) Signal Regiment (V)
- 1 July 1975 cadre disbanded

---

[207] 80 (Cheshire) Signal Sqn, 33 (Lancashire and Cheshire) Signal Regiment (V) formed 1 April 1967 from the regiment's signal section; redesignated 1973 as 80 (Cheshire Yeomanry) Signal Sqn.

North Irish Horse
- 1 April 1967 became D (North Irish Horse) Sqn, The Royal Yeomanry (V)[208]
- 1 April 1992 became an independent squadron as North Irish Horse (V)
- 1 July 1999 redesignated as B (North Irish Horse) Sqn, The Queen's Own Yeomanry (V)

Kent and County of London Yeomanry (Sharpshooters)

[I]
- 1 April 1967 became C (Kent & County of London Yeomanry) Sqn, The Royal Yeomanry (V); 8 October 1973 changed to '(Kent and Sharpshooters Yeomanry)'
- HQ (Kent and County of London Yeomanry) Sqn, The Royal Yeomanry (V) formed 1987.

[II]
1 April 1967 formed R (Kent and County of London Yeomanry) Bty, The London and Kent Regiment RA (T). That regiment reduced to cadre 1 April 1969 and used to form 265 Signal Sqn, 71 (Yeomanry) Signal Regiment (V), which was redesignated 1970 as 265 (Kent and County of London Yeomanry) Signal Sqn.

[III]
1 April 1967 formed A Kent and County of London Yeomanry (Sharpshooters) Coy, 8th (T) Bn The Queen's Regiment (West Kent). That battalion was reduced to cadre 1 April 1969 and companies lost their separate identities.

The Duke of Lancaster's Own Yeomanry
- 1 April 1967 amalgamated with 40th/41st RTR to form TAVR III units as The Duke of Lancaster's Own Yeomanry (Royal Tank Regiment) (T); reduced to cadre 1 April 1969 and dropped the (T).
- 1 April 1971 Duke of Lancaster's Own Yeomanry (Royal Tank Regiment) (V) formed from cadre as a HD infantry battalion
- 29 February 1972 redesignated The Duke of Lancaster's Own Yeomanry
- 1 April 1983 reroled as recce regiment in RAC
- 1 November 1992 disbanded and amalgamated with The Queen's Own Mercian Yeomanry (V) to form D (Duke of Lancaster's Own Yeomanry) Sqn, The Royal Mercian and Lancastrian Yeomanry (V)

---

[208] Also formed TAVR III units as North Irish Horse (T) 1 April 1967; reduced to cadre 1 April 1969 and cadre disbanded 1 April 1975. 69 (North Irish Horse) Signal Sqn, 32 (Scottish) Signal Regiment (V) formed 1 April 1969 from part of TAVR III unit. Transferred 1 April 1995 to 40 (Ulster) Signal Regiment (V).

The Leicestershire and Derbyshire (Prince Albert's Own) Yeomanry

[I]

- 1 April 1967 formed TAVR III units as The Leicestershire and Derbyshire (Prince Albert's Own) Yeomanry (T); reduced to cadre 1 April 1969 and dropped (T)
- 1 April 1971 cadre used to form The Leicestershire and Derbyshire (Prince Albert's Own) Yeomanry Sqn, 7th (V) Bn, The Royal Anglian Regiment
- 1 April 1975 redesignated as The Leicestershire and Derbyshire (Prince Albert's Own) Yeomanry Coy of battalion
- 1988 redesignated as C (Leicestershire and Derbyshire Yeomanry) Coy of battalion
- October 1992 transferred as 3rd Coy, 5th (V) Bn, The Royal Anglian Regiment[209]
- 1 April 1996 battalion converted and became 203 Sqn, 158 (Royal Anglian) Transport Regiment Logistic Corps

[II]

- 1977 B (Leicestershire and Derbyshire Yeomanry) Coy, 3rd (V) Bn The Worcestershire and Sherwood Foresters formed from part of The Leicestershire and Derbyshire (Prince Albert's Own) Yeomanry Coy, 7th (V) Bn, The Royal Anglian Regiment; officially formed by 1 April 1978
- 1 April 1992 became B (Leicestershire and Derbyshire Yeomanry) Sqn, The Royal Yeomanry (V)

The Queen's Own Lowland Yeomanry

[I]

- 1 Apr 1967 formed TAVR III units as The Queen's Own Lowland Yeomanry (T); reduced to cadre 1 April 1969 and dropped (T); also formed 225 (Queen's Own Lowland Yeomanry) Sqn, 154 Regiment RCT (V)
- 1 April 1975 cadre disbanded
- 1 November 1992 225 (Queen's Own Lowland Yeomanry) Fuel Tanker Sqn RCT converted as HQ (Lothians and Border Horse) Sqn, The Scottish Yeomanry (V)
- 1 July 1999 disbanded

[II]

- 222 Sqn, 154 (Lowland) Transport Regiment formed 1 April 1967 from 264 (Scottish) Regiment RCT (V)[210]
- Converted 1 November 1992 as B (Lanarkshire and Queen's Own Royal Glasgow Yeomanry) Sqn, The Scottish Yeomanry (V)

---

[209] Given the lack of a subtitle, this may be considered withdrawal of any connection to the former Yeomanry regiment. 203 Sqn RCT was the only one in the new regiment without a subtitle.

[210] Squadron thus had no prior connection to any Yeomanry unit.

- 1 July 1999 disbanded

The Northumberland Hussars
- 1 April 1967 amalgamated with other units to form TAVR III units as The Northumberland Hussars (T); reduced to cadre 1 April 1969 and dropped (T)
- HQ Sqn The Queen's Own Yeomanry (V), formed 1 April 1971 from cadre, redesignated November 1972 as N' (Northumberland Hussars) Sqn [still HQ Sqn]
- 1986, D (Northumberland Hussars) Sqn newly formed from elements NH Sqn, which was redesignated HQ (Northumberland Hussars) Sqn
- 1 July 1999 D (Northumberland Hussars) Sqn disbanded and HQ Sqn redesignated as D (Northumberland Hussars) Sqn

The Sherwood Rangers Yeomanry[211]
- 1 April 1967 became B (Sherwood Rangers Yeomanry) Sqn, The Royal Yeomanry (V)
- 1 April 1992 transferred as B (Sherwood Rangers Yeomanry) Sqn, The Queen's Own Yeomanry (V)
- 1 July 1999 transferred as S (Sherwood Rangers Yeomanry) Sqn, The Royal Yeomanry (V)

The Shropshire Yeomanry
- 1 April 1967 amalgamated with other units to form TAVR III units as The Shropshire Yeomanry (T); reduced to cadre 1 April 1969 and dropped (T); also used to form 95 (Shropshire Yeomanry) Signal Sqn, 35 Signal Regiment (V)
- 1 April 1971 cadre used to form RHQ and C (Shropshire Yeomanry) Sqn, The Mercian Yeomanry; 25 May 1973 The Queen's Own Mercian Yeomanry [a home defense infantry battalion]; reroled 1982 as recce regiment RAC
- 1 November 1992 became HQ (Shropshire Yeomanry) Sqn of The Royal Mercian and Lancastrian Yeomanry
- 1 July 1999 reorganized as B (Shropshire Yeomanry) Sqn of regiment

The North Somerset and Bristol Yeomanry
1 April 1967 formed TAVR III A Coy (North Somerset and Bristol Yeomanry), The Somerset Yeomanry and Light Infantry (T); that battalion was reduced to cadre 1 April 1969 and company identities lost

---

[211] Also formed TAVR III units as The Sherwood Rangers Yeomanry (T); reduced to cadre 1 April 1969 and dropped the (T). Cadre used 1 April 1971 to form A (Sherwood Rangers) Sqn, 3rd (V) Bn The Worcestershire and Sherwood Foresters Regiment. Redesignated 1 April 1975 as a company. In September 1992, absorbed into B Sqn, The Royal Yeomanry (V).

The Staffordshire Yeomanry (Queen's Own Royal Regiment)
- 1 April 1967 amalgamated with other units to form TAVR III units as The Staffordshire Yeomanry (Queen's Own Royal Regiment) (T); reduced to cadre 1 April 1969 and dropped (T)
- 1 April 1971 cadre used to form B (Staffordshire Yeomanry) Sqn, The Mercian Yeomanry (V); 25 May 1973 The Queen's Own Mercian Yeomanry (V) [a home defense infantry battalion]; reroled 1982 as recce regiment RAC
- 1 November 1992 became B (Staffordshire Yeomanry) Sqn, The Royal Mercian and Lancastrian Yeomanry (V)
- 1 July 1999 amalgamated with A (Warwickshire and Worcestershire Yeomanry) Sqn of regiment

The Queen's Own Warwickshire and Worcestershire Yeomanry
- 1 April 1967 formed TAVR III units as The Queen's Own Warwickshire and Worcestershire Yeomanry (T); reduced to cadre
- 1 April 1969 reduced to cadre and dropped (T); also used to form 67 (Queen's Own Warwickshire and Worcestershire Yeomanry) Signal Sqn, 37 (Wessex and Welsh) Signal Regiment (V)
- 1 April 1971 cadre used to form A (Queen's Own Warwickshire and Worcestershire Yeomanry) Sqn, The Mercian Yeomanry (V); 25 May 1973 The Queen's Own Mercian Yeomanry (V) [a home defense infantry battalion]; reroled 1982 as recce regiment RAC
- 1 Nov 1992 became A (Warwickshire and Worcestershire Yeomanry) Sqn, The Royal Mercian and Lancastrian Yeomanry (V)
- 1 July 1999 amalgamated with B (Staffordshire Yeomanry) Sqn as A (Staffordshire, Warwickshire and Worcestershire Yeomanry) Sqn of regiment

The Royal Wiltshire Yeomanry (Prince of Wale's Own)
- 1 April 1967 formed TAVR III B Coy (Royal Wiltshire Yeomanry), The Royal Wiltshire Territorials
- 1 April 1969 transferred as cadre unit under old designation
- 1 April 1971 cadre became B (Royal Wiltshire Yeomanry) Sqn, The Wessex Yeomanry (V) [HD infantry battalion]; The Royal Wessex Yeomanry (V) 8 June 1979; 1 Apr 1983 reroled as HD recce regiment in RAC

The Queen's Own Yorkshire Yeomanry
- 1 April 1967 formed TAVR III units as The Queen's Own Yorkshire Yeomanry (T); reduced to cadre 1 April 1969 and dropped (T)
- A Sqn The Queen's Own Yeomanry (V) formed 1 April 1971 from cadre; redesignated November 1972 as Y (Queen's Own Yorkshire Yeomanry) Sqn
- 1 July 1999 redesignated as Y (Yorkshire) Sqn

Appendix 2: Summary of Divisions and Brigades

For those units granted battle honours, it is relatively easy to determine where they served in combat, although it may be more difficult to ascertain periods of service without action, whether in the UK or abroad. Unlike the case with GHQ units (where brief notice can be given that the regiment was in North Africa, or with 21st Army Group, for example) it can be awkward to interrupt details of brigade or division assignments by interspersing the formation's movements as well. This Appendix, then, is intended to simply give a brief reference to the service of the armoured and cavalry divisions and of the armoured, tank and related brigades. Used in conjunction with the assignment detail in the main text, it allows the interested reader to determine where the unit was during the course of the war.

Divisions

Guards Armoured Division. Formed September 1941 in the UK by the conversion of Guards battalions. Landed in NW Europe late June 1944 and served through the end of the war. In June 1945 it was converted to infantry as Guards Division.

1st Armoured Division. Regular formation with its units at various locations in the UK. The infantry and one armoured regiment went to Calais May 1940; the remainder of the division was in France May-June 1940. It left the UK for Egypt in July 1941, arriving that November. It served in various battles through May 1943. Following refitting, it moved to Italy in May 1944 and was in action that September. At the end of the month it was withdrawn, slotted for dissolution as part of Eighth Army's replacement problems. The division ceased to be operational October 1944, although not officially disbanded until January 1945. The division's 2nd Armoured Brigade survived as a GHQ formation in Italy, and its engineers ended up in 25th Armoured Engineer Brigade.

1st Cavalry Division. Formed the end of October 1939 in the UK, mainly around horsed Yeomanry regiments, and soon sent to Palestine, where it arrived January 1940. It never operated as a complete formation with all three brigades, although it served in Syria and Iraq. In August 1941 it was converted as the 10th Armoured Division.

2nd Armoured Division. Formed December 1939 in the UK. It sailed for Egypt October 1940, arriving on New Year's Day. The bulk of the division moved into Libya, although elements were detached to provide a brigade group for Greece. The German offensive beginning 31 March 1941 quickly destroyed the division; the division HQ was captured 8 April 1941, and its units were placed under 7th Armoured Division the same date. The disbanding in May 1941 was simply a formality.

6th Armoured Division. The first of the new wartime divisions, organized October 1940 in the UK. It arrived in North Africa November 1942 and was committed, piecemeal, in Tunisia. Following the end of the campaign in May 1943, it remained in Africa until sent to Italy in March 1944. It first went into action May 1944, and served through the end of the war. In May 1945 it moved into Austria for occupation duties, and was renumbered the next year as 1st Armoured Division.

7th Armoured Division. A Regular formation, only partially formed; designated in August 1939 as the Mobile Division (Egypt), soon redesignated Armoured Division (Egypt), and not numbered as the 7th until February 1940. The Desert Rats served throughout the war in North Africa. Following a brief rest, it went to Italy in September 1943, staying until December 1943 when it was moved to the UK. The division began landing in Normandy on 7 June 1944. Fairly or not, its performance earned substantial criticism, with its commander and numerous other officers removed the beginning of August. Its next commander ended up being sacked as well. The division served throughout the campaign in NW Europe, and remained in Germany on occupation duties.

8th Armoured Division. Formed November 1940 from two army tank brigades redesignated as armoured. The division arrived in Egypt July 1942, but never served as a formation, with its armoured brigades and other units detached. It was disbanded 1 January 1943.

9th Armoured Division. Formed December 1940 from armoured brigades largely built around the old divisional cavalry regiments. It never saw service, although operational until May 1944. It was disbanded that July.

10th Armoured Division. Formed August 1941 in Palestine by the conversion of 1st Cavalry Division. It moved to Egypt the end of April 1942, and served at Alam el Halfa and El Alamein. It was then withdrawn from operations, and moved back to Palestine January 1943. From then on it was given a role as a training and holding organization. The 10th went back to Egypt September 1943, its role unchanged, and was disbanded there June 1944.

11th Armoured Division. Formed March 1941 in the UK, built in part around the newly activated wartime cavalry regiments. The division landed in NW Europe mid June 1944, and was in action throughout the campaign. It received the new Comet tanks February-March 1945. The division was disbanded February 1946 in Germany.

42nd Armoured Division. Formed November 1941 in the UK by conversion of the 42nd (East Lancashire) Infantry Division. It was disbanded October 1943 without service. Its armoured brigade and RE went to the 79th Armoured Division.

79th Armoured Division. Formed August 1942 as a conventional armoured division. It was reorganized in April 1943 and made responsible for the development and control of specialized armour. Its units were parceled out to support other formations beginning with the D-Day landings, and the division itself was basically a holding formation. It was disbanded August 1945 in Germany.

Brigades

1st Armoured Brigade. A Regular formation as 1st Light Armoured Brigade with 1st Armoured Division; transferred January 1940 to 2nd Armoured Division (brigade redesignated April 1940). The brigade sailed for Egypt in November 1940, and then served as a separate brigade group in Greece March-April 1941.It was next in action during the Gazala battles of May 1942, and ceased to be operational the next month (although it lingered to November as a HQ in charge of reorganization and tank delivery).

1st Armoured Reconnaissance Brigade. Formed the end of March 1940 in France, withdrawn to the UK 31 May 1940, and reorganized as 27th Armoured Brigade in November 1940.

1st Tank Brigade. A regular formation as 1st Army Tank Brigade, serving in France (with two of its three battalions) April-May 1940. After service with Home Forces, it went to Egypt in April 1941 and participated in a number of campaigns there. In 1943 it was re-equipped with CDL tanks. Returning to the UK April 1944, it became the CDL brigade in 79th Armoured Division and was broken up that October without further service.

1st Armoured Engineer Brigade. Formed in 79th Armoured Division as 1st Assault Brigade RE and redesignated in April 1945, its units supported 21st Army Group operations from D-Day to the end of the war. It was disbanded in July 1945.

1st Motor Machine Gun Brigade. Formed May 1940 in the UK. Converted October 1940 to 26th Armoured Brigade.

2nd Armoured Brigade. A Regular formation as 2nd Light Armoured Brigade (redesignated April 1940) assigned to 1st Armoured Division, the brigade was in France May-June 1940 then returned to the UK. It went to Egypt November 1941, serving in a variety of campaigns through May 1943. It then rested before going to Italy in May 1944, serving there for the remainder of the war (a separate brigade from September 1944).

2nd Armoured Reconnaissance Brigade. Formed the end of March 1940 in France, withdrawn to the UK 1 June 1940. It was redesignated June 1940 as 3rd Motor Machine Gun Brigade (later 28th Armoured Brigade).

2nd Motor Machine Gun Brigade. *See* 25th Tank Brigade

3rd Armoured Brigade. The Regular 1st Heavy Armoured Brigade, redesignated in April 1940; assigned to 1st Armoured Division. One regiment went to Calais in May 1940, and the remainder of the brigade served in France May-June 1940. It was detached in October and went to North Africa November 1940, serving under a number of formations. It was largely destroyed March-April 1941 while under 2nd Armoured Division. It ceased to be operational that September.[212]

3rd Motor Machine Gun Brigade. Formed June 1940 in the UK from 2nd Armoured Reconnaissance Brigade. Converted December 1940 to 28th Armoured Brigade.

4th Armoured Brigade. Originally the Heavy Brigade (Egypt) to February 1940 (4th Heavy Armoured Brigade until April 1940 redesignation), the 4th served in North Africa until May 1943. (Typically for the desert war, it served under a variety of formations, but most often under 7th Armoured Division.) It then served in Sicily and Italy as a separate brigade, moving to the UK in January 1944. Landing early in Normandy, the brigade served throughout the NW Europe campaign. It lasted in BAOR into 1948.

4th Cavalry Brigade. Formed the last day of October 1939 in the UK and assigned to 1st Cavalry Division. Landed in Palestine February 1940 and then served in Iraq and Syria. Converted August 1941 to 9th Armoured Brigade.

5th Guards Armoured Brigade. Formed in September 1941 (from 20th Guards Inantry Brigade) and assigned to Guards Armoured Division. Served in NW Europe from the end of June 1944. Converted June 1945 to infantry.

5th Cavalry Brigade. TA formation embodied September 1939 and assigned the next month to 1st Cavalry Division. Landed in Palestine February 1940 and then served in Syria, later returning to Palestine. Redesignated April 1942 as Deseret (5th) Cavalry Brigade, serving from June 1942 as fictitious 8th Infantry Division. Disbanded September 1943 in Palestine.

---

[212] One of the continuing controversies in sources is whether or not the brigade HQ was redesignated as HQ 32nd Army Tank Brigade, which took over its surviving units in September 1941. Despite the fact that it never operated again, Joslen (*Orders of Battle*) has the brigade HQ officially active until disbanded 11 January 1943. Presumably it was at zero strength throughout that period.

6th Guards Armoured Brigade. Formed in September 1941 (from 30th Guards Infantry Brigade) and assigned to Guards Armoured Division. Relieved January 1943 and redesignated **6th Guards Tank Brigade**. Assigned to 15th (Scottish) Mixed Division January-September 1943, then becoming a separate brigade. Served in NW Europe from the end of June 1944; redesignated **6th Guards Armoured Brigade** in February 1945. Converted June 1945 to infantry.

6th Cavalry Brigade. TA formation embodied September 1939 and assigned the next month to 1st Cavalry Division. Landed in Palestine February 1940. Converted August 1941 to 8th Armoured Brigade.

7th Armoured Brigade. Originally the Light Brigade (Egypt) to February 1941 (then 7th Light Armoured Brigade to April 1940), the 7th served in North Africa—mainly under 7th Armoured Division—until largely destroyed November 1941. Reformed, it was sent to Ceylon and then India, serving in the Burma debacle February-May 1942 (losing every tank but one). Remaining in India to October 1942, it went to the Middle East and served variously in Palestine, Syria and Egypt; assigned 10th Armoured Division June 1943-April 1944. It did not see action again until May 1944 when it moved to Italy, where it served for the remainder of the war as a separate brigade.

8th Armoured Brigade. Formed August 1941 in Palestine from 6th Cavalry Brigade and assigned to 10th Armoured Division. It went to North Africa February 1942, serving in various battles until May 1943; a separate brigade from late November 1942. Arriving in the UK December 1943, it landed in NW Europe on D-Day and served there the remainder of the war. It served on occupation duties in Germany until disbanded March 1946.

9th Armoured Brigade. Formed August 1941 in Palestine from 4th Cavalry Brigade and assigned to 10th Armoured Division. It went to North Africa May 1942, serving in various battles until January 1943 when it moved to Syria. with some time in Palestine as well; a separate brigade from May 1943. Briefly in Egypt March-April 1944, it sailed to Italy where it arrived in May. At the end of the war in Europe, the 9th was selected for redeployment to the Far East. It was moved (personnel only, by air) to the UK August 1945. It was disbanded some time later, with Japan's surrender obviating the transfer.

10th Armoured Brigade. Formed November 1941 by conversion of 125th Infantry Brigade of 42nd Infantry Division; released as 10th Tank Brigade July 1942 and disbanded November 1943 in the UK. Had role of holding and training reinforcements from October 1942 when placed under 48th Infantry (Reserve) Division.

11th Armoured Brigade. Formed November 1941 by conversion of 126th Infantry Brigade of 42nd Infantry Division; released as 11th Tank Brigade July 1942 and disbanded November 1943 in the UK. Had role of holding and training reinforcements from January 1943 when placed under 77th Infantry (Reserve) Division.

20th Armoured Brigade. Formed in the TA as 20th Light Armoured Brigade and redesignated in April 1940. Under 1st Armoured Division June-October 1940 and then assigned to new 6th Armoured Division. Relieved April 1942. In January 1943 its regiments were selected for conversion to armoured recce, and it supervised that until disbanded April 1943.

21st Tank Brigade. Formed in the TA as 21st Army Tank Brigade. Redesignated June 1942 when assigned to 4th Mixed Division. Went to NW Africa March 1943, serving in the Tunisian campaign. Relieved from 4th Infantry Division December 1943.[213] It moved to Italy May 1944, serving there the remainder of the war. It was not redesignated **21ˢᵗ Armoured Brigade** until June 1945. Disbanded later.

22nd Armoured Brigade. Formed in the TA as 22nd Heavy Armoured Brigade and redesignated April 1940. Assigned to 2nd Armoured Division January-October 190 when transferred to 1st Armoured Division. Moved to North Africa October 1941, serving in a number of battles under 1st and 7th Armoured Divisions until May 1943; it was assigned to 7th Armoured Division September 1942. It next fought in Italy September-December 1943 before moving to the UK. It landed in NW Europe early June 1944 and served the remainder of the war there. It remained in BAOR following the war; redesignated 7th Armoured Brigade January 1947 when 22nd reformed in the TA.

23rd Army Tank Brigade. Formed in the TA. Redesignated November 1941 as **23rd Armoured Brigade** upon assignment to new 8th Armoured Division. Moved to North Africa July 1942, serving to May 1943, primarily as a separate brigade. It was then in Sicily July-September 1943 and in Italy from September. Moved to Greece October 1944, where it served until disbanded April 1946.

24th Army Tank Brigade. Formed in the TA. Redesignated November 1941 as **24th Armoured Brigade** upon assignment to new 8th Armoured Division. Moved to North Africa July 1942, its only action was at Second Alamein under 10th Armoured Division. Its units were posted away January 1943 and the brigade HQ disbanded that March. (The designation of 24th Armoured Brigade was used as the notional command for dummy tank units 1943-44.)

25th Army Tank Brigade. Formed in the TA. (Designated 2nd Motor Machine Gun Brigade May-December 1940 and then reverted to prior designation.) Redesignated **25th Tank Brigade** June 1942 upon assignment to 43rd (Wessex) Mixed Division; transferred September 1942 to 1st Mixed Division; relieved November 1942. Sent to

---

[213] The 4th was the only mixed division to see combat as such.

NW Africa February 1943, serving in action to May. Following a rest there, it moved to Italy April 1944. Reorganized and redesignated January 1945 as **'B' Assault Brigade RAC/RE** and April 1945 as **25th Armoured Engineer Brigade**. Disbanded following the war.

26th Armoured Brigade. Formed October 1940 in the UK from 1st Motor Machine Gun Brigade and assigned to new 6th Armoured Division. Moved to NW Africa November 1942, serving in Tunisia, and then served in Italy from March 1944 through the end of the war. Moved with division to Austria following the war.

27th Armoured Brigade. Formed November 1940 in the UK by from 1st Armoured Reconnaissance Brigade and assigned to new 9th Armoured Division the next month. Assigned to 79th Armoured Division September 1942. Used to experiment with specialized armour and techniques beginning April 1943, in particular (from October 1943 when relieved from 79th Armoured Division) DD tanks. Landed at Normandy on D-Day and then broken up in France July 1944.

28th Armoured Brigade. Formed December 1940 in the UK from 3rd Motor Machine Gun Brigade and assigned to new 9th Armoured Division. Disbanded August 1944 without service.

29th Armoured Brigade. Formed December 1940 in the UK and assigned to new 11th Armoured Division March 1941. Landed in NW Europe June 1944 and served through the remainder of the war. Disbanded January 1946 in Germany.

30th Armoured Brigade. Formed December 1940 in the UK and assigned to new 11th Armoured Division March 1941. Relieved April 1942; assigned to 42nd Armoured Division May 1942 and then to 79th Armoured Division October 1943. Reorganized that month 3 with flail tanks. Like other parts of 79th Armoured Division, its units supported 21st Army Group operations from D-Day to the end of the war. Relieved August 1945 and disbanded in Germany that October.

31st Army Tank Brigade. Formed January 1941. Redesignated **31st Tank Brigade** May 1942 upon assignment to 53rd (Welsh) Mixed Division. Relieved September 1943 and became a separate brigade. Landed in NW Europe June 1944. Converted September 1944 to flamethrower tanks and assigned to 79th Armoured Division; from December 1944 also the parent formation for APC regiments. Like other parts of 79th Armoured Division, its units supported 21st Army Group operations to the end of the war. Remained in Germany on occupation duties until disbanded there April 1946.

32nd Army Tank Brigade. Formed September 1941 in Egypt, serving in various battles in North Africa until destroyed in Tobruk June 1942; brigade HQ officially disbanded 1 August 1942.

33rd Army Tank Brigade. Formed August 1941 in the UK.[214] Redesignated **33rd Tank Brigade** June 1942 as upon assignment to 3rd Mixed Division. Transferred May 1943 to 79th Armoured Division. Relieved August 1943 as a separate brigade. Redesignated March 1944 as **33rd Armoured Brigade**. Landed in NW Europe June 1944. Converted to Buffalos (LVTs) January 1945 and assigned to 79th Armoured Division. Disbanded August 1945 in Germany.

34th Tank Brigade. Formed December 1941 in the UK. Redesignated June 1942 as **34th Tank Brigade** upon assignment to 1st Mixed Division; transferred September 1942 to 43rd (Wessex) Mixed Division; relieved September 1943 as separate brigade Landed in NW Europe early July 1944 and served there the remainder of the war. Redesignated February 1945 as **34th Armoured Brigade**. Disbanded December 1945 in Germany.

35th Army Tank Brigade. Formed December 1941 in the UK by conversion of HQ 225th Infantry Brigade (Home). Redesignated August 1942 as **35th Tank Brigade**. Reorganized April 1943 with CDL tanks upon assignment to 79th Armoured Division. Relieved April 1944 and given the role of training reinforcements for 21st Army Group. Redesignated **35th Armoured Brigade** until 1945. Disbanded following the war.

36th Army Tank Brigade. Formed December 1941 in the UK by conversion of HQ 205th Infantry Brigade (Home). Redesignated August 1942 as **36th Tank Brigade**. Disbanded July 1943 in the UK.

(The designations of 74th and 87th Armoured Brigades were used as the notional command element of dummy tank units 1942-43 and 1944, respectively.)

137th Armoured Brigade. Formed July 1942 in the UK by conversion of 137th Infantry Brigade from 46th Infantry Division. Disbanded September 1943 in the UK.

Indian Army Brigades

50th Indian Tank Brigade. Formed near Poona October 1941 (formed from three regiments RAC; no Indian cavalry assigned until 1944). Served in the Arakan December 1944-February 1945, then withdrawn to India for further training. No British armour assigned after August 1945.

251st Indian Armoured Brigade. Formed July 1940 at Sialkot as 1st Indian Armoured Brigade and assigned to 1st Indian Armoured Division September 1940; renumbered October 1941 as 251st (and division as 31st). (No British element until November 1941.)

---

[214] HQ originally formed to supervise the training of infantry battalions converted to tank; in mid October 1941 the HQ was completed to establishment and it became an active brigade.

Relieved June 1942 and redesignated September 1942 as **251st Indian Tank Brigade**. Disbanded October 1943 without service.

252nd Indian Armoured Brigade. Formed from February 1940 as the Armoured Brigade, then 2nd Indian Armoured Brigade; assigned 1st Indian Armoured Division July 1940. (First British regiment joined September 1940.) Moved to Iraq July 1941 as a separate brigade group, serving there and in Persia; back to Iraq October 1941 and renumbered as 252nd Indian Armoured Brigade. (Last British regiment left January 1945. The brigade remained in Iraq until January 1946 when it returned to India.)

254th Indian Armoured Brigade. Formed April 1941 at Risalpur as 4th Indian Armoured Brigade and renumbered October 1941 as 254th. Assigned 2nd (32nd) Indian Armoured Division October 1941. (First British regiment joined May 1942.) Redesignated September 1942 as **254th Indian Tank Brigade** and relieved. Moved to the Imphal plain December 1943, serving there and in Burma until June 1945 when it moved from Rangoon to India.[215]

255th Indian Armoured Brigade. Formed June 1941 at Sialkot as 5th Indian Armoured Brigade, coming under 2nd (32nd) Indian Armoured Division; renumbered October 1941 as 255th. (No British regiment until May 1942.) Transferred April 1943 to 44th Indian Armoured Division; relieved March 1944. Redesignated August 1944 as **255th Indian Tank Brigade**. Moved to the Imphal plain October 1944, serving there and in Burma, not returning to India until after November 1945. No British regiment was assigned after January 1945.

267th Indian Armoured Brigade. Formed July 1943 Sialkot with three regiments RAC and assigned to 43rd Indian Armoured Division. On 1 April 1943 the brigade became 72nd Indian Infantry Brigade and its three regiments were converted back to infantry under their former titles. (In 1944 it would drop 'Indian' since it was always all-British.)

---

[215] 3rd Carabiniers remained with this brigade (redesignated as 3rd Indian Armoured Brigade December 1945) until April 1946.

Appendix 3: Battle Honours

The system of battle honours in the British Army developed over time, and the determination of what constituted a battle, what constituted participation in the battle, and what battles should be honored, was not always consistent, especially for the earlier wars. In simplest terms,

> The award of Battle Honours is primarily a system by which the Sovereign recognizes the presence of a regiment at, and its contributions to, a particular battle. Secondarily, it provides a means for that regiment to publicise its past glories by displaying the names of these battles.[216]

Battle honours are born on the regiment's colours. For the Second World War (as earlier), only cavalry/armoured and infantry regiments earned battle honours. The other arms and services have not received battle honours, nor did the Royal Marines.[217] Originally all battle honours were born on the colours, but the large size of infantry regiments and the huge number of battles in the First World War led to a decision that the regiments would each select ten battle honours for the colours. These are shown in printed lists either in bold type or in capital letters.

As was the case after the First War, a Battles Nomenclature Committee was established after 1945. It determined what constituted a battle, both in area and time, and an official name. Regiments then made application to a Battle Honours Committee, which determined entitlement. In addition to specific battles, there were also recognized campaigns (e.g., North Africa, with various possible combinations of years from 1940 to 1943), and these could also be claimed by regiments. Generally, a regiment eligible for a specific battle honour within the time and space of a campaign received the campaign honour as well. However, it was also possible for a regiment to receive the campaign honour without earning a battle honour as well. This allowed those which served in the theater, but not in a named battle, could still claim an honour.[218]

The earliest campaign honour, in terms of start date, is Norway. The next is North West Europe. This campaign honour has three possible dates: 1940 (the BEF), 1942 (Dieppe

---

[216] Anthony Baker, *Battle Honours of the British and Commonwealth Armies*, p 21.

[217] This was later changed in part for the Royal Artillery. Batteries were allowed claim a single honour—which they would have earned had they not been artillery—and make this 'honour title' part of their designation. An example from World War II is J (Sidi Rezegh) Battery RHA. Some batteries chose an earlier designation rather than a battle as their honour title, e.g., 16 Battery (Sandham's Company) RA

[218] As a general rule, more than half of the regiment/battalion must have participated in a battle to receive a battle honour, so participation by a detached company or squadron in a battle would not be recognized.

and other raids), and 1944-45 (21st Army Group). A regiment serving with both the BEF and 21st Army Group would show the honour as 'North West Europe, 1940 '44-45'. Abyssinia is a campaign honour that appears only with one British armoured regiment; British Somaliland or Persia do not appear on any. Iraq 1941 and Syria 1941 were campaign honours mainly found (for the British) in the regiments of 1st Cavalry Division. North Africa is another campaign honour that can have a variety of year dates, from 1940-43. It was followed by Sicily, and then Italy, with years between 1943-45 depending on actual service.

Greece had two distinct campaigns, 1941 and 1944-45. Crete, Madagascar, Malta and Middle East 1941-44 were campaigns that generally did not see British armour participate.

British armour also avoided Malaya 1941-42 and South East Asia 1941-42 [Hong Kong]. Burma is another long campaign, and year dates between 1942 and 1945 are possible.

Battle honours are always grouped by campaign, normally in date order, and begin with North West Europe, then North Africa/Sicily/Italy/Greece/Middle East, then Burma. Specific battle honours (if any) always precede the campaign honour. The Royal Tank Regiment provides a good example of the general scheme:

> Arras Counter-Attack, Calais 1940, St. Omer-La Bassee, Somme 1940, Odon, Caen, Bourgebus Ridge, Mont Pincon, Falaise, Nederrijn, Scheldt, Venlo Pocket, Rhineland, RHINE, Bremen, NORTH-WEST EUROPE 1940 '44-45, ABYSSINIA 1940, Sidi Barrani, Beda Fromm, Sidi Suleiman, TOBRUK 1941, Sidi Rezegh 1941, Belhamed, Gazala, Cauldron, Knightsbridge, Defense of Alamein Line, Alam el Halfa, EL ALAMEIN, Mareth, Akarit, Fondouk, El Kourzia, Madjez Plain, Tunis, NORTH AFRICA 1940-43, Primosole Bridge, Gerbini, Adrano, SICILY, Sangro, Salerno, Volturno Crossing, Garigliano Crossing, Anzio, Advance to Florence, Gothic Line, Coriano, Lamone Crossing, Rimini Line, Argenta Gap, ITALY 1943-45, GREECE 1941, BURMA 1942

Note that the regiment chose all of its campaign honours to show the breadth of its service, as well as selecting some notable specific battles. It appears that every regiment awarded El Alamein or Normandy Landing selected them for their colours.

A few Yeomanry regiments were converted to artillery or signals units during the war, but then reformed in the RAC in 1947. To recognize that service, they were awarded an Honorary Distinction, the badge of either the Royal Regiment of Artillery or the Royal Corps of Signals, with year dates (of service in that role) and then with scrolls for relevant campaigns. The Northumberland Hussars ended up with the most scrolls, five: 'North Africa', 'Greece', 'Middle East', 'Sicily', 'North-West Europe' Note that these are listed sequentially in time, unlike campaign honours.

Appendix 4: 21st Army Group Tank Strength June 1944—June 1945

This provides complete details of 21st Army Group tank strength just prior to D-Day. 21st Army Group was the largest British and Commonwealth force assembled during the war. It then provides the returns for December 1944, just past the mid point of the campaign. Finally, it provides the June 1945 strength, just after the end of the war.

This Appendix allows you to compare actual strength against theoretical establishments as well as the variety of tanks in use. Noteworthy is the number of Churchills in the tank brigades still armed with the long obsolete 6pdr gun. [219] While the returns show all armoured formations (e.g., 4th Canadian and 1st Polish Armored Divisions), this appendix is restricted to British only.

June 1944

7th Armoured Division
> Light: 44 Stuart V
> Cruiser: 36 Sherman VC, 201 Cromwell IV/V/VII, 24 Cromwell VI [261]
> Special: 28 Crusader AA, 8 Cromwell OP, 14 Cromwell ARV, 3 Valentine B/L

11th Armoured Division
> Light: 44 Stuart V
> Cruiser: 157 Sherman V, 36 Sherman VC, 62 Cromwell IV/V/VII, 6 Cromwell VI [261]
> Special: 28 Crusader AA, 8 Sherman V OP, 11 Sherman V ARV, 3 Cromwell ARV, 3 Valentine B/L

Guards Armoured Division
> Light: 44 Stuart VI
> Cruiser: 157 Sherman V, 36 Sherman VC, 59 Cromwell IV/V/VII, 6 Cromwell VI [258]
> Special: 18 Crusader AA, 8 Sherman V OP, 3 Cromwell OP, 11 Sherman V ARV, 3 Cromwell ARV, 3 Valentine B/L

4th Armoured Brigade
> Light: 33 Stuart III
> Cruiser: 157 Sherman II, 36 Sherman VC [193]
> Special: 20 Crusader AA, 8 Sherman II OP, 11 Sherman V ARV, 3 Valentine B/L

---

[219] However, it was regarded as a better antitank weapon than the 75mm gun on later marks.

8th Armoured Brigade
>Light: 33 Stuart III
>Cruiser 76 Sherman II DD, 95 Sherman III, 22 Sherman VC [193]
>Special: 20 Crusader AA, 8 Sherman III OP, 9 Sherman III ARV, 2 Sherman V
>ARC, 3 Valentine B/L

27th Armoured Brigade
>Light: 33 Stuart III
>Cruiser: 126 Sherman III, 38 Sherman V D, 29 Sherman VC [193]
>Special: 20 Crusader AA, 8 Sherman III OP, 9 Sherman III ARV, 2 Sherman V
>ARV, 3 Valentine B/L

30th Armoured Brigade
>Cruiser: 72 Sherman V, 180 Sherman V Crab [252]
>Special: 12 Sherman v ARV

33rd Armoured Brigade
>Light: 33 Stuart III
>Cruiser 157 Sherman I, 27 Sherman II [184]
>Special: 20 Crusader AA, 8 Sherman I OP, 6 Sherman V ARV, 3 Valentine B/L

1st Tank Brigade
>Cruiser: 50 Sherman I, 27 Sherman II; 162 Grant CDL [77 + 162 CDL]
>Special: 8 Sherman I OP, 6 Sherman V ARV, 3 Valentine B/L

6th Guards Tank Brigade
>Light: 12 Stuart V, 4 Stuart VI
>Cruiser: 4 Sherman V
>Infantry: 156 Churchill IV, 18 Churchill V/VIII [174; 164 with 75mm guns]
>Special: 11 Crusader AA, 8 Churchill IV OP, 11 Churchill ARV, 3 Churchill
>B/L

31st Tank Brigade
>Light: 33 Stuart III
>Cruiser: 4 Sherman V
>Infantry: 60 Churchill III, 12 Churchill IV, 31 Churchill VI, 18 Churchill V/VIII
>[121; 34 with 75mm guns]
>Special: 20 Crusader AA, 8 Churchill IV OP, 11 Churchill ARV, 1 Churchill
>B/L

34th Tank Brigade
>Light: 33 Stuart III
>Cruiser: 4 Sherman V
>Infantry: 90 Churchill III, 18 Churchill IV, 24 Churchill VI, 24 Churchill VII, 18 Churchill V/VIII [174; 59 with 75mm guns]
>Special: 20 Crusader AA, 8 Churchill IV OP, 11 Churchill ARV, 2 Churchill B/L

1st Assault Brigade RE
AVRE: not shown[220]
Special: 15 Churchill ARV

Other Units
15th/19th TKR Hussars: 75 Sherman V DD; 4 Stuart VI
141st Regiment RAC: 7 Churchill IV, 45 Churchill VII [Crocodile unit]

Total Tanks[221]

In this table, *Unit Equipment* represents what the establishments add up to; *Actual Total* is what the vehicles actually in the units add up; *With ARG* represents tanks in the hands of the Armoured Replacement Group; and *Reserve UE* is reserve unit equipment available outside the ARG.

	Unit Equipment	*Actual Total*	*With ARG*	*Reserve UE*
Cruiser Tanks				
Sherman I	207	207	52	75
Sherman II	276	260	50	50
	[76 DD]	[76 DD]		
Sherman III	316	316	150	150
Sherman V	937	951	178	232
	[175 DD]	[189 DD]		
Sherman IC	-	2	-	-
Sherman VC	316	316	24	18
Cromwell IV/V/VII	385	375	100	124
Cromwell VI [CS]	42	42	13	15
Challenger	-	-	-	18
Sherman V Crab	180	180	45	45
Grant CDL	162	162	-	-

[220] Not reported since these vehicles were not RAC types. In December 1944 the brigade had 131 AVRE, with another 35 in 21st Army Group (including reserves), for a total of 164.

[221] This table represents the total for 21st Army Group as a whole, not just the British formations detailed above. Otherwise it would distort the ratio of equipment on hand, reserves, etc. The other armoured formations are 4th Canadian and 1st Polish Armoured Divisions, and 2nd Canadian and Czech Armoured Brigades.

	Unit Equipment	Actual Total	With ARG	Reserve UE
Infantry Tanks				
Churchill III [6pdr]	150	150	-	-
Churchill IV [6pdr]	193	193	49	49
Churchill VI	56	56	30	3
Churchill VII	69	69	44	44
Churchill V/VIII [CS]	54	54	15	15
Light Tanks				
Stuart III	198	198	9	48
Stuart V	165	177	63	42
Stuart VI	158	52	11	3
Special Tanks				
Crusader AA	302	252	-	-
Sherman I OP	16	16	-	-
Sherman II OP	8	8	-	-
Sherman III OP	24	24	-	-
Sherman V OP	32	29	-	-
Churchill IV OP	24	24	-	-
Sherman III ARV	27	27	-	6
Sherman V ARV	101	93	12	17
Cromwell ARV	23	23	6	8
Churchill ARV	48	48	5	6
Valentine B/L	33	33	8	-
Churchill B/L	9	6	-	3

December 1944

7th Armoured Division

       Light: 31 Stuart

       Cruiser: 67 Sherman 17pdr, 196 Cromwell 75mm, 23 Cromwell CS [286]

       Special: 10 Sherman OP, 12 Cromwell ARV, 5 Crusader AA, 3 Valentine B/L

11th Armoured Division
>Light: 28 Stuart
>Cruiser: 139 Sherman 75mm, 74 Sherman 17pdr, 49 Cromwell 75mm, 7
>>Cromwell CS, 10 Challenger [279]
>Special: 9 Sherman ARV, 3 Cromwell ARV, 8 Sherman OP, 1 Valentine B/L

Guards Armoured Division
>Light: 36 Stuart
>Cruiser: 174 Sherman 75mm, 56 Sherman 17pdr, 70 Cromwell 75mm, 7
>>Cromwell CS, 11 Challenger [318]
>Special: 10 Sherman ARV, 3 Cromwell ARV, 8 Sherman OP, 2 Crusader AA, 1
>>Valentine B/L

79th Armoured Division
>Cruiser: 4 Sherman 75mm, 55 Sherman DD, 5 Sherman Crab [64]
>Infantry: 2 Churchill 75mm, 33 AVRE [35]
>Special: 214 Kangaroo, 6 Sherman ARV, 2 Churchill ARV, 1 Churchill B/L, 3
>>Ark

8th Armoured Brigade
>Light: 49 Stuart
>Cruiser: 149 Sherman 75mm, 66 Sherman 17pdr, 1 Cromwell 75mm [216]
>Special: 10 Sherman ARV, 6 Sherman OP, 1 Crusader AA, 3 Valentine B/L

29th Armoured Brigade[222]
>Light: 26 Stuart
>Cruiser: 112 Sherman 75mm, 48 Sherman 17pdr, 18 Cromwell 75mm, 31 Comet
>>[209]
>Special: 10 Sherman ARV

30th Armoured Brigade
>Cruiser 37 Sherman 75mm, 128 Sherman Crab [165]
>Special: 5 Sherman ARV

33rd Armoured Brigade
>Light: 31 Stuart
>Cruiser: 144 Sherman 75mm, 1 Sherman DD, 72 Sherman 17pdr [217]

---

[222] The brigade from 11th Armoured Division, withdrawn for conversion to Comet tanks but ended up in the Ardennes. 4th Armoured Brigade, normally a GHQ formation, was with the 11th Armoured Division in its place.

6th Guards Tank Brigade
> Light: 27 Stuart
> Cruiser: 5 Sherman 75mm
> Infantry: 48 Churchill 6pdr, 100 Churchill 75mm, 34 Churchill CS [182]
> Special: 12 Churchill ARV, 4 Churchill B/L

31st Tank Brigade
> Infantry: 13 Churchill 75mm, 12 Churchill CS, 90 Crocodiles [25+90]
> Special: 6 Churchill ARV

34th Tank Brigade
> Light: 33 Stuart
> Cruiser: 5 Sherman 75mm
> Infantry: 49 Churchill 6pdr, 108 Churchill 75mm, 38 Churchill CS [195]
> Special: 8 Churchill ARV, 3 Churchill B/L

1st Armoured Brigade RE
> Infantry: 131 AVRE
> Special: 5 Churchill ARV

Other Units
> VIII Corps: 9 Crusader AA
> XII Corps: 9 Crusader AA, 1 Cromwell ARV
> XXX Corps: 1 Sherman 75mm, 3 Cromwell 75mm, 5 Crusader AA
> 3rd Inf Div: 4 Crusader AA

Total Tanks[223]

Unlike the table for June 1944, this shows only actual tanks on hand and those with the Armoured Replacement Group. Also note that tanks are reported by main armament rather than by mark.

	Actual Total	*With ARG*
Cruiser Tanks		
Sherman 75mm	1,121	128
Sherman DD	56	9
Sherman 76mm	51	39
Sherman 17pdr	605	123
Cromwell 75mm	522	98
Cromwell CS (95mm)	55	9

---

[223] As with June 1944, these are the totals for all of 21st Army Group. The other armoured formations are still 4th Canadian and 1st Polish Armoured Divisions, and 2nd Canadian and Czech Armoured Brigades.

	Actual Total	*With ARG*
Comet	31	7
Challenger	21	11
Sherman V Crab	133	3

Infantry Tanks

Churchill 6pdr	115	7
Churchill 75mm	260	49
Churchill CS (95mm)	97	7
Crocodile	90	-
AVRE	164	2

Light Tanks

Stuart	431	90

Special Tanks

Crusader AA	51	2-
Kangaroo APC	214	12
Sherman OP	88	3
Sherman ARV	94	6
Cromwell ARV	24	3
Churchill ARV	36	3
Valentine B/L	9	2
Churchill B/L	8	3
Ark	3	-

June 1945

7th Armoured Division
>Light: 11 Stuart, 2 Alecto,[224] 28 Chaffee [41]
>Cruiser: 1 Sherman 75mm, 21 Sherman 17pdr, 1 Sherman 105mm, 90 Cromwell 75mm, 31 Cromwell CS, 87 Comet, 11 Challenger [242]
>Special: 4 Sherman ARV, 13 Challenger ARV, 3 dozers

11th Armoured Division
>Light: 32 Stuart
>Cruiser: 1 Sherman 75mm, 5 Cromwell 75mm, 26 Cromwell CS, 226 Comet [258]
>Infantry: 1 Churchill ARV, 1 Churchill B/L
>Special: 8 Cromwell OP, 16 Sherman ARV, 3 dozers

HQ 79th Armoured Division
>Infantry: 1 Churchill CS, 16 Crocodile
>Special: 2 Churchill ARV, 2 Churchill Ark

4th Armoured Brigade
>Light: 38 Stuart
>Cruiser: 102 Sherman 75mm, 67 Sherman 17pdr, 4 Sherman 105mm [173]
>Special: 4 Sherman OP, 13 Sherman ARV, 2 dozers

8th Armoured Brigade
>Light: 20 Stuart
>Cruiser: 114 Sherman 75mm, 66 Sherman 17pdr, 3 Sherman 105mm [183]
>Special: 10 Sherman ARV, 3 dozers

31st Armoured Brigade
>Light: 11 Stuart
>Infantry: 13 Churchill 75mm, 21 Churchill CS [34], 135 Crocodiles
>Special: 9 Churchill ARV, 4 dozers

33rd Armoured Brigade
Details for this unit appear to be missing from the source, other than 5 Sherman ARV. However, it was an LVT unit so those vehicles might not have been reported.

---

[224] This was a 95mm SP close-support vehicle on modified Harry Hopkins (Light Tank Mark VIII) chassis..

34th Armoured Brigade
>Light: 12 Stuart
>Cruiser: 15 Sherman 75mm
>Infantry: 50 Churchill 75mm, 7 Churchill CS [57], 15 Crocodile
>Special: 5 Churchill ARV, 3 Churchill B/L, 4 dozers

1st Armoured Engineer Brigade
>Light: 4 Chaffees
>Infantry: 28 AVRE
>Special: 1 Churchill ARV

Other Units
>VIII Corps: 3 Sherman 75mm, 1 Sherman DD, 3 Sherman 17pdr, 5 Cromwell 75mm, 1 Comet, 2 Churchill 75mm, 1 Churchill CS, 2 Cromwell OP, 1 Sherman ARV, 1 Cromwell ARV
>XXX Corps: 1 Sherman 75mm, 3 Cromwell 75mm
>3rd Infantry Division: 1 Cromwell ARV
>6th Airborne Division: 2 Cromwell 75mm

Total Tanks[225]

For this report, totals are those with units and those held in depots. As a reminder, Guards Armoured Division and 6th Guards Armoured Brigade had been converted to infantry and turned in all of their tanks.

	With Units	*Depots*
Cruiser Tanks		
Sherman 75mm	381	745
Sherman DD	1	90
Sherman 76mm	181	97
Sherman 17pdr	300	750
Sherman Crab	-	180
Sherman 105mm	32	50
Cromwell 75mm	154	314
Cromwell CS (95mm)	64	65
Comet	314	292
Challenger	24	26

---

[225] Figures are still for all of 21st Army Group. The other formations are 4th and 5th Canadian Armoured Divisions, and 1st Polish Armoured Division. The 1st and 2nd Canadian Armoured Brigades and Czech Armoured Brigade were present but either were not listed in the version on the web or I missed them while copying.

	With Units	*Depots*
Infantry Tanks		
Churchill 6pdr	-	47
Churchill 75mm	65	142
Churchill CS (95mm)	30	254
Crocodile	166	21
AVRE	28	223
Valentine 6pdr	16	9
Valentine 75mm	16	46
Valentine DD	-	60
Light Tanks		
Stuart	227	438
Locust	3	79
Alecto	3	32
Chaffee	32	109
Special Tanks		
Sherman ARV	60	107
Cromwell ARV	18	6
Churchill ARV	18	44
Sherman OP	17	23
Cromwell OP	13	-
Kangaroo APC	-	393
Churchill B/L	4	3
Valentine B/L	3	10
Ark	3	32
		-
Grant CDL	-	28
Dozer	17	6

Source: Peter Brown. '21st Army Group Tanks: British Tanks in Europe 1944-45'. November 1996 [based on 'Half Yearly Reports on the Progress of the Royal Armoured Corps' for June and December 1944]

Appendix 5: Tank Strengths, Tank Regiments in Italy, 1944-45

This Appendix is based on Eighth Army tank status reports, shown in tabular form by Chris Shillito, 'Churchill Tanks in Italy'.

21st Tank Brigade landed in Italy early May 1944 with the 12th and 48th RTR and the 145th Regiment RAC. That unit left 4 December 1944 to be disbanded, and was replaced by the North Irish Horse from 25th Tank Brigade.

25th Tank Brigade landed in Italy mid April 1944 with the North Irish Horse, 51st RTR and 142nd Regiment RAC. The latter left 18 December 1944 to be disbanded, while the North Irish Horse was transferred 4 December 1944 to the 21st Tank Brigade. In early January 1945 the 25th was reorganized as 'B' Assault Brigade RAC/RE, later 25th Armoured Engineer Brigade, with specialized armour (51st RTR and two assault regiments RE).

This list does not show all regiments, or the entire period for those shown.

For all months, dates are as of the end of the month unless otherwise indicated.

North Irish Horse
I: while in 25th Tank Brigade

	May 1944	Jun 1944	Jul 1944	Aug 1944	Sep 1944	Oct 1944	Nov 1944
Churchill I	6	6	6	6	6	6	0
Churchill III/IV	30	24	24	31	26	26	20
Churchill V (CS)	-	-	-	12	-	-	-
Churchill NA75	-	-	-	-	-	10	15
Churchill VII	-	-	-	-	-	2	3
Sherman I/II	17	18	21	11	12	3	3
Churchill ARV	3	4	4	3	6	3	-
ARK	-	-	-	-	-	2	3
Fascine	-	-	-	-	-	-	6

August 1944: 20th

North Irish Horse
II: while in 21st Tank Brigade

	Dec 1944	Jan 1945	Feb 1945	Mar 1945	Apr 1945
Churchill III/IV	29	27	22	24	16
Churchill V (CS)	6	7	9	9	9
Churchill NA75	16	18	17	18	14
Churchill VI[226]	-	-	-	-	-
Churchill VII	6	6	6	8	13
Sherman I/II	9	9	9	4	-

December 1944: 20th

12th Royal Tank Regiment
in 21st Tank Brigade

	Dec 1944	Jan 1945	Feb 1945	Mar 1945	Apr 1945
Churchill III/IV	25	23	20	18	16
Churchill V (CS)	6	8	9	9	9
Churchill NA75	6	6	7	13	14
Churchill VI[227]	-	-	-	-	-
Churchill VII	6	6	6	8	13
Sherman I/II	9	9	9	4	-

December 1944 : 20th

[226] However,. the regiment had 12 Churchill VI on 10 April and 6 on 20 April 1944, with none on 30 April 1944, the last date shown.
[227] However, the regiment also had 12 Churchill VI on 10 April and 6 on 20 April 1944, with none on 30 April 1944, the last date shown.

48th Royal Tank Regiment
in 21st Tank Brigade

	Dec 1944	Jan 1945	Feb 1945	Mar 1945	Apr 1945
Churchill III/IV	17	18	18	16	16
Churchill V (CS)	6	9	9	9	9
Churchill NA75	6	4	5	15	11
Churchill VII	3	3	3	7	16
Sherman I/II	20	18	17	4	-

December 1944 and February 1945: 20th

51st Royal Tank Regiment
in 25th Tank Brigade

	May 1944	Jun 1944	Jul 1944	Aug 1944	Sep 1944	Oct 1944	Nov 1944
Churchill I	6	6	5	4	4	6	6
Churchill III/IV	31	33	29	31	27	27	21
Churchill V (CS)[228]	-	-	-	-	-	-	-
Churchill NA75	-	-	-	-	7	15	15
Churchill VII	-	-	-	-	-	-	3
Sherman I/II	17	18	20	9	6	5	4
Churchill ARV	4	4	4	4	3	4	-
ARK	-	-	-	-	-	-	3
Fascine	-	-	-	-	-	-	4

August 1944: 20th

---

[228] However, the regiment had 11 on 10 August and 2 on 10 November.

142nd Regiment RAC
in 25th Tank Brigade

	May 1944	Jun 1944	Jul 1944	Aug 1944	Sep 1944	Oct 1944	Nov 1944
Churchill I	6	5	6	5	3	6	3
Churchill III/IV	30	24	24	31	26	30	20
Churchill V (CS)	-	-	-	12	-	-	-
Churchill NA75	-	-	-	-	10	16	15
Churchill VII	-	-	-	-	-	2	3
Sherman I/II	17	18	21	11	12	3	3
Churchill ARV	3	4	4	3	6	3	-
ARK	-	-	-	-	-	2	-
Fascine	-	-	-	-	-	-	6

August 1944: 20th

Appendix 6: Armoured Regiment 1945

Although issued just prior to the end of hostilities, this war establishment (II/157/1, effective 1 May 1945) basically tracks the prior November 1943 armoured regiment war establishment as modified November 1944 and early 1945. Those changes will be noted and discussed. 21st Army Group, however, changed from the establishment beginning January 1944 to accommodate use of the Sherman Firefly tank, and their alterations will also be noted..

	Headquarters	Headquarters Squadron	Three Squadrons (each)	Total
Officers	5	9	8	38
WO	1	4	1	8
Sgt/Staff Sgt	2	13	9	42
Rank and file	14*	169	133	582
Total all ranks	22	195	151	670
Attached		8	7	29
Total	22	203	158	699

* Includes an operator Royal Signals in one of the tanks; that individual is not shown in the details as one of the attached personnel.

Officers
Lieutenant Colonel, commanding; five Majors (one 2nd-in-command), Adjutant, Technical Officer, Liaison Officer, eight Captains,[229] 20 Subalterns, Quartermaster

Warrant Officers
regimental sergeant major, regimental quartermaster sergeant, technical quartermaster sergeant, mechanist quartermaster sergeant, four squadron sergeants major

Sergeants and Staff Sergeants
four squadron quartermaster sergeants, four mechanist sergeants, sergeant clerk, provost sergeant, signal sergeant, transport sergeant, technical storeman sergeant, 29 sergeants

Other Ranks
59 corporals (includes 11 lance sergeants), 523 troopers (includes 45 lance corporals)

Of the other ranks, 447 are tradesmen:

---

[229] The Adjutant and Technical and Liaison Officers are Captains.

carpenter and joiner, 13 clerks (two corporals), four driver mechanics, 90 driver mechanics AFV, 103 driver operators, five electricians, equipment repairer, gun fitter, 92 gunner mechanics, 89 gunner operators, six technical storeman, 39 vehicle mechanics

Of the other ranks, 135 are non-tradesmen:
22 batmen, butchery dutyman, 90 drivers IC, medical officers orderly, six motorcyclists, postman, five sanitary dutymen, five storemen, four water dutymen

Attached
Medical Officer RAMC, three armourers (one sergeant) and six vehicle mechanics (three sergeants) REME, 19 cooks ACC (one sergeant and one corporal)

	Headquarters	Headquarters Squadron	Three Squadrons (each)	Total
Tanks cruiser	4		17	55
Tanks close support*			2	6
Tanks, Light		11		11
Tanks AA		6		6
Scout cars		9	1	12
Motorcycles solo		8		8
Cars 4x4 4-seater	1			1
Jeeps (cars 5cwt 4x4)		8	1	11
Halftracks 15cwt personnel	1	5	3	15
Trucks 15cwt 4x4 GS		3	1	6
Trucks 15cwt 4x4 FFW		1		1
Trucks 15cwt 4x4 water		1	1	4
Lorries 3ton 4x4 GS		11	12	47
Lorries 3ton 4x4 Office		1		1
Lorries 3ton 4x4 Kitchen		1	1	4
Lorries 3ton 4x4 Machinery type I-30		1	1	4
Lorries 3ton 6x4 store		2	1	5
Armoured recovery vehicles			1	3

* Normal gun tanks in regiments equipped with the Sherman.

Note: although the details that follow indicate 'cruiser tanks', the actual establishment refers simply to tank, cruiser or infantry.

REGIMENTAL HEADQUARTERS

Cruiser Tank 1
> Lieutenant Colonel, Adjutant, sergeant, driver mechanic, driver operator

Cruiser Tank 2
> Major (2nd in command), regimental sergeant major, corporal gunner operator, driver mechanic AFV, *operator Royal Signals*

Cruiser Tank 3
> Subaltern, sergeant, gunner operator, driver mechanic AFV, driver operator

Cruiser Tank 4
> Intelligence Officer, corporal driver IC (intelligence duties), driver mechanic, gunner operator, driver operator

4-seater car 4x4
> corporal driver, driver IC

15cwt Halftrack
> driver IC

Note: the 15cwt halftrack and driver IC were added to the old WE in early 1945

HEADQUARTERS SQUADRON

Squadron Headquarters

Jeep (car 5cwt 4x4) 1
> Major (squadron commander), driver IC

Jeep (car 5cwt 4x4) 2
> Liaison Officer, driver operator

15cwt Truck FFW
> Captain (squadron 2nd in command), squadron sergeant major, driver operator

Note: the second jeep with Liaison Officer and driver operator were added to the old WE in late 1944

AA Troop

AA Tank 1
> Subaltern, driver mechanic, gunner operator, driver operator

AA Tank 2
> sergeant, driver mechanic AFV , gunner operator, driver operator

AA Tanks 3-6
> corporal driver operator, driver mechanic AFV, gunner operator, gunner mechanic

Note: the AA troops were disbanded in summer 1944. Although continued on this war establishment, there were no AA tanks in 21st Army Group in June 1945.

Reconnaissance Troop

Troop Headquarters

Light Tank 1
> Captain, driver mechanic, gunner operator, driver operator

Light Tank 2
>Subaltern, driver mechanic , gunner operator, driver operator

Three Sections (each)

Light Tank 1
>sergeant, driver mechanic , gunner operator, driver operator

Light Tanks 2-3
>corporal driver operator, gunner mechanic, gunner operator, driver mechanic

Note: in late 1944 the Recce Troop gained a Captain as commanding officer, retaining the Subaltern but eliminating one sergeant. In addition, some units replaced the second light tank at troop HQ with a scout car (Subaltern and driver operator), which eliminated two other ranks as well (driver mechanic and gunner operator from the light tank).

Intercommunications Troop

Scout car 1
>sergeant, driver operator

Scout cars 2, 3
>driver operator, corporal driver IC

Scout cars 4-8
>driver operator, driver IC

Scout car 9
>Technical Officer, driver operator

Note: in November 1944 the Technical Officer lost his scout car (replaced by a corporal driver IC) and moved to riding in an admin troop vehicle. However, in 1945 he got the scout car back.

Administrative Troop

Motorcycle
>provost sergeant

Motorcycles 2-7
>motorcyclist

Motorcycle 8
>batman

Car 5cwt 4x4 (Jeep) 1
>corporal driver IC

Car 5cwt 4x4 (Jeep) 2-5
>driver IC

Jeep (car 5cwt 4x4) 6
>Quartermaster, driver IC

15cwt Truck 4x4 GS 1
>squadron quartermaster sergeant, driver IC

15cwt Truck 4x4 GS 2
>sanitary dutyman, medical officer's orderly, driver IC

15cwt Truck 4x4 GS 3
>quartermaster sergeant (technical), sergeant storeman (technical), corporal clerk, batman, driver IC

15cwt Truck 4x4 water
>water dutyman, driver IC

Halftrack

      Medical Officer RAMC, batman, driver IC

Halftrack [ambulance] 1

      driver IC

Halftrack [ambulance] 2

      driver IC

Halftrack 1

      mechanist sergeant, 3 vehicle mechanics, driver operator

Halftrack 2

      equipment repairer, sergeant armourer, 2 armourers, corporal storeman (technical), driver IC

3ton 4x4 lorry GS 1

      transport sergeant, *cook ACC* (officers' mess), butchery dutyman, batman, driver IC

3ton 4x4 lorry GS 2

      carpenter and joiner, vehicle mechanic, corporal driver operator (relief), 3 driver mechanics (relief), 3 gunner operators (relief), 3 gunner mechanics (relief), driver IC

3ton 4x4 lorry GS 3

      postman, storeman, 3 batmen, driver IC

3ton 4x4 lorry GS 4

      electrician, gun fitter, driver IC

3ton 4x4 lorry GS 5

      sergeant, sanitary dutyman, driver IC

3ton 4x4 lorry GS 6

      clerk, driver IC

3ton 4x4 lorry GS 7

      clerk, driver IC

3ton 4x4 lorry GS 8

      regimental quartermaster sergeant, driver IC

3ton 4x4 lorry GS 9

      3 vehicle mechanics, driver IC

3ton 4x4 lorry GS 10

      storeman, clerk, driver IC

3ton 4x4 lorry GS 11

      2 clerks, driver IC

3ton 4x4 lorry office

      Signal Officer, signal sergeant, sergeant clerk, corporal clerk, driver IC

3ton 4x4 lorry kitchen

      sergeant cook ACC, *2 cooks ACC*, driver IC

3ton 4x4 lorry machinery I30

      electrician, driver mechanic

3ton 4x4 lorry store

      vehicle mechanic, technical storeman, 3 batmen, driver IC

Note: The slave battery carrier (a Lloyd Carrier) was replaced by the 3ton 4x4 lorry Machinery I30. The 3ton GS vehicle carrying the Signal Officer was replaced by a variant purpose-built as an office or a converted signals vehicle. Some 15cwt GS or FFW trucks were later replaced by halftracks. The 3ton stores lorry was later replaced by a purpose built version instead of an adaptation of the GS vehicle.

THREE SQUADRONS (EACH)

Squadron Headquarters 'A' or Fighting Portion

Cruiser Tank (close support) 1
> Major, sergeant, driver operator, gunner operator, driver mechanic

Cruiser Tank (close support) 2
> Captain (2nd in command), driver mechanic, gunner operator, gunner mechanic, corporal driver operator

Cruiser Tank 1
> squadron sergeant major, driver mechanic, gunner operator, gunner mechanic, driver operator

Cruiser Tank 2
> Captain, driver mechanic, gunner operator, gunner mechanic, driver operator

Car 5cwt 4x4 (Jeep)
> driver IC

Scout Car
> driver operator

Armoured Recovery Vehicle
> *sergeant vehicle mechanic REME*, *vehicle mechanic REME*, vehicle mechanic, driver mechanic

Note: While the establishment called for two close support tanks at squadron HQ, in Sherman-equipped regiments these were all normal gun-armed Shermans. This was true in Italy as well until September 1944 when regiments there received six Sherman IB (105mm) CS variants.

In 21st Army Group one tank (it is not clear which) was given up to bring the troops up to 16. It was officially returned in early 1945 but some regiments may have done so earlier. This would give the regiment 64 rather than 61 cruiser tanks.

Squadron Headquarters 'B' or Administration Portion

Truck 15cwt 4x2 GS
> squadron quartermaster sergeant, sergeant, driver IC

Truck 15cwt 4x2 water
> water dutyman, driver IC

15cwt Halftrack 1
> mechanist sergeant, 2 vehicle mechanics, driver operator (relief)

15cwt Halftrack 2
> *cook ACC* (officers' mess), driver IC

15cwt Halftrack 3
> 2 driver mechanics (relief), driver operator (relief), 2 gunner operators (relief)

3ton Lorry 4x4GS 1
> storeman, 5 vehicle mechanics, driver IC

3ton Lorry 4x4GS 2
> batman, driver IC

3ton Lorry 4x4GS 3
> batman, driver IC

3ton Lorry 4x4GS 4
        batman, driver IC
3ton Lorry 4x4GS 5
        clerk, corporal driver IC
3ton Lorry 4x4GS 6
        batman, driver IC
3ton Lorry 4x4GS 7
        gunner operator (relief), driver IC
3ton Lorry 4x4GS 8
        gunner mechanic (relief), sanitary dutyman, driver IC
3ton Lorry 4x4GS 9
        2 gunner mechanics (relief), driver IC
3ton Lorry 4x4GS 10
        corporal driver operator (relief), driver IC
3ton Lorry 4x4GS 11
        clerk, driver IC
3ton Lorry 4x4 GS 12
        driver IC
3ton Lorry 4x4 Kitchen
        corporal cook ACC, 3 cooks ACC, driver IC
3ton lorry 4x4 Machinery I30
        electrician, driver mechanic
3ton 4x4 lorry stores
        corporal storeman technical, 2 vehicle mechanics, gun fitter

Note: The slave battery carrier (a Lloyd Carrier) was replaced by the 3ton 4x4 lorry Machinery I30. The 15cwt GS truck could later be replaced by a 4x4 or a halftrack. The 3ton stores lorry was later replaced by a purpose built version instead of an adaptation of the GS vehicle.

             Five tank troops (each)
Cruiser Tank 1
        Subaltern, corporal driver operator, gunner operator, gunner mechanic, driver mechanic
Cruiser Tank 2
        sergeant, driver operator, gunner operator, gunner mechanic, driver mechanic
Cruiser Tank 3
        corporal, driver operator, gunner operator, 2 gunner mechanics, driver mechanic

In 21st Army Group

             Four tank troops (each)[230]
Cruiser Tank 1
        Subaltern, corporal driver operator, gunner operator, gunner mechanic, driver mechanic
Cruiser Tank 2
        corporal, driver operator, gunner operator, gunner mechanic, driver mechanic
Cruiser Tank 3
        corporal, driver operator, gunner operator, 2 gunner mechanics, driver mechanic

---

[230] At least in 1944, one of the tanks from squadron HQ came down to fill out one of the troops.

Cruiser Tank (Firefly)
>sergeant, gunner operator, gunner mechanic, driver mechanic

Note: Regiments gradually increased the number of Fireflys, trying to get to two per troop. The original establishment for a division was 36 (12 in each regiment). In December 1944, Guards Armoured Division had 56, 7th Armoured Division 67 and 11th Armoured Division (with 4th Armoured Brigade) a full 74. Its 29th Armoured Brigade (due to switch over to Comets) had 48 Fireflys, 8th Armoured Brigade had 66, and 33rd Armoured Brigade 72.

All of the regiments except those in 22nd Armoured Brigade (7th Armoured Division) were equipped with the Sherman. The 22nd had the Cromwell, and thus its squadron HQ had two of the Cromwell CS version (either Mk VI or Mk VIII) and two gun-armed tanks. One of the latter would have been given up to the bring the four troops to 16 tanks total. In theory the Challenger would have replaced the Firefly in these regiments, but so few were actually in service with 21st Army Group that this seems unlikely. For example, even in June 1945 7th Armoured Division had 21 Sherman Firefly and 11 Challengers; in the prior December, as noted, it had no Challengers but 67 Sherman Firefly.

Appendix 7: Tank Regiment 1943

The last wartime War Establishment for a tank regiment [still technically a tank battalion] was II/154/2 with an effective date of 30 November 1943. At this point there was little real difference between armoured and tank regiments other than their tanks, and the May 1945 war establishment for armoured regiments was also used for the remaining tank regiments. As noted in the main text, it is impossible to reconcile the information within the only known published copy of this war establishment.

	Headquarters	Headquarters Squadron	Three Squadrons (each)	Total
Officers				38
WO				8
Sgt/Staff Sgt				41
Rank and file				582
Total all ranks				670
Attached				28
Total				699

Officers
Lieutenant Colonel, commanding, Major (2nd in command), four Majors, Adjutant, Technical Officer, Liaison Officer, eight Captains, 20 Subalterns, Quartermaster[231]

Warrant Officers
Regimental Sergeant Major, Regimental Quartermaster Sergeant, Quartermaster Sergeant (Technical), Mechanist Quartermaster Sergeant, four Squadron Sergeants Major

Sergeants/Staff Sergeants
Three squadron quartermaster sergeants, four mechanist sergeants, sergeant clerk, provost sergeant, signal sergeant, transport sergeant, sergeant (technical storeman), 29 sergeants

Other Ranks
59 corporals, 523 troopers

Of the other ranks, 444 are tradesmen:carpenter and joiner, 13 clerks, 94 driver mechanics, 103 driver operators, 5 electricians, equipment repairer, gun fitter, 92 gunner mechanics, 89 gunner operators, 6 storemen (technical), 39 vehicle mechanics

---

[231] The adjutant and the technical and liaison officers are captains, the quartermaster is a subaltern.

Of the other ranks, 135 are non-tradesmen:[232]
22 batmen, butchery dutyman, 90 drivers IC, medical orderly, 6 motorcycle orderlies, postman, five sanitary dutymen, five storemen, four water dutymen

Attached
Medical Officer RAMC, three armourers and six vehicle mechanics (three sergeants) REME, 19 cooks ACC

	Headquarters	Headquarters Squadron	Three Squadrons (each)	Total
Tanks infantry	4		16	52
Tanks infantry close support			2	6
Tanks, light		11		11
Tanks, observation post	2			2
Tanks AA		6		6
Scout cars		9	1	12
Motorcycles solo		10		10
Cars 4x4 4-seater	1	1	1	5
Jeeps (cars 5cwt 4x4)		9		9
Halftracks 15cwt personnel	1	5	3	15
Trucks 15cwt 4x2 GS		3	1	6
Trucks 15cwt 4x2 FFW		2		2
Trucks 15cwt 4x2 water		1	1	4
Lorries 3ton 4x4 GS		13	11	
Lorries 3ton 6x4 store		1	1	4
Lorries 3ton 4x4 kitchen		1	1	4
Armoured recovery vehicles			1	3
Carrier slave battery		1	1	4

Two vehicles in the HQ Squadron's Admin Troop tow 20mm AA guns on trailers.

In the details that follow, the vehicles are probably correct, but the personnel shown cannot be made to square with the overall numbers.

---

[232] Note that these two groups add up to 579, leaving three rank and file unaccounted for.

REGIMENTAL HEADQUARTERS

Churchill Tank 1 (control)
> Lieutenant Colonel, sergeant, driver mechanic, gunner operator, driver operator

Churchill Tank 2 (rear link)
> Major (2nd in command), regimental sergeant major, corporal driver mechanic, gunner operator, *operator Royal Signals*

Churchill Tank 3
> Intelligence Officer, driver mechanic, corporal gunner operator, gunner mechanic, driver operator

Churchill Tank 4
> Adjutant, sergeant, gunner operator, driver mechanic, driver operator

4-seater car 4x4
> Subaltern, corporal driver IC, driver IC

Halftrack
> Driver IC

The December 1943 war establishment also included the following vehicles, which were removed in 21st Army Group prior to D-Day:

Tank Observation Post 1
> sergeant, driver mechanic, driver operator, gunner mechanic

Tank Observation Post 2
> driver mechanic, gunner operator, corporal driver operator, gunner mechanic

Each included a seat for an observation officer from the RA.

HEADQUARTERS SQUADRON

Squadron Headquarters

Car 4-seater 4x4 [may be replaced by Jeep]
> Major (squadron commander), squadron sergeant major, corporal clerk, driver IC

Jeep (car 5cwt 4x4)
> Captain Liaison Officer, batman driver

15cwt Truck FFW
> Captain (squadron 2nd in command), 2 driver operators

AA Troop[233]

AA Tank 1
> Subaltern, driver mechanic, gunner operator, driver operator

AA Tank 2
> sergeant, driver mechanic, gunner operator, driver operator

AA Tanks 3-6
> corporal driver operator, driver mechanic, gunner operator, gunner mechanic

---

[233] Removed after Normandy, the AA troops remained in the May 1945 war establishment but were not reformed.

Reconnaissance Troop

Troop Headquarters
Light Tank 1
       Subaltern, driver mechanic, gunner operator, driver operator
Light Tank 2
       sergeant, driver mechanic, gunner operator, driver operator
Three Sections (each)
Light Tank 3 (6, 9)
       sergeant, driver mechanic, gunner operator, gunner mechanic
Light Tanks 4-5 (7-8, 10-11)
       corporal driver operator, gunner mechanic, gunner operator, driver mechanic

Note: in late 1944 the Recce Troop gained a Captain as commanding officer, retaining the subaltern but eliminating one sergeant. This raised the officer total from 37 to 38.

Intercommunications Troop

Scout car 1
       Subaltern, driver operator
Scout car 2
       sergeant, driver operator
Scout car 3
       driver operator, corporal driver IC
Scout cars 4-8
       driver operator, driver IC
Scout car 9
       Technical Officer, driver operator

Administrative Troop

Motorcycle
       provost sergeant
Motorcycle 2
       corporal motorcyclist
Motorcycles 3-10
       Motorcyclist
Jeeps (car 5cwt 4x4) 1-8
       Driver IC
15cwt Truck 4x2 GS 1
       mechanist quartermaster sergeant, 2 vehicle mechanics, driver IC
15cwt Truck 4x2 GS 2
       transport sergeant, batman, gunner operator (relief), 4 gunner mechanics (relief)
15cwt Truck 4x2 GS 3 [officers mess equipment]
       2 batmen, *cook ACC (officers mess)*, driver IC
15cwt Truck 4x2 GS 4 [officers mess baggage and rations]
       signal sergeant, 3 batmen, driver IC
15cwt Truck 4x2 GS 5
       Quartermaster, driver IC
15cwt Truck 4x2 GS 6 [medical stores]
       medical officer's orderly, driver IC

15cwt Truck 4x2 water
    water dutyman, driver IC
15cwt Halftrack 1 [fitters and tools]
    mechanist sergeant, 2 vehicle mechanics, driver operator
15cwt Halftrack 2
    3 driver mechanics (relief), 3 gunner operators (relief), driver IC
15cwt Halftrack 3
    Medical Officer RAMC, driver operator
15cwt Halftrack [for the collection of casualties]
    driver IC
15cwt Halftrack [for the collection of casualties]
    driver IC
3ton 4x4 lorry GS 1[234] [carries anti-gas stores]
    regimental quartermaster sergeant, technical quartermaster sergeant, corporal clerk, technical storeman, driver IC
3ton 4x4 lorry GS 2 [carries petrol]
    batman, driver IC
3ton 4x4 lorry GS 3 [carries petrol]
    Sergeant (relief), driver IC
3ton 4x4 lorry GS 4 [carries petrol]
    corporal driver operator (relief), driver IC
3ton 4x4 lorry GS 5 [carries ammunition]
    corporal driver operator (relief), driver IC
3ton 4x4 lorry GS 6 [carries ammunition]
    batman, driver IC
3ton 4x4 lorry GS 7 [carries ammunition]
    batman, driver IC
3ton 4x4 lorry GS 8 [carries ammunition]
    clerk, driver IC
3ton 4x4 lorry GS 9 [carries ammunition]
    clerk, driver IC
3ton 4x4 lorry GS 10 [carries ammunition]
    clerk, driver IC
3ton 4x4 lorry GS 11[235] [carries MT stores]
    sergeant technical Storeman, corporal technical storeman, sanitary dutyman, driver IC
3ton 4x4 lorry GS 12 [carries armourers and carpenters tools]
    sergeant armourer REME, lance corporal armourer REME, armourer REME, carpenter and joiner, sanitary dutyman, driver IC
3ton 4x4 lorry GS 13 [carries baggage and blankets; tows 1ton trailer]
    storeman, postman, equipment repairer, batman, driver IC
3ton 4x4 lorry GS 14 [office use]
    Sergeant Clerk, corporal clerk, driver IC
3ton 4x4 lorry kitchen
    squadron quartermaster sergeant, *sergeant cook ACC, 2 cooks ACC*, butchery dutyman, storeman, clerk, driver IC

---

[234] Tows a 20mm AA gun.
[235] Tows a 20mm AA trailer.

3ton 6x4 lorry store [carries stores and vehicle mechanics tools]
>6 vehicle mechanics, technical storeman, driver IC

Carrier, starting and charging (slave battery)
>electrician, driver mechanic

Note: The slave battery carrier (a Lloyd Carrier) was later replaced by the 3ton 4x4 lorry Machinery I30. The 3ton office lorry was originally a GS lorry, and was later replaced by a purpose-built office vehicle.

THREE SQUADRONS (EACH)

Squadron Headquarters 'A' Fighting Portion

Churchill Tank 1 (CS)
>Major (squadron commander), sergeant, driver operator, gunner operator, driver mechanic

Churchill Tank 2 (CS)
>Captain , squadron sergeant major, driver mechanic, gunner operator, driver operator

Churchill Tank 3
>Captain, driver mechanic, gunner operator, gunner mechanic, corporal driver operator

Scout car
>gunner mechanic (relief), driver operator

Armoured Recovery Vehicle Mk I
>*sergeant vehicle mechanic REME, mechanic REME*, vehicle mechanic, driver mechanic

Squadron Headquarters 'B' Administration Portion

Car 4-seat 4x4
>squadron quartermaster sergeant, batman, driver IC

Truck 15cwt 4x2 GS [carries officers mess equipment]
>3 batmen, driver IC

Truck 15cwt 4x2 water
>water dutyman, driver IC

15cwt Halftrack 1
>mechanist sergeant, 2 vehicle mechanics, driver operator (relief)

15cwt Halftrack 2
>gunner mechanic (relief), 4 gunner operators (relief), driver operator (relief), driver IC

15cwt Halftrack 3
>sergeant, 2 driver mechanics (relief), 2 driver operators (relief)

3ton Lorry 4x4 GS 1 [carries ammunition]
>vehicle mechanic, driver IC

3ton Lorry 4x4 GS 2 [carries ammunition]
>vehicle mechanic, driver IC

3ton Lorry 4x4 GS 3 [carries ammunition]
>sanitary dutyman, driver IC

3ton Lorry 4x4 GS 4 [carries ammunition]
>gunner mechanic (relief), driver IC

3ton Lorry 4x4 GS 5 [carries ammunition]
> gunner mechanic (relief), driver IC

3ton Lorry 4x4 GS 6 [carries petrol]
> vehicle mechanic, driver IC

3ton Lorry 4x4 GS 7 [carries petrol]
> corporal clerk, driver IC

3ton Lorry 4x4 GS 8 [carries petrol]
> clerk, driver IC

3ton Lorry 4x4 GS 9 [carries baggage and blankets, tows 1ton trailer]
> sergeant storeman, driver IC

3ton Lorry 4x4 GS 10
> 2 gunner mechanics (relief), driver IC

3ton Lorry 4x4 kitchen [carries rations]
> *corporal cook ACC, 4 cooks ACC*, driver IC

Carrier, Starting and Charing (slave battery)
> electrician, driver mechanic

3ton 6x4 Lorry stores [carries stores and mechanics tools]
> corporal storeman technical, 4 vehicle mechanics

Note: The slave battery carrier (a Lloyd Carrier) in the original establishment was replaced by a 3ton 4x4 lorry Machinery I30. The 3ton 6x4 stores lorry may have been a later replacement of the original 4x2 adaptation of the GS vehicle.

Five tank troops (each)

Churchill Tank 1
> Subaltern, corporal driver operator, gunner operator, gunner mechanic, driver mechanic

Churchill Tank 2
> sergeant, driver operator, gunner operator, gunner mechanic, driver mechanic

Churchill Tank 3
> corporal driver operator, gunner operator, 2 gunner mechanics, driver mechanic

Appendix 8: Armoured Car Regiment 1943

The final war establishment for an armoured car regiment was III/236/2, effective 30 November 1943.

	Headquarters	Headquarters Squadron	Four Squadrons (each)	Total
Officers	5	6	11	55
WO	1	4	1	9
Sgt/Staff Sgt	1	9	9	46
Rank and file	20	112	134	628
Total all ranks	27	131	145	738
Attached	-	9	5	29
Total	27	140	150	767
LMGs .303" for 'B' vehicles		9	5	29

Officers
Lieutenant Colonel commanding, six Majors (one second in command), five Captains, Adjutant, Liaison Officer, Technical Officer, 32 Subalterns, Intelligence Officer, Signals Officer, Transport Officer, Quartermaster

Warrant Officers
Regimental Sergeant Major, Regimental Quartermaster Sergeant, Quartermaster Sergeant (technical), Mechanist Quartermaster Sergeant, five Squadron Sergeants Major

Sergeants/Staff Sergeants
Five Squadron Quartermaster Sergeants, four mechanist sergeants, provost sergeant, signals sergeant, Transport NCO, Clerk, Technical Storeman, 32 Sergeants

Other Ranks
80 corporals (includes 18 lance sergeants), 548 troopers (includes 55 lance corporals)

Of the other ranks, 364 are tradesmen
carpenter and joiner, 16 clerks, 72 driver mechanics, 127 driver operators, two electricians, equipment repairer, 41 gunner mechanics, 73 gunner operators, seven storemen (technical), 24 vehicle mechanics

Of the other ranks, 264 are non tradesmen:
38 batmen, butchery dutyman, 120 drivers IC, five drivers IC (for intelligence duties), medical officers orderly (lance corporal), 17 motorcyclists, postman (lance corporal), four regimental police, five sanitary dutymen, seven storemen, 60 troopers, five water dutymen

Attached Personnel
Medical Officer RAMC, four armourers REME (one a sergeant), and 24 cooks ACC (five are corporals).

	Headquarters	Headquarters Squadron	Four Squadrons (each)	Total
Armoured cars	3		16	67
Armoured cars AA		5		5
Scout cars		13	13	65
Motorcycles solo	3	8	3	23
Car, 2-seater 4x2		2 [1]*		2 [1]
Car, 4-seater 4x4	2	[1]	1	6[7]
Jeeps (cars 5cwt 4x4)	3		1	7
Trucks 15cwt 4x2 GS		3		3
Trucks 15cwt 4x2 office		1		1
Trucks 15cwt 4x2 water		1	1	5
Trucks 15cwt 4x2 FFW		1	1	5
Trucks 15cwt 4x4 personnel		1	4**	17
Lorries 30cwt slave battery		1	1	5
Lorries 3ton 4x4 GS		8	5	28
Lorries 3ton 4x4 mobile kitchen		1	1	5
Lorries 3ton 4x4 stores		1	1	5

* One 4x2 2-seater car later replaced by 4-seater 4x4 car.
** Includes three White scout cars, which were sometimes later replaced by halftracks.

REGIMENTAL HEADQUARTERS

Motorcycle solo[236]
>   signal sergeant

Motorcycle
>   corporal motorcyclist

Motorcycles 2-3
>   motorcyclist

4 seater car 4x4
>   Intelligence Officer, corporal driver IC (for intelligence duties), clerk, driver IC

4 seater car 4x4
>   regimental sergeant major, sergeant, driver IC

5cwt cars 4x4 (Jeep) 1-3
>   driver IC

Armoured Car 1
>   Lieutenant Colonel, corporal gunner mechanic, driver mechanic, gunner operator, driver operator

Armoured Car 2
>   Major (2nd in command), driver mechanic, driver operator, gunner operator, gunner mechanic

Armoured Car 3[237]
>   Signals Officer, Adjutant, driver mechanic, driver operator

---

HEADQUARTERS SQUADRON

Squadron Headquarters

4 seater car 4x4
>   Major, squadron sergeant major, corporal clerk, driver IC

2-seater car 4x2
>   Captain, driver IC

AA Troop[238]

AA Armoured Car 1
>   Sergeant, driver mechanic, driver operator, gunner mechanic

AA Armoured Car 2
>   Sergeant, driver mechanic, driver operator, gunner operator

AA Armoured Car 3-5
>   corporal gunner mechanic, driver mechanic, driver operator, gunner operator

---

[236] One version available shows this individual in the intercommunications troop. Perhaps he was assigned there but operated with RHQ, where the other version shows him..

[237] All versions of the war establishment I have seen only show four instead of five personnel here. It may be that, like the armoured regiment RHQ, a signal operator from the supporting Royal Signals section rode in this vehicle.

[238] It appears that most regiments disbanded their AA troops in 1944, but this seems done on an individual basis and not all at one time.

Intercommunications Troop
Scout car 1
>Liaison Officer,[239] driver operator

Scout cars 2-4
>corporal driver IC, driver operator

Scout cars 5-12
>driver operator, driver IC

Scout car 13
>sergeant, driver operator

Administrative Troop
Motorcycle
>provost sergeant

Motorcycles 2-5
>regimental policemen

Motorcycles 6-7
>motorcyclist

15cwt truck 4x2 GS 1
>Quartermaster, corporal clerk, clerk. batman, driver IC

15cwt truck 4x2 GS 2
>Technical Officer, clerk, driver IC

15cwt truck 4x2 GS 3
>*cook ACC (for officers mess)*, batman, driver IC

15cwt truck 4x2 office
>sergeant clerk, corporal clerk, 2 clerks, driver IC

15cwt truck 4x2 water
>water dutyman, driver IC

15cwt truck 4x2 FFW
>Transport Officer, 2 driver operators, driver IC

15cwt truck 4x4 personnel[240]
>*Medical Officer RAMC*, medical officer's orderly, gunner operator (relief), driver IC

30cwt lorry slave battery[241]
>2 electricians, driver IC

3-ton lorry 4x4 GS 1 (carries petrol)
>sergeant technical storeman, technical storeman, driver IC

3-ton lorry 4x4 GS 2 (carries petrol)
>transport sergeant, driver IC

3-ton lorry 4x4 GS 3 (carries ammunition)
>technical storeman, vehicle mechanic, postman, driver IC

3-ton lorry 4x4 GS 4 (carries ammunition)
>regimental quartermaster sergeant, equipment repairer, storeman, driver IC

---

[239] The liaison officer and his scout car would be at the HQ of the formation for which the regiment was working. The other 12 remained with the regiment, but might be found forward with the squadrons.
[240] Medical stores. Replaced by armoured 15cwt 4x4 White scout car.
[241] Later replaced by 3ton machinery lorry I30.

3-ton lorry 4x4 GS 5 (carries regimental stores)
> technical quartermaster sergeant, corporal technical storeman, vehicle mechanic, carpenter and joiner, driver IC

3-ton lorry 4x4 GS 6 (carries HQ squadron stores)
> squadron quartermaster-sergeant, 2 storemen, sanitary dutyman, driver IC

3-ton lorry 4x4 GS 7 stores (carries baggage and blankets)
> sergeant armourer, 3 armourers, driver IC

3-ton lorry 4x4 GS 8
> 8 batmen, 2 gunner operators (relief), 3 gunner mechanics (relief), driver IC

3-ton lorry 4x4 mobile kitchen
> *corporal cook ACC, 2 cooks ACC*, butchery dutyman, driver IC

3ton lorry 4x4 stores (carries vehicle stores, spare parts, mechanics' tools)
> mechanist quartermaster sergeant, 2 vehicle mechanics, driver IC

FOUR SQUADRONS (EACH)

Squadron Headquarters ('A' or fighting portion)

Motorcycle solo
> corporal motorcyclist

Motorcycles solo 2-3
> motorcyclist

4 seater car 4x4
> driver IC (for intelligence duties), driver IC

5cwt car 4x4 (Jeep)
> driver IC

Scout car (squadron command)
> driver-operator

Armoured Car 1
> Major, driver mechanic, driver operator, gunner mechanic

Armoured Car 2
> Captain, gunner mechanic, gunner operator, driver operator

Armoured Car 3
> Subaltern, gunner mechanic, gunner operator, driver operator

Armoured Car 4
> squadron sergeant major, driver operator, gunner mechanic, driver mechanic

Squadron Headquarters ('B' or admin portion)

Truck 15cwt FFW
> Transport Officer, 2 driver operators, driver IC

Truck 15cwt 4x4 personnel
> 4 gunner mechanics (relief), 2 gunner operators (relief), driver IC

Truck 15cwt water
> water dutyman, driver IC

Lorry 3-ton GS 1
> squadron quartermaster sergeant, 2 clerks, driver IC

Lorry 3-ton GS 2
> mechanist sergeant, 5 vehicle mechanics, driver IC

Lorry 3-ton GS 3
    technical storeman, driver IC
Lorry 3-ton GS 4
    7 batmen, driver IC
Lorry 3-ton GS 5
    sanitary dutyman, driver IC
Lorry 3-ton kitchen
    corporal cook ACC, 4 cooks ACC, driver IC
Lorry 3-ton stores
    storeman (non-technical), driver IC
Lorry 30cwt slave battery[242]
    electrician Royal Signals, driver IC

Heavy Troop[243]
Armoured Car 1
    Subaltern, driver operator, gunner operator, driver mechanic
Armoured Car 2
    sergeant, driver operator, gunner operator, driver mechanic
Scout car
    corporal driver operator, driver IC

Support Troop[244]
Scout car
    Subaltern, driver operator
Truck 15cwt 4x4 personnel 1
    Sergeant, 4 troopers, driver IC
Trucks 15cwt 4x4 2-3
    5 troopers, driver IC

Five Troops (each)
Armoured Car 1
    Subaltern, gunner operator, driver mechanic
Armoured Car 2
    Sergeant, gunner operator, driver mechanic
Scout Car 1
    2 driver operators
Scout Car 2
    driver operator, driver IC

---

[242] Later replaced by 3ton 4x4 machinery lorry I30.
[243] The two armoured cars tended to be AEC Mk III in 21st Army Group and (until they wore out) the T12 halftrack in the Mediterranean; each was equipped with a 75mm gun.
[244] The 15cwt trucks were replaced by the White scout car, and from 1944 in at least some cases by the M5 halftrack.

Appendix 9: Armoured Reconnaissance Regiment, Type 'B'

The final version of the armoured recce regiment was War Establishment II/156/1, effective 5 November 1943. As noted in the main text, only the regiments serving in Italy 1944-45 fought under this establishment. Regiments in 21st Army Group were turned into de facto armoured regiments spring 1944.

	Headquarters	Headquarters Squadron	Three Squadrons (each)	Total
Officers	5	9	9	41
WO	1	4	1	8
Sgt/Staff Sgt	2	9	10	41
Rank and file	11	138	146	587
Total all ranks	19	160	166	677
Attached		9	7	30
Total	19	169	173	707

Officers
Lieutenant Colonel commanding, five Majors (one second in command), Adjutant, Technical Officer, seven Captains,[245] Intelligence Officer, Signal Officer, 23 Subalterns,[246] Quartermaster

Warrant Officers
regimental sergeant major, regimental quartermaster sergeant, quartermaster sergeant (technical), mechanist quartermaster sergeant, four squadron sergeants major

Sergeants and Staff Sergeants
four squadron quartermaster sergeants, three mechanist sergeants, provost sergeant, signal sergeant, transport sergeant, clerk, storeman (technical), 29 sergeants

Rank and File
75 corporals (includes 14 lance sergeants), 512 privates (includes 45 lance corporals)

Of the rank and file, 454 are tradesmen:
carpenter and joiner, 13 clerks, 4 driver mechanics, 96 driver mechanics (AFV), 122 driver operators, five electricians, equipment repairer, 84 gunner mechanics, 91 gunner operators, six storemen (technical), 31 vehicle mechanics

---

[245] The Adjutant and Technical Officer are Captains.
[246] The Intelligence and Signal Officers are Subalterns.

Of the rank and file, 133 are non tradesmen:
24 batmen, butcher dutyman, driver IC (for intelligence duties), 86 drivers IC, medical officers orderly (lance corporal), four motorcyclists, postman (lance corporal), five sanitary dutymen, five storemen, five water dutymen

Attached
RAMC (Medical Officer), REME (three armourers [one sergeant and one lance corporal], six vehicle mechanics AFV [three sergeants]), ACC (20 [includes four corporals])

The establishment detail shows an operator from the Royal Signals in one of the RHQ tanks, but he is not listed on the war establishment itself.

	Headquarters	Headquarters Squadron	Three Squadrons (each)	Total
Tanks cruiser	4		12	40
Tanks close support			2	6
Tanks, Light			10	30
Tanks AA		5		5
Scout cars		19	1	22
Motorcycles solo		6		6
Cars 4x4 4-seater		2	1	5
Jeeps (cars 5cwt 4x4)		7		7
Halftracks 15cwt personnel		2	2	8
Trucks 15cwt 4x2 GS		4		4
Trucks 15cwt 4x2 personnel			1	3
Trucks 15cwt 4x2 FFW		1		1
Trucks 15cwt 4x2 office		1		1
Trucks 15cwt 4x2 water		2		2
Trucks 15cwt 4x4 personnel		1		1
Lorries 3ton 4x4 GS		9	11	42
Lorries 3ton 6x4 store		2	1	5
Armoured recovery vehicles			1	3
Carrier slave battery		1	1	4

REGIMENTAL HEADQUARTERS

Cruiser Tank 1
> Lieutenant Colonel, Adjutant, sergeant, driver mechanic AFV, driver operator

Cruiser Tank 2
> Major (2nd in command), regimental sergeant major, corporal driver mechanic, driver operator, *operator Royal Signals*

Cruiser Tank 3
> Subaltern, sergeant, gunner operator, driver mechanic AFV, driver operator

Cruiser Tank 4
> Intelligence Officer, corporal driver IC (intelligence duties), driver mechanic, gunner operator, driver operator

HEADQUARTERS SQUADRON

Squadron Headquarters

Car 4-seater 4x4 1
> Major, batman, driver IC

Car 4-seater 4x4 2
> Technical Officer, corporal driver IC

Truck 15cwt 4x2 FFW
> Captain (squadron 2nd in command), squadron sergeant major, batman, driver operator

AA Troop

AA Tank 1
> Subaltern, driver mechanic (AFV), gunner operator, driver operator

AA Tank 2
> sergeant, driver mechanic (AFV), gunner operator, driver operator

AA Tanks 3-5
> corporal driver operator, driver mechanic (AFV), gunner operator, gunner mechanic

Reconnaissance Troop

Scout cars 1-2
> Subaltern, driver operator

Scout car 3
> sergeant, driver operator

Scout cars 4-5
> driver operator, corporal driver operator

Scout cars 6-12
> driver operator, driver IC

Intercommunications Troop

Scout car 1
> sergeant, driver operator

Scout cars 2, 3 and 6
> driver operator, corporal driver IC

Scout cars 4-5
> driver operator, driver IC

Scout car 7
> Subaltern, driver operator

Administrative Troop

Motorcycle 1
> provost sergeant

Motorcycle 2
> corporal motorcyclist

Motorcycles 3-5
> motorcyclists

Motorcycle 6
> batman (for medical officer

Car 5cwt 4x4 (Jeep) 1
> corporal driver IC

Cars 5cwt 4x4 (Jeep) 2-7
> driver IC

Truck 15cwt 4x2 GS 1
> Quartermaster, batman, driver IC

Truck 15cwt 4x2 GS 2
> sanitary dutyman, medical officer's orderly, driver IC

Truck 15cwt 4x2 GS 3
> quartermaster sergeant (technical), sergeant technical storeman, corporal clerk, driver IC

Truck 15cwt 4x2 GS 4
> equipment repairer, *sergeant armourer REME, 2 armourers REME*, technical storeman, driver IC

Truck 15cwt 4x2 office
> Signal Officer, signal sergeant, sergeant clerk, corporal clerk, driver IC

Trucks 15cwt 4x2 water1-2
> water dutyman, driver IC

Truck 15cwt 4x4 personnel
> driver operator

15cwt Halftrack 1
> Medical Officer, driver operator

15cwt Halftrack 2
> mechanist quartermaster sergeant, 2 vehicle mechanics, driver operator

Lorry 3ton GS 1
> regimental quartermaster sergeant, corporal clerk, 3 clerks, driver IC

Lorry 3ton GS 2
> sanitary dutyman, electrician, driver IC

Lorry 3ton GS 3
> 2 batmen, clerk, driver IC

Lorry 3ton GS 4
> storeman, 2 vehicle mechanics, driver IC

Lorry 3ton GS 5
> storeman, vehicle mechanic, driver IC

Lorry 3ton GS 6
>> *4 cooks ACC*, butchery dutyman, driver IC

Lorry 3ton GS 7
>> transport sergeant, *cook ACC*, 3 batmen, driver IC

Lorry 3ton GS 8
>> carpenter and joiner, 3 driver mechanics, 3 driver operators, 3 gunner operators, 3 gunner mechanics, driver IC

Lorry 3ton GS 9
>> postman, driver IC

Lorry 3ton store 1
>> 2 vehicle mechanics, technical storeman, driver IC

Lorry 3ton store 2
>> squadron quartermaster sergeant, technical storeman, driver IC

Carrier slave battery
>> electrician, driver mechanic

THREE SQUADRONS (EACH)

Squadron Headquarters 'A' or Fighting Portion

Cruiser Tank close support 1
>> Major, sergeant, driver mechanic, gunner operator, driver operator

Cruiser Tank close support 2
>> Captain (2nd in command), driver mechanic, gunner operator, gunner mechanic, corporal driver operator

Cruiser Tank 1
>> Captain, driver mechanic, gunner operator, gunner mechanic, corporal driver operator

Cruiser Tank 2
>> squadron sergeant major, corporal driver mechanic, gunner operator, gunner mechanic, driver operator

Scout car
>> Subaltern, driver operator

Squadron Headquarters 'B' or Administration Portion

Car 4-seater
>> squadron quartermaster sergeant, batman, driver IC

Truck 15cwt 4x2
>> *cook ACC*, 2 batmen, driver IC

15cwt Halftrack 1
>> mechanist sergeant, 4 vehicle mechanics, driver operator

15cwt Halftrack 2
>> driver IC

Lorry 3ton GS 1
>> sanitary dutyman, driver IC

Lorries 3ton GS 2-3
>> vehicle mechanic, driver IC

Lorry 3ton GS 4
> driver IC

Lorry 3ton GS 5
> corporal driver IC

Lorry 3ton GS 6
> *4 cooks ACC*, driver IC

Lorry 3ton store
> corporal technical storeman, vehicle mechanic, driver IC

Carrier slave battery
> electrician, driver mechanic, gunner mechanic, driver operator

Armoured recovery vehicle Mk I
> driver mechanic, vehicle mechanic, *sergeant vehicle mechanic REME*, *vehicle mechanic REME*

Five tank troops (each)

Cruiser Tank 1
> Subaltern, driver operator, gunner operator, gunner mechanic, corporal driver operator

Cruiser Tank 2
> sergeant, driver mechanic, gunner operator, gunner mechanic, driver operator

Light Tanks 1-2
> driver operator, gunner operator, gunner mechanic, corporal driver operator

21st Army Group

The recce troop in HQ squadron was changed to 11 light tanks, matching the equivalent unit in armoured regiments.

In the sabre squadrons, the five troops changed to three cruiser tanks each. This gave the regiment 61 cruisers (six close support).

Cruiser Tank 1
> Subaltern, driver operator, gunner operator, gunner mechanic, corporal driver operator

Cruiser Tank 2
> sergeant, driver mechanic, gunner operator, gunner mechanic, driver operator

Cruiser Tank 3
> corporal driver operator, gunner operator, 2 gunner mechanics, driver mechanic

Appendix 10: Reconnaissance Regiment 1943

The final war establishment for regiments, Reconnaissance Corps, was II/251/2, effective 17 December 1943. When the Reconnaissance Corps was absorbed into the RAC the next month, these became reconnaissance regiments RAC.

	Headquarters	Headquarters Squadron	Three Squadrons (each)	Total
Officers	5	9	9	41
WO	1	3	1	7
Sgt/Staff Sgt	3	17	18	74
Rank and file	23	153	166	674
Total all ranks	32	182	194	796
Attached	4	11	2	21
Total	36	193	196	817
LMGs .303 inch	3	12	36	123
PIAT	2	7	9	36
Mortars 2"		4	7	25
Mortars 3"		6		6
Gun 6pdr AT		8		8

Officers[247]
Lieutenant Colonel commanding, five majors, six captains, adjutant, technical officer, 26 subalterns, quartermaster

Warrant Officers
regiment sergeant major, regimental quartermaster sergeant, mechanist quartermaster sergeant, five squadron sergeants major

Sergeants/Staff Sergeants
four squadron quartermaster sergeants, signal sergeant, intelligence sergeant, three mechanist sergeants, provost sergeant, transport sergeant, orderly room clerk, storeman (technical), 61 sergeants

Other Ranks
107 corporals (includes 19 lance sergeants), 567 troopers (includes 52 lance corporals)

---

[247] The adjutant and technical officer are captains, the quartermaster a subaltern.

Of the other ranks, 263 are tradesmen: four carpenters and joiners, eight clerks, 131 driver mechanics, 95 driver operators, two electricians, two equipment repairers, four fitters (gun), five storemen (mechanical), 12 vehicle mechanics

Of the other ranks, 411 are non tradesmen: 14 batmen, 20 batmen drivers, butchery dutyman, 64 drivers IC, 36 gun numbers (for AT guns), six intelligence personnel, four medical officers orderlies, 30 mortar men (six for 3" and 24 for 2"), 22 orderlies, post orderly, four sanitary dutymen, 12 signallers, five storemen, three transport corporals, 192 gun numbers and riflemen

Attached
RAMC: medical officer; RAOC: shoemaker (corporal); REME: four armourers (includes one sergeant and one corporal); ACC: 15 cooks (includes two sergeants and one corporal)

	Headquarters	Headquarters Squadron	Three Squadrons (each)	Total
Armoured cars	1		9	28
Light reconnaissance cars	2	1	7	24
Carriers Lloyd		12		12
Carriers universal		6	21	69
Motorcycles solo	7	24	8	55
Cars 4x4 4-seater	1			1
Jeeps (cars 5cwt 4x4)		7	1	10
Trucks 15cwt 4x2 GS	1	8	1	12
Trucks 15cwt 4x2 water		1	1	4
Trucks 15cwt 4x4 personnel[248]	3	3	9	33
Lorries 3ton 4x4 GS		7	5	22

REGIMENTAL HEADQUARTERS

Motorcycle 1
  provost sergeant
Motorcycle 2
  intelligence sergeant
Motorcycles 3-7
  intelligence trooper
4-seater car 4x4
  Lieutenant Colonel, batman, driver IC or batman driver

[248] Can be replaced by White scout cars or haltracks.

Light reconnaissance car 1[249]
>   driver operator, driver mechanic

Light reconnaissance car 2
>   Technical Officer, driver operator, batman driver

Armoured car
>   Subaltern, driver operator, driver mechanic

15cwt Truck 4x4 personnel[250]
>   Major, Captain adjutant, 2 driver operators, batman driver

15cwt Truck 4x2 GS
>   *Sergeant cook ACC, 2 cooks ACC,* driver IC

15cwt Truck 4x4 personnel[251]
>   regimental sergeant major, sergeant orderly room clerk, 2 clerks, intelligence trooper, driver IC

15cwt Truck 4x4 personnel[252]
>   *Medical Officer RAMC,* medical officer's orderly, driver IC

HEADQUARTERS SQUADRON

Squadron Headquarters

Motorcycles 1, 2
>   orderly

15cwt Truck 4x4 personnel[253]
>   Major, squadron sergeant major, driver operator, clerk, batman driver

Light reconnaissance car
>   Captain, driver operator, batman driver

Signal Troop

Motorcycle 1
>   signal sergeant

Motorcycle 2
>   sergeant

Motorcycle 3
>   corporal signaler

Motorcycles 4-11
>   signaler

Car 5cwt 4x4 (Jeep) 1[254]
>   signaler, driver operator

Car 5cwt 4x4 (Jeep) 2-3
>   signaler, driver operator

---

[249] For the CO's use in action.
[250] Can be replaced by White scout car.
[251] Can be replaced by White scout car.
[252] Can be replaced by White scout car.
[253] Can be replaced by White scout car.
[254] Detached to RHQ for CO's use.

15cwt Truck 4x2 GS
>Captain Signal Officer, batman driver

15cwt Truck 4x4 personnel[255]
>4 driver operators, driver IC

Mortar Troop
Troop Headquarters
Car 5cwt 4x4 (Jeep)
>Subaltern, batman driver

Three Mortar Sections (each)
Motorcycle
>sergeant

15cwt Truck 4x2 GS[256]
>mortarman, driver IC

Carrier universal mortar 1[257]
>sergeant, 3 mortarmen, driver mechanic

Carrier universal mortar 2[258]
>corporal, 3 mortarmen, driver mechanic

Anti Tank Battery
Battery Headquarters
Motorcycles 1-2
>orderly

Car 5cwt 4x4 (Jeep)
Captain, batman, driver IC

Two Anti Tank Troops (each)
Motorcycle
>orderly

Car 5cwt 4x4 (Jeep)
>Subaltern, batman driver

15cwt Truck 4x2 GS[259]
>sergeant, driver IC

Two Sections (each)[260]
>Lloyd Carrier 1[261]
>>sergeant, 3 gun numbers, driver mechanic

>Lloyd Carrier 2[262]
>>corporal gun number, 3 gun numbers, driver mechanic

---

[255] Can be replaced by White scout car.
[256] Carries 72 rounds of 3" mortar ammunition.
[257] Carries 3" mortar and 66 mortar rounds.
[258] Carries 3" mortar and 66 mortar rounds.
[259] Carries stores and 6pdr ammunition.
[260] Each section has a Bren LMG and a 2" mortar.
[261] Tows 6pdr AT gun and carries 24 rounds of ammunition.
[262] Tows 6pdr AT gun and carries 24 rounds of ammunition.

Lloyd Carrier 3[263]
> lance corporal gun number, gun number, driver mechanic

Administrative Troop

Motorcycle 1
> transport sergeant

Motorcycle 2
> orderly

Motorcycles 3-4
> *armourer REME*

15cwt Truck 4x2 GS 1
> Quartermaster, corporal postman, batman driver

15cwt Truck 4x2 GS 2
> clerk, driver IC

15cwt Truck 4x2 water
> water dutyman, driver IC

15cwt Truck 4x4 personnel[264]
> Subaltern, mechanist quartermaster sergeant, sergeant storeman (technical), vehicle mechanic, batman driver

3-ton Lorry 4x4 GS 1
> 2 vehicle mechanics, storeman (technical), 2 electricians, equipment repairer, driver IC

3-ton Lorry 4x4 GS 2
> storeman (technical), gun fitter, 3 vehicle mechanics, driver IC

3-ton Lorry 4x4 GS 3
> *sergeant armourer REME, armourer REME,* sanitary dutyman, driver IC

3-ton Lorry 4x4 GS 4
> carpenter and joiner, equipment repairer, *corporal shoemaker RAOC,* storeman, driver IC

3-ton Lorry 4x4 GS 5
> regimental quartermaster sergeant, driver IC

3-ton Lorry 4x4 GS 6
> storeman, driver IC

3-ton Lorry 4x4 GS 7
> squadron quartermaster sergeant, *sergeant cook ACC,. corporal cook ACC, 4 cooks ACC,* butchery dutyman, driver IC

THREE SQUADRONS (EACH)

Squadron Headquarters 'A' or Fighting Portion

Motorcycle
> orderly

Light reconnaissance car
> Major, driver operator, driver mechanic

Car 5cwt 4x4 (Jeep)
> squadron sergeant major, driver IC

---

[263] Carries 30 rounds of 6pdr ammunition and Bren LMG.
[264] Can be replaced by White scout car.

15cwt Truck 4x4 personnel 1[265]
        Captain, driver operator, driver IC
15cwt Truck 4x4 personnel 2[266]
        clerk, 2 driver operators, driver IC
15cwt Truck 4x4 personnel 3[267]
        medical officer's orderly, batman driver

Squadron Headquarters 'B' or Administration Portion

15cw Truck 4x2 GS
        carpenter and joiner, driver IC
15cwt Truck water
        water dutyman, driver IC
15cwt Truck 4x4 personnel[268]
        mechanist sergeant, 2 vehicle mechanics, driver IC
3-ton Lorry GS 1
        sanitary dutman, driver IC
3-ton Lorry GS 2
        transport corporal, driver IC
3-ton Lorry GS 3
        storeman, storeman (technical), gun fitter, driver IC
3-ton Lorry GS 4
        4 driver operators, driver IC
3-ton Lorry GS 5
        squadron quartermaster sergeant, *2 cooks ACC*, driver IC

Three scout troops (each)

Troop Headquarters
Motorcycle 1
        sergeant
Motorcycle 2
        orderly
Armoured car
        Subaltern, driver operator, driver mechanic
Carrier Universal
        Subaltern, 2 driver operators, driver mechanic
Reconnaissance Section
Armoured cars 1-2
        sergeant, driver operator, driver mechanic
Light reconnaissance car 1
        corporal, batman, driver mechanic
Light reconnaissance car 2
        corporal, diver operator, diver mechanic

---

[265] Can be replaced by White scout car.
[266] Can be replaced by White scout car.
[267] Can be replaced by White scout car.
[268] Can be replaced by White scout car.

Two Carrier Sections (each)[269]

Carrier universal 1

      sergeant, corporal, driver mechanic

Carriers universal 2-3

      corporal, trooper, driver mechanic

Assault Troop

Troop Headquarters

15cwt Truck 4x4[270]

      Subaltern, sergeant, driver operator, 2 mortarmen for 2" mortar, batman driver

Motorcycle

      Orderly

Four Sections (each)[271]

15cwt Truck 4x4[272]

      corporal, lance corporal, 5 troopers, driver IC

---

[269] Each section has a PIAT and a 2" mortar.

[270] Can be replaced by a halftrack. The vehicle carries a PIAT as well as the 2" mortar.

[271] Each section has a Bren LMG.

[272] Can be replaced by a halftrack.

Appendix 11: Airborne Armoured Reconnaissance Regiment 1944

The first and only war establishment for this regiment was I/138/I, effective 18 October 1944.

	Headquarters	Headquarters Squadron	Support Squadron	Two Squadrons (each)	Total
Officers	6	7	6	6	31
WO	1	4	1	1	8
Sgt/Staff Sgt	1	6	6	6	25
Rank and file	13	101	67	51	283
Total all ranks	21	118	80	64	347
Attached	-	11	-	-	11
Total	21	129	80	64	358
LMGs .303" [includes vehicle mounts]	4	6	8	15	48
MMGs .303" (Vickers)			8		8
PIATs	3	4		3	13
Mortars, 2"				6	12
Mortars, 4.2"			4		4
Boyes rifle [vehicle mounts]				3	6

Officers
Lieutenant Colonel commanding, four Majors (one second in command), Adjutant, Technical Officer, five Captains,[273] Intelligence Officer, Signal Officer, 16 Subalterns,[274] Quartermaster

Warrant Officers
regimental sergeant major, regimental quartermaster sergeant, quartermaster sergeant (technical), mechanist quartermaster sergeant, four squadron sergeants major

Sergeants/Staff Sergeants
four squadron quartermaster sergeants, mechanist, clerk, storeman (technical), transport sergeant, 17 sergeants

Rank and File
31 corporals (includes six lance sergeants), 252 troopers (includes 23 lance corporals)

---

[273] The Adjutant and Technical Officer are captains.
[274] The Intelligence and Signal Officers are subalterns.

Of the rank and file, 143 are tradesmen:
five clerks, 20 driver mechanics AFV, 24 driver mechanics, 59 driver operators, two electricians, 15 gunner operators, two storemen (technical), 16 vehicle mechanics

Of the rank and file, 140 are non tradesmen:
10 batmen, four batmen drivers, butchery dutyman, 43 drivers IC, medical officers orderly, four mortarmen, 47 motorcyclists, 26 machine gunners, provost corporal, sanitary dutyman, water dutyman

Attached
RAMC (medical officer), REME (sergeant and lance corporal armourers), ACC (eight cooks)

	Headquarters	Headquarters Squadron	Support Squadron	Two Squadrons (each)	Total
Tanks, Light				4	8
Tanks, Cruiser		8			8
Scout Cars	2		2	8	20
Carriers, Universal			8	6	20
Motorcycles, solo	10	10	21	6	53
Cars, 4-seater		2			2
Jeeps (5cwt 4x4 cars)	3	14	6	2	27
Trucks, 15cwt 4x2		1			1
Trucks, 15cwt 4x2 water		1			1
Lorries, 3-ton 4x2 GS		5			5
Lorries, 3-ton 4x2 kitchen		1			1
Carriers, slave battery		1			1

REGIMENTAL HEADQUARTERS

Motorcycle 1
       Liaison Officer
Motorcycle 2
       corporal motorcyclist
Motorcycles 3-10
       motorcyclist
5cwt car 4x4 (Jeep) 1
       Lieutenant Colonel, Adjutant
5cwt car 4x4 (Jeep) 2
       Intelligence Officer, driver operator

5cwt car 4x4 (Jeep) 3
>Major (2nd in command), sergeant clerk, driver operator

Scout car 1
>Signal Officer, corporal driver operator

Scout car 2
>regimental sergeant major, driver operator

HEADQUARTERS SQUADRON

Squadron Headquarters

5cwt car 4x4 (Jeep)
>Major, squadron sergeant major, driver operator

Intercommunications Troop

Motorcycle 1
>sergeant motorcyclist

Motorcycle 2
>corporal motorcyclist

Motorcycles 3-8
>motorcyclist

Motorcycles 9-10
>vehicle mechanic

Airborne Administrative Troop

5cwt car 4x4 (Jeep) 1
>Quartermaster, squadron quartermaster sergeant, driver IC

5cwt car 4x4 (Jeep) 2
>Technical Officer, vehicle mechanic

5cwt car 4x4 (Jeep) 3
>Subaltern, clerk

5cwt car 4x4 (Jeep) 4
>mechanist quartermaster sergeant, 2 vehicle mechanics

5cwt car 4x4 (Jeep) 5
>*Medical Officer RAMC*, medical officer's orderly, driver IC

5cwt car 4x4 (Jeep) 6
>mechanist sergeant, 2 vehicle mechanics

5cwt car 4x4 (Jeep) 7
>*sergeant armourer REME, lance corporal armourer REME*, driver mechanic, driver IC

5cwt car 4x4 (Jeep) 8
>transport sergeant, 2 drivers IC

5cwt car 4x4 (Jeep) 9
>provost corporal, 2 vehicle mechanics

5cwt car 4x4 (Jeep) 10
>corporal driver IC, 2 vehicle mechanics

5cwt car 4x4 (Jeep) 11-13
>vehicle mechanic, driver IC, driver mechanic

Carrier, slave battery
  electrician, vehicle mechanic

Seaborne Party

4 seater cars 1-2
  batmen driver
15cwt GS Truck 4x2
  Subaltern, regimental quartermaster sergeant, driver IC
15cwt Truck 4x2 water
  water dutyman, friver IC
3ton Lorry 1
  Subaltern, storeman (technical), driver IC
3ton Lorry 2
  quartermaster sergeant (technical), sergeant storeman (technical), storeman (technical), clerk, driver IC
3ton Lorry 3
  vehicle mechanic, storeman, 4 batmen, driver IC
3ton Lorry 4
  2 clerks, 3 batmen, sanitary dutyman, corporal driver IC
3ton Lorry 5
  corporal clerk, electrician, 3 batmen, sanitary dutyman, corporal driver IC
3ton Lorry 6
  corporal clerk, electrician, 3 batmen, driver IC
3ton Lorry kitchen
  corporal cook ACC, 7 cooks ACC, butchery dutyman, driver IC
Cruiser tank 1
  Captain, sergeant, 2 driver mechanics AFV
Cruiser tanks 2-3
  corporal driver operator, 2 driver operators, gunner operator, driver mechanic AFV
Cruiser tanks 4-5
  corporal driver operator, gunner operator, driver mechanic AFV
Cruiser tanks 6-8
  gunner operator, 2 drivers mechanics

Note: Cromwells had a crew of five; six of the eight would complete their crews from the Locust crew members.

SUPPORT SQUADRON

Squadron Headquarters
Motorcycle 1
  squadron sergeant major
Motorcycles 2-3
  motorcyclist
5cwt car 4x4 (Jeep)
  Captain, squadron quartermaster sergeant, 2 driver operators

Scout car
      Subaltern, driver operator

Two MMG Troops (each)
Carrier universal MMG 1
      Subaltern, driver operator, machine gunner, driver mechanic
Carrier universal MMG 2
      sergeant, 2 machine gunners, driver mechanic
Carrier universal MMG 3-4
      corporal driver IC, 2 machine gunners, driver mechanic

Heavy Mortar Troop
5cwt car 4x4 (Jeep) 1
      Captain. 2 driver operators
5cwt car 4x4 (Jeep) 2[275]
      sergeant, driver operator, mortarman, driver IC
5cwt car 4x4 (Jeep) 3[276]
      corporal driver IC, driver operator, mortarman, driver IC

Infantry Support Troop
Motorcycle 1
      sergeant
Motorcycles 2-3
      corporal motorcyclist
Motorcycles 4-18
      motorcyclist
Scout car
      Subaltern, driver operator

EACH SQUADRON

Squadron Headquarters
Motorcycle 1
      corporal motorcyclist
Motorcycles 2-6
      motorcyclist
5cwt car 4x4 (Jeep) 1
      squadron sergeant major, driver operator, driver IC
5cwt car 4x4 (Jeep) 2
      squadron quartermaster sergeant, driver operator, driver IC
Scout car 1
      Major, sergeant
Scout car 2
      Captain, driver operator

---

[275] Draws mortar trailer.
[276] Draws mortar trailer.

Heavy Troop

Light tank 1
>   Subaltern, gunner operator, driver mechanic AFV

Light tank 2
>   sergeant, gunner operator, driver mechanic AFV

Light tanks 3-4
>   corporal driver operator, gunner operator, driver mechanic AFV

Three Troops (each)

Carrier universal 1
>   Subaltern, driver operator, machine gunner, driver mechanic

Carrier universal 2
>   corporal driver IC, driver operator, machine gunner, driver mechanic

Scout car 1
>   sergeant, driver operator

Scout car 2
>   driver operator, driver IC

Appendix 12: Armoured Engineers

This Appendix covers the war establishments of assault RE (later armoured engineer) regiments and squadrons in 21st Army Group.

Headquarters, Assault Regiment RE (Armoured Engineer Regiment)

This war establishment (XIV/902/1) is probably from July 1944, although it is possible that that the RHQ (unlike the squadrons) did not change during the summer. It was intended to be self-contained, so that it could operate apart from brigade HQ. Neither brigade nor regiment ever actually operated as a tactical headquarters—the various squadrons commonly operated apart in support of particular formations or units.

RHQ had seven officers (lieutenant colonel, major, three captains and two subalterns), two warrant officers, and 52 other personnel for an aggregate of 61. The only available source does not show a medical officer or any ACC cooks, although there is a kitchen truck. The regiment was supported by a signals section and a large light aid detachment REME.

There were two scout cars, with the remaining vehicles those typical of a headquarters: six motorcycles, five jeeps, one 4-seater 4x4 car, five 15cwt trucks (three GS and two FFW), and four 3ton lorries (two GS, one kitchen, one office). In lieu of any water trucks there was a water trailer.

Each regiment originally controlled four squadrons. This was officially reduced to three in December 1944 although most had their fourth squadron detached prior to that.

Assault Squadron RE (Armoured Engineer Squadron)

War Establishment XIV/900/1, effective 22 July 1944

	Personnel	Equipment
Sqn HQ		2 ARRE, 1 ARV
Admin Trp		2 scout cars
Trp *x3*	2/60	6 AVRE, 1 scout car

This war establishment was effectuated following D-Day. The major change from the D-Day organization was the withdrawal of one troop per squadron to form a training regiment. Troops were large units and could operate away from the regiment.

The squadron had nine officers and 230 other ranks for an aggregate of 239 personnel. The exact distribution other than for the troop was not shown in the source; they had three officers and 50 other ranks between them.. No medical officer or ACC cooks are shown in the source.

Squadron HQ had two AVREs, nine motorcycles, two jeeps, a 4-seater 4x4 car and a Churchill ARV. The Admin Troop had two scout cars, three 15cwt trucks (GS, office and water), ten 3ton 4x4 lorries (two stores, kitchen, seven GS), and a Loyd carrier slave battery. One of the vehicles towed a welding trailer.

The troop HQ had a scout car and motorcycle (captain, driver and orderly). There were two AVRE sections, each of three Churchill AVREs, one led by a subaltern and one by a sergeant. In addition, there are four 4ton 4x4 GS lorries (two with Petard bombs and General Wade charges, one with petrol, and one with baggage and small arms ammunition). Some 21 support personnel also had to fit into these lorries.

Overall the squadron had 20 AVRE, five scout cars, a Churchill ARV, and the assorted jeeps, car, trucks and lorries and motorcycles.

If the only change from the D-Day squadron was the loss of a troop, that squadron would have had 302 personnel and 26 AVRE.

Assault Squadron RE (Armoured Engineer Squadron) [Buffalo]

The war establishment above remained in effect for these units, although the equipment was modified. There may have been some personnel changes as well, since the LVTs did not require the six man crews of the AVRE.[277] All but one of these squadrons changed back to AVREs in 1945.

Squadron HQ had two LVTs in place of the AVREs but was otherwise the same for vehicles, as was the admin troop. Each of the three troops had six LVTs (in place of the AVREs) and a Weasel (in place of the scout car), along with the four3ton lorries and a motorcycle.

Assault Squadron RE (Armoured Engineer Squadron) [Terrapin]

There is no known separate war establishment for the single squadron that converted to operating the Terrapin, although it is known that it had 40 of those vehicles and was still organized in three troops. The normal crew of twofor a Terrapin (vs. the six of an AVRE) allowed it to operate more vehicles.

Squadron HQ was the same, except that the two AVREs were replaced by four Terrapins. The admin troop was also unchanged. The three troops were similar to those in the Buffalo squadron, but with 12 Terrapins in place of six LVTs, a Weasel, only two 3ton GS lorries, and a motorcycle.

---

[277] Each AVRE crew included a vehicle commander (subaltern, sergeant or lance sergeant), corporal demolition NCO, driver, co-driver/loader, mortar man, and operator.

Assault Park Squadron RE (Armoured Engineer Park Squadron)

In May 1944, 149th Assault Park Squadron RE was combined with HQ 1st Assault Brigade RE. The two were made separate again in January 1945. The squadron was officially made a separate unit again the 18th of that month.[278]

War Establishment XIV/903/1, effective 1 January 1945

	Personnel	Equipment
Sqn HQ	2/45	
Park Trp *x3*	1/79	

The squadron had five officers and 282 other ranks, for an aggregate of 287, plus nine ACC cooks. It did not have sufficient vehicles to move all of its personnel and equipment in one lift. Aside from various trucks and related vehicles, the squadron had 12 lightly armoured Caterpillar D7 Angledozers [US bulldozers], also known as a Tractor, crawler, Class II. These could be loaned to squadrons on an as-needed basis.

Squadron HQ had 47 personnel and three of the ACC cooks. Vehicles were a 4-seater 4x4 car, jeep, seven motorcycles, a 15cwt office truck, a 15cwt GS truck, 3ton kitchen lorry , two different 3ton 4x4 machinery lorries, and five 3ton 4x4 GS lorries (one for petrol and the others for tools, stores, baggage, etc.)

The squadron had three identical park troops, allowing one per regiment, each with 80 personnel and two ACC cooks. In addition to four armoured angledozers, there was a jeep, five motorcycles, 15cwt 4x2 FFW truck, 15cwt 4x2 GS truck, 3ton 6x4 Coles Crane Mk IV, and nine 3ton 4x4 GS trucks (one for petrol), along with the 3ton 4x4 kitchen truck. The troop had two 6ton tractors (such as AEC Matador) with 18ton multiwheel trailers, allowing it to carry two of the four dozers at a time to a work site. These were replaced where possible with Scammel Artillery Tractors and 20ton trailers.

Assault Dozer Squadron

The Centaur Assault Dozer was created to improve capabilities above what the Caterpillar dozers could provide. Based on a tank chassis, it was better armoured and had the same road speed as a tank, allowing it to travel on its own instead of being towed. These were provided to one squadron around November 1944, under War Establishment XIV/901/1 effective that month. The squadron had six officers and 225 other ranks; 231

---

[278] It may be presumed—but is not know for sure—that its establishment during 1944 would have been similar insofar as the park troops are concerned.

aggregate. No ACC cooks are shown, although there is a kitchen lorry.[279] There were four scout cars and 36 tank dozers, along with an ARV.

Headquarters had three officers and 57 other ranks (60 total). There were a scout car, a 4-seater 4x4 car, a jeep, five motorcycles, three 15cwt trucks (GS, office and water), eight 3ton 4x4 GS lorries, a 3ton 4x4 stores binned lorry, a 3ton 4x4 mobile kitchen, and an ARV.

Each of the three troops had an officer and 56 other ranks (57 total). There was a scout car, 12 tank dozers, four motorcycles, and six 3ton 4x4 GS lorries.

Assault Training Regiment

One squadron was withdrawn from a regiment following D-Day for training and replacement duties, since there was no depot system for replacing the trained engineers in the brigade. Each of the other squadrons contributed a troop, and the new regiment was in place by September 1944. In December 1944 it also took over the experimental unit (F Wing) and ended up designated as 557 Assault Training and Experimental Establishment.

War Establishment XIV/951/1 (effective July 1944)

	Personnel		Equipment
RHQ	4/20		
HQ Sqn	5/119		2 ARK, 1 ARV
Sqn *x3*	6/20		
▶ Sqn HQ		2/16	2 AVRE, 1 ARK
▶ Trp *x4*		1/1	6 AVRE

Total assigned personnel were 27 officers and 199 other ranks (226 in total), or roughly the size of a squadron. However, the regiment processed all replacements for 1st Assault Brigade RE (later 1st Armoured Engineer Brigade). There were also a medical officer RAMC and 27 ACC cooks. Of the 78 AVREs and five ARKs, half were operational replacements and half training vehicles.

The small RHQ had only four motorcycles as assigned vehicles. The HQ squadron had an admin troop and a park troop, and most of the vehicles. The admin troop (there was no separate squadron HQ) had a car, jeep, 15cwt GS truck, five motorcycles and 25 3ton 4x4 GS lorries (one FFW). The park troop had two Humber scout cars, two ARKs, two armoured angledozers, and work vehicles: one 15cwt compressor truck, one 3ton Coles Crane, one 3ton Machinery Type X lorry, and a Federal 604 20ton 6x4 articulated transporter, along with a motorcycle and slave battery carrier.

---

[279] As elsewhere in this appendix, the ACC cooks may simply be missing from the available copy of the war establishment.

The training squadron had only a motorcycle and car (FFW) in addition to the armoured vehicles, each troop had a single motorcycle.

Appendix 13: Operation Coronet

Operation CORONET was the planned invasion of Japan in late 1945 or early 1946. The British would have contributed a corps to this effort, along with air and naval forces. The organization for several armoured units is shown in a secondary source and provides a look at how the British might have reorganized some units for the type of fighting expected.[280]

1st Royal Gloucestershire Hussars
    RHQ: 4 Churchill VII, 3 Churchill AVLB, 2 Churchill IV OP
    3 Squadrons, each
        Squadron HQ: 2 Churchill VII, 2 Churchill VIII CS
        5 Troops, each 3 Churchill VII
    Recce Troop: 11 Stuart VI, 11 Humber scout cars[281]

8th Royal Tank Regiment from 9th Armoured Brigade
    RHQ: 4 Churchill NA75 and VII, 3 Churchill ARV
    A and C Squadrons, each
        Squadron HQ: 2 Churchill VII, 2 Churchill VIII CS
        4 Troops, each 3 Churchill VII
    B Squadron,
        Sqn HQ: 4 Crocodiles
        4 Troops, each 3 Crocodiles
    Recce Troop: 11 Stuart VI, 11 Humber scout cars

4th Royal Tank Regiment of 4th Armoured Brigade
    RHQ: 4 trucks and some M29 Weasels
    3 Squadrons, each
        Sqn HQ: 1 Buffalo II
        5 Troops, each 2 Buffalo II, 5 Buffalo IV

---

[280] Mark Bevis, *British and Commonwealth Armies 1944-45*, p 84.
[281] Two of each vehicle at troop HQ and three sections, each with three of each vehicle.

Abbreviations

AA	Anti Aircraft
AAI	Allied Armies in Italy; title used for a time by 15th Army Group
ACC	Army Catering Corps [formed March 1941]
AFV	Armoured Fighting Vehicle
Armd	Armoured
ARV	Armoured recover vehicle
Atk	Anti tank
ATR	Anti tank rifle
B/L	Bridgelayer
Bn	Battalion
CDL	Canal Defence Light [cover name for tanks with searchlights]
Coy	Company
CS	Close Support
DD	Duplex Drive [kit to allow tanks to wade in to shore]
FFR	Fitted for Radio; replaced later in the war by FFW
FFW	Fitted for Wireless
FWD	Four-wheeled drive; in use to around 1942, thereafter shown as 4x4
GHQ	General Headquarters
Gp	Group
HQ	Headquarters
I	Infantry [tank]
L of C	Line of Communications
LR[C]	Light Reconnaissance [Car]
LVT	Landing Vehicle, Tracked; (A) indicates armoured variant, (R) a rocket-armed variant
ME	Middle East
MG	Machine Gun
Mk(s)	Mark(s); i.e., different versions
MV	Motor Vehicle
N	North (generally, as in N Africa for North Africa)
NW	North West

OCTU	Officer Cadet Training Unit
PAIForce	Persia and Iraq Force
PIAT	Projector, Infantry, Anti tank
Pln	Platoon
QF	Quick Firing [gun]
RAC	Royal Armoured Corps
RAOC	Royal Army Ordnance Corps
RE	Royal Engineers
Recce	Reconnaissance
Regt	Regiment
REME	Royal Electrical and Mechanical Engineers [created October 1942 from part of the RAOC
RHQ	Regimental Headquarters
RM	Royal Marines
RTC	Royal Tank Corps
RTR	Royal Tank Regiment
Spt	Support
Sqn	Squadron
TA	Territorial Army
Trp	Troop
WE	War Establishment: the personnel, vehicles and organization of a unit
WO	Warrant Officer. By the end of the war there were two classes of warrant officer: WO I (the highest) and WO II. A third class existed to 1941, the WO III, who commanded platoons or the equivalent in lieu of a subaltern.

Sources

This represents the principal sources actively consulted for this work. However, use was made of additional material as well, especially campaign histories.

8th Armoured Brigade. History published at Hannover, March 1946, available online [2012] at www.warlinks.com/armour/8th_armoured/index.php

Badges and Emblems of the British Forces, 1940. (Published by Deep River Armory, Inc [Houston, TX]; copyright 1968 by Arms and Armour Press; this is a reprint of work published in 1940)

Beale, Peter. 'Be Unprepared: The Motto of the British armoured forces from 1930 to 1945'. A précis of his 1998 book, *Death by Design: The fate of British tank crews in World War II*; delivered as a talk to the Royal United Services Institution of New South Wales in 2002; online at www.9thrtr.com/tech/Be%20Unprepared.htm. (Beale is also the author of 9th RTR's history, *Tank Tracks at War*.)

Bellis, Malcolm A. *Regiments of the British Army 1939-1945 (Armour and Infantry).* (London: Military Press International, 1994)

_____. *The British Army Overseas, 1945—1970.* (Published by Malcolm A. Bellis, 2001)

Bevis, Mark. *British and Commonwealth Armies 1939-43.* (Helion Order of Battle Vol. 1) (Solihull: Helion & Company, 2001)

_____. *British and Commonwealth Armies 1944-45.* (Helion Order of Battle Vol. 2) (Solihull: Helion & Company, 2003)

Bingham, Maj James. *Crusader-Cruiser Mark VI.* (AFV Profile 8) (Windsor, Berks: Profile Publications Ltd, n.d.)

_____. *Cromwell and Comet.* (AFV Profile 25) (Windsor, Berks: Profile Publications Ltd, 1971)

Brayley, Martin [J.]. *The British Army 1939-45 (1): North-West Europe.* (Osprey Men-at-Arms Series, No. 354) (Oxford: Osprey Publishing Ltd, 2001)

_____. *The British Army 1939-45 (2):Middle East & Mediterranean.* (Osprey Men-at-Arms Series, No. 368) (Oxford: Osprey Publishing Ltd, 2002)

_____. *The British Army 1939-45 (3): The Far East*. (Osprey Men-at-Arms Series, No. 375) (Oxford: Osprey Publishing Ltd, 2002)

Brown, Peter. '21st Army Group Tanks: British Tanks in Europe 1944-45.' November 1996 [based on 'Half Yearly Reports on the Progress of the Royal Armoured Corps' for June and December 1944 and June 1945] The web site on which this was posted has disappeared.

_____. 'British Armoured Cars in Europe 1944-1945'. [based on 'Half Yearly Reports on the Progress of the Royal Armoured Corps' for June and December 1944 and June 1945; supplemented by additional research by Mr. Brown; originally published in *Armored Car* No 35 (June 1996),] online [2012] at www.warwheels.net/BritACsInEurope44_45BROWN.html

_____. 'British Armoured Car Production Figures 1945'. [based on the production section of the 'Half Yearly Report on the Progress of the Royal Armoured Corps' for June 1945, with some supplementary material.] Online [2012] at www.warwheels.net/BritishArmouredCarProductionFiguresArticleBROWN.html

Carver, Brig R. M. P. *A Short History of the 4th Armoured Brigade*. (Published in Germany, July 1945; available online [2005], warlinks.com/armour/)

Chadwick, Tony. War Establishments. Online [2012] at www.warestablishments.net/ [contains copies of a variety of war establishments, and is especially complete for recce units of all types]

Chamberlain, Peter and Chris Ellis. *British and American Tanks of World War Two. The complete illustrated history of British, American and Commonwealth tanks 1939-1945.* (London: Cassell, 2000; first published 1969)

_____. *M3 Medium (Lee/Grant)*. (AFV Profile 11) (Windsor, Berks: Profile Publications Ltd, n.d.)

Chappell, Mike. *British Battle Insignia (2): 1939-45*. (Osprey Men-at-Arms Series, No. 187) (London: Osprey Publishing Ltd, 1987)

Cole, Howard. *Formation Badges of World War 2: Britain, Commonwealth and Empire.* (London: Arms and Armour Press, 1973)

Crow, Duncan. *British and Commonwealth Armoured Formations (1919-46)*. (Windsor, Berks: Profile Publications Ltd, 1972)

Davis, Brian L. *British Army Cloth Insignia, 1940 to the Present*. An Illustrated Reference Guide for Collectors. (London: Arms and Armour Press, 1985)

Davy, Brig G. M. O. *The Seventh and Three Enemies*. (Heffer and Sons, n.d. [1953?]) [At one time available online as a text file]

Doherty, Richard. *Only the Enemy in Front (Every Other Beggar Behind...): The Recce Corps at War 1940-1946*. (London: BCA, 1994)

_____. *The British Reconnaissance Corps in World War II*. (Osprey Elite 152) (Oxford; Osprey Publishing Ltd, 2007)

Edwards, Maj T. J. *Regimental Badges*, First Edition. (London: Ernest Benn Ltd, 1980; reprint of 1951 book)

Ellis, Chris and Peter Chamberlain. *Light Tanks M1-M5*. (AFV Profile 4) (Windsor, Berks: Profile Publications Ltd, n.d.)

Fletcher, David. *Matilda Infantry Tank 1938-45*. (Osprey New Vanguard 8) (Oxford: Osprey Publishing Ltd, 1994)

_____. *Crusader and Covenanter Cruiser Tanks 1939-45*. (Osprey New Vanguard 14) (Oxford: Osprey Publishing Ltd, 1995)

_____. *Universal Carrier 1936-48: The 'Bren Gun Carrier' Story*. (Osprey New Vanguard 110) (Oxford: Osprey Publishing Ltd, 2005)

Flint, Keith. *Airborne Armour: Tetrarch, Locust, Hamilcar and the 6th Airborne Armoured Reconnaissance Regiment 1938-50*. (Solihull: Helion & Company Ltd, 2004)

Forty, George. *British Army Handbook 1939-1945*. (Phoenix Mill: Sutton Publishing Ltd, 1998)

Frederick, J. B. M. *Lineage Book of British Land Forces, 1660—1978*. (2 vols) (Wakefield, Yorkshire: Microform Academic Publishers, 1984)

French, David. *Raising Churchill's Army: The British Army and the War Against Germany 1919-1945*. (Oxford: Oxford University Press, 2000)

Hart, Stephen Ashley. *Montgomery and 'Colossal Cracks': The 21st Army Group in Northwest Europe, 1944-45*. (London: Praeger Series in War Studies, 2000)

Hodges, Peter and Michael D. Taylor. *British Military Markings 1939-1945*. [revised and expanded edition] (Retford, Notts: Cannon Publications, 1994)

Hogg, Ian V. *British & American Artillery of World War 2*. (London: Arms and Armour Press, 1978)

Hughes, David, James Broshot, and Alan Philson. *The British Armies in World War Two: An Organizational History*. Volume One: British Armoured and Cavalry Divisions. (Published by George F. Nafziger [West Chester, OH], 1999)

_____. *The British Armies in World War Two: An Organizational History*. Volume Two: Polish, Australian, Canadian, South African and Indian Armoured and Cavalry Divisions; British Regular Infantry Divisions. (Published by George F. Nafziger [West Chester, OH], 2000)

Hughes, David, James Broshot and David A. Ryan. *The British Armies in World War Two: An Organizational History*. Volume Three: British Infantry, Mountain, Reserve and County Divisions; Independent Infantry Brigade Groups; Deception Divisions and Dummy Brigades. (Published by George F. Nafziger [West Chester, OH], 2001)

Hughes, David, David A. Ryan and Steve Rothwell. *The British Armies in World War Two: An Organizational History*. Volume Four: British Tank and Armoured Brigades; 79th Armoured Division; Armoured Car Regiments; African, Malayan and other Colonial Forces. (Published by George F. Nafziger [West Chester, OH], 2002)

Jewell, Brian. *British Battledress 1937-61*. (Osprey Men-at-Arms 112) (London: Osprey Publishing Ltd, 1981)

Joslen, Lt. Col. H. F. *Orders of Battle, Second World War, 1939-1945*. History of the Second World War, United Kingdom Military Series (London: HM Stationary Office, 1960 in two volumes; reprinted London: The London Stamp Exchange, 1990 in one volume)

Kempton, Chris. *'Loyalty and Honour': The Indian Army, September 1939-August 1947*. Part II: Brigades (Milton Keynes: The Military Press, 2003)

Kemsley, Capt W. and Capt M. R. Riesco. *The Scottish Lion on Patrol: Being the story of the 15th Scottish Reconnaissance Regiment 1943-1946*. Online [2012] at www.15threcce.org/ScottishLionOnPatrol.html

Kennedy, Gary J. 'Battalion Organisation During the Second World War' web site, at [2012] www.bayonetstrength.150m.com/British/british_army.htm [However, information on armoured regiments formerly contained here has disappeared, and it now appears confined to infantry only]

Ladd, James D. *By Sea By Land: The Royal Marines 1919—1997*. (London: HarperCollins, 1998)

Ladd, J[ames] D. 'Royal Marine Tanks at Normandy,' *AFV G-2*, Vol 6, No 6 (January-February 1979), 6-12.

Lord, Cliff and Graham Watson. *The Royal Corps of Signals: Unit Histories of the Corps (1920-2001) and its Antecedents*. (Solihull, West Midlands: Helion & Co Ltd, 2003)

Macksey, Kenneth. *The Tanks: The History of the Royal Tank Regiment, 1945-1975*. (London: Arms and Armour Press, 1979)

Mills, T. F. http://regiments.org/regiments/index.htm. Mr. Mills created the premier web site on the British and Commonwealth armies; unfortunately the site disappeared and apparently will not be recreated. A version of the site can be found at web.archive.org/web/20060118065023/http://www.regiments.org/default.htm

National Archives. www.nationalarchives.gov.uk/catalogue/default.asp?j=1 Online catalogue of war diaries from the following record groups: WO 166 (Home forces, Second World War), WO 169 (Middle East, Second World War), WO 170 (Central Mediterranean Forces, British Element, Second World War), WO 171 (Allied Expeditionary Force, North West Europe (British Element), Second World War), WO 172 (British and Allied Land Forces, South East Asia, Second World War), WO 175 (Allied Forces, North Africa, British Element, Second World War), and WO 267 (British Army of the Rhine)

Owen, Frank and H. W. Atkins. *The Royal Armoured Corps*. Described on the cover as 'The First Official Account of The Royal Armoured Corps' and on the title page as prepared for the War Office by Messrs. Owens and Atkins. (London: HMSO, n.d.; text completed August 1944)

Pakenham-Walsh, Maj Gen R. P. *History of the Corps of Royal Engineers*, Vol VIII. (Chatham: The Institution of Royal Engineers, 1958)

Perrett, Bryan. *Tank Tracks to Rangoon: The Story of British Armour in Burma*. (London: Robert Hale, 1978)

304

_____. *Churchill Infantry Tank 1941-51*. (Osprey New Vanguard 4) (Oxford: Osprey Publishing Ltd, 1993)

Place, Timothy Harrison. *Military Training in the British Army, 1940-1944: From Dunkirk to D-Day*. (London: Frank Cass Publishers, 2000)

Platz, William E. 'The Indian Army Reconnaissance Squadron of 1944' *AFV G-2*, Vol 4, No 2 (February 1973).

_____. 'Marking British Vehicles: A Guide for Serious Modelers, Part 9: Sherman Medium Tanks, Part I' *AFV G-2* Vol 6, No 5 (October-November 1978), 15-19

_____. 'Marking British Vehicles: A Guide for Serious Modelers, Part 10: Sherman Medium Tanks, Part 2' *AFV G-2* Vol 6, No 6 (January-February 1979), 17-20

_____. 'Marking British Vehicles: A Guide for Serious Modelers, Part 11: Sherman Medium Tanks, Part 3' *AFV G-2* Vol 6, No 8 (August-September 1979), 40-42+

_____. 'Marking British Vehicles: a Guide for Serious Modelers, Part 12: Grant Medium Tanks, Part 1' *AFV G-2* Vol 6, No 9 (January-February 1980), 41-43

_____. 'Marking British Vehicles: a Guide for Serious Modelers, Part 13: Grant Medium Tanks, Part 2' *AFV G-2* Vol 6, No 10 (January-February 1981), 37-39+

Regimental Web Sites[282]
◊ 1st Queen's Dragoon Guards [1st King's Dragoon Guards and Queen's Bays], [2005] www.qdg.org.uk/index.php—includes detailed history to 1942 and armament details for the entire war
◊ Royal Scots Dragoon Guards [3rd Carabiniers and Royal Scots Greys], [2005], www.army.mod.uk/scotsdg/history_and_traditions/history_timeline.htm—exceptional for an official site, with detailed history for both regiments including references to all of the battle honours, this page no longer exists
◊ The Queen's Royal Hussars [3rd TKO, 4th QO, 7th QO, and 8th KRI Hussars], [2005], www.qrh.org.uk/history.htm—good historical summaries for all four regiments
◊ The Queen's Royal Lancers [16th/5th and 17th/21st Lancers], [2005], www.qrl.uk.com/h_home.html—fairly good historical summaries for both regiments

---

[282] While an attempt to locate and view all regimental web sites (official or otherwise) was made, only those with some degree of usable historical information are given here. The official sites in particular now provide very cursory histories or none at all..

◊ 2nd Royal Tank Regiment, three paragraphs on World War II [2005]
www.army.mod.uk/2rtr/regimental_history/index.htm; another page that no
longer exists
◊ 9th Royal Tank Regiment, [2005] www.9thrtr.com—a copy of that regiment's War
Diary from June 1944 to June 1945, with additional explanatory material and
maps. It also contains the text of their history, *Tank Tracks*, and other historical
material.
◊ Royal Gloucestershire Hussars, [2005] www.glosters.org.uk/hussars.
html—summary history of the two wartime regiments
◊ North Irish Horse, [2005] www.nih.ww2site.com/nih/index.html—
created by a World War II veteran of the regiment, includes the war
diary, battle reports, and a variety of material
◊ Royal Wiltshire Yeomanry, [2005] www.yeomanry.co.uk/—detailed history of the
regiment
◊ Yorkshire Yeomanry, [2005] www.army.mod.uk/qoy/y_squadron/
y_squadron_history.htm—very brief summary histories of the three regiments
{QO Yorkshire Dragoons, Yorkshire Hussars, East Riding Yeomanry]

Ryan, David A., David Hughes and James Broshot. *The British Armies in World War
Two: An Organizational History*. Supplement One: Orders of Battle 1939 to 1941.
(Published by George F. Nafziger [West Chester, OH], 2001)

Ryan, David A., David Hughes and Steve Rothwell. *The British Armies in World War
Two: An Organizational History*. Supplement Two: Orders of Battle 1941 to 1942.
(Published by George F. Nafziger [West Chester, OH], 2002)

Ryan, David A., Steve Rothwell and David Hughes. *The British Armies in World War
Two: An Organizational History*. Supplement Three: Orders of Battle 1942 to 1944.
(Published by George F. Nafziger [West Chester, OH], 2003)

_____. *The British Armies in World War Two: An Organizational History*.
Supplement Four: Orders of Battle 1944 to 1945. (Published by George F. Nafziger
[West Chester, OH], 2005)

Sampson, June. 'Force of the Phantom'. *Kingston Guardian*, 20 February 2004, online
[2005] at www.kingstonguardian.co.uk/news/features/
display.var.462004.0.force_of_the_phantom.php

Schillito, Chris. 'The Churchill N. A. 75'. Formerly online at his site [2012]
www.armourinfocus.co.uk/a22/index.htm

_____. 'Churchill Tanks in Italy'. [Based on Eighth Army tank status reports].
Formerly online at his site [2012] www.armourinfocus.co.uk/a22/index.htm

Smart, Nick. *Biographical Dictionary of British Generals of the Second World War*. (Barnsley: Pen & Sword Books Ltd, 2005)

Taylor, Dick. *Warpaint: Colours and Markings of British Army Vehicles, 1903-2003.*. (Sandomierz I, Poland: STRATUS s.c., 2008 [Vol I], 2009 [Vol II], 2011 [Vol III], 2012 [Vol IV])

Trux Super Factsheets. Published by Trux Models (Yeadon, Leeds). These are copies of various 21st Army Group war establishments, along with additional data and information. Those used were:[283]
>   WE 2109 Phantom: GHQ Liaison Regiment [HQ GHQ Liaison Regiment, Army Squadrons, Army Group Squadrons]
>   WE 2110: Reconnaissance Regiment
>   WE 2111 Armoured Car Regiment
>   WE 2112: Armoured Reconnaissance Regiment [both the Armoured Recce Regiment and Armoured Regiments in 22nd Brigade]
>   WE 2113 Armoured Regiment [Sherman]
>   WE 2114 Armoured Regiment [Comet]
>   WE 2115 Tank Regiment [includes Crocodile Regiment]
>   WE 2117 Assault Regiment RE [HQ Assault Regiment RE, Assault Squadron RE, Assault Squadron RE, Amphibious]
>   WE 2119 Armoured Divisional Signals
>   WE 2120 Armoured Brigade Headquarters [Armoured and Tank Brigades 1944 and Armoured Brigade 1945]
>   WE2124, Divisional Royal Electrical and Mechanical Engineers
>   WE 2126 Assault Brigade RE [HQ Assault Engineer Brigade, 149 Assault Park Squadron, 557 Assault Training Regiment]

Van der Bijl, Nicholas and Paul Hannon. *The Royal Marines 1939-93*. (Osprey Elite Series, No. 57) (London: Osprey Publishing Ltd, 1994)

Vanderveen, Bart H. *The Observer's Fighting Vehicles Directory of World War II*, rev. ed. (New York: Frederick Warne & Co. Inc., 1972)

---

[283] The 'WE' number represents their catalog number, not an actual British Army war establishment designation. These and virtually every other 21st Army Group war establishments are now online, at ww2talk.com/forum/trux-21st-army-group/. The online material are the establishments, without the additional material included in the publications. However, there are also extensive sections on equipment and transport. The old site, truxmodels.co.uk/, included some BEF 1940 war establishments as well, but they were not transferred.

War Diaries. Electronic copies of the war diaries of the following regiments are available at Robert Cull's 'WWII: A British Focus' web site, [2012] www.warlinks.com/armour/index.php:

- 11th Hussars (Prince Albert's Own)
- 6th Royal Tank Regiment
- 2nd Royal Gloucestershire Hussars
- 3rd County of London Yeomanry (Sharpshooters)
- 4th County of London Yeomanry (Sharpshooters)
- North Irish Horse

Those for the North Irish Horse can also be found at the regiment's web site (see above)

Watson, Graham E. Material provided by Dr. Watson on BAOR's demobilization 1945-47 was helpful in determining a number of inactivation/suspended animation dates.

White, B. T. *British Tanks and Fighting Vehicles, 1914—1945* (London: Ian Allen, 1970).

_____. *Valentine, Infantry Tank Mk III*. (AFV Profile 6) (Windsor, Berks: Profile Publications Ltd, n.d.)

_____. *Armoured Cars*. (AFV Profile 21) (Windsor, Berks: Profile Publications Ltd, 1970)

Wilson, Edward. *Press on Regardless: The Story of the Fifth Royal Tank Regiment in World War Two*. (Staplehurst: Spellmount Ltd, 2003)

Windrow, Martin. *Tank and AFV Crew Uniforms Since 1916.* (Carrollton, Texas: Squadron/Signal Publications, 1979)

Zaloga, Steven J. *Sherman Medium Tank 1942-45*. (Osprey New Vanguard 3) (Oxford: Osprey Publishing Ltd, 1978)

_____. *M3 Infantry Half-Track 1940-73*. (Osprey New Vanguard 11) (Oxford: Osprey Publishing Ltd, 1994)

www.ingramcontent.com/pod-product-compliance
Lightning Source LLC
Chambersburg PA
CBHW062035090426

42740CB00016B/2916